8/03

The Irish War of Independence

Ireland

Coleraine

Letterkenny

DONEGAL

Derry

DERRY

ANTRIM

Larne

Donegal

Ulster

Omagh

BELFAST

Moneygold
25 October 1920

TYRONE

Enniskillen

Lisburn
22 August 1920

Sligo

MAYO

SLIGO

Armagh

DOWN

Newport

FERMANAGH

Monaghan

MONAGHAN

Newry

Kilmeena
19 May 1921

Castlebar

ROSCOMMON

LEITRIM

Cavan

CAVAN

Dundalk

Westport

Scramogue
23 March 1921

Carrowkennedy
3 June 1921

Tourmakeady
3 May 1921

Ballinalee

Clonfin
1 February 1921

LOUTH

Clifden

Connacht

Tuam

Roscommon

Longford

LONGFORD

Drogheda

Navan

WESTMEATH

Mullingar

MEATH

Balbriggan
21 September 1920

Galway

GALWAY

Athlone

Leinster

DUBLIN

DUBLIN

OFFALY

KILDARE

Ennistymon
22 September 1920

Borrisokane
26 June 1920

Kildare

Naas

Rineen
22 September 1920

CLARE

Modreeny
3 June 1921

Roscrea

Portlaoise

WICKLOW

Ennis

Nenagh

LAOIS

Wicklow

Kilrush

Limerick

TIPPERARY

Thurles

Carlow

Soloheadbeg
21 January 1919

Kilkenny

CARLOW

WEXFORD

LIMERICK

Kilmallock
28 May 1920

O Cashel

Tralee

Lackelly,
2 May 1921

Tipperary

Cahir

Dingle

Munster

Clonmel

Wexford

Headford Junction
21 March 1921

Clonbannin
5 March 1921

Mallow 28 September 1920

WATERFORD

Rosslare

Killarney

CORK

Fermoy
7 September 1919

Coolavokig
25 Feb. 1921

Dripsey
28 Jan. 1921

Clonmult
20 Feb. 1921

Dungarvan

Kenmare

Macroom

Youghal

Kilmichael
28 Nov. 1920

CORK

Bantry

Bandon

Crossbarry, 19 March 1921

Upton Station 15 Feb. 1921

━━━━━ Provincial border

━━━━━ Rep. of Ireland / N.Ireland border

The Irish War of Independence

Michael Hopkinson

McGill-Queen's University Press
Montreal & Kingston • Ithaca

© Michael Hopkinson 2002
Published in the United States and Canada by
McGill-Queen's University Press

ISBN 0-7735-2498-3

Published simultaneously in Ireland by
Gill & Macmillan Ltd
Hume Avenue,
Park West,
Dublin 12

Index compiled by Helen Litton
Map supplied by EastWest Mapping
Print origination by Carole Lynch
Printed by Creative Print and Design Wales

The paper used in this book comes from the wood pulp of managed forests. For every tree felled, at least one tree is planted, thereby renewing natural resources.

McGill-Queen's University Press acknowledges the financial support of the Government of Canada through the Book Publishing Industry Development Program (BPIDP) for our publishing activities.

National Library of Canada Cataloguing in Publication

Hopkinson, Michael
        The Irish War of Independence / Michael Hopkinson.

Includes bibliographical references and index.
ISBN 0-7735-2498-3

        1. Irish Republican Army—History. 2. Ireland—History—1910–1921. I.
        Title.

DA962.H66 2002   941.7082'1   C2002-902781-0

5 4 2 3 1

'I always think that it is entirely wrong to prejudge the past.' William Whitelaw, on his arrival in Belfast as Secretary of State for Northern Ireland.

(By kind permission of Lady Celia Whitelaw)

Contents

17   The North-East and the War of Independence   153
18   The American Dimension   165
19   The Peace Process   177
20   The Path to the Truce   192
     Conclusion   198

     Appendices   204
     Notes   217
     Bibliography   245
     Index   257

List of Illustrations

The Chief Secretary of Ireland, Ian Macpherson, moving the first reading of what eventually became the Government of Ireland Act 1920. This was the Act that effected the partition of Ireland. (Courtesy of The Illustrated London News Picture Library)

British troops searching a car in Dublin (courtesy of Independent Newspapers Ltd)

Countess Markievicz (courtesy of Irish Times Newspapers Ltd)

B Company Auxiliary Division, RIC, 1921 (courtesy of Hulton Getty)

Arthur Griffith and Éamon de Valera (courtesy of Hulton Getty)

Troops in the grounds of Jervis Street Hospital, November 1920 (courtesy of the National Library of Ireland, ref. no. Hog/Len A17)

Royal visit to Belfast, June 1921: from left, Lady Greenwood, Sir Hamar Greenwood, Lady Carson and Sir James Craig (courtesy of Hulton Getty)

General Richard Mulcahy (courtesy of the National Library of Ireland, ref. no. KE 195)

Lord FitzAlan of Derwent (left), the last Lord Lieutenant of Ireland, takes the salute. (Courtesy of the National Library of Ireland, ref. no. Hog/Len A26)

Michael Collins (courtesy of Hulton Getty)

The Custom House on fire (courtesy of Hulton Getty)

A tank used as a battering ram during an army search (© Popperfoto)

In the ruins of the Custom House (courtesy of the National Library of Ireland, ref. no. Hog/Len A24)

Refugees escaping from Balbriggan following its destruction by the Black and Tans (courtesy of Hulton Getty)

Seán MacEoin and Seán Moylan (courtesy of the Irish Times Picture Library)

Éamon de Valera

Members of Cumann na mBan recite the rosary outside Mountjoy Jail on 25 April 1921, the morning that Thomas Traynor was hanged. (Courtesy of the National Library of Ireland, ref. no. Hog/Len A22)

A troop raid (courtesy of Hulton Getty)

Terence MacSwiney (courtesy of the National Library of Ireland, ref. no. R 12945)

David Lloyd George (courtesy of Hulton Getty)

Forces of the Crown: a member of the DMP, a regular soldier and two Black and Tans (courtesy of Hulton Getty)

Black and Tans confiscate property taken from Liberty Hall, the headquarters of the Irish Transport & General Workers' Union. (Courtesy of Hulton Getty)

Sir Hamar Greenwood (courtesy of Hulton Getty)

Irish delegates at the Treaty negotiations in London: Arthur Griffith is on the extreme left with Robert Barton next to him. Desmond FitzGerald is standing left. Erskine Childers is seated right. (© Popperfoto)

British troops on parade on the great square of the Royal Barracks (now Collins Barracks) (courtesy of the National Library of Ireland, ref. no. Hog/Len A9)

Seán T. O'Kelly left, Eoin MacNeill second from left, and Éamon de Valera second from right (© Popperfoto)

W.T. Cosgrave (courtesy of the RTE Archives — Cashman Collection, CD no. 509/057)

Acknowledgments

I am grateful to the British Academy, the Leverhulme Trust and the Carnegie Trust for supplying research grants for this project, and to the Institute of Irish Studies at Queen's University, Belfast for the award of a one-year visiting Fellowship. Over the years, many of the ideas in this book have been aired to various helpful audiences: the Irish-Australian Conference in Perth, the Hertford College Oxford Research Seminar, the Ulster Committee of Historical Sciences and the Institute of Irish Studies Seminars at Queen's. I am also indebted to the University of Stirling's sabbatical leave scheme.

The staff of the many libraries I have worked in have all been extremely professional and efficient. Particular mention should be made of the late Peter Young and his successor Victor Laing at the Irish Military Archives, and Seamus Helferty in UCD Archives. Sister Raphael of the Catholic Archives in Perth, Western Australia and Patricia McCarthy of the Cork City Archives went far beyond the call of duty in helping me.

The friendship and hospitality of Tim Pat Coogan, Diarmuid O'Connor and Rodney and Susan Thom made my stays in Dublin most enjoyable and productive. Michael MacEvilly has been a constant source of assistance and encouragement along with other Irish historians who have never been less than generous. Michael MacEvilly, Seán O'Mahony, Eamonn Gaynor and Meda Ryan have supplied valuable comments on the chapters on local areas. Michael MacEvilly, Tim Pat Coogan, Diarmuid O'Connor, Jim Fleming, Liam Cosgrave and Eunan O'Halpin have kindly supplied private documents to me. In Australia, Bob and Lesley Reece, my wonderful friends, and John Corr and Ian Chambers, my first and most supportive students, are among many there who made my time so pleasurable. At Stirling University, my research student Robert Lynch has offered a willing ear and sound advice. Fergal Tobin originally suggested this book and is the most genial and sympathetic of editors. Deirdre Rennison Kunz has seen the book to press in the most sympathetic and tactful of manners.

Michael Hopkinson
Stirling, June 2002

Chronology

1913   25 November: Founding of Irish Volunteers.

1914   24 April: Gunrunning at Larne, Bangor and Donaghadee.
24 July: Arms landing at Howth.
4 August: Britain declares war on Germany: start of First World War.
18 September: Home Rule Bill receives Royal Assent.

1915   19 May: Coalition government formed in Britain.
1 August: O'Donovan Rossa funeral: oration by Patrick Pearse.

1916   21 April: Arrest of Sir Roger Casement at Fenit, County Kerry.
24 April: Proclamation of the Irish Republic.
24–29 April: The Easter Rising.
23 December: First Irish Volunteers released from Frongoch internment.

1917   5 February: Count Plunkett elected MP for North Roscommon.
9 May: Joe McGuinness elected MP for South Longford.
11 July: Eamon de Valera elected MP for East Clare.
11 August: W.T. Cosgrave elected MP for Kilkenny.
25 September: Thomas Ashe dies on hunger strike in Mountjoy Prison.
25/26 October: Sinn Féin Convention.
27 October: Irish Volunteer Convention.

1918   12 April: Irish Convention Report issued.
18 April: Military Service Act passed in British parliament.
21 April: Anti-conscription pledge signed throughout Ireland.
17/18 May: German Plot arrests.
21 June: Arthur Griffith elected MP for East Cavan.
7 October: Publication of President Wilson's Fourteen Points.
11 November: Armistice signed ending First World War.
3 December: Election Pact in Ulster agreed.
14 December: General Election.
30 December: Election results announced: Sinn Féin victory.

1919   11 January: Sir Ian Macpherson replaces Edward Shortt as Chief Secretary.
21 January: First meeting of Dáil Éireann. Soloheadbeg ambush.

22 January: Opening of Irish Race Convention at Philadelphia.

24 January: South Tipperary proclaimed a military area.

3 February: De Valera, Seán McGarry and Seán Milroy escape from Lincoln Prison.

6 March: Announcement of release of Irish political prisoners.

4 May: Irish-American delegation arrives in Dublin.

13 May: Rescue of Seán Hogan at Knocklong.

22 June: De Valera arrives in USA.

12 September: Proscription of Dáil Éireann.

19 December: Attempted assassination of Lord French at Ashtown.

1920   15 January: Local elections.

21 January: Assistant Commissioner Redmond, DMP, shot dead in Dublin.

25 February: Government of Ireland Bill introduced into House of Commons.

19 March: Tomás MacCurtain, Lord Mayor of Cork, shot dead.

26 March: Alan Bell, RM, shot dead by IRA.

29 March: Sir Nevil Macready appointed GOC Irish Command.

3 April: IRA burning and destruction of income tax offices and evacuated RIC barracks.

Sir Hamar Greenwood appointed Chief Secretary.

12 April: General Strike called in support of hunger strikers in Mountjoy.

14 April: Release of political prisoners from Mountjoy.

22 May: General Sir Henry Tudor appointed Police Adviser in Ireland.

28 May: IRA attack on Kilmallock RIC barracks.

8 June: Results of County Council and Rural elections.

20/24 June: Riots in Derry City.

17 July: DC Smyth shot dead in Cork.

21 July: Attack on Catholic shipyard workers in Belfast.

23 July: Cabinet discussion of Irish situation in London.

9 August: Restoration of Order in Ireland Bill receives Royal Assent.

12 August: Arrest of Terence MacSwiney, Lord Mayor of Cork.

22 August: Shooting dead of D/I Swanzy in Lisburn.

25/30 August: Riots in Belfast.

20 September: Shootings and reprisals at Balbriggan.

14 October: Shooting dead of Seán Treacy.

25 October: Death of Terence MacSwiney on hunger strike.

1 November: Execution of Kevin Barry.

12 November: Arthur Griffith calls off remaining hunger strikes.

21 November: Bloody Sunday.

26 November: Arrest of Arthur Griffith, Eoin MacNeill and Eamon Duggan.

28 November: Kilmichael ambush.

1 December: Start of Archbishop Clune's peace initiative.
3 December: Galway County Council Peace Resolution.
5 December: Father O'Flanagan telegram to Lloyd George.
10 December: Proclamation of Martial Law in Cork, Kerry, Limerick and Tipperary.
11 December: Cork City burnings.
23 December: Government of Ireland Bill enacted.
24 December: De Valera returns to Dublin.
29 December: First official reprisal at Midleton.

1921   4 January: Martial law declared for Clare, Wexford, Waterford and Kilkenny.
7 March: Shooting dead of George Clancy, Mayor of Limerick, and Michael O'Callaghan, ex-Mayor of Limerick.
19 March: Crossbarry.
21 March: Headford Junction attack.
14 May: De Valera and Sir James Craig meet in Dublin.
24 May: General election in Northern Ireland.
25 May: Burning of Dublin Custom House.
22 June: King George V speech opening Belfast parliament.
24 June: Lloyd George invites de Valera to conference.
8 July: British, Sinn Féin and Southern Unionists meet in Dublin.
9 July: Truce agreed.
11 July: 12 noon, Truce begins.
16 August: Second Dáil meets.
6 December: Signing of Anglo-Irish Treaty.

Introduction

The Irish War of Independence has provoked a massive amount of interest; IRA guerrilla warfare and Black and Tan reprisals have rivalled the issue of the British government's culpability for the Great Famine as the most emotive subject in modern Irish history. A familiar and popular story has usually been told in the form of biographies, memoirs and narrative accounts of heroic victory against the odds, of dramatic raids and ambushes, of hunger strikes and prison resistance. The Black and Tans have become the most well-known symbol for perfidious Albion in Irish communities world-wide. The best-selling books written by veterans of the conflict, notably Tom Barry in *Guerilla Days in Ireland,* Dan Breen in *My Fight for Irish Freedom* and Ernie O'Malley in *On Another Man's Wound,* have had a huge influence on popular perception. Whole shelves in bookshops are devoted to biographies of Michael Collins with publishers' blurbs talking of 'the man who won the War'.[1] There is still something of a national obsession with attaching blame and responsibility for the divisions which followed the conflict.

The reasons for the undying fascination are readily apparent. Biographies are a particularly colourful form of historical writing; all states, especially young ones, romanticise their founding fathers. The divisions of the revolutionary period dominated Irish politics and society for a very long time afterwards and affected historical interpretation. In his long career, Eamon de Valera always felt the need to put the record straight about the 1919–23 years.[2] The new perspectives offered by many scholars on the period since the 1960s have had little effect on the popular consciousness. Neil Jordan's film *Michael Collins* (1997) has had a much more powerful effect than any scholarly work has done or is ever likely to do.[3]

To revise the traditional nationalist account of the conflict, even in the new century, is not an easy task. Sensitivities are acute: even mild correctives are easily distorted into accusations of bias on one side or the other. Both Irish and British governments have been extremely reluctant to release documents of the period. The Public Record Office at Kew in London held back a considerable amount of material at the end of the original official fifty-year closure time and since then has opened up files in a most selective fashion, inviting speculation as to the criteria used and the secrets still to be revealed, possibly in another fifty years. The mysteries of the release process have been even greater in the Northern Ireland Public Record Office where for a time some historians appeared to be given preferential treatment. In the Irish Republic, there have only recently been considerable gains in the opening up of official files. However, the Bureau of Military History papers have long been a subject of official procrastination and delay.[4] The demands of the historian are still clashing with the civil service and governmental obsession for secrecy after the passage of eighty years.

In a notorious recent academic article,[5] the medieval historian Brendan Bradshaw argued that the 'beneficent legacy' of the nationalist version of Irish history should not be tampered with. In his view, history has a public function to support 'the rich heritage of the aboriginal Celtic civilisation': in other words, myths may be untrue but destroying them threatens national culture and stability. As I write, the remains of Kevin Barry and another nine executed IRA men which have been disinterred from Mountjoy Prison are to be reburied at Glasnevin following a full state funeral on 14 October 2001. Evidently political parties today still need to make the connection with their revolutionary past. In recognition of the danger of upsetting susceptibilities, much of the writing on the War of Independence and the Civil War has been cautious in tone and restricted in scope: surprisingly the 1919–23 period, in contrast to the debate about the Easter Rising, has not featured strongly in the whole revisionist saga.[6]

We are constantly told that Civil War politics are dead: to judge by much recent literature, Civil War history is very much alive. In this self-confident time in the history of the Irish Republic, many historians are taking an unsympathetic view of republicanism in the revolutionary era. Tom Garvin's brilliant *1922: The Birth of Irish Democracy* celebrates the state's achievement of stability in reaction against the long-dominant neo-republican de Valera orthodoxy. Michael Laffan has referred to an 'almost accidental revolution' and Kevin Myers keeps up a regular barrage against the nationalist consensus in his columns in the *Irish Times*.[7]

In the mid-1970s, Charles Townshend's *The British Campaign in Ireland, 1919–1921* and David Fitzpatrick's *Politics and Irish Life, 1913–21* pioneered fresh scholarly perspectives on the period. Eunan O'Halpin and John McColgan have laid bare the chaos and confusion of the last years of Dublin Castle rule.[8] It is no longer unquestioningly accepted that there was a symbiotic relationship between the IRA and the people. The limited and heavily localised nature of the fighting is now appreciated, and it is broadly agreed that the IRA's achievements were more in the Intelligence and publicity spheres than in the purely military. Pioneering work on localities has addressed the social make-up of the IRA and their motivation.[9] It remains true, however, that the central questions posed by the War are still being neglected: these relate to how and why a large measure of independence for the twenty-six counties was won, and whether that achievement was at the expense of Partition. There should be consideration of how necessary the use of violence was, and whether something akin to Dominion Status could have been won without it. Why was the British government willing in July 1921 to offer a settlement far in advance of anything offered before?

Implicit in much of the writing on the subject, both British and Irish, has been the assumption of a kind of inevitability. This applies particularly to the amount of violence used and the establishment of Partition. Hindsight can be a barrier to proper consideration of the choices faced and the mistakes made at the time. The very existence of the Free State/Republic and of the province of Northern Ireland has precluded examination of alternative outcomes from 1919 to 1921. This goes beyond the reluctance of historians to look at hypotheses, and concerns their relationship with their entire culture and upbringing.

The role of violence in the revolution, if not glorified, has been broadly accepted with little questioning. Unsurprisingly, the focus for so long was on the atrocities of Black and Tans and Auxiliaries, and less attention was paid to IRA excesses. A comforting distinction was often made between IRA violence in the 1919 to 1921 period and that in the 1970s and 1980s. The assumption was that a mandate existed for violence in the revolutionary era but not thereafter. Recently Peter Hart has brought out how much of the fighting amounted to tit-for-tat killing, in Cork as well as Belfast.[10] What Hart says for Cork may well not apply equally to other counties, but the issue desperately needed an airing.

There was much criticism at the time of IRA activities. The Sinn Féin victory in December 1918 did not amount to an acceptance of a physical force revolution and the issue was never put to the test. It was British coercion, and particularly the reprisals from the summer of 1920, that transformed popular attitudes. The same people who had deep reservations about the IRA and its methods in 1920–21 later exulted over what had been achieved. In 1920, Cardinal Logue said of Michael Collins and his lieutenants: 'No object would excuse them, no hearts, unless hardened and steeled against pity, would tolerate their cruelty.' Two years later, Logue felt that Collins had been transformed into 'a young patriot, brave and wise'.[11]

The part that political and passive resistance tactics played in gaining independence has only lately been accorded due importance;[12] sensational fighting narratives win a much readier audience. When, however, the priority was on politics and diplomacy in 1919 they achieved little. Two historians have addressed the key issue. On the one hand Ronan Fanning has argued that 'there is not a shred of evidence that Lloyd George's Tory-dominated Government would have moved from the 1914-style niggardliness of the Government of Ireland Act of 1920 to the larger, if imperfect, generosity of the Treaty if they had not been impelled to do so by Michael Collins and his assassins.'[13] By complete contrast, Roy Foster has written of the eventual offer of Dominion Status: 'whether the bloody catalogue of assassination and war from 1919–21 was necessary in order to negotiate thus far may fairly be questioned.'[14]

The high level of violence from mid-1920 followed on decisions made by the British government to adopt a coercive rather than a conciliatory policy. Historians have underrated how near a negotiated settlement was in December 1920. The escalation of the War in late 1920 and the first six months of 1921 caused not only a terrible waste of many lives but also an appalling long-term embitterment in Anglo-Irish relations. This is the study of tragedy and is not something to glory in.

The subject of the relationship of the north-east to the War has been largely avoided. This can be explained by Partitionist attitudes on both sides of the border. Southern historians have frequently bypassed the subject and taken an almost possessive attitude, apparently considering the War a twenty-six-county affair. Dermot Keogh's *Twentieth-Century Ireland: Nation and State*[15] leaves the North out entirely, and only recently have there been separate studies of the Northern Catholic minority. Accounts written from a Unionist perspective have sought to defend,[16] and even justify, the intransigent policies of the Northern government. The siege mentality has extended to the historical profession. Underlying both approaches is again the assumption of the inevitability of Partition. The history of the Government of Ireland Bill was anything but predictable, and the British government's crucial backing for the hard-line Unionist policies of 1920–21 has rarely been sufficiently analysed. As at the end of the twentieth century, stances taken were frequently less hard-line than they appeared to be on the surface, and retrospective accounts by contemporaries tended to emphasise consistency and dogmatism as opposed to flexibility.

The place of the fighting between 1919 and 1921 in the overall context of the Irish Revolution has rarely been debated. The Irish have been strikingly reluctant to use the term 'revolution', almost as reluctant as the British were to use the term 'war'.[17] This is perhaps because the Civil War and its legacy of eternal bitterness and mistrust divorced the new state from an objective evaluation of its revolutionary roots. The Irish equivalent of Bastille Day is Easter Monday 1916; it has been easier for Irish nationalists to associate themselves with failed uprisings than with the successful guerrilla warfare following the First World War. This relates to the difficulty of finding an appropriate title for the conflict and hence for this book.[18]

To use the terms 'War of Independence' or 'Anglo-Irish War', as with 'Derry'/'Londonderry', reveals an implicit bias. Many republicans know it as 'The Tan War' and some resort to the ubiquitous Irish euphemism 'The Troubles'. For decades, the British followed the official lead at the time: it was a rebellion. Of late they have used the neutral-sounding term 'Anglo-Irish War', ignoring the fact that many Irish fought on the British side. The conflict had strong elements of a civil as well as a colonial war. Apart from the consideration that the War of Independence is a happier-sounding title, it is a more appropriate expression of the nationalist demand, though the independence achieved was geographically limited to twenty-six counties and constitutionally limited to a form of Dominion Status. Whatever nomenclature is used, events should be placed in a wider chronological framework than the immediate post-First World War context. It was the Ulster Crisis of 1912–14 and the First World War which represented the point of no return for the British government. The years 1919 to 1921 were the crucial final stages in a revolution, albeit an unfinished one.

The structure of this book aims to focus on specific issues and to avoid the straitjacket of traditional narrative history. A purely chronological approach would be confusing, as events jump geographically from Kerry to London to Dublin, though there has to be a sense of development over time also to understand events. What results is, in the rather stuffy language of the historian, an 'analytical narrative'. As far as possible, British and Irish aspects are kept apart in order to clarify issues; some overlapping and repetition cannot be avoided. This structure allows separate chapters on easily-defined subjects such as the North and on Irish America, and on the War as it progressed in the localities. Thus also, due highly-focused attention can be given to peace initiatives. It is hoped that in this way justice can be given to many disparate themes which can too easily be lost in the relentless flow of a narrative.

PART I

~

GATHERING STORM

1

BRITISH RULE IN IRELAND

'The present conflict between the opposing forces in Ireland has its roots in
the failure of English statecraft and administration to rule Ireland.'
G.C. Cockerill, Memorandum on Ireland 1919–20.[1]

At the time of the Third Home Rule Bill's introduction in 1912, a
measure of self-government for Ireland appeared to be on the brink
of being achieved. The House of Lords veto had been removed,
seemingly ensuring passage of the legislation. Optimism was shattered by the strength and effectiveness of Ulster Unionist resistance supported
by an opportunistic Conservative Party; by 1914 the whole basis of internal
security was threatened and the Liberal government's dithering underlined
their lack of conviction over the issue. The beginning of the First World War
allowed the Bill to be passed, but with its operation suspended until a time not
later than the end of the conflict, and with the further caveat that an amending
Bill would make special provision for all or part of Ulster.

It is doubtful if this limited measure of devolution could have produced a long-
term settlement.[2] What is clear, however, is that the Ulster Crisis brought the gun
back into Irish politics and together with the First World War undermined constitutional nationalism. Catholic nationalists of all shades viewed the failure to
stand up to Ulster and to force the passage of Home Rule as the ultimate British
betrayal. Vast numbers of moderates became radicals almost overnight. From
then on any appeal to a so-called middle ground was hopeless. In this wide context the Easter Rising should be seen as the consequence of the revolutionary
developments of the preceding four years. Long before the end of the War, a settlement along Home Rule lines was inconceivable and the Irish Parliamentary
Party's leader, John Redmond's hopes for Anglo-Irish rapprochement devastated.[3] The British government, however, did not choose to recognise these realities.

While the Easter Rising in the long term revived militant, advanced nationalism, in the short term it placed a higher premium than ever on the need for
a speedy Home Rule settlement. Lloyd George's initiative of the summer of

1916, which attempted to achieve immediate implementation of Home Rule, together with the exclusion of the six north-eastern counties, foundered on Cabinet disunity and Southern Unionist resistance.[4]

Recourse was then made to the delaying action of the Irish Convention of 1917–18, which was motivated by the desire to appease international, particularly American, opinion.[5] Lloyd George then commented: 'In six months the war will be lost . . . the Irish-American vote will go over to the German side. They will break our blockade and force an ignominious peace on us, unless something is done . . . to satisfy America.'[6] By this time, the transformed Sinn Féin Party had achieved a dominant position in Irish politics against the background of British prevarication, delay and pinpricking coercion. The conscription crisis of the spring and summer of 1918 sounded the final death knell of Home Rule hopes and with them of the Irish Parliamentary Party.

The British administration of Ireland in its final years demonstrated in a dramatic and concentrated manner all the vices which had existed within it for hundreds of years. The system was in its death throes before the reorganisation of the Irish Volunteers and the formation of the Dáil government between 1917 and 1919.

The failure of British administration in Ireland owed much to structural and institutional weaknesses. A separate government, based in Dublin Castle, survived the Act of Union of 1800–1801 and changed little in form during the course of the following one hundred and twenty-one years. It consisted of a multitude of Departments and Boards, some autonomous from London, some overlapping with each other. The Castle was meant to run the country as well as to advise the British government on policy, and became a watchword for unaccountable and inefficient rule, criticised on every front for its top-heavy bureaucracy. The French observer Louis Paul-Dubois described it as 'A world in itself, a city within a city. It is at once the palace of the viceroy, a military barrack, the seat of administration, and the office of the secret police . . . omnipotent and omniscient.' The Liberal politician John Morley saw it as: 'the best machine that has ever been invented for governing a country against its will'.[7] The evolution of accountable parliamentary government in Britain during the course of the nineteenth century found no parallel in Ireland.

The vestiges of an archaic colonial administration remained. The office of Lord Lieutenant, the representative of the Crown in Ireland, survived, his relationship to the Chief Secretary problematic. One commentator likened that office to a 'useless and idle pageant' and the historian Kieran Flanagan concluded that the Viceroy 'symbolised the incomplete nature of the Act of Union and the notion of Ireland as a separate nation'.[8] Increasingly the holders of the post became like constitutional monarchs, associated with symbolism and ritual, while the Chief Secretary became more powerful, largely because of his role in the Cabinet and in the Commons.

Long-term improvements in communications meant that the Chief Secretary's frequent visits to London contrasted with the Viceroy's permanent residence in Dublin. The Chief Secretary became dependent on Westminster and on the Prime Minister's patronage. The position was usually given to a junior politician as a sinecure rather than for any perceived knowledge of or ability in Irish affairs. Time in the office averaged two years.

Some sympathy is due to the Chief Secretaries because of the range of skills required — headship of the bureaucracy and representative of Irish affairs in Westminster and Whitehall, administrator and trouble-shooter, constantly travelling back and forth across the Irish Sea. At various times the balance between Lord Lieutenant and Chief Secretary changed, dependent on the political weight and the personalities involved. In the running of Dublin Castle the office of Under-Secretary was usually the most important one: he became a full-time civil servant, permanently stationed in Dublin.[9]

The system was full of potential for disharmony both within Dublin Castle and between Dublin and Westminster. At sundry times British politicians talked of modernising it but little change occurred. Lord John Russell wrote in 1847: 'A separate government — a separate court — and an administration of a mixed nature, partly English and partly Irish, is not of itself a convenient arrangement. The separate government within fifteen hours of London appears unnecessary — the separate court a mockery — the mixed administration the cause of confusion and delay.' At another time Russell declared that he 'found the relationship between the Irish and the United Kingdom administrations clumsy, and even absurd'.[10]

The preservation of the status quo was in part due to the fact that the administration acted as a career route and boosted status, particularly for the Anglo-Irish ascendancy. In an open letter to the Lord Lieutenant in 1905, the writer R. Barry O'Brien commented: 'It is notorious that the highest positions in the Government of Ireland have been and are filled by Protestants, almost wholly to the exclusion of those who professed the religion of the nation . . . It has well been said that the government of a country must partake of the character of the people.'[11] Any change was seen by the Unionists as a step to undermining the whole Union, while Home Rule supporters saw reform as insufficient and as a barrier to self-government. Nobody within Ireland argued for the preservation of Dublin Castle on the grounds of its effectiveness or efficiency.

A major consequence of the introduction of the Third Home Rule Bill was that self-government was seen as inevitable. During the time of Augustine Birrell's Chief Secretaryship, 1907–16, Catholics took an increasing proportion of administrative posts. The Easter Rising, however, destroyed any hope of a smooth transition from colony to devolution. During the ensuing martial law period, Prime Minister Asquith talked of abolishing the positions of both Viceroy and Chief Secretary and making a single Cabinet Minister responsible for Irish government.[12] After the collapse of Lloyd George's attempt to produce immediate Home Rule in the summer of 1916, the old system was restored, with the recall of Lord Wimborne as Viceroy and the appointment of the obscure lawyer H.E. Duke as Chief Secretary. From that time the

existence of a Coalition government with a Tory majority meant the reversal
of what has been called 'the greening of Dublin Castle',[13] although some
Catholics held on to important jobs.

Patricia Jalland has sought to re-establish Birrell's historical reputation, and
George Boyce together with Cameron Hazelhurst has made a case for the usually poorly-regarded Duke. In response, Eunan O'Halpin has pointed to
Birrell's inept administration of security, Duke's inability to take policy initiatives and his frequent recourse to Whitehall on trivial matters.[14] Such debate,
however, should be put in a wider context. Second-rate politicians like Duke,
Ian Macpherson and Hamar Greenwood were chosen because major figures
declined the job. Lloyd George refused the supremo position in 1916 and
from 1917 Walter Long preferred a liaison role to that of returning to the
Chief Secretaryship. H.A.L. Fisher looked the other way when asked about his
availability for the office in 1920.[15]

While various Chief Secretaries have received much of the blame for the
shortcomings of British rule in Ireland, the primary responsibility should rest
with Westminster. Up to 1912, Birrell was the longest-serving and, in terms of
legislative accomplishments, among the most successful of Chief Secretaries:
he even relished living in Ireland and read widely in Irish history and literature.
Following the Ulster Crisis and the Easter Rising, it was not Asquith's reputation
but Birrell's, and that of Matthew Nathan the hardworking and sympathetic
Under-Secretary, which suffered.[16]

The structural and institutional weaknesses were the consequence of unsympathetic and ill-thought out British policy towards Ireland. There had been no
debate about the system of government at the time that the Union was implemented. The abolition of the Irish parliament had been motivated by defence
considerations and passed in a manner calculated to deepen an Irish sense of
grievance. Sir James Dougherty, Under-Secretary 1908–14, declared: 'We have a
quasi-separate government, and . . . the people of Ireland look to what they call
"the Castle" despised as it is by many, for advice and guidance, and, above all,
they make it the repository of their complaints.'[17]

The Union proved a disastrous halfway house with few of the virtues of either
a centralised or a devolved government, thus enabling all Irish grievances and
problems to be blamed on it. Under the Act, Irish considerations were all too
frequently subjugated to British political demands: there was an unwillingness
to relate British political philosophy to Irish needs, most dramatically demonstrated during the Great Famine. Beginning with Catholic emancipation, necessary reforms were reluctantly made and badly delayed.

Irish policy was often determined by British party political considerations:
reforms were adopted because of the value of Irish votes at Westminster or
opposed because it suited electoral needs. For all his talk of morality in politics
and of a mission to pacify Ireland, Gladstone had strong political reasons for
introducing the First Home Rule Bill.[18] The vicissitudes of British rule encouraged the growth of Catholic nationalism. When constructive measures were

passed — the Disestablishment of the Church of Ireland in 1869; the sundry Land Acts of the late nineteenth and early twentieth centuries; the eventual founding of a Catholic university; the democratisation of local government in the last years of the nineteenth century and the introduction of Home Rule legislation — it was a matter of too little, too late, and was not the product of any coherent underlying philosophy.

These changes served only to heighten demands for self-government and to bring about the birth of Northern Unionism. Arguably if the various strands of constructive Unionism had been used to tackle Irish grievances in the earlier years of the nineteenth century, wide elements of Irish opinion could have become reconciled to the Union. It may be true also that Ulster's resistance to a separate Dublin parliament could have been overridden in the late nineteenth century, before its two political parties became organised under the one banner of Ulster Unionism. This would have required, however, a sustained and empathetic approach to Irish affairs which was never exhibited by any British government. The traditional British skill of compromise leading to consensus could not be made to apply to Ireland where a radical reassessment was called for in government, society and economy.

Underlying all was a fundamental lack of sympathy for the Catholic Irish, often amounting to racism. Many of the leading figures responsible for British administration in Ireland in the period of the War of Independence expressed contempt for the Irish. Walter Long, who led Southern Unionist opinion and had an Irish wife, in arguing for strong government commented: 'It is the only form of government which the Irish understand. They are very quick, and when they see that disloyalty not only goes unpunished but is sometimes even rewarded they naturally do not hesitate to indulge in their own tastes.' Harold Spender reported Lloyd George as saying that 'Ireland had hated England and always would. He could easily govern Ireland with the sword; he was far more concerned about the Bolsheviks at home.'[19]

In the spring of 1920, Winston Churchill wrote to his wife of a 'diabolical strain' in the Irish character and continued: 'I expect it is that treacherous, assassinating, conspiring trait which has done them in in the bygone ages of history and prevented them from being a great responsible nation with stability and prosperity.' In the midst of detailed consideration of Irish policy in January 1921, Bonar Law declared the Irish to be 'an inferior race'; when commiserating with Ian Macpherson on his appointment as Chief Secretary in January 1919, General Macready commented: 'I cannot say I envy you for I loathe the country you are going to and its people with a depth deeper than the sea and more violent than that I feel against the Boche.'[20]

In the political context the importance of the fact that a Coalition government, dominated increasingly by Conservatives, existed from 1915 cannot be overstressed. The problem with reconciling Tory and Liberal views within the administration meant that it served no-one's political interest to raise the Irish Question unless it was absolutely necessary. Throughout the government's history, up to its collapse in 1922, Ireland had the potential to destroy it.[21] While the Tory party were less militant in their support of the Ulster Loyalist cause than they had been pre-First World War, they still appeared implacable in resistance to any talk of an all-Ireland settlement or of Dominion Status. It is additionally true that the overwhelming demands of the World War and the settlement after it meant that other issues were sidelined.

The decision to extend conscription to Ireland, taken on 25 March 1918, is an excellent example of blinkered Westminster policies towards Ireland. The German offensive of that time provided an apparently sound pretext but the consequence was to unify all nationalist opinion. As a sop to Liberals within the Coalition, the prospect of imminent legislation on Home Rule was coupled with conscription. Lloyd George confided to Lord Oranmore that a Home Rule Bill had to be offered 'to satisfy Labour sentiments and American feeling, but that if no one in Ireland approved of it, it might be doomed'. The government was seemingly oblivious to the reality that Irish opinion had by now rejected any such idea of limited devolution. The step was taken against the advice of all the Irish administration. Duke resigned over it, commenting: 'The worst thing that could happen would be to support the introduction of Conscription and not to carry it through.' This fear was to be completely realised.[22]

The Cabinet, advised by Lord French who had undertaken a mission to Ireland, was confident that they could override any opposition. The conscription decision resulted in the transformation of Dublin Castle. Originally the intention had been that the Lord Lieutenancy be put into commission with the appointment of three Lord Justices — Lord French to control military aspects, Lord Midleton and the Lord Chancellor Campbell to be responsible for political issues. The rôle of the Chief Secretary was to be downgraded to that of political spokesman at Westminster. When Midleton refused the terms offered, French became Viceroy with the clear assurance that his position amounted to military supremo. French reminded Lloyd George in October 1918 that he had been sent to Ireland 'to exercise the full functions of a Governor-General de jure and de facto' and at another time talked of a quasi-military government.[23]

It was expected in the beginning that French's Irish background and personal popularity, together with his positive attitude to Home Rule, would make him a popular appointment, but his time in the office proved a disastrous end to his public service career. French was a poor administrator and revealed all the bone-headed stubbornness which military men often demonstrate in political contexts. In February 1920, Lord Justice Ross told Walter Long that French 'has no local knowledge and like all great soldiers he has no knowledge of civil administration. The consequence has been a series of most serious blunders.' W.E. Wylie, the Law Adviser in Dublin Castle, wrote: 'A dear old man Lord French. A kindly honest Gentleman brave and courteous but I often wondered how the first British Expeditionary Force . . . ever got back from Mons in 1914.'

While in office, French soon retreated from any support for Home Rule. Eight months after coming to Dublin he commented: 'Every day that has passed since I became viceroy of Ireland has proved more clearly the unfitness of Ireland for any form of Home Rule, now, or in the immediate future.' French was always to be a firm supporter of coercive policies to deal with Irish resistance.[24]

The Lord Lieutenant's intransigent attitudes were probably hardened by the appointment of Edward Saunderson, son of the old Unionist leader, as his chief aide. Saunderson was a protégé of Walter Long and a bigoted Protestant of the worst order. In January 1919 Saunderson told Long: 'I have been waging steady war with the dirty elements in Dublin Castle. When you see His Ex. you would do him a very good turn if you would impress on him that when he is dealing with Catholic officials like MacMahon (the Under Secretary) he should be careful what he says. He has the open-hearted ways of a soldier and does not realise . . . the Catholic Church are making (efforts) to get hold of the machine.'[25]

Long was the major influence on French and the British government. He was a Wiltshire landowner and traditional Tory who had inherited land in County Wicklow, became Chief Secretary in 1905 and later leader of the Irish Unionist Party. In 1918 Long chaired the committee with the brief to draw up Home Rule legislation parallel with the implementation of conscription. By that time Long was supporting a federalist solution as a means of reconciling Ulster and Tory opinion to a measure of Irish self-government. Such views won little support in Britain and were of supreme irrelevance in Ireland. Long was obsessed by what he saw as the link between Sinn Féin and the ultimate horror of the Bolshevik menace.[26] It was extremely ironic that when he was Chief Secretary, Long had insisted that his position be defined as superior to that of the Lord Lieutenant. In 1918 and 1919, however, he supported virtually dictatorial powers for the Viceroy.

For the next two years, French and Long dominated British policy on Ireland at a time when the War Cabinet was preoccupied with more pressing issues and Ireland was regarded as a tiresome diversion. Long stated: 'the Irish Government have been given practically a free hand; and I am not aware that they need any additional authority.'[27]

In late April 1918 Edward Shortt was appointed Chief Secretary. A barrister and junior minister, Shortt, who was fifty-six, was a Liberal MP for Newcastle-upon-Tyne. He was descended on his mother's side from a County Tyrone family.[28] Neither Shortt's greater sympathy for Irish nationalism nor the reduction in power of his office augured well for the harmonious running of Dublin Castle. The Lord Lieutenant and the Chief Secretary were to disagree on a whole host of matters — French was to countermand Shortt's instruction that old members of the Ulster Volunteer Force hand in arms, and Shortt was to be extremely critical of French's administrative reforms.[29]

For a time French played down talk of divisions, telling Long in June: 'I could not really wish for a better Chief Secretary to work with. He is full of courage, energy and go. Although he is an out-and-out Radical and Nationalist, he is always ready and willing to listen to views other than his own . . . I really like him very much.' By October, French was telling the Prime Minister: 'Unless Mr Shortt can be induced to change his methods, I do not consider it will be to the general advantage that he and I should any longer be associated together in the government of Ireland.' French claimed that Shortt was igno- rant about Irish conditions and was interested only in the Irish vote in Britain. He concluded: 'The fact of the matter is Mr Shortt . . . both openly and secret- ly, has opposed my policy from the first.'[30]

French's first prominent act in office was to order the so-called German Plot arrests. A large proportion of the Sinn Féin leadership were imprisoned on the flimsiest of grounds. When the material justifying the arrests was published in 1921, it pertained almost entirely to pre-1918 evidence.[31] The action would appear to have been intended to demonstrate French's hard line but only served to ensure radical nationalist control of Sinn Féin.

With the aim of following A.J. Balfour's perceived successful time as Chief Secretary in the late 1880s,[32] French planned administrative, social and eco- nomic reforms to follow on coercive measures. A particular stress was placed on employment schemes for demobilised officers and on changes to the machinery of government. French established an Executive Council, which sat between May 1918 and August 1919 and had the sensible aim of bringing together politicians, civil servants, soldiers and lawyers. The Chief Secretary was excluded and there was no accountability to parliament. French himself headed the Military Council which again aimed at the rationalisation of the loosely-controlled system.

Finally, an Advisory Council met from October 1918 and was intended, as Long absurdly claimed, to form 'a representative body of Irishmen from all parts of the Island to discuss . . . the various problems of government'.[33] The members were all Southern Unionist and had no political mandate whatsoever. Shortt and French disagreed as to whether the Council should be advisory or consultative. Evidently Long and French wanted it to replace a Home Rule parliament and were fiercely opposed by Shortt, who was perhaps responsible for a report in *The Times* of 13 December entitled 'Irish Reconstruction — A Muddle'.

The whole idea of economic reconstruction was stillborn. French's health problems in the first months of 1919 aided the collapse of his feeble adminis- trative experiment. In early 1919, he was initially attracted to R.B. Haldane's ideas for administrative reform as a basis for political reconciliation. Haldane had been responsible for major changes to the British machinery of govern- ment and had visited Dublin in January 1919. He suggested that a commission of three be set up, representing Southern nationalist, Ulster Unionist and independent interests and that, if consensus was arrived at, Dominion Status should be granted for the whole of Ireland. Long reacted with horror to these suggestions and it is clear that they were the product of an administrative mind quite divorced from political realities.[34]

2

BACKGROUND TO THE
IRISH REVOLUTION

At the beginning of 1910, the future for radical varieties of Irish nationalism appeared to be dim. The Irish Parliamentary Party (IPP) held virtually undisputed sway at elections and the Irish Republican Brotherhood (IRB) with a membership of only around 1,500 seemed to have no concrete revolutionary plans: a few years earlier James Joyce had seen Dublin as the centre of paralysis.[1] By 1918 the situation had been transformed: the IPP was on the swift track to oblivion and was being replaced by an advanced nationalist coalition led by a new resurgent Sinn Féin Party and the Irish Volunteers, soon to be known as the Irish Republican Army (IRA).

The immediate causes for the radicalisation of Irish nationalism were the Ulster Crisis, the effects of the First World War, and the Easter Rising and its aftermath. Nonetheless there had been massive changes in attitudes before and since the fall of Parnell in the late 1880s/early 1890s which were also critical in explaining the speed of the Irish revolution. In retrospect the IPP had reached its zenith with the introduction of the First Home Rule Bill in 1886 and had been on the decline even before the disastrous Parnell split. In these years a whole host of social, cultural and political movements developed an appeal which was never to be effectively countered by the IPP.

The Gaelic Athletic Association (GAA) was the most popular of all, appealing particularly to the young and soon the object of a clash between the IRB and the Catholic Church for its control. Its county-based structure was a focus for local pride and identity centred on small towns. To start with the Irish language movement, the Gaelic League, established in 1893, had had far fewer members than the GAA, but by the first decade of the new century it had led a successful campaign for compulsory teaching of the Irish language in schools and had established itself widely in urban areas.[2] The cultural revival was reinforced by the work of W.B. Yeats, Lady Gregory and J.M. Synge amongst many others, and by the foundation of the Abbey Theatre in Dublin.

The commemoration of the centenary of the 1798 Rebellion and the organisation of protest against the royal visits of Queen Victoria and Edward VII resulted in the formation of political pressure groups, most notably Cumann na nGaedheal and Arthur Griffith's National Council, both of which amalgamated with the more radical and Northern-based Dungannon Clubs to form Sinn Féin in 1907. By advocating economic protectionism to develop Irish industry, Griffith looked forward to planning for an independent Ireland's future. His advocacy of passive resistance tactics against British rule and for the boycott of Westminster by Irish MPs provided the blueprint for what occurred in 1919. The movement had the potential to provide a bridge between constitutional and physical force nationalists.[3]

These institutions, comprising what became known as the New Nationalism, had very different aims and philosophies but were unified by their resistance to British cultural influences. They must be placed in the context of changes in both society and in the economy, and particularly in the enormous growth of communications. Irish society was becoming much more mobile; the migrant experience within Ireland as well as the emigrant experience had vast repercussions. Many of the young escaped their small town backgrounds and went to work in Dublin and other towns in the growing service and local government occupations. Much of the support for the New Nationalist organisations was amongst civil servants and school teachers. This degree of social mobility only heightened the realisation that most higher positions were barred to Catholics. The British government's belated reforms in this period ironically aided this burgeoning sense of Irish identity.[4]

The precise relationship between the elements of the New Nationalism and the achievement of the Irish revolution has recently been questioned. Nevertheless, the reminiscences of a massive number of Sinn Féin and IRA veterans tell of the importance of the GAA and the Gaelic League in their rising consciousness: the Christian Brothers' schools taught future revolutionaries the traditional version of Irish history, centring on the magic dates of 1798, 1848 and 1867. Memories abound of the influence of local schoolteachers and of parents relating the collective folk memory of the Famine and of the Fenians.[5]

Women were uneasy partners in what became the Sinn Féin coalition. They played an independent and forceful role within the Gaelic Revival through an organisation called Inghinidhe na hÉireann [Daughters of Eireann] and especially in the campaign against royal visits. The IPP's negative approach to women's rights, and particularly the suffrage, helped to ensure that the sympathy of politically-active women would gravitate to more radical forms of nationalism. There were, however, strains in the relationship between the female suffragists and nationalists.[6]

Cumann na mBan was formed in 1914 as an auxiliary to the Irish Volunteers. Eoin MacNeill affirmed: 'There would be work to do for large numbers who could not be in the marching line. There would be work for the women.' This was a contrast to the more militant independent days of the Ladies' Land

League of 1881–2. Despite this the Proclamation of the Irish Republic in 1916 guaranteed equal rights and equal opportunities for all citizens, and women had a crucial role, occasionally involving fighting, in the Rising. Women were even more essential after the massive number of internments which followed.[7]

Between 1917 and 1921 Irish nationalists hit upon the most appropriate and successful methods of resisting the British administration: a mixture of guerrilla warfare and passive resistance with a high priority given to intelligence and propaganda and the sidelining of progressive social ideas. On the surface the military and political wings of the movement combined to mutual advantage, although all kinds of tensions were suppressed and would fester into enormous future problems. Underlying everything was the rejection of British rule together with the IPP which meant that a consensus existed for advanced nationalism.

The Easter Rising succeeded in arousing the latent nationalist consciousness in spite of the tactics adopted and because of the British government's coercive reaction. To take over prominent buildings, and at that not the most appropriate ones, to set up a hopelessly-confused plan of operations with Germany, America and the provinces, and not even to block the communication route for British reinforcements from Kingstown to the centre of Dublin, were all to invite disaster. Apart from its slipshod planning, the Rising demonstrated the absurdity of nineteenth-century notions of romantic revolution at a time of huge advances in military technology. To virtually court the execution, or at least imprisonment, of the leadership and to potentially decimate the fighting force were strange ways to expect to win a war.[8]

In the recesses of the General Post Office, Michael Collins shook his head with disgust at the impractical tactics and the chaos caused by the strategy. It is often argued that the sacrifice of Pearse, Clarke and their comrades proved to be justified by subsequent events. However, Irish revolutionary socialism was never to recover from the loss of the intellectual and charismatic leadership of James Connolly. The Rising also produced a good deal of recrimination within the nationalist ranks. Many, notably Éamon de Valera and Cathal Brugha, blamed the IRB for what went wrong and argued that in future the reliance should be on public institutions and that the secret organisation should be wound up. The leadership of the Cork Volunteers was put on trial by the IRB for surrendering their arms, and the Kerry leaders were heavily blamed for the debacle of the arms landing and the arrest of Sir Roger Casement on Fenit Strand.[9] Thus the legacy of 1916 had negative as well as positive effects.

Nonetheless, the Cork IRA leader and historian Florrie O'Donoghue held that the Rising had served its purpose by restoring the soul of the nation, and its memory played an important role in the regeneration of advanced nationalism. The cult of the 1916 martyrs and the religious symbolism of Eastertide underpinned the development of the Sinn Féin movement during 1917.[10] The choice of individuals connected with the Rising as candidates at crucial by-elections established this link at the same time as completely different political strategies were adopted. The emphasis was to be on responding to general opinion rather than, as in 1916, being in advance of it.

The tactics and ideology of the new Sinn Féin movement had been set out in Arthur Griffith's *The Resurrection of Hungary*, published in 1904: abstention from the Westminster parliament by the Irish MPs, formation of an independent government and a counter-state. The Sinn Féin Party, however, emerged by a process of trial and error through the course of 1917. The breakdown of Lloyd George's Home Rule initiative in the summer of 1916, the various acts of coercion by the authorities resulting in the arrests of nationalists on often ridiculously trivial grounds, and the long-winded futility of the Irish Convention all played into the hands of advanced nationalists. For much of 1917 there was a battle between contending personalities and inchoate institutions to fill the vacuum left by the decline of the IPP. A vital decision was that taken to contest all by-elections, so deserting the abstentionist orthodoxy and republican purity, and thus anticipating a similar decision in the 1980s by nationalists in Northern Ireland. Some opposed the move, warning of the consequences if the elections were lost.

The first gamble was taken at the North Roscommon election of February 1917, when Count Plunkett, the father of Joseph Plunkett executed in 1916, was comfortably elected. Only after his victory did Plunkett make clear his decision to abstain from Westminster.[11] After much urging, Joe McGuinness, detained in Lewes Prison, reluctantly agreed to stand in the South Longford election of May 1917, on the priceless slogan 'put him in to get him out'. This time the victory was marginal and probably decided by the last-minute intervention of Archbishop Walsh of Dublin warning of the evils of Partition. Longford was much less favourable territory for advanced nationalism than Roscommon had been and Walsh's secretary, Monsignor Michael J. Curran, concluded that the election was 'an almost fatal blow to the (Parliamentary) Party'.[12] The largest triumph of all came with de Valera's landslide at the East Clare election in July 1917. By the time of William T. Cosgrave's success at the Kilkenny City poll a month later, Sinn Féin victories had become the norm, although the party suffered reverses at the South Armagh, East Tyrone and Waterford City contests in early 1918.[13]

During 1917 and 1918 there was a certain vagueness about the Sinn Féin programme. The Convention of October 1917 which brought about the unity of the party under de Valera's Presidency, adopted a compromise by which disillusioned constitutional nationalists, members of the original Sinn Féin clubs, IRB men and Volunteers could all be brought together. It was agreed that a republic should be the desired objective but that a referendum would be held on the precise form of government once independence had been achieved. Nothing was said about the means by which British authority should be removed, and all could agree on the desirability of an appeal to an international post-World War peace conference and the formation of an independent government.[14]

It was widely admitted in retrospect that the election triumphs of 1917 and 1918 represented more a rejection of the Parliamentary Party than a clear support for Sinn Féin. Collins confided that the 'declaration of a Republic was really in advance of national thought'. There was a deliberate emphasis on moderation and respectability which included the calculated wooing of the Catholic Church.[15] All elements within Irish society supported the resistance to conscription and by their withdrawal from Westminster over it the IPP's MPs conceded the shrewdness of Sinn Féin's abstentionist policy. In the rise of advanced nationalism, the conscription crisis was a far more decisive moment than the Easter Rising.

By contrast to Sinn Féin, the military side of the movement had no preconceived plan. The move away from the obsession with preparation for a general rising towards the adoption of guerrilla methods did not occur because of any inspired revelation in the post-Rising prisons and internment camps; rather it evolved in response to changed circumstances. Fintan Lalor in Young Ireland days and, more recently, Bulmer Hobson had theorised about defensive warfare tactics, of methods to compensate for the disparity in strength between rebels and British forces, but there is no evidence that their ideas were studied and consciously taken up.[16] In contrast to later guerrilla fighters who learned from the Irish experience, there was no blueprint for such methods at that time. *An tÓglach*, the journal of the IRA, responded to events and did not direct them.

Even as late as 1921, British authorities talked of the possibility of a general rising being attempted and there is evidence that at various times IRA leaders had not totally abandoned such notions.[17] Tomás MacCurtain and Terence MacSwiney, Sinn Féin and Volunteer leaders in Cork City, in suggesting a wave of barracks attacks, in early 1920, visualised a concerted uprising: the principle behind hunger-striking corresponded with Pearse's blood-sacrifice ideology. The post-1916 development of the Volunteers was dictated by circumstances: the scarcity of arms and the consequences of absurdly inept British policy. During 1917 and 1918, the Volunteers were reorganised on a local basis: the attempt to establish centralised direction followed.

In the absence of anything other than small supplies of arms, training was at best rudimentary. The Volunteers were organised along conventional British lines in companies, battalions and brigades; the company usually corresponded with a village or parish, the brigade with single counties. Officers were unpaid and elected and units were self-financing. The leaders tended to be local notables, footballers, hurlers, or Gaelic League enthusiasts, chosen often without reference to military ability. John McCoy, reminiscing about his battalion in South Armagh, commented: 'Our first capt. was selected for his fine physique, football ability and his decency of character. He was a local farmer without the organising ability or the sense of discipline necessary to make a successful officer.'[18] All this made for an uneven geographical spread of the movement, for parochial attitudes and failure of co-ordination between areas. This was only partly compensated for by the cross-fertilisation of ideas and lasting friend-ships fostered in places like Frongoch in Wales, where many had been interned after 1916.

An enormous boost was given to the revival of the Volunteers by external events. The staged release of internees to ecstatic receptions from December 1916 until the following spring, vividly contrasted with the hostility shown on their departure. In September 1917, Thomas Ashe, hero of Ashbourne in the Rising and President of the Supreme Council of the IRB, died as a consequence of force-feeding during a hunger strike in Mountjoy Prison. This played a cru-cial role in the reactivation of the Dublin Brigade which organised a massive funeral procession through the city streets.[19]

The disproportionate speed of the movement's growth in certain areas had much to do with the incidence of by-elections. A high profile was gained by the Volunteers in canvassing and guarding the ballot boxes and the influx of lead-ers from all over the country helped with recruitment and training. Volunteers in Longford and South Armagh testified that elections there transformed their brigades. Longford veterans recalled that the South Longford election gave the first impetus to recruitment, the conscription crisis the second. A local offi-cer in South Armagh reported: 'There was little Volunteer organisation in evi-dence in the constituency before the election and after it Companies were functioning in almost every parish area. The war-like conditions which these new Volunteers had to face during the election campaign and the sacrifices and physical strain demanded from them — and cheerfully undertaken — produced a splendid morale which was a most valuable asset later on in the Tan War.'[20]

A Volunteer meeting in March 1917 in Dublin re-established the National Executive and a Convention in October, meeting just after the Sinn Féin one, strove to bring together the political and military branches; de Valera assumed the Presidency of the Volunteers as well as that of Sinn Féin. In March 1918 a General Headquarters Staff (GHQ) was set up with Richard Mulcahy as Chief of Staff, and Michael Collins as Director of Organisation.[21] With few arms to distribute and no means of enforcing control, GHQ to start with could exer-cise little authority over provincial commands but did have potential for edu-cation and co-ordination.

Nevertheless, O'Donoghue was correct to emphasise: 'The democratic organisation of the Volunteers and the impossibility in the circumstances of any tight control by the headquarters staff permitted and encouraged the development of local initiative on a scale quite abnormal in a regular army.' The cell-like structure of the clandestine IRB with its insistence that members only knew the identity of their immediately superior officer reinforced this localism.[22]

The most vital boon for the Volunteers came with the planned extension of conscription to Ireland in the spring of 1918. Monsignor Michael J. Curran wrote: 'It would be difficult to over-state the paramount importance of the fight on conscription.' Every county reported a considerable rise in membership figures and details were drawn up for resistance in the event of its implementation. The Volunteers now appeared to be popular opponents of alien authority and many moderates joined the movement, which was akin to what happened in 1914. The numbers fell off again following the removal of the conscription threat, but the crisis had done much to raise the importance of the military wing of advanced nationalism vis-à-vis the political side.[23]

It was the conscription crisis which finally brought both the church and moderate opinion into line with the Sinn Féin outlook. The hierarchy's hardline resistance to physical force nationalism had mellowed somewhat by 1917. Their attitude to the Easter Rising had been ambivalent and bishops followed opinion rather than led it when it came to criticism of the Irish Parliamentary Party and the British government in 1917. There was, and remained, a divide between older and younger priests, with the latter sharing the sympathy of their small farmer class backgrounds to advanced nationalism. Individual bishops, however, like Bishop Fogarty of Killaloe, publicly supported Sinn Féin. The Catholic hierarchy's enthusiastic participation in the popular campaign against conscription was a rare example of opposition to established government on their part.[24]

Although the new consensus gave the appearance of unity, there were many signs of strain within the coalition itself. Many Volunteers were cynical about the political strategy and impatient about the lack of military activity. The diaries of Liam de Róiste, Gaelic revivalist and TD for Cork City, reveal a long-standing opposition to what he regarded as the autocratic attitudes of the Volunteers in Cork to his passive resistance beliefs. On 20 October 1917, de Róiste wrote: 'the military side of the movement is now actively and aggressively working to dominate the civil side and to take all control and direction of civil as well as military affairs . . . Every man who is not a Volunteer or in the good graces of the chiefs of the Volunteers is to be pushed aside from responsible positions in Sinn Féin.'[25]

In the early post-Rising days, Sinn Féin and Volunteer activities had been practically interchangeable, but military men increasingly developed a contempt for politicians. There was an ill-defined and confused relationship between institutions. The Volunteer organisation predated the reconstituted Sinn Féin Party and its prior allegiance was to its own Executive. In a clear statement of its purpose, it became customary during 1919 for the Volunteers to be called the Irish Republican Army. Matters were further confused by the continued existence of the IRB. The secret society, dating back to 1857, made clear that its Supreme Council claimed to be the highest authority in the absence of an actual republican government: its constitution was reformed in 1919 to allow for recognition of the Dáil, but allegiance was conditional on that body adhering faithfully to the tenets of republicanism.[26]

The IRB formed an elite within the expanding Volunteers and often caused tensions and divided loyalties. The IRA GHQ consisted almost entirely of IRB men. Some Volunteers were profoundly disturbed that membership of secret societies was forbidden by the Catholic Church. The future leader of the Dublin Brigade IRA, Frank Henderson, rejected an invitation from Seán O'Casey to join the IRB. He wrote: 'I explained to him that I understood from the Pronouncement of the Bishops in their Pastorals on "Secret Societies" that they prohibited the IRB.' Others felt that they were being excluded from a charmed inner circle, controlled by Collins.[27]

It has become the norm to depict the IRB's role after 1916 as progressively less significant. Many have argued that it became redundant as the size and strength of the Volunteers/IRA increased. Contemporaries on both sides of the Treaty debate like to give this impression. Andy Cooney said: 'We treated it as a joke', and Richard Mulcahy said that its meetings consisted of nothing more than a roll call and that policy was in no way affected by consideration of secret society membership.[28] It suited the interests of these two to say this and their argument downgrades the important part the IRB played in the War and the divisions that followed it. IRB men formed a network of arms smugglers on boats and in ports at home and abroad; Collins relied on them as if they were part of an extended family and their mutual loyalty underpinned the methods used with such success in the Irish revolution. At the local level tensions within the IRA can often be ascribed to attitudes to the IRB.

These confused relationships between institutions encouraged the emergence of contending and charismatic leaders. Sinn Féin, the Volunteers and the IRB provided powerbases for ambitious men. By the end of 1917, Éamon de Valera was the dominant political personality and Michael Collins rose to pre-eminence in military matters due to his strength within the IRB and the Volunteer GHQ.

Born in Manhattan in 1882 to an Irish mother and Spanish father, de Valera had been brought up in County Limerick by his grandparents. A mathematics teacher, he came to the Volunteers through the Gaelic League and sprang to fame as the last surviving commandant of the Easter Rising; Boland's Mill in 1916 was the last military action that de Valera was ever to be directly involved in. As the victorious Sinn Féin candidate at the East Clare by-election in July 1917, de Valera displayed his political talents and he soon became the chief conciliator and diplomat within Sinn Féin ranks. His aloof manner aided his rise to the top and he became the most appropriate middleman between hardline republicans like Cathal Brugha and Austin Stack and moderates like Arthur Griffith. De Valera's imprisonment from May 1918 until February 1919 strengthened his nominal control of the movement. He was always to believe that the route to Irish independence lay through diplomacy and international recognition.[29]

In his Intelligence summary of the War, Brigadier-General Ormonde Winter expressed his firm belief that the IRA lacked a natural and popular leader.[30] This only goes to show the amazing lack of knowledge and judgment of the Head of British Intelligence. Allowing for romanticisation of Michael Collins by many at the time and since, it remains true that Collins was the most charismatic and efficient of Irish revolutionaries. While he took advantage of favourable circumstances, it is impossible to argue that any colleague could have adequately replaced him. Collins inspired a remarkable degree of personal loyalty as well as provoking suspicion and antagonism amongst others. Colonel Charles Russell recalled that Collins 'was everything' and Frank Thornton, of his Intelligence staff, commented that he 'was a man with a determination to make a complete success of everything he put his hands to'.[31]

Collins was born in West Cork in 1890 and his time working in post offices and banks in London between 1906 and 1916 is a key to his mindset. An avid reader of Conan Doyle and other Edwardian writers, Collins was heavily influenced by his British experience as well as by his participation in Gaelic revivalism in London societies. He returned to Dublin just prior to the Rising, in which he played a background part at the GPO, and was interned in Frongoch. A range of accounts from fellow detainees tell of Collins' commanding position within that university of revolution. On release in December 1916, his influence with Tom Clarke's widow led to his taking control of the Prisoners' Dependants Fund, which in part was a front for the IRB's revival. Collins' legendary energy and immense administrative ability had by the end of 1917 made him indispensable.[32]

The reservations held by many concerning Collins' rather brash and domineering personality were shown by colleagues preferring Mulcahy over him as Chief of Staff of the Volunteers in 1918, but it was soon apparent who called the shots in the organisation. Possessed of an amazing memory, he insisted on punctuality and was intensely aware of negative stereotypes about the supposedly slovenly, lazy Irish character. Collins' correspondence reveals a personal involvement with all the intricate and complex negotiations over arms supplies and all the other IRA activities. Direct, plain-speaking, hard drinking and very sociable, Collins was regularly found by men from the provinces sitting in the snug of Devlin's Bar in Parnell Square masterminding operations with his encyclopaedic knowledge.[33]

Already Collins had realised the central importance of a spy network, and had set up an Intelligence organisation. He used his contacts in British ports and in London to supply war material. While Collins was only narrowly elected to the Sinn Féin Executive in October 1917, he was to surprise many with his political abilities and proved the most efficient of administrators in the Dáil government as Minister of Finance.[34]

Arthur Griffith was an essential, if at times marginal, figure within the Sinn Féin coalition. He was considerably older than most of his colleagues and remained wary of physical force nationalism. His stress on the virtues of passive resistance became less relevant as the military conflict intensified.[35] Cathal Brugha and Austin Stack personified the survival of the unbending and intransigent Fenian tradition. They grew to resent Collins' all-encompassing aura and were much friendlier with de Valera. Richard Mulcahy, the IRA Chief of

Staff, shared a public service background with Collins but was quite different in terms of personality, being dour, unclubbable and sober. Collins and Mulcahy had a mutual respect and worked well together.[36] Beneath the superficial unity of Sinn Féin, therefore, were tensions and rivalries relating both to ideology and to personality.

The post-Rising Sinn Féin and Volunteer revival initially went hand in hand with agitation on the land question, caused by the absence of emigration during the World War years as well as the repercussions from previous land legislation, which had worsened income differentials within farming communities. In the western counties much of the popularity for advanced nationalism was related to land hunger, and Sinn Féin activists participated in cattle drives on grazier land during 1917 and 1918. Michael Brennan, the major IRA leader in East Clare, soon warned of the divisive effects of agrarian agitation and his attitude was in line with that of GHQ. British military and police sources were convinced that the spectre of Bolshevism lay behind political protest and failed to see how conservative the Sinn Féin movement had become. The Labour Party decided not to contest the 1918 general election for fear of splitting the nationalist vote, but they got precious little in return for this act of self-denial.[37]

The Irish revolution was not to be concerned with the redistribution of wealth. Sinn Féin and the IRA continued to be overwhelmingly dominated, with a few local exceptions, by the small farmer class and by artisans and traders in urban areas. They did reflect majority opinion within the twenty-six counties and represented an emerging ruling class but excluded others; many disparate interests in Irish society, including Southern Unionists, prosperous farmers, farm labourers and the working class in general were largely unrepresented in the Dáil. The historian Fergus Campbell has stressed the importance of the survival of land protest in the west as demonstrated by the continuity in membership between the United Irish League of the early years of the twentieth century and the Sinn Féin party post-1916. The widespread agrarian agitation of 1920, threatening the security of so many graziers, had the potential to move the Irish revolution in a more radical direction. If it is true, however, that the Irish revolution was not 'innately conservative', by 1921 social considerations had been overwhelmed by narrowly political ones.[38]

International aspects contributed considerably to the favourable prospect for advanced nationalism. US President Woodrow Wilson has commonly been depicted as an enemy of the Irish nationalist cause. It was Wilson, though, who gave enormous assistance to Sinn Féin in 1917 and 1918 by propagating the doctrine of self-determination and continually stressing to worldwide audiences the rights of small nations and the evils of imperialism. Not only did Wilson's espousal of a new, liberal world order place the British Empire on the defensive, it enabled the Irish nationalists to recover from the pro-German associations of 1916. The German support for the Easter Rising had done much to harm the Irish cause in American eyes but by 1918 exile nationalism had won back a lot of its respectability and popularity. Wilson was to disappoint Irish hopes of him, but had done a lot to ensure the Sinn Féin victory of 1918.[39]

The electoral strategy embraced by both Sinn Féin and the Volunteers reached its apogee in the Sinn Féin victory at the December 1918 General Election. For months before there could have been little doubt, except in confused British minds, about the outcome of that election. The German Plot arrests of May 1918, in the midst of the stand-off over conscription, had driven even more moderate opinion into the arms of Sinn Féin. Michael Collins was forewarned by his Intelligence sources of the planned arrests and with other IRB colleagues went into hiding: de Valera and other moderates chose to accept imprisonment and remained in jail long beyond the General Election.[40] This meant that more radical nationalists controlled the Sinn Féin nominations for constituencies.

At the election Sinn Féin won seventy-three seats, Unionists twenty-six and the Parliamentary Party six. The result had more to do with the collapse of the IPP, as shown by the twenty-five uncontested seats Sinn Féin won, than it did with any popular understanding of the precise aims of the Sinn Féin party and how it hoped to realise them. To a large extent the IPP had given up before the campaign started. In electoral percentage terms the Sinn Féin vote was somewhat less impressive at 48 per cent of the electorate, or 65 per cent in the twenty-six counties excluding the north-east. Apart from the university seats, the only IPP successes were in the north-east and these were aided by an electoral pact with Sinn Féin guaranteeing them both some seats. Personation and multi-voting was rife but could not have affected the overall result. The huge majority of the new and younger voters, now including women over twenty-eight and all working-class men, went with the new consensus. A political revolution could not be stopped.[41]

PART II

BEGINNING

3

OUTLINE OF THE WAR
JANUARY 1919–JUNE 1920

~

The Anglo-Irish War, as the conflict is most often known, has been widely accepted as beginning on 21 January 1921, when Dáil Éireann met publicly for the first time and an ambush occurred at Soloheadbeg, in County Tipperary. This saw the shooting dead of two Royal Irish Constabulary (RIC) constables, the first such fatalities since the Easter Rising. The extremely limited and episodic nature of the hostilities during the rest of 1919 scarcely merits the term 'war'. There was nothing inevitable about the gradual escalation of the conflict which by the autumn of 1920 consisted of comparatively widespread guerrilla warfare.

Irish resistance in these months had not been planned and to a considerable extent happened because of the ineptitude of British policy, exacerbated by the social and economic repercussions of the First World War. The key developments in the achievement of Irish independence, involving the alienation of a large majority of the population of the twenty-six counties of the south and west from the British administration, had long preceded January 1919 and had been graphically illustrated by the result of the 1918 General Election.

The first meeting of the Dáil, held in the Mansion House in Dublin, was concerned more with winning publicity for the cause, both at home and abroad, than with establishing a working legislature and government. Only a minority of those elected could attend, as a high number had been interned following the German Plot arrests. Two grandiose documents, the Declaration of Independence and a 'Message to the Free Nations of the World', were read out (Appendixes C and D). In a token act of gratitude for the Labour Party's abstention from the General Election, the Democratic Programme was passed, suggesting economic and social priorities which were never to be fulfilled. Three envoys, Count Plunkett, Arthur Griffith and Éamon de Valera, were chosen to present the Irish case at the Paris Peace Conference. They were never to be given safe conducts to attend.

On 3 February, before the next meeting of the Dáil, held between 1 and 4 April, Michael Collins and Harry Boland engineered the escape of de Valera and two colleagues from Lincoln Jail. Shortly after, the British released the remaining internees. In April the Dáil session was far better attended and a greater attempt could be made to establish a counter-government and policy. A team of Ministers was appointed: de Valera became President of the Council of Ministers. It soon became evident, however, that the political strategy was producing few results: Irish claims to be heard at the Peace Conference were rejected and the attempt to build up a counter-state became more a matter of rhetoric than concrete achievement.

The popular revival of Irish-American nationalism in the months following the First World War had initially given grounds for hope that international pressure could be crucial in the fight for independence. Such optimism was behind de Valera's mission to the United States between June 1919 and December 1920. Though the Irish question proved a complicating element in Anglo-American relations, the Sinn Féin leadership exaggerated the extent and importance of American support, which never went beyond fund-raising and expressions of sympathy at State government and US Congressional level.

Of much greater significance was the Dáil's authorisation at its 10 April meeting of the RIC boycott. This policy had been followed by the Volunteers at a local level during the two preceding years and the attack on the police provided the basis for the IRA's whole campaign thereafter. To attack the RIC was to undermine the crucial arm of British control in Ireland. The Soloheadbeg ambush resulted from an impatience felt by gunmen with what they perceived to be the slowness and lack of action of the Sinn Féin leadership. The action of Seán Treacy, Dan Breen and their comrades in the South Tipperary Brigade was unauthorised by the Volunteer GHQ and widely denounced at the time as morally indefensible, amounting to murder. The British authorities soon declared South Tipperary a Special Military Area, forcing Breen, Treacy and company to go on the run.

The dramatic follow-up to Soloheadbeg came on 13 May when Seán Hogan, one of the ambushers who had later been captured, was rescued from a train at Knocklong in County Limerick, with again two RIC men killed. In March a Resident Magistrate, J.C. Milling, had been shot dead in Westport and in June D/I Hunt was killed in broad daylight in the centre of Thurles. Such incidents were small in number but had a profound effect on the British and on popular perception, both in Britain and in Ireland.

Of even more importance was the undermining of the G Division (the detective branch) of the Dublin Metropolitan Police Force (DMP) by the shooting policy of Collins and his Intelligence unit, implemented by the Squad, his elite gunmen. The basis of British Intelligence in Dublin was shattered by the end of the year and attempts to stage a counter-coup only resulted in the assassination in January 1920 of D/I Redmond, brought in from the north with the specific brief to track Collins down, and the shooting dead in March of Alan Bell, who had been investigating the source of IRA Intelligence and finance.

British policy in the post-World War months had been rudderless and confused. The preoccupation with the Paris Peace Conference and with immediate economic and social concerns made for an unwillingness to confront seemingly intractable Irish issues. The existence of a Tory-dominated Coalition government made any Irish initiatives even less likely. Throughout 1919 there was little interference from Whitehall with the Dublin Castle administration of Lord French and the Chief Secretary Ian Macpherson, appointed in January. The fervent reactionary Sir Walter Long continued to play a dominant role in Irish affairs in London. French and Macpherson put a priority on security but won little support in London for their preferred policy of martial law in the south and west, which was ruled out at this time of troop demobilisation. In the hope that the Dáil and the Dáil government would collapse, the British authorities delayed until September before proscribing them, fearing to award them undue prominence.

By the end of 1919, the British government was forced to introduce new Irish constitutional legislation. If an initiative had not been taken, the suspended Third Home Rule Act of 1914 would have had to have been implemented on the conclusion of the Peace Treaties in the spring of 1920. The messy compromise of the Government of Ireland Bill was introduced in December 1919 and took a whole year to be passed through parliament.

The Bill made provision for the establishment of two devolved parliaments and administrations, one in Dublin and the other in Belfast. A Council of Ireland, to consist of representatives from both parts of Ireland, was proposed to supposedly offer some basis for a future united Ireland. For all the attempt to stress that this legislation was in conformity with prevailing notions of self-determination and majority rights, it amounted to little more than an appeasement of Northern Unionism. In response to pressure from Belfast Protestants, the original nine-county province was changed to six in order to ensure an entrenched Unionist majority. British policy-makers were well aware that it was inconceivable that Southern opinion would accept such limited devolution as well as Partition.

During the course of 1919, a perception developed in Dublin Castle and Whitehall that the police were in crisis. There was an extreme reluctance to use the army to put down what was regarded as an irritating rebellion. Experienced troops were lacking in an army overstretched by imperial responsibilities: throughout the conflict there was a determination to refute any suggestion that there was a war going on. Political and practical considerations both applied.

In order to minimize attacks on the RIC, from the autumn of 1919 police barracks in large parts of the south and west, particularly in remote rural areas, were evacuated. This dramatically illustrated the collapse of British rule and enabled the establishment of some elements of a counter-state, notably the republican courts. In December 1919, the bungled assassination attempt on

Lord French succeeded in frightening British opinion out of its post-First World War apathy over Ireland. January 1920 was to see a considerable stepping-up of the British military effort as the realisation belatedly penetrated the official mind that something larger than a short rebellion was taking place.

From the beginning of 1920, the IRA's GHQ was sufficiently confident to give authority for attacks on some police barracks, first in Cork and then in many other counties. This was the start of a wave of such attacks in the ensuing seven months. The prime aim was to capture much-needed arms and ammunition but the side-effects were to provoke a crisis in Whitehall and Dublin Castle. On the Easter weekend arson attacks on evacuated RIC barracks and government offices were authorised: around 300 police barracks and twenty-two income tax offices were burned. Local government elections in January and June 1920 demonstrated the continuing Sinn Féin majority and strengthened nationalist control over local affairs.

As early as the autumn of 1919, the fateful decision had been made to augment the police by the raising of auxiliary forces largely from demobbed troops. The infamous label of 'Black and Tans' was soon attached to these mercenaries whose numbers increased rapidly though 1920. The killing of Tomás MacCurtain, Lord Mayor of Cork, on 19 March in his home, in all probability by members of the RIC, anticipated the degeneration of the conflict into tit-for-tat killings and reprisals. In January a new internment policy, involving co-operation between military and police, had been implemented, but was soon diluted, and collapsed in April when protesting hunger strikers were released by the British authorities.

These developments led to the appointment of a committee under the leadership of Sir Warren Fisher, Head of the British Civil Service, to enquire into the workings of Dublin Castle. Its disturbing conclusions led to the purging of the old administration and the appointment of new men who appeared to represent a changed outlook. Sir Nevil Macready became GOC, General Sir Henry Tudor was appointed Police Adviser, Sir Hamar Greenwood Chief Secretary, and a team of seconded civil servants led by Sir John Anderson, the new Joint Under-Secretary, arrived to breathe new life into a tired and discredited administration.

In May and July the British Cabinet undertook its first major review of Irish policy since the end of the First World War. Many elements within and without government advocated negotiations with Sinn Féin and the offer of a settlement well in advance of the Government of Ireland Bill. The argument for that seemed to succeed over the arguments advocating hardline coercive policies. Initially the Greenwood administration was identified with conciliatory policies but it quickly became apparent that Lloyd George was to follow a hawkish line.

Historians have imposed a pattern to the events in these months which conveniently forgets how reactive, confused and unplanned actual developments were on both sides. The question arises as to what would have happened if the British had reformed their administration and their policy far earlier and striven to detach moderate from hardline Irish nationalists during 1919. The unpopularity of the IRA's physical force policy in the early months of the conflict paled in comparison to the hatred and fear engendered by the Auxiliary police: British policy continually handed publicity gifts to the Irish resistance. A final chance to reform existed for the British government in these months and was predictably spurned.

4

BRITISH ADMINISTRATION 1919–APRIL 1920

~

B y the start of 1919 it was apparent that French, the Lord Lieutenant, and Shortt, the Chief Secretary, could no longer co-exist. H.A.L. Fisher quoted Shortt as saying that 'French is now entering under the influence of Saunderson, his private secretary, a little knot of Kildare Club men and . . . relations are very strained.' Shortt thought it best that both he and French be recalled, but French's prestige saved him for the time being: thus it was Shortt alone who was relieved of office in January 1919.[1] He was replaced by the Junior War Minister, Ian Macpherson. Macpherson was a Highland Presbyterian Scot and longterm Liberal MP: he had been Under-Secretary of State for War between 1914 and 1916. Originally keen to stress his Home Rule beliefs, Macpherson showed little evidence of liberal views during his tenure. He testified that he entered an administration where 'everyone was quarrelling' and that Lloyd George had never consulted him about taking the job. Soon Macpherson was to describe Shortt as 'the worst of all Chief Secretaries . . . I have never heard one man of any shade of political opinion in Ireland say a kind thing about him. People talk about Duke. In my judgement, he attempted to do his work well and with an honest endeavour. The fact remains that when I went there Ireland was in a hopeless mess.'[2]

Both with regard to personal compatibility and to views on policy, French had every reason to welcome Macpherson. Long told French on 14 January: 'I am sure Macpherson will be amenable to advice and a certain amount of direction. I was with him at the War Office and formed a very high opinion of his capabilities. I think he has also a very charming personality! It will be a wonderful change.' By May, Long was telling the Prime Minister: 'Macpherson is doing splendid work: it is impossible to speak too highly of him. He is cool, determined, courageous, and has all the . . . broad common sense of the Scotchman. He gets on excellently with French, is very popular in the country;

and considering he has only been in office a very few months I am really amazed at the position which he has made for himself.'[3]

Macpherson's fourteen months as Chief Secretary represented the high-water mark of reactionary conservatism. While it would be unfair to blame him for the collapse of British rule in Ireland which occurred during this period, it is impossible to make any positive case for his stewardship. Even by the standards of other Chief Secretaries, Macpherson spent little time in Ireland, a fact only partly excused by poor health. In January 1920, French told Lord Londonderry: 'Macpherson is a great help and a staunch ally but he is away always in the House of Commons or electioneering. Moreover, his health is not good, and this continual strain is, I fear, telling badly upon him.' Sir John Ross told Long in the same month: 'The Chief Secretary is excellent but is in bad health — is rarely here and has got out of touch.'[4]

French and Macpherson were united on the need to pursue a strong coercive policy leading to the banning of Sinn Féin, the Volunteers and other nationalist institutions in November 1919. They supported the introduction of martial law and other changes in the law to expedite convictions. Long and Bonar Law resisted all these measures except the banning of Sinn Féin because of limited military and police resources. The Lord Lieutenant and Chief Secretary saw no need to distinguish between moderate and militant elements of Sinn Féin, holding that firm action would allow the broad body of the population to free themselves from intimidation. They argued that the Sinn Féin electoral success represented a rejection of the Irish Parliamentary Party and a response to physical threats more than an expression of republican conviction. Like many another British politician both before and since, they believed that a few extremists were the problem and that the usual order would be restored once these were dealt with.[5]

Such an outlook resulted in misplaced optimism about Sinn Féin's decline throughout Macpherson's time in office. The establishment of the Dáil on 21 January 1919 was not taken seriously. French had told Long on 14 January: 'Perhaps I am sanguine, but I believe the end of it will be that these seventy-three devils will very soon go bag and baggage over to Westminster' and Long agreed, writing: 'I think when they find that they cannot draw their salaries, that they cannot do anything in Ireland, they will probably come over.' Even as late as December 1919, French persisted in a superficial and optimistic analysis: 'The real feeling of the country was never in favour of a Republic, or indeed, any form of complete separation. The mass of the people voted as they did for fear of what would happen to them if they acted otherwise.' French went on to criticise the 'weak and vacillating stand' of the British Government and to say that the Irish people were 'not a deep thinking people'.[6] At a time when Sinn Féin was going through a critical process of definition, Dublin Castle's intransigent outlook, which allowed scope for no political initiative, only served to weaken the British administration. While French and Macpherson argued for a strong militarist policy, police barracks were evacuated in large areas of the south and the west from the autumn, and the Republican counter-state began its chequered life.

During Macpherson's time as Chief Secretary the views of the deeply conservative Assistant Under-Secretary, Sir John Taylor, dominated in Dublin Castle. Taylor was the most blinkered of administrators and the most fervent of Catholic Unionists. Both the civil servant G.C. Duggan and the lawyer W.E. Wylie, in their memoirs, present a picture of a narrow-minded, humourless and pedantic man backed up by the cheese-paring attitudes of Maurice Headlam, the Treasury Remembrancer. 'Like the Turk,' wrote Duggan, Taylor 'could brook no brother near the throne'. Wylie remembered that Taylor 'was an exponent of the old style of Castle Government. He was a Unionist and could see no possible good in anyone who was not a Unionist also.'[7] An ill-disguised sectarianism was demonstrated in the sidelining of James MacMahon, the Under-Secretary. Originally, Long had welcomed MacMahon's appointment as offering a valuable link with the Catholic hierarchy, but now he was seen as a security risk. In January 1920, French reported that MacMahon 'is now quite estranged from all of us owing to his violently Catholic tendencies, so we have to short-circuit him and make Taylor superintend all the Castle work. He, however, (Taylor) is perfectly splendid.' A month earlier, French told Macpherson: 'The anomalous position of MacMahon and Taylor is causing me a great deal of worry. Efficient government is quite impossible as things are at present and steps must be taken at once to cut MacMahon off from any access to papers or documents which really matter. I am sure that the man whom he is employing as private secretary is utterly unreliable.' French decided to take MacMahon away from all security responsibilities, concluding: 'The Place seems to be honeycombed with spies and informers . . .'[8]

French and Macpherson's long campaign against the Catholic RIC Inspector-General Joseph Byrne, culminating in his messy replacement at the end of 1919, reveals a similar story of narrow, confused administration with strong overtones of sectarianism. Again Long and Saunderson helped to fan the flames. During the course of 1919, the leadership came to blame Byrne for many of the RIC's problems. French argued that pay, conditions and resources were not the problem but rather internal matters within the force, and accused Byrne of running down the Intelligence system. It is not completely clear why Byrne was held in such poor regard, although he opposed suggestions that the police be reinforced by non-Irish recruits and favoured the centralisation of the police. In May 1919, Long wrote to the Prime Minister: 'I have satisfied myself from the information I have received from several reliable quarters that the Head of the Police, Colonel Byrne, has lost his nerve.' French concluded of Byrne: 'in my opinion he has been one of the greatest impediments we have had in Ireland to the cause of law and order.'[9]

With no justification, Byrne was seen as a security risk. Long held that positioning a Catholic at the head of the RIC had caused 'a leakage in high quarters which has led to the defeat of justice'. The pettiness of the criticism is shown by the complaints against Byrne for not attending the funeral of DI Hunt in Thurles in the summer of 1919 — Byrne was in Westport at that time and unable to get there but visited the town soon afterwards. Lloyd George supported the campaign against Byrne, telling French: 'as to Byrne, I am afraid you are right. He is an able and intelligent man but has always given the impression of an official who is overwhelmed with the hopelessness of his task. That is not the spirit in which you can face a conspiracy like that with which you have to deal in Ireland.' Initially, Chief Commissioner Smyth was brought in from Belfast to understudy Byrne, with the clear intention that he should soon take over the top job.[10]

By December, French and Macpherson had decided to remove Byrne from office, sending him on leave. Macpherson suggested that as a sop Byrne be given a colonial governorship. Difficulties over pension rights prevented Byrne from being sacked and discussion over that brought Sir Warren Fisher, Head of the Civil Service and Permanent Secretary at HM Treasury, for the first time face-to-face with the problems of Irish administration. Fisher became a long-term supporter of Byrne, both at that time and when Long opposed Byrne's application to become Head of the Secret Service in December 1921. Fisher described Byrne's treatment as 'one of the most tragic instances on record of injustice to a public servant'. Aided by a carefully placed article in *The Times*, Fisher prevented Byrne from being officially dismissed.[11] In the meantime, however, Smyth, with the Dublin leadership's enthusiastic backing, had filled the position. Fisher's impassioned defence of Byrne did not involve any positive claim for Byrne's effectiveness as an administrator. There can be no doubt, however, that he had been the victim of religious discrimination.

While the British government generally interfered little with the Castle administration during 1919, a particular intervention had disturbing consequences. Few incidents better illustrated the implicit tension between Dublin Castle and Westminster than the saga of the Irish-American delegation's tour of Ireland in May.[12] Three prominent Irish-Americans — Frank P. Walsh, a leading labour lawyer, Edward F. Dunne, former Governor of Illinois and Michael J. Ryan, a Philadelphia lawyer — had been appointed by the Philadelphia Race Convention to press the Irish cause at the Paris Peace Conference. It was their pressure which led to President Wilson saying to Lloyd George that until the Irish Question was settled 'it was bound to affect not only the relations which ought to exist between England and the US but . . . would inevitably affect the relations of England with the colonies.' The delegation was given to believe by Wilson's close adviser, Colonel House, that prospects were good for a meeting between them and Lloyd George. Meanwhile, the British Prime Minister agreed to safe conducts for them to visit Ireland.[13]

The delegation's visit to Ireland was stage-managed by Sinn Féin. The delegates addressed the Dáil and the British military increased the publicity value by raiding the Dáil on the same day and by preventing them from visiting Westport, which was in a proscribed area. The trio, on their return to Paris, issued a melodramatic report on their Irish experiences, placing a heavy emphasis on their harassment by the British forces and on the poor economic and social conditions they encountered.[14]

The delegation's visit appeared to have British official approval. *The Times* wrote: 'There is a general impression, however fantastic it may be, that the three Irish Americans have come to Ireland with the approval of President Wilson and with Lloyd George's consent as an agent of the Irish Republican policy and that when they return to Paris the Prime Minister will consider their demand for international recognition of the Irish Republic at the Peace Conference. In other words the country is being asked to believe that the Republican movement has descended from the region of idealism into that of practical politics.'[15] The Unionist response was predictably outraged and even Macpherson was forced to ask probing questions of Lloyd George: 'The presence of the Irish Delegation from America embarrassed us. We did not and do not know how to act. French and I, if I may say so, had both confidence in yourself and we recognised that there might be something behind it all and we did not take the action which the conduct of these men deserved.' Macpherson concluded that the visit 'has given Sinn Féin an importance which it never hoped to have, and has undone the work which I set myself to do here at great personal risk — viz. restore the spirit of confidence to law abiding citizens'. Lloyd George responded to the blast of criticism by blaming House for misleading him as to the purpose and likely character of the delegation's visit.[16] As a consequence, Lloyd George not only played into the hands of Sinn Féin publicity but also was responsible for straining Anglo-American relations.

Since the end of the First World War the government had shown no inclination to introduce any major Irish legislation, resisting all pressure on the issue in the House of Commons. To avoid the Third Home Rule Bill coming into effect as a consequence of the finalisation of the Versailles Peace Treaty, an alternative policy had to be decided upon. In October 1919 the Irish Situation Committee was set up under Long's chairmanship to consider the question. Their protracted discussions arrived at a seemingly artful compromise which was, with a few changes, accepted by the government.

They started from the premise that 'in view of the situation in Ireland itself, of public opinion in Great Britain and still more of public opinion in the Dominions and the United States of America, they cannot recommend the policy either of repealing or of postponing the Home Rule Act of 1914.' The determination was to avoid the break-up of the Empire and any coercion of Ulster. Three options were considered: a Home Rule Parliament for all Ireland with exclusion of part of Ulster allowed for by county option or by some form of plebiscite; a single parliament with strong safeguards for Ulster amounting to veto powers or, finally, the establishment of two separate parliaments with a Council of Ireland 'to promote as rapidly as possible, and without further reference to the Imperial Parliament the union of the whole of Ireland under a single legislature'.

The Committee felt that a plebiscite would inflame passions and in reject-ing the first option was anxious to remove direct British rule from any part of Ireland. It was felt that the second alternative would satisfy no one and would prevent the projected parliament from being effective. The third choice was accepted as removing British control of domestic issues and circumventing Ulster's resistance to a Dublin parliament. In conclusion, they emphasised their attachment 'to doing everything possible to promote Irish unity without in any way infringing the freedom of Ulster to decide its own relation to the rest of Ireland'.[17] The Cabinet agreed with the logic of these conclusions and soon was largely concerned about whether the new Parliament should apply to six or to nine counties.[18]

For all the use of language which conformed with the contemporary stress on consent and self-determination, the Government of Ireland Act was the product of expediency and should be interpreted in a purely British political context. It was well understood that there was never any prospect of Southern nationalist — moderate or advanced — agreement to the Bill or subsequent Act, nor any serious expectation that Ulster could be attracted 'by kindness' into a united Ireland. Lord Birkenhead told Lord Oranmore that the Cabinet's chief aim was to satisfy American opinion; Birkenhead concluded: 'If Sinn Féin declared definitely against it, he could not see the good of forcing it on them against their wishes.'

The Council of Ireland had been included as a palliative for world opinion and in no way represented a serious commitment to Irish unity. Ulster loyalists had been provided with a veto on Irish unification. The Bill was a classic com-mittee compromise, a means by which Tory and Unionist opinion could be reconciled to a Dublin parliament. In a purely British political context, it had its strengths, but in no other.

From his Liberal coalitionist standpoint, H.A.L. Fisher, a member of Long's Committee, said that he 'admitted the defects of the Bill', but still insisted: 'it was the best that could be got from the existing Government. It would at least accomplish two essential things: it would take Ulster out of the Irish Question which it had blocked for a generation and it would take Ireland out of English party controversies.'[19]

The Bill had a long-drawn-out passage through Parliament for virtually all of 1920. The debates on it were poorly attended and the government showed little inclination to accelerate its passage. Walter Long became alarmed about the possibility that Lloyd George was deliberately delaying matters in order to achieve a peace settlement by amending the legislation.[20] Despite official denials, amendment was always a possibility. Few major Acts can have lasted so long from such confused and inglorious beginnings.

The worst of all examples of Dublin Castle's ineptitude occurred in the midst of the personnel changes made to the top administration in April 1920. The chaotic handling of the Mountjoy Prison hunger-strike crisis finally brought home to the British government the need for radical reform of the administration, and directly led to the appointment of a committee under Sir Warren Fisher to examine Dublin Castle.

Both convicted and remand prisoners arrested in the police/military swoops of January 1920 had gone on hunger strike, demanding political status. Originally Dublin Castle took a hard line on the issue, but when faced by massive demonstrations in Dublin culminating in a general strike, agreed to parole for unconvicted prisoners. Confusion then set in and all categories of detainees were released in error. W.E. Wylie, the law adviser in the Castle, who was working on the cases commented: 'Jailbirds, political prisoners, petty thieves, every damn one of them. I nearly fainted when I heard of it.' The decision took place while Sir John Taylor was on a month's leave: he was never to return. The mistake occurred because all the starving prisoners regardless of category were taken outside the prison to see doctors. French decided, as he put it: 'to make the best of the blunder that had been committed' by releasing all those who had been medically examined. Of the ninety released, thirty-one were convicted prisoners. The affair raised grave doubts about the competence and resolve of the British administration and had a bad effect on the morale of the security forces.[21]

Major changes were made in the Castle both before and after the Fisher Report. A new outlook as well as new personnel would, it was hoped, help to improve the situation. The changes marked an end to the drift in British policy towards Ireland. In late March, General Sir Nevil Macready was appointed Commander-in-Chief, replacing Lieutenant-General Shaw.

Shaw had been on a temporary commission and in a weak position, dependent on his long association with French. He had little clout with Whitehall. In common with many others at the time, he was deeply hurt by his abrupt dismissal. For months before, Churchill had been keen to appoint Field Marshal Robertson, of the Rhine Command, to the position; both Churchill and the King were offended when Lloyd George short-circuited the appointment process by installing Macready without consultation. Macready was appointed not just because of his social and political association with the Prime Minister. He also had relevant experience as Commissioner of the London Metropolitan Police and from his time as military leader in support of the civil authority both in Belfast and in the Tonypandy miners' strike in 1912.[22]

Macready insisted that his considerable personal financial demands be met, he was awarded £5,000 as disturbance allowance, and he refused to take over joint police and military command, suggesting instead that a special police adviser be chosen, with a deputy to act as Head of Intelligence. Accordingly Major-General Sir Henry Tudor was appointed police adviser and later that year became Chief of the RIC. Macready's preferred choice, Lieutenant-General Sir Edward Bulfin, had shown good sense in rejecting the approach. Brigadier-General Ormonde Winter became Head of Intelligence and Tudor's Deputy.[23] Thus it was that a military man became police supremo and a police specialist took over military command.

From the start Macready saw no future in purely coercive policies and supported a settlement in advance of the Government of Ireland Bill. No doubt affected by his experience in Ulster in 1914, he was a fierce critic of Ulster loyalism. In a memorandum of 24 May 1920, he wrote: 'From a soldier's standpoint, the easiest and simplest solution of present difficulties would be martial law, and the consequent suspension of the Civil Courts, etc. Given sufficient troops, the country could be reduced to comparative quietude.' Macready, however, did not believe that British opinion would tolerate this and felt that it would only increase resistance to British rule. He concluded: 'Coercion has been tried in the past and has failed. Will the situation be any worse in the future if a policy of giving the people the very fullest measure of Self-Determination within the Empire is tried?' Macready admitted that there were positive and moderate people within Sinn Féin and poured scorn on notions of a Bolshevik conspiracy. He was to be criticised by Churchill for using the word 'proletariat' in a communication to the Cabinet.[24]

In early April Macpherson was replaced by Sir Hamar Greenwood as Chief Secretary. Though health reasons were cited, it is clear that he was pushed out and was unhappy with this decision. Warmly supporting the appointment of the Fisher Committee, French brazenly distanced himself from the previous administration: 'During the last year the position has become greatly accentuated by the fact that Macpherson completely ostracised . . . MacMahon, and would not permit him to fulfil his proper functions. Consequently there was always a missing link in the chain of responsible government.' He urged Macpherson as strongly as he possibly could to put an end to this but Macpherson would do neither one thing or the other 'and this is really the cause of the frightful mistakes which are constantly made.'[25] French was the sole survivor of the spring purges though thereafter he was very much marginalised. Lord Riddell said of French to Lloyd George: 'I think he is done'; Lloyd George replied: 'Yes, he has been through a lot and I doubt whether he is the man he was.'[26]

The last Irish Chief Secretary, Sir Hamar Greenwood, was by no means the most distinguished. Making allowance for the absence of private papers and the impossible task he faced in defending the Black and Tans, it is extremely difficult to restore Greenwood's reputation. Brought up in Canada, he became a barrister, was a lifelong teetotaller, Liberal MP for Sunderland and Secretary for Overseas Trade. He was not the first choice but was a firm Lloyd George loyalist, destined to move over to the Conservative Party after the end of the Coalition government. An effective, if limited, public speaker, Greenwood clearly enjoyed wearing formal finery and attending official functions. He would have made a better Lord Lieutenant than Chief Secretary. G.C. Duggan commented that Greenwood was incapable of handling more than one idea at a time and his public utterances and letters reveal a naive optimism in the most desperate of times. Lord Oranmore described him as: 'a Canadian bagman and a windbag at that'. His wife, Lady Margery Spencer, who was from a landed background, was much more highly regarded in social and political circles.[27]

5

THE DÁIL AND THE
DÁIL GOVERNMENT

Few knew precisely what they were voting for when they voted Sinn Féin in December 1918. It had been made clear that those elected would abstain from the Westminster parliament and that an appeal would be made to the Paris Peace Conference, but there was less clarity over the form a new assembly should take and whether a republic should be declared to exist. The abstentionist policy ran considerable risks: the lack of Irish representation would leave Northern Unionists and a few Southern Unionists and remnants of the Irish Parliamentary Party as the only Irish voices in the Commons, and a Partition settlement would be made considerably easier to implement. In addition, there was the danger that any independent assembly would be easily ridiculed and the publicity for the Irish cause, formerly so easily gained at Westminster, would be lost.

The decision to press ahead with the establishment of Dáil Éireann was by no means inevitable. Two meetings in Dublin early in January decided to hold a public first meeting of the Dáil on 21 January 1919. Of the seventy-three Sinn Féin members elected, only twenty-six attended this meeting. Many, including de Valera, were still in prison. Michael Collins found other things to do. The proceedings were presided over by Cathal Brugha, and were chiefly concerned with gaining public attention, particularly abroad.[1] A grandly-phrased Declaration of Independence (Appendix C) proclaimed: 'The Irish electorate has . . . seized the first occasion to declare by an overwhelming majority its firm allegiance to the Irish Republic . . . We, the elected Representatives of the ancient Irish people in National Parliament assembled, do, in the name of the Irish nation, ratify the establishment of the Irish Republic and pledge ourselves and our people to make this declaration effective by every means at our command.' A Message to the Free Nations of the World (Appendix D) called 'upon every free nation to uphold her national claim to complete independence as an Irish Republic against the arrogant pretensions of England founded in fraud and sustained only by an overwhelming military occupation'. De Valera, Count Plunkett and Griffith were chosen to represent the Irish cause at Paris. As a way of thanking the Labour Party for their non-participation in the election, a diluted Democratic Programme was passed which committed the new assembly 'to make provision for the physical, mental and spiritual well-being of the children' and 'a sympathetic native scheme for the care of the Nation's aged and infirm'.

Ernest Blythe, a founding member of the Dáil and a future senior minister in the Free State government, later described this event as 'the beginning of a persistent campaign of make-believe and self-deception which has continued to do harm right down to the present day . . . If we had not committed ourselves in January 1919 to Propaganda-Over-All and Propaganda-All-The-Time it would have been realised that there was no existing Republic to be maintained or defeated and that it was the duty of the Dáil, at that junction, to decide in a spirit of realism . . . having regard to the fact that it had become obvious that an All-Ireland Republic was utterly unattainable without the prior consent of the opposing Northern Protestants (who) were in an unassailable position.'

Blythe felt that if de Valera, Griffith and Cosgrave had been able to attend the first meeting, a wiser strategy would have been adopted.[2] The declaration of a Republic was to make it difficult for any future compromise with the British government and was at the heart of the debate between idealist and pragmatist in the Treaty and Civil War period. Blythe was correct to point out that the new assembly's policy made partition the more likely. Nonetheless the gamble taken in January 1919 was in many ways remarkably effective as a means of furthering the revolution in the twenty-six counties. The Dáil and its government appeared to legitimise the IRA's actions and, for all the unreality often involved, made coherent and concrete the advanced nationalist cause. Senator Michael Hayes, another of the first TDs, in an article emphasising the importance of the political side of the movement, wrote that the Dáil was 'a source of authority, a symbol of resistance, rather than a legislative assembly'.[3] In time, the existence of the Dáil meant that the British had an institution with which to negotiate, thus enabling the political side of the movement to assert its own importance.

By the time the Dáil next met in April, the context had been dramatically altered. On the same day that the Dáil had first met publicly, 21 January, two RIC men had been killed in the ambush at Soloheadbeg, thus starting the erratic attacks on the police which continued on a small scale through the rest of the year.[4] Then, on 3 February, de Valera, together with Seán Milroy and Seán McGarry, escaped from Lincoln Prison.

De Valera had obtained wax impressions of the prison master key using melted candles and the chaplain's key. A replica key was made and smuggled back inside a cake. After overcoming a last-minute hitch, Collins and Harry Boland effected the escape. Ironically, given de Valera's antipathy to the IRB, de Valera stayed with Collins' secret society intimates in Manchester before being smuggled across to Dublin, where he hid for another short period.[5] Even at this early stage, de Valera was determined to base his immediate operations in the United States. He opposed plans for a public reception in Dublin for him, and Collins described the cancellation decision as equivalent to Daniel O'Connell's failure to go ahead with the Clontarf meeting in 1843.[6]

The remaining German Plot prisoners were released from British jails immediately following the death in the influenza epidemic of Pierce McCan, a Tipperary TD.[7] At the next meeting of the Dáil between 1 and 4 April, fifty-two attended, the largest number at any session during the conflict. De Valera was elected as President of the Council of Ministers and a series of other ministers appointed: Griffith became Home Affairs Minister, Count Plunkett was placed in charge of Foreign Affairs, Collins went to Finance, Cosgrave to Local Government and MacNeill to Industries. Later the Cabinet was expanded to eleven. Another session between 10 and 12 April announced the beginning of a bond sale and backed the police boycott.[8]

A month elapsed before the next meeting when the Dáil was given an immense fillip by the attendance on 9 May of the Irish-American delegation. Their leader, Frank P. Walsh, addressed the gathering and a false impression was given of official American backing for the cause to be heard at the Paris Conference. The *Irish Times* commented that 'three weeks ago none save fools and fanatics believed in the possibility of an Irish Republic' but that now attitudes had been transformed.[9]

Concrete plans for the establishment of a counter-state began in June, when a commission was set up to examine the country's resources, together with plans for a land bank, an afforestation scheme, fishing and an Irish language project. More practically, a system of arbitration courts was approved and a consular system established, and on 19 June, Mulcahy ordered the Army to set up a republican police force.[10]

This force would be structured according to the company, battalion and brigade pattern of the Army, and in November it was made clear that it should be a separate body. The distinction between the two organisations was more theoretical than real, however. Placing the new force under the nominal control of the Home Affairs Department proved ineffective and the quality of recruit to this force was a huge problem up to and beyond the Truce. The collapse of the RIC in large areas of the country had left a huge space which was never to be adequately filled until after the revolution.[11]

On 11 September, the British authorities proscribed the Dáil and hence-forward meetings became irregular and necessarily secret. At the end of November, Sinn Féin, the Gaelic League, the Volunteers and Cumann na mBan were also banned. Between September 1920 and July 1921, there were only eight meetings of the Dáil. Frequently members complained that they were given no notice of meetings. In such circumstances it was inconceivable that any government business could be carried out effectively and that the institution could be accountable to its electorate. There were, however, some notable successes, especially in finance and the courts, and it was crucial that the structure was kept intact.[12]

Underlying these developments were acute tensions between the political and military sides of the movement as to the preferred direction of policy. Originally many in Sinn Féin ranks had had faith in passive resistance proving effective, and during the first half of 1919 the more militant leadership became extremely alarmed about the lack of action. Collins told Austin Stack in May 1919: 'We have too many of the bargaining type already . . . It seems to me that official SF is inclined to be ever less militant and ever more political theoretical.'[13] Liam de Róiste in his diaries continually emphasised how the Cork IRA despised his brand of moral resistance and declared that he was one of the few in the Dáil who was not on the run and had not been in prison. In August 1919 an officer in the Meath Brigade IRA wrote that 'prominent Volunteers seem to encourage amongst them a feeling of contempt for the political side of the movement, and put it down as constitutionalism.'[14]

Both Griffith and de Valera were opposed to the shooting of policemen and would have been happier if the conflict had proceeded on different lines.[15] De Valera's misplaced trust in the appeal to the Paris Peace Conference and then to the United States for recognition demonstrated his doubts about a military strategy as well as his own aversion to fighting. His talents were in the diplomatic and political field; he always skilfully cultivated a personal image of detachment, dignity and a certain cold hauteur which goes far to explaining his peculiar dominance. Although a poor orator, he emanated natural authority. It was remarkable that his decision to spend eighteen months in the United States at the height of the conflict was never publicly challenged.

De Valera only returned after Griffith was arrested in November 1920 and Collins became acting President. Griffith's role in the conflict was obscure and he appeared largely ignorant of military developments, concentrating on publicity and propaganda. The division between politicians and military men was not a straightforward one between moderates and hardliners: Brugha and Stack, both staunch republicans, were much closer to de Valera than to Collins. The compromise achieved at the Sinn Féin Convention in October 1917 was to prove illusory.

The 1918 General Election had represented the peak of Sinn Féin achievement. As the war intensified, the political party's organisation declined and the Dáil government took over most of the party's functions. De Valera was at pains to ensure that the same men were not both Sinn Féin and Dáil government officials.[16] To a considerable extent, the divisions between Sinn Féin and the IRA amounted to a generation gap: while the IRA was primarily a young man's organisation, Sinn Féin consisted of mature men preferring rhetoric and administration. Long before the escalation of the fighting from the beginning of 1920, the Sinn Féin policy had demonstrably failed: no coherent passive resistance strategy was ever formulated and the appeal to the Paris Peace Conference never had any hope of succeeding. Seán T. O'Kelly was sent to

Paris to represent the Irish case but his pompous correspondence with the Great Powers produced nothing. It was inconceivable that Britain would withdraw from Ireland as a consequence of the establishment of the Dáil or in response to international pressure. Some form of military confrontation was a virtually certain result of the political developments. Any prospect that passive resistance could even be tried for any length of time was soon overtaken by the reality of British reaction to developing guerrilla warfare.

The Sinn Féin activist and author Darrell Figgis argued that the physical force side of the movement, led by the IRB, had hijacked the cause because moderates were in prison following the German Plot arrests at the time of the Dáil's formation. Father Patrick Gaynor, a Sinn Féin activist in Clare, claimed that passive resistance had never been given an opportunity to work and that the unfortunate dominance of the military side was the key to understanding the Civil War divisions. 'In truth', he stated, 'if a shot had never been fired we should have won the war to an equal extent. The progress might have been slow, but . . ., on the other hand, if there were no fighting, there would have been no need for a Truce, no consequent lowering of morale, no need to enter negotiations with Britain on her terms, and — best of all — no Civil War.'[17] It was physical force, however, both Irish and British, which was to provide the motor for change.

It is true, as both Blythe and Gaynor argued, that the contribution of the political side has been underrated. Blythe stressed that Terence MacSwiney's death did as much for Irish freedom as a dozen ambushes.[18] The activities of the flying squads appeal far more easily to the popular memory than that of the revolutionary administrator. Andy Cope, the British Under-Secretary in the Castle from the summer of 1920, held that the relative success of the republican courts undermined British government authority more than any IRA actions. Foreign journalists were keen to emphasise the Dáil government's successes. On 5 July 1920, Robert Lynn wrote in the *Daily News*: 'So far as the mass of the people are concerned the policy of the day is not an active, but a passive policy. Their purpose is not to attack the Government, but to ignore it, and to build up a new Government quietly by its side.' A day later he wrote of the republican courts: 'nothing so marvellous has grown up out of the ground in Ireland since the coming of the Normans.' As in so many other respects, the perception was what mattered. In August the liberal British journal *The Nation* went so far as to claim: 'The central fact of the present situation in Ireland is that the Irish republic exists.'[19]

On two occasions militant but non-violent tactics were used to demonstrable effect: mass protests in the spring of 1920, centring on Mountjoy Jail in Dublin and later at Wormwood Scrubs in London in support of political status for prisoners, played a large role in bringing about the British government's decision to release the hunger strikers.[20] From May 1920, railway workers, inspired by the action of British dockers in refusing to work on Polish ships bound for Russia, banned the transport by rail of soldiers and war material. The action was surprisingly successful and for several months produced no effective British response; troops were often left stranded on driverless trains and on remote platforms. Crucially, though, no support was forthcoming from British unions nor was there sufficient financial backing. Eventually in November, the British government threatened to withdraw grants from the railway companies and the strike ended abruptly in December.[21]

There was never any hope that a republican government could operate in a meaningful way. The financial resources were absent and talk about collecting tax revenues and land annuities was never put into effect. As Minister of Finance, Collins led a Loan Drive, which was launched in September 1919. A short propaganda film was produced with Collins, seated at a desk, receiving cheques from a procession of republican notables, including Mrs Kathleen Clarke, widow of Tom, and Arthur Griffith. In his efficiency at running the Drive and his whole Department, Collins showed administrative skills unsuspected in Irish revolutionaries. Despite limited press coverage and the support of only three Catholic bishops, the Loan raised £380,000, an impressive amount considering the absence of the wealthy in Sinn Féin ranks. Even more important was the more than $5,000,000 raised in America in another Loan Drive, though much of that was used to finance the Irish delegation in the US, including payment for de Valera's expensive hotel bills. Only $3,000,000 was sent to Ireland and the whole issue was to plague the Free State government throughout the 1920s. Collins was particularly critical of the small sum contributed in Britain, which, together with France, contributed £11,719. The total financial resources, however, could only finance a skeleton counter-state.[22]

Most of the Dáil government's Ministries existed more for their propaganda value than for any functioning reality. The commission set up to survey the country's resources took an eternity to report, the land bank never had the resources to fulfil its ambitions of redistribution of land and the heightening of British military activities from the autumn of 1920 killed off any idea that aspirations in education and culture could be attained, as in fact it stifled most other governmental plans. The abilities of individual ministers were a factor in explaining the success or otherwise of various departments. Ernest Blythe castigated Eoin MacNeill, Minister of Industry, saying: 'He not only did not attempt to create a department, but he practically never attended a meeting of the ministry.' Austin Stack, Minister for Home Affairs, showed little administrative grasp, his department being dismissed contemptuously by Collins.[23]

The military perception following the war was that the civil side had hopelessly failed to back up the military effort. A GHQ memorandum commented: 'No single Government Department has been the slightest assistance to the Army and some of them have been a serious drag . . . Indeed the Army is not without grounds for quoting the words of Bleuker. "What has been gained by the heart's blood of the soldiers these scribblers will yet lose cowardly and infamously . . ." The plain fact is the our Civil Services have simply played at governing a Republic, while the soldiers have not played at dying for it.' From his

Cork perspective, Liam Lynch wrote: 'We must admit that all civil organisations, county councils, Sinn Féin Clubs and all other organised bodies were an absolute failure during the last phase of hostilities. If anything, they were a burden on the army — why even the civil government failed.'[24] Such judgments were harsh: it was all but impossible for the counter-state to work properly and whatever success was gained was dependent on the military.

Any possibility of a radical programme being followed soon died in the course of 1919. Discussion of the merits of co-operative schemes in the farming and fishing industries never advanced beyond the theoretical. The Democratic Programme of social welfare reforms was never followed up. Kevin O'Higgins was later to comment: 'We were probably the most conservative-minded revolutionaries that ever put through a successful revolution.'[25] For the most part, British constitutional forms were followed by the Dáil. The chief achievements of the Dáil in the courts and local government owed little to planning but all to expeditious circumstances.

The much-acclaimed Dáil courts amounted to a revolution from below. In June 1919 the Dáil had made provision for arbitration courts but the spread of these throughout the west, particularly in early 1920, was a product of land hunger and agitation, together with the collapse of the British legal system. The Dáil only established a court system in the summer of 1920 when the vacuum in the judicial system had already been filled by locally set up courts. Solicitors had realised that their living depended on an acceptance of the transferred authority. Even Southern Unionists were forced to admit that the courts operated fairly and efficiently. In terms of the land question, the courts tended to side with the status quo. Enforcement of the courts' decisions meant relying on the IRA in the guise of the Republican Police Force. The role, however, of criminal and circuit courts as the conflict intensified was necessarily limited and it was generally admitted that the court system had major problems in functioning at all from the autumn of 1920.[26]

There was little initiative taken in local government until the Sinn Féin victories in the local government elections of 1920. As a result of the urban council elections of January, Sinn Féin won control in nine out of eleven corporations, and in the county council elections in June, in twenty-nine out of thirty-three councils. Despite this, the Department of Local Government was slow to respond, doing little other than organising a commission and ordering councils to pass resolutions swearing allegiance to the Dáil. There were to be enormous problems providing the necessary staff to oversee a new system and in collecting rates and revenues. It was Dublin Castle's abandonment of all aid to the new authorities on 29 July 1920 which forced them to face their responsibilities and find ways to cope.

A series of economies and cost-cutting measures had to be implemented at once, with only limited financial support from the Dáil. Workhouses were consolidated into single institutions and tuberculosis hospitals closed; in some counties the mentally-ill were left uncared for and destitute, though care continued to be provided through religious orders.[27] By the time of the Truce, much of the Irish social and legal system was in a state of collapse following the demise of British administration and the false promise of the Dáil government. In social and economic affairs the revolution was reactive rather than proactive.

At the time and since, British sources have proclaimed the effectiveness of republican propaganda. General Macready in particular contrasted the speed and opportunism of the Irish with the ineptitude of British efforts. Only in September 1920 was Basil Clarke made head of the Castle's News Bureau, and he was soon associated with the failure to counter in any coherent way the wave of propaganda resulting from the deaths of Terence MacSwiney and Kevin Barry. Lines of communication between the various publicity agencies were confused and often overlapped. Both the military and political leadership in the Castle were obsessed with the hostile coverage by Irish newspapers, and the clumsy arrest of the owners of the *Freeman's Journal* in October 1920 was totally counter-productive.[28]

The Dáil's Propaganda Department was run on a relative shoestring and was frequently heavily criticised by the Irish military and political leadership. Desmond FitzGerald, the Director of Publicity between May 1919 and his arrest in February 1921, had considerable success in establishing contacts with foreign journalists in London but was berated for poor administration. When the novelist and republican convert Erskine Childers took over, de Valera regarded this as a huge change for the better. The establishment of a number of consuls in assorted centres was part of the publicity drive. During the Paris Peace Conference, Seán T. O'Kelly sought to present the Irish cause to world leaders and was later joined in Paris by George Gavan Duffy and Erskine Childers. While individual consuls cultivated sympathetic journalists, they achieved little.[29]

The chief organ of republican publicity was the *Irish Bulletin*, first published in November 1919, appearing five times a week and circulated internationally. Its interminable list of atrocities and repressive acts provided a major source for journalists writing in many other publications at home and abroad. So big was its reputation that the British brought out a fake edition in late March of 1921.[30]

For all the volume of propaganda, the greatest effect was almost certainly achieved by visiting British journalists, and most notably Hugh Martin in the *Daily News*. The eyewitness reports by muckraking correspondents were much more readable, colourful and entertaining than the propaganda sheets and came with dramatic photographs of burning buildings and the suffering and terrified populace. Irish newspapers frequently printed extracts from reports by these foreign correspondents.[31] While it was important that a free press exposed British atrocities to world attention, events actually spoke for themselves. It is doubtful that Britain could have hidden the harsh truth from the rest of the world.

The return of de Valera from America, in late December 1920, brought a change of emphasis within the republican government. De Valera adopted a much more hands-on approach than Griffith and was immediately critical of guerrilla warfare methods. He made it clear that the stress should be on larger actions with international opinion in mind. In the first meeting of the Dáil after his return, Roger Sweetman, a Wexford TD, and Liam de Róiste expressed profound reservations about the morality of physical force. Even though Sweetman resigned and de Róiste remained a marginal figure, they had hinted at unbridgeable divisions within the Sinn Féin coalition. Remarkably, de Valera suggested that Collins should go as Irish representative to the US and the conclusion is unavoidable that a power struggle was under way. Collins is reported to have said 'the long whore won't get rid of me that easily.' Soon Brugha's criticisms of Collins' and Mulcahy's handling of arms accounts exacerbated these tensions. It was only after the Truce that this serious schism became explicit for all to see.[32]

The British thought that the divisions were straightforward ones between moderate politicians and hardline militarists: they gave orders that de Valera was not to be arrested but conducted massive searches for Collins. This was understandable and illustrates how effectively the republican movement created the impression that its military and political branches were working together harmoniously. In February 1921, Sir Warren Fisher, while bemoaning the absence of unity of command on the British side, overrated the unity of the Irish side. He thought that the military and political sides worked as an efficient team. In March de Valera made the Dáil explicitly responsible for IRA actions. For all the tensions within nationalist ranks, it was crucial that the appearance of unity was maintained.[33]

6

BRITISH SECURITY FORCES

THE POLICE

The most decisive development of the War of Independence may well have been an unseen one: the evacuation of a large number of RIC barracks in rural areas in the last months of 1919 and early 1920. Alarmed by the murders of many of their colleagues and threatened by the likelihood of attacks on their barracks, RIC men were living in siege-like conditions. Tudor was told by two RIC sergeants: 'It is obvious that small garrisons all over the country would simply be . . . isolated islands' and that the men would become 'cock-shies for Sinn Féin'. Chief Secretary Macpherson reported on 8 March 1920 that: 'There are very few RIC barracks which the local Volunteers could not destroy in a very short time, assuming of course that they are determined and able men.'[1] The Sinn Féin boycott and IRA attacks had left the police incapable of pursuing their normal functions. Police barracks in rural areas were usually small terraced private houses in village centres and were easy to attack. From the summer of 1920 larger barracks were protected by steel shutters and sandbags. To destroy the RIC presence was to move against the heart of British administration in the localities; to make it impossible to hold courts or to protect witnesses and to back up the work of the tax collector and the bailiff.

It is easy to understand why the evacuation took place but more difficult to explain why Dublin Castle and the British government allowed matters to reach this pass. Sir Edward Carson told Bonar Law that he was 'at a loss to know why the Irish Government had given up keeping police in small districts: the moment the police were removed the district fell outside British control and anyone who objected to law breaking was left defenceless.' The Attorney-General declared that it 'possibly had been a mistake to move the police from the barracks but there was no alternative. The barracks were small buildings with no accommodation for troops.' Speaking of his Connaught home, Lord Desart said that he knew that 'the withdrawal of the patrols before General

Macready took office had been unfortunate in his part of the world.' The Southern Unionist deputation to Bonar Law in April 1920 concluded: 'The evacuation of police stations has been undoubtedly a grave mistake, which if not remedied must prove fatal. All the abandoned police stations should be re-occupied, and the police should be placed in a position to carry out their normal duties.'[2] For this to happen, they stated that 'adequate military co-operation' would be necessary.

Shortly before his removal as GOC Army, General Shaw said: 'It became obvious before the end of 1919 that matters had got beyond the power of the police to handle.' The Dublin Metropolitan Police's authority was ruined even more effectively and dramatically by means of the ruthless attack on its 'G' Division by Collins' Squad. In July, Macready wrote: 'The Dublin Metropolitan Police are, in my opinion, quite past redemption.' By that time there was little more optimism about the future of the RIC either. Sir John Anderson told Greenwood: 'The morning I arrived in Dublin the Inspector-General of the RIC stated in my presence that he was in daily fear of . . . wholesale resignations from the force or of his men running amok.' Macready reported County Inspector Marrian saying that half the force were acting as Sinn Féin informers and 'the other half prepared owing to strain to become assassins' and that he feared a break-up of all the Southern units.[3]

The organisation of the force had long been outmoded. An editorial in the *Constabulary Gazette* in 1918 said that the force was 'a wooden velocipede — a marvellous invention fifty years ago'. Two years earlier it commented: 'The RIC may be likened unto a noble mansion of the early Victorian era, still occupied but showing visible signs of decay.'[4]

During 1918 French blamed the police's problems on the British government's refusal to pay adequately, pointing out that they were more badly remunerated than their British equivalents. Increasingly, however, French switched his criticisms to the forces themselves, particularly to the leadership. In late December 1919, French argued that the attacks on 'G' Division and the RIC were 'the result of weakness, want of foresight and incapacity on the part of our own officials who signally failed to make instant and proper use of the powers which the Cabinet freely gave us'. Early in January 1920, French wrote to Macpherson: 'Matters here are really getting beyond the control of the police, and a time is rapidly approaching when I shall have to tell the Government that it will be impossible for me to carry on any longer without martial law.'[5] When the committee which French appointed to enquire into the performance of the DMP gave their report, they demonstrated considerably more sympathy with the force than the Viceroy had. They stressed that: 'these murders and intimidation must destroy the morale of any police force no matter how good it may be.'[6] They also appreciated that it was useless to blame the DMP for its lack of patrols given the current situation.

French's judgmental attitude demonstrated a failure to understand the depth of the problems and to empathise with the impossible position the police had been placed in. Up to the recent past, to join the RIC had been a socially acceptable move for the general Catholic population, although in times of crisis the armed force became easy targets for physical force movements and popular protest. The alienation of most of the south and west from British authority post-1912 transformed that situation. In that context, it was hardly surprising that recruitment failed to keep pace with resignations. By the beginning of 1919 the effective numbers of the RIC at 9,300 were considerably below strength. Action was only taken at the end of the year to remedy the situation. By July 1920, numbers had risen to 11,110, and 14,212 by the end of June 1921.[7]

During 1919 in large parts of Ireland, RIC men became estranged from their own communities. When two constables were attacked on 28 September in Berrings, near Blarney, as they left church, no one would testify against their attackers. A local police officer reported: 'Several respectable Nationalists — not of course Sinn Féiners — told me that the people are in a state of terror from the Sinn Féiners and afraid to speak to, or have any communication with, the police.' While many may have had reservations about the IRA's assassination policy, few were willing to inform on their neighbours. When DI Hunt was shot in the main street of Thurles in July 1919, the population stood aside and refused to offer information afterwards.[8]

As part of the reorganisation of the Castle administration in spring 1920, Major-General Sir Henry Tudor arrived on the scene. Tudor's qualifications and abilities were gained in the Artillery and he lacked the flexibility and sensitivity required in police work. His hardline policies were supported by Churchill but he was viewed rather contemptuously by Macready and senior civil servants in Dublin Castle. While he will always be associated with the Black and Tans, G.C. Duggan praised Tudor's administrative abilities and his strengthening of transport and arms resources. After the conflict, Tudor served in Palestine, and later distanced himself in Newfoundland, where he survived to the ripe old age of ninety-five.[9]

The government's most notorious decision, however, had been made months before. From mid-1919 there had been talk in Dublin Castle of enlarging the RIC and militarising the conflict by recruiting ex-soldiers. This had been opposed by the RIC's Inspector-General Byrne and it was only after his clumsy removal that authority was given in November 1919 to recruit what became known as the 'Black and Tans'. Recruitment began near the end of 1919 and for the first six months averaged approximately one hundred per month. Their considerable expansion in numbers and their notoriety dated from summer 1920 but the government's disastrous policy of a hybrid force had been established. The speedy and ill-thought-out nature of this new force was demonstrated by the fact that they were forced by the lack of available uniforms to wear a mixture of khaki army trousers and green police tunics, thus earning the derisive nickname 'Black and Tans' after a Limerick Hunt. The new men had little training and no disciplinary code imposed on them.[10]

In July 1920, a further force was organised composed of veteran army offi-cers, to be known as the Auxiliary Division of the RIC. These Auxiliaries, although a distinct force with a separate uniform, both at the time and since have tended to be confused with the Black and Tans. In May 1920, the Cabinet had asked Churchill, as Secretary of State for War, to consider the feasibility of a 'special Corps of gendarmerie' to work within the RIC structure. It was con-cluded that such a force would take too long to assemble and instead the new independent battalion units were to be directly administered by the War Office.[11]

In all, 2214 were recruited including 281 who had been decorated for gal-lantry and three holders of the VC. Their pay of £1 a day, the highest in any uni-formed police force in the world at that time, was the obvious inducement. They were given six-month contracts, easily extended to a year, and were sent to active IRA areas in self-contained companies. An extremely confused rela-tionship developed with the rest of the RIC and the army, who had little direct control over them. Much depended on the ability of the individual Auxiliary company commander. The whole force did not merit the widespread oppro-brium it has received: the company based at Macroom which was ambushed at Kilmichael was not, it appears, particularly unpopular in the locality.[12] Nonetheless, the history of the force is a disastrous one. Fifty-nine Auxiliaries were declared unsuitable in the first three months of 1921 and there were nearly forty cases of destruction associated with them.[13]

The reputation of the Auxiliaries was not enhanced by the resignation of their Commander, Brigadier-General F.P. Crozier, when proceedings were abandoned against cadets caught robbing and looting in Trim in the spring of 1921. It is likely that some Auxiliaries were psychological casualties of the Great War and some had joined because they were unable to adjust to peace-time; however, the major problem was that they were given no clear definition of their role and no preparation for dealing with guerrilla warfare.[14]

The introduction of the Black and Tans, and later of the Auxiliaries, and the increasing involvement of the army from the beginning of 1920 was essentially an attempt to win back the ground lost by the RIC's evacuation of so many areas and the DMP's surrender: that ground, however, could never be fully recovered. Before the police force was militarised, British authority had given up without a fight being offered. The responsibility lay with the government in its failure to appreciate in time the gravity of the situation that confronted the police and in the methods they used to reinforce them.

THE ARMY

For political reasons the British government determined that the main responsi-bility for dealing with the challenge from the IRA should fall to the police and that the military should be confined to a supporting role. Bonar Law wrote to French at the end of 1919: 'I am very glad that you are making this effort to improve the police for am sure that the more you can preserve order by a civil rather than a military force the better.' This was the one consistent aspect of British policy. There was a commitment to avoiding the word 'war' or to recognising its de facto existence and thus an insistence on referring to the conflict as an internal British rebellion. The IRA recognised this and took advantage by concentrating their activities on attacking the RIC and the DMP, rarely targeting the army until the summer of 1920. The military, therefore, appeared as a bystander as the crisis developed and were increasingly critical of police failings in what they correctly assessed as essentially a military emergency.[15]

Even had the government been desirous of increased military involvement, it would have been difficult in the post-World War One context. Demobilisation and the threat of labour crises at home together with the manpower demands of colonial areas meant there had been a drop in troop numbers. In January 1919 French told the Chief Secretary of 'the dangerously rapid withdrawal of troops from Ireland'. Three months later General Shaw drew the attention of the Cabinet 'to the serious shortage of troops with which we are threatened'. By that time Shaw was pointing out the need for nine extra battalions. Churchill, the new Secretary of State for War, agreed to send only one battalion and was stressing the need to reduce army numbers in Ireland from 57,000 to 40,000.[16] In November 1919, Brigadier-General Brind stated that the minimum number of bayonets, that is efficient infantry, needed was 25,000 with 10,000 other fighting men and 5,000 administrators. The total number of soldiers in Ireland at that time came to 37,529. Despite such warnings, by January 1920 there were only thirty-four of the required thirty-six infantry divisions in Ireland; furthermore six were due to disband and many were understaffed. In April 1920 Sir Henry Wilson, the Chief of Imperial General Staff, wrote in his diary that general army recruitment had dropped from 1000 a day to 100 a day.[17]

The problem was also one of quality and experience within the army. General Loch told French that he felt numbers were sufficient but 'I feel bound to point out that the discipline and consequently the effectiveness of the Army is not what it was.' There was a particular shortage of experienced NCOs. Sir Edward Carson referred to the soldiers in Ireland as 'little more than boys'[18] and General Shaw expressed his concern about the 'indifferent quality of the troops' and their inadequate training.

The military were ill-suited to the passive role assigned to them and to the police tasks they were often forced to carry out. Many commented at the time that the RIC stress was always on decentralisation and small localised operations, while the army was suited to centralised command and large-scale manoeuvres. This all led to a feeling in army ranks that the government was only playing at combating the IRA.[19]

By January 1920 the army was aware of the police's inability to crush the IRA. Initially the military were given the major role in the deportation policy of that month with wide-ranging powers to arrest and deport suspects, but the instructions were soon modified by insistence that each case would have to be approved by authorities in London. The struggle to arrest the right people only heightened the failings in police intelligence. Military frustration with the vacillations in government policy came to a head over the release of convicted prisoners following the hunger strikes of April 1920. Soon after, a government order cancelled the powers granted in the preceding January to arrest rebel leaders. There was a widespread feeling that the efforts to deport had been futile.

Both the army's official 'Record of the Rebellion in Ireland' and 'The History of the Sixth Division' saw this as a pivotal moment. The former observed: 'The release of the hunger strikers and the cancellation of policy . . . nullified the effect of the efforts made by the Crown Forces during the three preceding months. The situation reverted to that obtaining in January, 1920, and was further aggravated by the raised moral of the rebels, brought about by their "victory", and a corresponding loss of morale on the part of the troops and police, accompanied by a natural irritation at seeing the release of men who had been engaged in cowardly outrages, and whose arrest had entailed untiring efforts, attended by considerable hardship and loss of life . . . Up till May, 1920, the rebel movement had been engineered by a comparatively few extremists, who, by enlisting the more desperate men of the country and stiffening their ranks with professional "gunmen", had succeeded in terrorizing certain districts and in gaining adherents to their policy of systematic outrages. The complete domination of Sinn Féin had, however, not been brought about at this time. There was still a considerable portion of the community, notably the farmers and tradesmen, who only desired peace, and who looked upon the IRA rather than the Crown Forces as being the obstacle to peace. But for the unfortunate lack of troops, and the ease with which a few armed men can terrorize Irishmen of moderate views, it is possible that, had the Government policy of January, 1920, been vigorously pursued, the inhabitants might have been relieved of this armed terrorism; and a situation in time created when a political solution might have had a reasonable chance of success on lines which the majority of Irishmen, unterrorized, would have approved.'[20]

No doubt this exercise in counter-factual history takes far too sanguine a view of what could have been achieved by military methods and distorts the relationship between the IRA and the general population, but it is, nonetheless, an accurate reflection of military angst.

The government's eventual realisation of the depths of the crisis led to Shaw's replacement in the spring of 1920. From the start Macready was extremely critical of the police and alarmed about the youth and inexperience of many of his troops. He put the priority on increasing the mobility of the army who up till that time he realised had been deployed in 'purely passive defence of localities, buildings etc'. In meetings with the Cabinet, Macready demanded eight extra battalions and considerable improvement in military transport. It would appear that by increasing mobility Macready aimed to re-occupy previously evacuated areas. His requests for men were only reluctantly granted and it was stipulated that authority would only be given on Macready's absolute insistence at each stage of the process. Two months later Sir John Anderson was reporting: 'The military forces in the country were insufficient in numbers and so far as rank and file were concerned quite raw, and for the immediate purpose of giving support to the civil authority in the ordinary task of maintaining law and order throughout the country almost useless.'[21]

As in so many other areas, half measures had been resorted to; military and political authority remained confused and the army's position was left ill-defined and weak. Nothing illustrated the army's anomalous position better than the bizarre story of the capture and imprisonment of Brigadier-General C.H.T. Lucas. Lucas was kidnapped on 26 June 1920, together with Lieutenant-Colonels Tyrell and Danford, while fishing at Kilbarry, in the north of County Cork. Liam Lynch and Seán Moylan were amongst those in the IRA party, which used two cars. Tyrell and Danford escaped in a shoot-out, but Lucas' month-long imprisonment proved a publicity triumph for the IRA. The official Sixth Division British Army Record commented that the affair became a regular staple for music-hall comedians. While Sinn Féin publicity exaggerated Lucas' seniority, the episode caused considerable embarrassment. Macready had no fears concerning Lucas' long-term safety, but soon it was inconceivable that senior military personnel should be unprotected when off duty.[22]

Lucas' imprisonment was a mixed blessing for the IRA. Obviously they had no prison facilities and the units that guarded him were thus inhibited from other activities. He was passed from Cork to Limerick to Clare and back to Limerick and left, perhaps deliberately, with an opportunity to escape, which he accordingly did on 30 July. Farcically, he immediately drove into an ambush at Oola but escaped again.[23]

Lucas and his captors had enjoyed each other's company. Tom Malone recorded that they had to buy a certain brand of pipe tobacco for Lucas, and that they played bridge and tennis together. Mark Sturgis, a leading civil servant in Dublin Castle, writes of Lucas: 'He was well treated and got some fishing and night poaching.' Lucas was concerned about the poaching until told that the local gamekeeper was Seán Carroll, one of his captors.[24] A few short months later it would be beyond belief that a British soldier could be treated with such chivalry.

From the summer of 1920 the army did become more involved in the War, but only as a consequence of being more frequently attacked. In July General Jeudwine, in command of the Fifth Division, concluded: 'The enemy is making war on us while we are not making war on him but are vegetating in passive defence, maintained with difficulty.' Throughout 1920 the government had the option of placing Ireland on a war footing or of genuinely seeking a settlement — calamitously it settled for a police war. Jeudwine commented: 'There must be either war or peace. The present policy viewed from a military standpoint can only end in disaster. If the Government elects for war it must be waged with all the resources of war unsparingly used, and it must begin at once and fought to a finish. The more drastic, complete and immediate the measures taken the less will be the cost, and the quicker the end will be reached. If the Government elects for peace, it must pursue peace openly at once, and make an offer of terms.'[25]

INTELLIGENCE

It has become customary to depict the War as an Intelligence triumph for the IRA and, together with success on the publicity side, to contrast this with their military limitations. There has, however, been much exaggeration of the effectiveness of IRA Intelligence, particularly in the provinces. In his survey of the Intelligence war, Brigadier-General Winter took issue with the generally favourable British view of the IRA machine. Given their advantage of local knowledge and control of the postal and telephone systems, Winter held that they should have done much better, pointing to their failure to install an effective filing system backed up by photographs of prominent targets. For instance, the documents seized from Éamon Duggan's legal office were found hidden away chaotically among his clients' briefs.

The overall success of the IRA in the Intelligence conflict owed most to the alienation of large segments of the Catholic population from acceptance of British rule, and an underlying feeling that the non-implementation of a Home Rule settlement had undermined any moral authority of the British government. Winter commented: 'To all intents and purposes, the Intelligence Service had been operating in a completely hostile country, without any of the advantages conferred by the proclamation of war'.[26]

The collapse of British authority in Ireland is dramatically illustrated by the state of Intelligence. On 3 January 1920 Lord French wrote: 'Our Secret Service is simply non-existent', and later that same month added: 'Outside the city of Belfast there exists practically no special detective force.' On the military side the history of the Fifth Division concluded: 'We were much hampered in 1920 by the unavoidable weakness of the military intelligence service . . . There were no secret service agents, and the officer or soldier who tried to pose as a local Irishman was found out immediately. All our intelligence officers became marked men.' Government sources were agreed in attributing long-term responsibility for this to Birrell's neglect of security services before and after the Easter Rising.[27] The period of the First World War had seen a failure of liaison between military and police systems in Ireland, and, in striking contrast to Fenian times, an inability to infiltrate the various institutions of advanced nationalism.

In 1919 outside Dublin the major reliance was still on the RIC's Crimes Special Branch which had been useful in appraising local developments but deficient in the methods of collecting and collating information. The army's 'Record of the Rebellion in Ireland' states: 'The first difficulty was that prior to 1920 there was no intelligence organised on modern lines with complete and up-to-date records and capable of being developed and expanded without

dislocation into an effective intelligence organisation such as had been created in London and in the various theatres of war, during 1914–18.

'The Crimes Special Branch depended much more on personal and local
knowledge than on organisation and methodical recording . . . The branch
was all so secret that no one was allowed to know anything about it . . . The
unwise economy which reduced the personnel of the Crimes Special Branch
made it almost impossible to keep adequate, up-to-date and reliable records
and files. Moreover, nearly every "Crimes Special" report was laboriously written out in long-hand and copies were seldom kept. They were passed backward
and forward between the central and subordinate officers, thus greatly increasing the opportunities for discovering their contents. The result was that when
those men, whose knowledge would have been invaluable during 1920 and
1921, were murdered, the intelligence system in Ireland collapsed for the time
being and had to be built up afresh.'[28]

The situation with regard to the detective force, the 'G' Division, of the
Dublin Metropolitan Police was more dramatic: Collins' Squad had chosen
them as the central target of their assassination policy. During 1919 five of the
Political Detective Branch were murdered and another disabled for life. When
Assistant Commissioner Redmond was sent from Belfast to reorganise the force,
he was soon assassinated in January 1920. Not surprisingly, there were no volunteers for the detective service and many transferred to the uniform force.
The Report of the Enquiry into the DMP of the spring of 1920 concluded:
'Inside information of real value is almost impossible to maintain' and while
the identities of police force members were known to Sinn Féin, the converse
was not true. In fairness to the DMP, the Report pointed out that the military
and Scotland Yard had been equally unsuccessful.

Following the near miss of the IRA's attempt to assassinate Lord French in
December 1919, and the shooting of Redmond, the British authorities at last
gave priority to reforming Intelligence.[29] A small, secret committee, including Alan Bell, a veteran of detective work in Land League days, was forced to
consider the consequences of what G.C. Duggan described as the virtual
extermination of the Intelligence system. Bell has generally been depicted at
this time as leading an investigation into the location of Sinn Féin bank
accounts but it is clear from his personal papers that he was involved in detective work relating to the French and Redmond shootings. While the committee was still sitting, Bell was shot dead by Collins' men: the fact that he was
unarmed and unprotected and travelling on his regular route by public transport between Monkstown and the city of Dublin says little for his own idea of
sensible precautions.

In January 1920 the military participation in deportation raids made the army
well aware of the failings of RIC Intelligence. The GHQ Record concluded: 'It
was not . . . understood how completely the RIC service of information was
paralysed until it was decided to arrest . . . a large number of extreme Sinn
Féiners in the hope that the deportation of a few hundreds would put a stop to

the Sinn Féin movement. It was then found that the local RIC could give little reliable information about such persons beyond a statement that so and so was "a bad boy" or "a bad article". The police lists were out of date and to them every Sinn Féin club was a battalion. The lists were eventually compiled with their assistance, but the IRA status of the person whom it proposed to arrest was in all cases supplied by military intelligence officers.'[30] Appreciation of such realities was no doubt behind the establishment of a somewhat shadowy military Intelligence organisation, under Lieutenant-Colonel Walter Wilson, which appears to have had some limited success but was to be plagued by poor relations with the police and overlapping authority.[31] It was at this time also that an increasing role in Irish affairs was given over to Basil Thomson's Scotland Yard organisation. Trained spies were sent over to infiltrate the IRA with James Byrnes (alias Jameson) and H.J. Quinlisk soon meeting a ghastly fate on the outskirts of Dublin and Cork respectively.

The enlistment and training of Intelligence agents in London reflected despair over the situation in Ireland. A First World War veteran from Essex, Byrnes had operated as an undercover agent in socialist circles in London, where he became acquainted with Art O'Brien, Collins's key contact in London. O'Brien gave him letters of introduction and recommendation to Collins. The expectation was that Byrnes would supply arms and information on the IRA.[32]

While in Dublin, Byrnes used several aliases, the most common one being Jameson, and travelled ostensibly as a jewellery salesman. Details of his movements remain shrouded but it is clear that he alone among Intelligence agents succeeded in actually meeting Michael Collins. It seems that at an early stage, Byrnes' identity became known through Collins' contacts in the Castle. He was probably used as a double agent for some weeks thereafter.[33]

In late January 1920, Byrnes was shot dead in the northern outskirts of Dublin by members of the Squad, led by Paddy Daly. Daly testified: 'I told him that we were satisfied he was a spy, that he was going to die, and that if he wanted to say any prayers he could do so. The spy jumped to attention immediately and said, "You are right. God bless the King. I would love to die for him." He saluted and there was not a quiver on him. The papers we found in his possession were notes of his various appointments, and sufficient evidence to hang him. The few small bits of jewellery were only fakes. In the meantime Tom Cullen again went into the Granville Hotel and collected all his luggage. From it we discovered he was in charge of a group here. The day after he was shot we decided we would investigate the group, but when we went for them they were gone. They had left on the mail boat that night.'[34]

A few months later Walter Long, in an obvious reference to Byrnes, commented that they had lost their best spy. At that time also, Quinlisk, an ex-member of Casement's brigade, was engaged on similar work and was tracked down in Cork city as a consequence of mail being intercepted. His killing marked the completion of one of the first tasks of Florrie O'Donoghue's

Intelligence network.[35] These spies and D/I Redmond had been brought to Dublin with the specific brief to eliminate Collins; Collins remained at large, they paid the price. British Intelligence was forced to regroup and re-assess.

Following the appointment of Brigadier-General Ormonde Winter, to be known in Dublin as 'O', a new priority was given to Intelligence, but the lines of command between police and military remained blurred. Winter had little experience in secret service work and was frequently criticised by his Castle superiors. Sir John Anderson wrote of Winter: 'His show is thoroughly bad and I don't see it getting any better . . . He has worked devilish hard and we mustn't let him down but the job is too vital to be left in the wrong hands.'[36] Winter was an all too easily satirised figure. G.C. Duggan commented: 'At first . . . one would imagine him the typical Colonel of light comedy — slight and small, dapper, delicate of speech, eyeglass set in eye.' Mark Sturgis saw him as looking like: 'a wicked little white snake . . . He is as clever as paint, probably entirely non-moral, a first class horseman, a card genius, knows several languages, is a super sleuth, and a most amazing original. When a soldier who knew him in India heard he was coming to Ireland, he said "God help Sinn Féin, they don't know what they're up against." ' Winter has been criticised by the historian Keith Jeffery for being obsessed by cloak and dagger work, as opposed to the mundane work of building up dossiers on suspects.[37] It is difficult to judge, however, how much responsibility for the limitations should be ascribed to him personally rather than the impossible task he was set; as in all aspects of Irish administration, the initiative had been lost for good long before his arrival.

Winter's new system took a long time to implement. He only moved into the Castle in late autumn 1920 and had major problems centralising authority under his command due to continuing rivalry with the military. His new local centres, aiming at integrated control, began to be set up in December and were only fully established just before the Truce. There was, however, a considerable increase in the amount of information picked up on raids. From August 1920 to July 1921, 6311 raids and searches were carried out in the Dublin district.[38] There were some notable Intelligence coups: the capture on two occasions of Richard Mulcahy's papers; the successful raid at the end of December 1920 on the Dawson Street flat of Eileen McGrane, one of Collins' agents, and the seizing of sensitive material in Austin Stack's and Michael Collins' offices.[39] The IRA attacks on the morning of Bloody Sunday were proof of increased pressure from British Intelligence sources. By the spring of 1921, both de Valera and Collins were increasingly concerned that the net was closing in around them.

In a long memorandum reviewing his work in Dublin,[40] Winter admitted the peculiar difficulties of dealing with guerrilla warfare. He adopted the usual patronising, and worse, attitude to the Irish, commenting: 'The Irishman, without any insult being intended, strongly resembles a dog, and understands firm treatment, but, like the dog, he cannot understand being cajoled with a piece of sugar in one hand whilst he receives a beating from a stick in the other.'

Somewhat mysteriously, Winter felt that the conflict had produced no effective Irish leaders but admitted that rewards for captures of IRA men had met with no success. He confessed that his use of bloodhounds had proved ineffective and ascribed the limited results stemming from eavesdropping equipment in prison cells to the fact that: 'the acoustics of a cell are generally bad, and a microphone of English manufacture seems ill-adapted to the Irish brogue.' He seems belatedly to have realised that the most successful aspects of Intelligence work related to that on captured documents rather than melodramatic plots.

The GHQ 'Record of the Rebellion in Ireland' admitted the limitations of the Intelligence effort but put the primary responsibility for this down to the vicissitudes of government policy and the lack of central political direction. It commented: 'It is probable that what handicapped the service of information more even than the difficult conditions in Ireland was doubt as to what was the real policy of the Government, while the Government probably found it difficult to define their policy owing to their lack of information as to what really was happening and as to the trend of events. The result was a compromise between conciliation and coercion and a state of affairs which was neither peace nor war.'

Moving on to criticise the confusion between and the duplication of effort of the various secret service agencies, the Record notes that: 'A sort of hermaphrodite intelligence service' resulted. 'There was no reason why the broad principles, on which British Intelligence was based during the war, should not have been followed in Ireland, for they are generally admitted to have been sound and to have achieved successful results. But neither the police nor the Civil Government had had any experience of them. The result was an organisation which was false in conception and over-centralised in practice. Military intelligence on the other hand was too much decentralised . . . This faulty organisation in both police and military branches of the intelligence can be traced back to uncertainty as to the main policy.'[41]

7

BRITISH POLICY AT THE CROSSROADS: APRIL–AUGUST 1920

~

I
n mid-April 1920, a committee of three was appointed to examine the workings of Dublin Castle. Sir Warren Fisher, the Permanent Secretary to the Treasury and Head of the Civil Service, led it and was assisted by Alfred Cope, Second Secretary in the Ministry of Pensions, and R.E. Harwood, Assistant Secretary of the Treasury. The original idea for this appears to have come from Downing Street. Despite his considerable responsibility for the failings of British administration, French enthusiastically associated himself with the project. 'Government administration in Ireland', French stated, 'is . . . just as bad as it is possible for it to be.' French complained that both his Chief Secretaries had disregarded his attempts to reform the system by means of his three Councils.[1]

On receipt of the Report, Austen Chamberlain, the Chancellor of the Exchequer in the Coalition government, commented: 'I was prepared for none too satisfactory an account of the Irish Administration, but the Report submitted by Sir W. Fisher and the greater detail given by his subordinates disclose a condition both of administration and staff which is worse than anything that I had anticipated.' Fisher's Report was accompanied by a supplementary one from Cope and Harwood and by an even more biting letter from Fisher. The cutting language used avoided any of the habitual caution and reserve of civil service vocabulary.[2]

Fisher's Report began: 'The Castle Administration does not administer. On the mechanical side it can never have been good and is now quite obsolete; in the infinitely more important sphere (a) of informing and advising the Irish Government in relation to policy and (b) of practical capacity in the application of policy it simply has no existence.' The inefficiency in administration was attacked as well as the failure of civil government to assert sufficient control over the military and the police. Cope and Harwood found that there had been too much concentration of work in the hands of the Assistant

Under-Secretary, Taylor, and the Principal Clerk, Connolly, which had reduced the Under-Secretary MacMahon to the level of, in Fisher's words, 'a routine clerk', having no role in policy decisions. Cope and Harwood recommended drastic reorganisation of the Administrative Division of the Chief Secretary's Office with the employment of seconded personnel from Whitehall. Fisher was especially critical of MacMahon, writing that he 'is not devoid of brains, but lacks initiative, force, and driving power'.

MacMahon's removal, however, was not advised for fear of upsetting Catholic sensitivities and losing MacMahon's contacts with the Catholic hierarchy. Instead the appointment of the Chairman of the Board of Inland Revenue, Sir John Anderson, as Joint Under-Secretary was recommended. Fisher argued that in such an arrangement Anderson 'would rapidly acquire the real control'. Fisher further suggested that Sir John Taylor should not return to the Castle, as forty-three years' service entitled him to retirement, and that he should be replaced by Cope. It was argued that the Administration should be physically removed from the Castle, 'the associations of which are a heavy sentimental handicap' and that the Lord Lieutenancy should be abolished 'with its atmosphere of pinchbeck royalty'. In what was to be a persistent theme in the coming year, Fisher recommended unity of command for the Crown Forces and civil control of the RIC by 'a really able and powerful Civil Servant'.

In his supplementary report, Fisher criticised the quality of the political advice offered by Dublin Castle. He described the existing government, apart from Macready: 'as almost woodenly stupid and quite devoid of imagination. It listens solely to the ascendancy party and . . . never seemed to think of the utility of keeping in close touch with opinions of all kinds.' Fisher went on to argue that Dublin Castle had made the critical mistake of failing to understand the breadth of the Sinn Féin movement. The proscription of Sinn Féin had only served to rally moderate opinion behind the hardliners.[3]

All the new officials who came to Dublin Castle in the spring and summer of 1920 confirmed Fisher's judgment about the chaotic state of the administration and the collapse of police and governmental authority. Sir Hamar Greenwood, the new Chief Secretary, told Bonar Law: 'There is a sloppiness in administration and a lack of cohesion in the protective forces that is amazing.' Macready reported: 'Before I had been there three hours, I was honestly flabbergasted at the administrative chaos that seems to reign here.' The General was particularly critical of the police and its leadership.[4]

Macready, Anderson and Wylie continually reported that the Government of Ireland Bill had no public support, and remained opposed to the implementation of martial law. They saw no prospect of any short-term military solution. While admitting that they were exceeding their remit, Macready and Anderson supported the establishment of links with Sinn Féin and the offer of some kind of Dominion Status. Anderson told the Cabinet: 'The brute fact, which cannot be ignored, is that, broadly speaking, the entire population in the South and West, so far as it is not actually hostile, is out of sympathy with the Government and cannot be relied upon to co-operate in the carrying out of even the most reasonable and moderate measures.' Macready criticised government policy and administration by saying it had: 'been allowed to drift into such an impasse that no amount of coercion can possibly remedy it'. He felt that the British public would not support martial law for any length of time and concluded that having tried the coercion policy in one form or another for so long, it would be a good thing to go right to the other extreme.[5]

Fisher had delivered the epitaph to the old Dublin Castle administration. Most of his suggested administrative and personnel reforms were quickly implemented, although his policy suggestions were apparently disregarded. His criticisms were somewhat harsh on individuals and insufficient emphasis was given to the underlying weaknesses of the system. The most obvious omission was any discussion of how much Dublin Castle's failure was down to the British government itself. It was, after all, Lloyd George who had appointed French and Macpherson and who had not interfered with their handling of government. Fisher's suggested remedies did not involve a fundamental restructure of the administration nor any improvement in the channels of communication between Dublin and Westminster; no change was suggested in the anomalous position of the Chief Secretary. In all probability, however, Fisher realised that such conclusions were academic because Dublin Castle was doomed.

Between May and July a large team of civil servants seconded from the Treasury, the Home Office and the Scottish Office arrived in Dublin. Initially they stayed at the Marine Hotel, Kingstown, in line with Fisher's desire for a break with the old Dublin Castle set-up. By the early autumn, however, security considerations forced the new administration into the Castle.[6] Significantly, Anderson was given the same financial powers as the Secretary to the Treasury in Britain, thus abolishing the cumbersome system of submitting requests to Whitehall and the office of Treasury Remembrancer. It is a major irony that the system was modernised shortly before its demise.

The three most important of the seconded officials were Anderson, Cope and Mark Sturgis. Anderson came from a middle-class background in Edinburgh. He graduated with the best First Class science degree of his year from Edinburgh University and followed the then usual practice of sitting the British civil service exams, where again he gained the highest marks of all. Anderson had worked in the Colonial Office and the Treasury and became a key figure administering National Insurance. He was widely regarded as the ablest civil servant of his time. Shortly before his appointment to Dublin, his first wife had died. W.E. Wylie and G.C. Duggan, colleagues of Anderson in the Dublin administration, were to assess him as the most competent man they had ever met — cool, logical, quick to get to the heart of a problem and the master of his brief. Wylie and Sturgis, however, pointed out that Anderson lacked the common touch and could appear aloof and somewhat pompous. Sturgis recorded: 'Lady Greenwood says when she talks to him she feels like a little girl waiting to be rebuked and that he treats Hamar too much like a child!'

In practice, Anderson proved to all intents and purposes the head of British government in Ireland. He was much sharper than Greenwood and his opinion was more highly regarded in Westminster. Because of his position and personality, Anderson had better relations with the military and police than did other members of the civil service junta, particularly Cope. He and Macready enjoyed many a civilised conversation over whiskies in the Castle. Anderson's time in Dublin was valuable preparation for his later illustrious career as Head of the Home Office, Governor of Bengal and his non-party political role as Home Secretary and Chancellor of the Exchequer during the Second World War.[7]

Alfred Cope, universally known as Andy, aroused extremes of reaction. He is rather a shadowy figure because of the undercover rôle Lloyd George gave him and the non-survival of relevant papers. Many republicans have been keen to blame Collins' relationship with Cope for bringing about division in nationalist ranks. Leading members of the British forces depicted Cope as being all but a Sinn Féiner. Cope came from a labour aristocracy background: his father was a bottle manufacturer, and he was born near Kennington Oval. At one time Cope had been a leading Customs detective. Nervous and highly-strung by temperament, Cope perhaps revealed a social discomfiture by his unwillingness to delegate. Sturgis, in his Diaries, finds it difficult to avoid a patronising tone when Cope is under discussion. Appointed as Under-Secretary, Cope had the public duty of improving the administrative machinery of the Castle but was also given the brief, it seems by Lloyd George, to establish links with Sinn Féin. He was to remain in Ireland for a period after the Anglo-Irish Treaty acting as the chief liaison with the new Irish government.[8]

In all but name, Sturgis was Anderson's deputy. For fear of upsetting Cope, he was never given the title of Assistant Under-Secretary. From a landed class background, educated at Eton and Christ Church, Oxford, and married to the aristocrat Lady Rachel Wharnecliffe, Sturgis was an unlikely career civil servant. He had been a personal secretary to the then Prime Minister, Herbert Asquith, but was easily bored by detail, and had been relieved to surrender his current post as Special Commissioner for Income Tax. Despite early doubts, his move to Dublin represented something of a liberation, enabling him to live the life of a country squire and develop his passion for horses and racing in a congenial environment. He played the part of a diplomatic attaché, organising social functions in the Castle, teaching Anderson to ride and calming Cope's nerves. Beneath his insouciant manner, Sturgis had great ability in easing fraught relationships and had a great fund of common sense. His entertaining, if self-consciously written, Diaries give a vivid, personalised account of day-to-day events during the last months of the British administration in Ireland.[9]

The Anderson-Cope-Sturgis triumvirate offers an ironic commentary on the British class system. When asked how three such diverse characters came to work together, Sturgis replied: 'Jonathan came in by the front door — Andy . . . came in by the back door and I came in by the drawing room window.'[10]

The seconded civil servants had been Warren Fisher's appointments and Fisher continued to be a strong influence on them. Anderson and Sturgis frequently dined with Fisher on their visits to London, broadly followed his advice on policy and kept in regular correspondence. The Law Adviser, William E. Wylie, quickly identified himself with the new officials in a social context in addition to the formal one and regarded them as a breath of fresh air.

Wylie was from Northern Irish Presbyterian stock. He had been a Special Prosecutor following the Easter Rising and a Crown Prosecutor in 1919–20. Wylie became a fierce advocate of Dominion Home Rule and for amendment of the Government of Ireland Act: he was used by Macready to put such views to Lloyd George and Bonar Law in the spring of 1920. Disappointed when the British government intensified its policy of coercion, Wylie tabled his resignation in the late summer of 1920 but was eventually cajoled out of it by his close friends, Anderson and Sturgis. Wylie achieved the considerable distinction of being appointed a judge by the British in 1920 and by the Irish Free State in 1924.[11]

Cope was put in charge of improving the machinery of government and by June was able to report considerable progress. As a result of the personnel changes, sounder advice was being given to the British Cabinet. The new regime, however, had its weaknesses. Greenwood's position became anomalous and he was often ignored by the civil service junta. G.C. Duggan, an official in the Castle, felt that Ireland was being governed by civil servants. Cope's personality and his ill-defined position created tensions between the civil and military/police authorities. Nothing was done about unity of command. Liaison between Dublin and Westminster remained a problem. Again much depended on how individuals got on with each other. Anderson and Macready had particularly good relations, but Macready strongly disliked Cope and there were acid relations between the military and police leaders. The system only worked at all because of Anderson's ability and the respect it engendered on all sides.[12]

For all their ability the new guard had their limitations. They shared with Macready a lack of sympathy with Northern Unionism. Sturgis, for instance, strove successfully to avoid setting foot at all in Belfast and the very mention of Cope's name sent shudders through Unionist ranks. Duggan and Wylie argued that Anderson and Sturgis would never understand the Irish, and there remained tensions between Irish and British civil servants, exacerbated by the fact that the British ones were better paid. The crucial weakness, however, was that the new regime did not control Irish policy. Fisher's Report had brought about administrative reform but his political advice was rarely followed.

A few weeks after his arrival, Macready sent Wylie to London to recommend a change of policy akin to Dominion Status to Lloyd George. Wylie told the Prime Minister that Sinn Féin would welcome such a settlement and Lloyd George replied: 'that he personally would agree but the British Government was a Coalition and I would have to convince Bonar Law'. Bonar Law and Sir Edward Carson, the Northern Unionist leader, were called in with the latter proving surprisingly sympathetic to Wylie's views. Lloyd George concluded matters by saying: 'I will not break the Coalition for Ireland.'[13]

By July important elements in the press and the church had come out in favour of a Dominion Status settlement.[14] The Cabinet's first discussion of the grim realities occurred in a meeting with Irish officials on 31 May. Greenwood there displayed his superficial grasp of affairs by ascribing the difficulties to American financial backing of 'thugs'. He argued: 'The real difficulty in Ireland is not so much the big issue of putting down crime as the inadequacy and sloppiness of the instruments of Government. We can only rely on the Navy, military and RIC.' While martial law was rejected on grounds of impracticality, emergency legislation was discussed to speed up the course of justice. The raising of another auxiliary police force was also discussed. With characteristic frankness, Churchill declared: 'What strikes me is the feebleness of the local machinery. After a person is caught he should pay the penalty within a week. Look at the tribunals which the Russian Government have devised. You should get three or four judges whose scope should be universal and they should move quickly over the country and do summary justice.' Bringing out the distinction between public and private appreciation of realities, Curzon stated: 'We have got to a state of open civil war in Ireland and not merely civil, it is as bad as against the Germans.'[15]

A second meeting of the British Cabinet with Irish government officials and James Craig, representing Northern Unionist interests, on 23 July was described by H.A.L. Fisher as the first wide-ranging review of Irish policy since the War. Never were the policy options and divisions to be so clearly expressed. The discussion opened with an amazingly frank address by Wylie. Sturgis reported 'Wylie gave it to them hot and strong I'm told' and Fisher referred to Wylie's 'brilliant speech'. Wylie began by saying that within two months if nothing was done the RIC would cease to exist outside the six counties. He pointed out that the British machinery of government no longer operated in large areas of the country. Wylie considered that Sinn Féin were well capable of government and consisted largely of idealists: their support was the product of genuine grievance that the British had failed to deliver on Home Rule. He felt that Sinn Féin would agree to a county option for Ulster and to the retention of British defence interests in Ireland. Wylie's bleak account of the situation went uncontradicted and his views were supported by Anderson, Macready, MacMahon and Cope. Anderson stressed that the implementation of martial law would be counterproductive and Macready doubted whether the Army could implement it.

The opposite view was put forward by Tudor who argued for drastic methods 'to crush the present campaign of outrage'. He recommended courts-martial for all crimes, the use of ID cards, the insistence on passports to enter Ireland, widespread internment outside Ireland and the use of flogging for various offences. Tudor concluded: 'The whole country was intimidated, and would thank God for strong measures.' To no-one's surprise Long, Birkenhead and Balfour supported Tudor's recommendations and Churchill went even further in advocating the use of a Northern Special Constabulary in the South. Curzon stated 'the arming of Ulster was a most fatal suggestion.' Churchill stressed that he was not opposed to further amendment of the Government of Ireland Bill but was completely opposed to any surrender to violence. At the end of the meeting Churchill asked Wylie if he condoned murder. Wylie replied that 'I had condemned murder beside the bodies of murdered men and in the presence of the murderers and that it was more than he had ever done speaking from the safety of the House of Commons.'

While opinion at the meeting split along generally predictable lines, both Curzon and Austen Chamberlain sided with a more moderate policy. Lloyd George did not express any clear opinion but said that if the view of the Dublin Castle officials was made known to the public it would be impossible to go on with the Government of Ireland Bill. Craig did not disagree with Wylie's analysis but insisted that any amendment of devolved powers in the Act be granted to the six counties as well.[16]

The next day Thomas Jones, Private Secretary to Lloyd George, wrote a memorandum to the Prime Minister clearly setting out the policy alternatives. Either, he held, they must have 'the rigorous application of force by means of courts martial, the suspension of civil government, the stoppage of trains and motors, the withholding of pensions and generally the infliction of a rapidly increasing paralysis upon the country' or 'an immediate attempt to conclude a pact with the leaders of Sinn Féin and the revolutionists'. Jones urged the Prime Minister to make a speech on the subject 'very soon'.[17]

The 23 July debate provides the essential background to the plethora of peace initiatives before and after. Lloyd George was not to accept the suggestions made by those he had appointed to Dublin. Instead an erratic coercion policy was followed and the association of conciliation with Greenwood's Chief Secretaryship conclusively ended. The responsibility for that rested with Lloyd George.

Despite the fact that the doves appeared to have won the argument at the 23 July meeting, the Government's subsequent policy was actually hawkish. Having been guillotined through parliament, The Restoration of Order in Ireland Act became law on 9 August. The Defence of the Realm Act (DORA) which, together with The Criminal Law and Procedure (Ireland) Act of 1887, had provided the legal basis for emergency powers, was now near the end of its limited time-span. Moreover there was an awareness of the chronic need to replace the non-functioning court system. The new legislation incorporated the relevant DORA provisions with new powers. Amongst other measures the jurisdiction of courts-martial was extended to cover offences against the ordinary civil law: courts-martial could now employ the death penalty; courts of summary justice, consisting of two Resident Magistrates, would be established; military courts of enquiry would replace the coroners' courts and powers given to suspend government payment to local authorities.[18]

The Act appeared to represent a triumph for the hard-liners within the Coalition. An editorial in *The Times* argued that it meant 'the complete collapse of the Irish legal system' and that there was no justification for it 'save that of stern necessity . . . its introduction robs the present system in Ireland of any semblance of normality and, indeed, of permanency.'[19] The Act was a halfway house towards martial law and was essentially a compromise. There remained an unwillingness to confront problems in the relationship between the civil and the military authorities.

The confusion between civil, police and military structures and the refusal to establish any unity of command was a key element in the collapse of British authority. Warren Fisher and Mark Sturgis continually harped on this weakness. Sturgis asserted: 'I cannot find anybody who does not agree that we have come back to this, that what we lack is Unity of Command. It is extraordinary to me that Lloyd George who saw so clearly the need for it in France does not seem to see the absolute necessity for it here.'[20]

In a deeply pessimistic and hard-hitting memorandum to the government in February 1921, Sir Warren Fisher devoted his greatest scorn to this issue, while simultaneously exaggerating the effectiveness of the Irish chain of command: 'As regards the "executive" arrangements of Government to "protect life and property" in Ireland, I can see no grounds for optimism at all. On the Sinn Féin side, the exponents of physical force work as a team under single direction: there is no question of divided control or responsibility. On the Government side . . . not only is the use of force not singly directed, but even as between the three elements now existing there is little evidence of effective cooperation. On the contrary there are to my mind undoubted signs of an untimely lack of sympathy and comprehension in attitude and of liaison in working, so that there isn't even the next best thing to unity of direction, namely a real alliance between separate controls.'[21]

Throughout the late summer and autumn of 1920 the vexed issue of reprisals caused Macready's contempt for the police to harden. Relations between Macready and Tudor were cool and Macready and Anderson were heavily critical of Winter. The situation was further complicated by Churchill's friendship with and support for Tudor and by Sir Henry Wilson's contempt for all politicians, to whom he referred as 'frocks'.

The unity of command issue should be seen as more the consequence of rather than the basic reason for maladministration. Everything stemmed from the Cabinet's refusal to acknowledge the depth of the crisis. Administrative failings mirrored the ambiguity of British attitudes both within and without the Cabinet. There was an extreme reluctance to opt for either of the dire alternatives of conciliation or full-scale coercion in the post-war years of economic recession and labour crises. Events were therefore to be the only arbiter in the determination of policy. Furthermore, the new administration in Dublin Castle was acutely aware that increased military involvement, even if successful in the short term, could not but inflame and worsen the situation ultimately. Any attempt to rationalise the command structure should have involved much more efficient Dublin Castle — Whitehall communications. As after the Easter Rising, little was done in this respect.

PART III

APOGEE

8

THE IRISH INTELLIGENCE SYSTEM AND THE DEVELOPMENT OF GUERRILLA WARFARE UP TO THE TRUCE

~

To a considerable extent, the War of Independence was more an Intelligence triumph for the IRA than a military one. Collins' Intelligence organisation became legendary and the template for later anti-colonial struggles. The Fenian movement of the 1860s had been riddled with informers; now Irish informers would infiltrate the British administration in a reversal of roles.

During 1917 Ned Broy, a confidential clerk in the DMP Headquarters in Baggot Street, had wanted to give information to the Volunteers, having become convinced that armed rebellion was necessary. It was several months before an intermediary introduced him to Collins, and Broy was one of those who gave advance warning of the German Plot arrests. Broy passed on copies of all material going through his hands up to his arrest in early 1921 and reported to Collins every twenty-four hours.[1]

In Dublin Castle itself, Joe Kavanagh supplied information from 1916 onwards until his death, from natural causes, in 1919, and his place was then taken by Jim MacNamara. David Neligan, another counter-agent, was prevailed upon to enter the British Secret Service after leaving the DMP. The many other agents who were scattered through the whole British administration in Dublin included Lily Merrin, a typist in the British Command HQ in the Castle. Nancy O'Brien, a cousin of Collins, also passed material on from within the Castle. Important contacts were made with the regular police in Dublin. It was DMP men in the Rathmines and Donnybrook stations who supplied the names and addresses of those assassinated on the morning of Bloody Sunday.[2]

Collins only became Director of Intelligence at GHQ in 1919 but before that had built up his network of agents and spies. Liam Tobin, his deputy, Tom Cullen and Frank Thornton were the dominant figures in his Intelligence staff and they collected information by sleuthing, and directed activities of the Squad. In the heart of the war, in meetings in a café at the bottom of Grafton Street, British agents, in complete ignorance of whom they were talking to, told Tobin and Cullen who the important figures in Collins' Intelligence system were.

By 1919 Collins was extending his network to the provinces very successfully and establishing contacts in the RIC, the post offices and the railways. Informers were active even in areas where the IRA was poorly organised; Seán Kavanagh, a Gaelic League teacher in Naas, for instance, supplied crucial information on the RIC from his contact with Sergeant Gerry Maher.[3] Police codes were known even before the police knew them themselves. The Intelligence organisation within most IRA brigades, however, was much less impressive and was frequently criticised by GHQ. To a considerable extent, Florrie O'Donoghue's system of spies and agents in Cork mirrored that of Collins in Dublin, but was the only such example.

Over plans for attacks on British government ministers in London, the Intelligence system almost overextended itself. Both in 1918 and 1921, schemes were hatched to send Intelligence agents and gunmen to the city. In 1918, matters never got beyond the theoretical stage, but in 1921, various officers did cross the Irish Sea with murder in mind. In later years, Mulcahy was keen to dissociate himself and Collins from any involvement in this and labelled it as Cathal Brugha's harebrained scheme. Brugha wanted individual gunmen to have responsibility for the assassination of each targeted Cabinet Minister, and Seán MacEoin was amongst those selected for the task. MacEoin recorded Mulcahy and Collins countermanding Brugha's instructions, ridiculing the idea of a thick Midlands brogue fooling anyone in London. Frank Thornton, however, records travelling to London and describes the crazy event in which Seán Flood, spying out the land, unknowingly knocked Lloyd George to the ground when running out of Westminster Underground station. It was fortunate in every sense that this remained an obscure sideshow.[4]

Collins' achievement and that of his agents was enormous. The British, ironically enough, were his keenest admirers, many wondering how he could cycle brazenly round Dublin without detection by them.[5] It has been claimed on somewhat dubious grounds that there were no photographs of Collins available. Collins took advantage of the fact that large numbers of civil servants, railway workers, hotel porters and so on were more than willing to leak information, at very great personal risk, in a way that would have been inconceivable ten years before. This change of attitudes reflected the rejection of the British administration following on the Ulster Crisis and the failure to implement Home Rule. The Intelligence system, as in all twentieth-century colonial struggles, provided the essential precondition for the development of guerrilla warfare.

The progress of the war can be assessed in distinct stages, each evolving according to the success or failure of the preceding one. The basis for later developments lay in the police boycott applied first in the localities in 1917 and 1918, and legislated on by the Dáil as soon as possible in April 1919. As in Land League days, the recourse to ostracisation was an ideal means of satisfying the advocates both of passive resistance and physical force.

The police were the most visible face of the British administration in the provinces and acted as the chief Intelligence agents for the government. The fact that they were armed meant that they could assume the character of an alien occupying force. It was hardly surprising that the boycott and the raids for arms on policemen resulted in the sporadic killings of 1919; eleven RIC men were killed in 1919 in addition to four members of the Dublin Metropolitan Police and twenty were wounded. These figures increased greatly in 1920 to 143 RIC killed, 197 wounded and even more in 1921 to 205 killed and 291 wounded.[6]

There was often considerable public sympathy for the police following individual shootings, but when retaliatory measures in the form of proscription of societies and the curbing of social events and travel were introduced, this evaporated quickly. Attacks on police barracks were the appropriate next stage. There was nothing novel in this and individual police huts had been raided in West Cork and Kerry in 1918, but a whole wave of such attacks occurred from January 1920, reaching a climax in the summer of that year.

In 1919, GHQ had refused permission for Michael Brennan in Clare and Terence MacSwiney in Cork to raid a whole series of barracks in rapid succession. They feared that such an escalation of the conflict was distinctly premature when arms supplies were very sparse and training was at a very early stage. When authority was given for a limited number of attacks, first in Cork in January 1920, GHQ held that the actions themselves would be useful as training. By that time the local units were desperate for action and often acted on their own initiative regardless of Dublin's sanction.

One bold incident in December 1919 stands out. In previous months there had been a whole series of plans to assassinate Lord French, including one to take place during a victory parade outside Trinity College, Dublin. Finally French's convoy was attacked on the 19th near Ashtown Station, by Phoenix Park, after the Viceroy's return from his house in County Sligo. The hastily organised attack by two parties failed because French was travelling in the first rather than the second car of four. Two RIC men were wounded and a Sligo-born Volunteer, Martin Savage, killed. Despite Lloyd George's callous comment to Macpherson that 'they are bad shots', the incident had a profoundly unsettling effect on British police and military morale.[7] In IRA terms it had been a hugely risky endeavour. If it had been successful, the whole British attitude to the War would surely have changed and an enormous amount of pressure would have been put on an ill-prepared IRA. As it was, the IRA was fortunate in its failure. The time for successful ambushes lay in the future.

The move to limited military actions was encouraged further by the failure of Sinn Féin's political policies during 1919. The appeal to the Paris Peace

Conference had produced nil results and de Valera's search for recognition of
the Dáil government in the US was predictably producing only sympathy. Any
chance that political success would render military action redundant no
longer existed. The prime reason for the IRA's concentration on targeting
police stations lies in the fact that they were the tangible emblems of British
rule and to attack them had symbolic and psychological implications which
were even more important than the physical ones. In appreciation of the siege-
like conditions for the RIC in much of rural Ireland, the police garrisons were
evacuated from the autumn of 1919.[8]

A majority of the raids on barracks were unsuccessful in straight military
terms. Often there was a breakdown in planning and co-ordination, mines failed
to detonate and Volunteers' nerves failed. To attack buildings situated right in
the midst of towns or in a fortified isolated location required a considerable
amount of logistical planning as well as courage. In many cases buildings were
evacuated after a failed raid; to some extent therefore the IRA actions against
the police were continuing a process already begun by the British themselves.
Nonetheless, successful attacks had massive political significance, demonstrating more dramatically than anything else the collapse of British authority.

A whole legend built up around the heroic story of barracks attacks: they
became the repositories of local pride. This is well reflected in the number and
popularity of accounts in often excruciating detail frequently serialised in
newspapers for many decades to come. The story of brave assaults on buildings
and running pitched battles appealed to a readership keen to identify with the
glorious rebels and against the wicked oppressors.[9]

From the autumn of 1920, raids on police barracks became much less frequent. In the last seven months of the war the taking of Rosscarbery Barracks
is the only example of a successful attack. Firing on police buildings by that
time amounted to little more than sniping, sometimes with the aim of bringing the police out into the open. IRA successes had led to a greater concentration of the RIC in heavily fortified stations, often backed up by the army.
Military barracks could only be raided by ruse or with internal assistance, as at
Mallow Barracks in October 1920. In the late summer of 1920, attention
turned to the planning of ambushes.

The most vulnerable aspect of the police and military presence had become
the supply convoys, bringing food, equipment and reinforcements, particularly
during the period in which the railway industry refused to carry troops. From
the Irish perspective, the switch to ambushes had much to do with the formation
of flying columns resulting from the increasing number of men living on the
run. The growing pressure of raids by the police and military and the effect of
The Restoration of Order in Ireland Act forced the IRA to concentrate men
and arms in elite units from the late summer of 1920. Again circumstances,
rather than any military manual, had dictated change.

The preferred size of the columns was around twenty-five, although numbers substantially varied. For large operations units often collaborated. In

memoranda ordering the formation of columns, GHQ claimed that they were an excellent means of providing training and liked to give the impression that they controlled operations, though this was far from the case.[10] The very nature of the column activities meant that the emphasis was on local knowledge, spontaneity and flexibility. On many occasions while permission was being sought from brigade or GHQ, opportunities were lost. Where central direction was useful was in Intelligence planning and in the blocking of communications which involved co-ordination across parish or county lines. On receipt of reports on ambushes, GHQ was able to analyse mistakes and to refine future tactics. Nonetheless, the story of flying columns is largely a matter of decisions and actions taken on the spot; men like Tom Barry and Seán Moylan were essentially maverick figures, suspicious of any outside control and relating principally to their own column men. A successful column became a matter of intense local pride.

The ambush was the ideal form of offensive and defensive warfare. It was the means by which the disparity in armed resources between the two sides could be made irrelevant. By trial and error, the IRA had stumbled on the type of warfare, with some reference to the Boer War, extensively copied since from Latin America to Vietnam, in which the advantage of a committed and motivated force, local knowledge and support outweighs the numerical superiority and vast armed resources of the occupying force. The impact of an ambush on Irish and British opinion was to be gauged in many other terms than in the strictly military; as with the Tet offensive in South Vietnam in January 1968, Crossbarry (see pages 111–12) hardly constituted a victory, yet it had tremendous consequences for morale and in political perception.

The British had all the disadvantages of fighting a war without a definite front. Shortly after the Truce, Sir John Anderson wrote: 'We have been fighting on a hopelessly extended front . . . hitherto we have presented a front of almost infinite extension with our local Post Offices, Income Tax Offices and individual members of every branch of the civil administration scattered all over the country and easy prey to the enemy, who has taken toll of them at will.'[11] The British were dependent for supplies and provisions on an almost entirely alienated population and the ambush was the physical manifestation of this hostility. Whatever doubts or moral misgivings some of the population may have harboured about the use of violence, their support lay with their local men.

The column had the crucial advantage of surprise; the IRA was able to choose the time and place of attacks and had the additional advantages of a detailed familiarity with the terrain and the availability of safe houses. The British constantly complained that they could not identify the enemy and that the column men did not wear uniforms and merged imperceptibly back into the local community.

From an enemy perspective, the ambush was a cowardly form of warfare: newspaper and military accounts constantly related how ruthless killers hid behind hedges, shot RIC men and soldiers in the back using dum-dum bullets for maximum trauma, and had no respect for the conventions of warfare. Such descriptions appeared to justify all the racist stereotypes about the barbaric Irish. From the IRA's perspective, however, for part-time, untrained Volunteers, with virtually no experience under fire and pathetic resources, to tackle the military might of the British Empire was a huge gamble and involved considerable courage. Too many attacks in the locality followed by a spate of reprisals risked antagonising the surrounding community: the IRA as well as the Black and Tans were blamed for the spread of outrages.

A successful ambush involved a major amount of planning and there was often a long wait in appalling conditions in which nerves and physical endurance were tested to their limits. Anxiety was no doubt increased by the number of times abortive attacks preceded successes. Even the major reverses, at Clonmult and the Dublin Custom House for instance, would have been much worse if it had not been for the courage and commitment shown.

To an even greater extent than the police barracks attacks, the psychological effects and the ensuing publicity of the ambushes vastly exceeded their military significance. In terms of the scale of the fighting, Kilmichael and Crossbarry appear piffling affairs by comparison with the Somme but they still had enormous consequences for British policy in Ireland. Successful ambushes made a deep impression on the public consciousness and remain the stuff of legend in the Irish countryside; signposts in Cork or Tipperary direct the traveller to ambush sites and not to stately homes. The considerable majority of planned attacks failed, and the traditional nationalist account has romanticised the brutal and complex truth, but what mattered to the war's outcome were the comparatively few successes. Together with the Intelligence war in Dublin these were the decisive events of the conflict.

Broadly speaking, successful ambushes became more difficult to accomplish as time went on. During 1921 in many areas there was a progressive concentration on smaller-scale activities and especially the blocking of communications. The British authorities drew the necessary conclusions from disasters like Kilmichael and became adept at counter-measures. Journey times and routes were varied and often changed at the last minute, cycle and single lorry patrols were abandoned for ordered well-protected convoys using troops and armoured cars. IRA prisoners were used as hostages to safety on many convoys, and classes in the combating of guerrilla warfare were started. In implicit admiration of the IRA columns, the British used similar small units to track down the rebels.

IRA success in ambushes guaranteed a massive British reaction in a locality and effectively immobilised any further guerrilla activity for some time. Frequently also a worryingly high proportion of the extremely limited ammunition was exhausted in a single fight. By no means all IRA victories produced substantial captures of war material, which was always a prime aim.

The issues of how far IRA actions were controlled and regulated by their GHQ and whether there was any political authority and democratic accountability for

DESIGNED "TO SETTLE ONCE AND FOR ALL THIS AGE-LONG DIFFERENCE": THE HOME RULE BILL THE SECOND READING.

CARRIED BY A RECORD MAJORITY. THE NEW HOME RULE BILL: MR. IAN MACPHERSON, CHIEF SECRETARY FOR IRELAND (SINCE RESIGNED) MAKING HIS INTRODUCTORY SPEECH.

The Chief Secretary of Ireland, Ian Macpherson, moving the first reading of what eventually became the Government of Ireland Act 1920. This was the Act that effected the partition of Ireland.

British troops searching a car in Dublin

Countess Markievicz

*B Company Auxiliary
Division, RIC, 1921*

*Arthur Griffith and
Éamon de Valera*

Troops in the grounds of Jervis Street Hospital, November 1920

Royal visit to Belfast, June 1921: from left, Lady Greenwood, Sir Hamar Greenwood, Lady Carson and Sir James Craig

General Richard Mulcahy

Lord FitzAlan of Derwent (left), the last Lord Lieutenant of Ireland, takes the salute.

Michael Collins

The Custom House on fire

A tank used as a battering ram during an army search

In the ruins of the Custom House

their work have been hotly debated. While Richard Mulcahy was determined to make out that there was an ordered chain of command and a response to instructions from Dublin, a range of testimony from provincial sources contradicts this. The issue had major implications for the later debate in the Treaty and Civil War period: pro-Treaty sources stressed the regular character of the IRA between 1919 and 1921 in order to bring out the irregularities of military resistance to the Treaty. The constitutional authority for IRA actions remained a strong bone of contention throughout the twentieth century, with the Provisional IRA continually harking back to the all-Ireland mandate allegedly given in 1918.[12]

The evidence for making a judgment on the extent of central control is limited and patchy. IRA column men were well aware of the dangers of correspondence being captured: Tom Barry and Seán Moylan had a deep contempt for what they regarded as 'pen pushers' in the command structure. Their emphasis was on action, not paperwork and with that went the conviction that they were fighting the war where it mattered. To read the detailed correspondence in the Mulcahy Papers of communication between GHQ and the country units is to receive a misleading impression of an ordered and tightly-knit fighting force. In any case GHQ policy tended to be reactive rather than proactive — flying columns had already been set up in some localities before GHQ officially sanctioned them. There is evidence, however, that Dublin was able to exercise restraint at particular times and had some success at coordinating activities overall. Longford appears a good example of how close relations with GHQ go some way to explaining the IRA's comparative success there; Cork exemplifies an area proud of its success achieved while largely independent from Dublin. GHQ always struggled with the fact that they had few means at their disposal to implement their wishes. Only in 1921 were organisers sent out from Dublin on a large scale to work up backward regions. As Andy Cooney pointed out, this implicitly revealed a preceding failure of communication. The arrival of those organisers usually made for acute tensions with the local men and proved counter-productive in many cases. The peculiar relationship between Dublin and the localities required considerable tact.

The major attempt to restructure came with the introduction of Divisions in 1921. By the time of the Truce, divisionalisation had been completed only in the southern and northern brigades and even there it seems to have had only limited significance. The idea behind this appears to have stemmed from meetings between the First Cork and Tipperary Brigades about the need for effective co-operation across county boundaries, and was eagerly adopted by GHQ who realised that it could take the pressure off strong fighting areas. GHQ communication with the provinces could thereby be simplified by delegation to another layer of management.

A 'Memorandum on the Divisional Idea' affirmed: 'it will make things very much simpler for GHQ by . . . diminishing the number of units coming directly in contact with GHQ. This will enable . . . more attention to be given to the main problems of each individual area and a much closer co-operation being carried out between the several Divisional areas. The machinery of administration will be greatly simplified, and there should be a very pronounced increase in speed and efficiency of working.' Priority was given to building up the northern brigades. A whole host of memoranda were written, rather pompously setting out the aims and objectives of each division. With regard to the Second Northern Division, GHQ argued: 'The six Carsonia counties form a bridgehead for the English in Ireland. Consequently, this area is the best . . . in which to direct an Irish offensive.'[13] This was little more than wishful thinking as there is no evidence of any concrete plans.

Also underlying this restructuring was the feeling that IRA work should be spread more evenly throughout the country. *An tÓglach* wrote on 1 March 1921: 'In other parts of the country . . . things are still very unsatisfactory. It effects no credit on the Volunteers in these districts that they should leave the gallant men of the South to bear all the brunt of the enemy's activities and thus help to make the military problems much simpler for the enemy.'

Many problems became attached to this new structure: there was strong opposition, especially from the Cork Brigades, and representatives from Kerry One did not even attend the meeting setting up the First Southern Division. It was pointed out that appointments to the new staffs took valuable men away from the fight and created unnecessary bureaucracy and obfuscation.[14] The new units were far too large and unwieldy and contradicted the fact that IRA success owed most to small, highly mobile local units. It was probably fortunate that the system had not been properly tested by the time the Truce came.

Formal responsibility for IRA actions was only taken by the Dáil in the spring of 1921. In 1919 Cathal Brugha had insisted that an Oath of Allegiance should be sworn to the Dáil by individual IRA members. This appears to have been motivated by a desire to challenge IRB authority and did little to change realities.[15] Key Dáil ministers like Arthur Griffith seem to have been completely unaware of IRA plans and the general contempt for politicians remained within the fighting units.

Despite the headline successes of the IRA and the effectiveness of some of its flying columns in the latter part of 1920, in many ways they had been forced on to the defensive by the increasing British military and Intelligence pressure. The risks taken on the morning of Bloody Sunday, 21 November 1920, amounted to an acknowledgment of that, and large-scale triumphs like Kilmichael a week later increased the British counter-offensive even more. Collins' willingness to negotiate for a Truce in December 1920 showed his concern about the war's progress. The increase in the number of incidents and in the casualty figures in the first six months of 1921 hide the fact that there was a switch to smaller objectives: hardly any barracks raids and a large increase in attacks which disrupted communications, such as blowing up roads and bridges, intercepting mail and telecommunications. From the spring of 1921 onwards, the IRA in the most active areas spent most of its time avoiding capture and demands increased for other areas to shoulder the burden. By early July 1921 there were 4,500 IRA internees, compared to an estimated figure of around 2,000 active men.

Meanwhile in Dublin the Intelligence net was closing around the Dáil government's offices and the IRA leadership. In May 1921, the British forces discovered the premises of the Home Affairs Department and in the same month Collins had a narrow escape when his office was attacked. Collins reported to Art O'Brien: 'Things have been very hard. In fact, too hard.' In another letter, Collins wrote: 'I am somewhat late in replying as the enemy brushed shoulders with me Thursday and with my staff. They didn't get very much, but they got a few things that I would much rather they had not got . . . They just walked into the office where they expected to find me working. The information was good, and I ought to have been there at the time. It happened, however, that I was not. Neither was my staff. It was the most providential escape yet. It will probably have the effect of making them think that I am even more mysterious than they believe me to be, and that is saying a good deal.' The imprisonment of Ned Broy in February had greatly weakened Collins' Intelligence network. Mulcahy later commented that if it had not been for the Truce it would have been necessary to stage another Bloody Sunday to break the threat from the British Secret Service. The botched attack on the Custom House in May 1921 (see page 103) must have deepened depression within GHQ.[16]

The premier reason for IRA concern in both Dublin and the provinces was the chronic shortage of arms and particularly ammunition. Florrie O'Donoghue denied that a delegation from Cork to GHQ in May 1921 had pleaded for a truce because of the scarcity of war material, but did not hide the fact that there had been a major problem. Considerable hope had been invested for several months before that in big gun-running plans. During 1920 and 1921, there was frequent talk of the arrival of major arms shipments from the Continent and from the United States. Little actually arrived.[17] The prime example of this is the following complex Italian arms saga which went on for the first six months of 1921.

In December 1920 Liam Deasy and Florrie O'Donoghue came to Dublin for discussions with GHQ. It was then decided to send a representative from Cork to organise the purchase and shipment of perhaps six hundred rifles and a massive quantity of ammunition from Italy in what would have been the first large gun-running operation since the Easter Rising. A senior IRA man from Cork, Mick Leahy, was chosen, due to his experience as a marine engineer, to travel to Genoa and arrange the deal. Myross Strand, near Glandore Harbour, on the south-west Cork coast, was to be the landing place. Plans were made for the distribution of these arms and for nearly one hundred dumps to be prepared. Before travelling to the Continent, Leahy had to meet Collins and get a false passport. He found himself caught up in the celebration of Tom Cullen's wedding and was taken aback by the casual behaviour of Collins' entourage. They in turn were appalled when Leahy asked for a lemonade rather than strong drink. This boded ill for what was to follow.

In Italy, initial negotiations conducted through Donal Hales, another brother in the famous Bandon republican family, went well with leading sources in the Italian government. The money, however, never came and Leahy was left in the lurch begging for financial support and desperately going to and fro between Paris and Genoa. The reasons for the collapse of the deal remain obscure. Sources close to Collins suggest that British Intelligence became cognisant of the plan; some Cork IRA men argue that Collins aborted the scheme having become preoccupied with the chance of a truce. Leahy himself related that he never knew the reason. Whatever the truth, the affair seriously deepened the rift between Cork and Dublin.[18]

During the negotiations over the Italian arms, Pax Whelan, the Waterford IRA leader, had argued that the Waterford coast was much better suited to the clandestine landing of arms than was that of West Cork. Through the spring of 1920, meetings were held with agents in Germany to land arms at Helvick Head but nothing came to fruition until after the Truce.[19]

At the very end of the conflict, the prospect of importing Thompson machine-guns appeared as an exciting answer. Easy to store and well-suited to urban fighting with their rapid fire, these guns would have been far better than the often antiquated, faulty and cumbersome assortment of arms the IRA possessed. Despite protracted negotiations for the purchase of one thousand in the United States only a few arrived, and those were used in only one major offensive. Two US Army officers, Major James Dineen and Captain Patrick Cronin, travelled to Ireland to instruct IRA men in the guns' use. On 16 June, Customs men and agents of the Department of Justice and police descended on Pier Two, Hoboken, New Jersey, and seized 495 Thompson machine guns, together with ammunition and spare parts. This consignment had been stored for some time in Hertford, Connecticut and the plan was evidently to ship them only when a large quantity had been assembled. The great expectations of deliverance from the arms crisis had therefore been dashed.[20]

9

THE WAR JULY–DECEMBER 1920

I t was in the late summer of 1920 that the character of the War abruptly changed. Before, it had consisted of erratic and limited actions but following The Restoration of Order in Ireland Act and the resultant change in IRA tactics, the conflict became widespread, brutal and ruthless on both sides.

The nature of guerrilla warfare is inextricably bound up with retaliation and reprisal. From the Balkans to Africa independence struggles developed into tit-for-tat violence. The popular memory of the war in 1920 and 1921 is one of burning villages and rampant Black and Tans, confirming the impression of a conflict between oppressor and oppressed. A central, if unstated, aim of the IRA was to provoke a harsh response and hence to court publicity and international sympathy; the onset of the spate of reprisals was also a consequence of the British government's failure to define the conflict as a war and their use of police in a military role without a clear code of discipline.

The Black and Tans and Auxiliaries were effect rather than cause; however appalling their deeds they were the product of Lloyd George's policies. Lady Violet Bonham Carter commented in the *Daily News* in April 1921: 'We have to feel sorry for the Black and Tans. They are risking their lives every day . . . and losing their souls in carrying out duties which no Englishmen should have been asked to perform.' *The New Statesman* emphasised on 25 September 1920: 'In Ireland, under existing conditions it is inevitable that the armed forces of the Crown should at times get out of hand. They are compelled to operate in small detachments not always under effective control, and the shooting down of comrades by invisible forces constitutes a provocation which men with arms in their hands find it difficult to resist, no matter how good their discipline. But with the auxiliary constable . . . there is clear evidence that methods of terrorism are adopted less from passion than from policy.'

The war's first major reprisal was the army's response by the burning of buildings in the town to the attack on the church patrol at Fermoy, County Cork on 7 September 1919. Macready's claim that only four reprisals were the work of the army was certainly an underestimate; ironically it was the Auxiliary Police who moved in to quell the violence following the military's attack on the centre of Mallow on 28 September 1920. Nonetheless as would be expected from the IRA concentration on attacking the police, the retaliation was primarily the work of the RIC and particularly its auxiliaries. Isolated reprisals took place in the first half of 1920 — in April in Nenagh and Limerick, in June in Bantry and in Fermoy again later that month following the capture of General Lucas.[1]

A torrent of tit-for-tat violence began with the RIC attack on Tuam after the shooting of two of their men on 20 July. The pattern of almost instantaneous response to ambushes or shootings was set — the burning of public buildings, shops and factories. Creameries, regarded as recruiting agencies for the IRA as well as essential elements of the local economy, became particular targets beginning in April and especially from August onwards. In all over one hundred were destroyed. Sir Horace Plunkett was left to bewail, in the correspondence pages of the British and Irish press, the assault on his beloved project.[2]

The list of reprisals in the late summer and autumn of 1920 reads like a sombre catalogue of small towns throughout the length and breadth of the south and west: Thurles, Upperchurch and Limerick in late July, Templemore on 16 August, Balbriggan on 21 September, Ennistymon, Lahinch and Miltown Malbay on 22 September, Trim on 27 September and Mallow a day later, Boyle on 5 October, Listowel, Tralee and Tubbercurry also in October, Templemore again on 1 November and Ballymote and Granard on 4 November.

Due to its geographical situation twenty miles north of Dublin, the Balbriggan reprisal gained the most notoriety. Following the fatal shooting of Constable Burke, Black and Tans from the nearby training base in Gormanstown descended on the town, killing two suspected IRA men, burning the local hosiery factory, destroying forty-nine houses and four pubs and driving much of the population to camp out in the surrounding fields. For all Greenwood's failure to come clean on the matter in the House of Commons, Dublin Castle was in no doubt as to who was responsible. Sir John Anderson wrote to Mark Sturgis: 'It is quite clear from the evidence that the burning was organised, and countenanced by the officers in charge.' The conclusions of the Military Enquiry were kept secret. Sturgis commented: 'Tudor quite agreed yesterday to my view that had they confined themselves to the dignified shooting of the two prominent Sinns, notorious bad men, the reprisal would have been not so bad — the burning spoilt the whole thing. Still worse things can happen than the firing up of a sink like Balbriggan . . .'[3]

Nothing in the conflict had remotely the same effect on domestic and international opinion as did reprisals. Photographs of ruined buildings provided the sorriest of commentaries on British administration of Ireland at a time when imperialism was at its least popular and the rights of small nations uppermost in international councils. An editorial in the *Observer* (12 September 1920) spoke of 'the immense weakening of Britain's moral position throughout the world' and the *Daily Mail* on 1 October wrote 'Britain, France, the Continent, America . . . half the world is coming to feel that our Government is condoning vendetta and turning a blind eye upon the execution of lawless reprisals . . . the slur on our nation's good name becomes insufferable.' The height of the reprisal season coincided with the American Presidential campaign.

There was increasing concern amongst Liberals in the Cabinet, notably H.A.L. Fisher and Edwin Montagu, the Secretary for India, about the outrages. Fisher wrote to the Prime Minister on 16 November 1920 about the Chief Secretary's admission that reprisals had occurred. 'We cannot, of course, allow this state of things to continue. Apart from the fact that these acts of lawless violence offend the conscience of English people, they cannot, I am persuaded help us to achieve the object which we have in view . . . That they will exasperate and embitter the temper of Ireland and contribute to give us a bad name in the world is equally certain . . . I am quite sure that public opinion in this country will not tolerate the continuance of these burnings and lootings by soldiers and policemen. The only result of them will be to induce Englishmen to say that if we can only govern Ireland by such means as these, we had better not govern Ireland at all . . . I trust, therefore, that we shall have no more wrecked creameries and burnt factories in Ireland.'[4]

Eye-witness accounts from leading journalists, most notably Hugh Martin in the *Daily News*, had a much stronger effect on popular attitudes than the predictable propaganda of the *Irish Bulletin*. The situation was made worse when Martin and some newspaper colleagues were roughly treated by British troops on a tour of County Kerry.[5] With the sole exception of the right-wing press, especially the *Morning Post*, editorial opinion savagely attacked the reprisals. The press reports demonstrated well the massive impact which such incidents had on small communities and the society and economy for many miles around. The names Balbriggan and Ennistymon will always be synonymous with the term reprisal.

The general context behind the spate of reprisals in the late summer and autumn of 1920 is easily explained: the stepping-up of attacks on the police from June, the armed forces' frustration at the consequences of the hunger strike releases in March, the inability successfully to prosecute gunmen and a general feeling that conciliatory methods had failed. The rage after colleagues were shot in the back by men in civilian dress and after ambushes is readily understandable. What is less easily explained is the frequency and number of outrages.

Several journalists at the time thought that a policy had been authorised by high authority. The *Westminster Gazette* concluded in September 1920 that Balbriggan, Tuam, Trim and Mallow were 'instances of a system deliberately organised'. *The Times* wrote on 21 September: 'in view of the wide area covered by the reprisals, it is difficult to believe that the occurrences at Balbriggan can have been entirely the result of a spontaneous outburst of resentment on the part of justifiably incensed policemen. There seems to have been behind it a directing influence.'

Sir Henry Wilson related in his Diary of 24 September 1920: 'Capt Shore on Tudor's Staff in Dublin had a long talk with Winston and me. Shore talks in the calmest way of murdering the SFs. He told us he had certain SFs marked down and at the slightest show of resistance they will be shot . . . Winston told me that PM had told Tudor that he (Tudor) could rely on LG to back him.' In June 1920, Divisional Commissioner Colonel Smyth appeared to give his men licence to retaliate. In October, Sturgis quoted Cope as saying: 'The RIC are *not* out of hand but are systematically led to réprise by their officers.' The targeting of particular buildings in many of the outrages points to planning rather than mindless retaliation.[6]

There appears to have been considerable sympathy for such a policy from the most senior politicians. Sir Henry Wilson in early July reported Lloyd George as having an 'amazing theory that Tudor, or someone, was murdering 2 S.F.'s to every loyalist the S.F. murdered', and holding that counter-murder was the best response to IRA outrages. After seeing Lloyd George in October, Lord Riddell confided in his diary: 'I came away with the conclusion that this is an organised movement to which the Government are more or less assenting parties.' Sir Maurice Hankey recorded the Prime Minister telling Lord Grey that he 'strongly defended the murder reprisals'. Lloyd George went on to say that reprisals 'had from time immemorial been resorted to in difficult times in Ireland; he gave numerous instances where they had been effective in checking crimes; he quoted two eminent nationalists who had told him in confidence that the Irish quite understood such reprisals, and that they ought not to be stopped.' Hankey summed up: 'The truth is that these reprisals are more or less winked at by the Government.'[7]

Lloyd George expressed a preference for shooting rather than burning. Sturgis recorded Cope's view of reprisals: 'If this is so it's tragic that these men cannot see that indiscriminate burning is idiotic and a little quiet shooting equally effective — and to shoot a known bad man who, if he hasn't just shot your comrade, has no doubt shot somebody else, is morally much more defensible than this stupid blind work.' Tudor signally failed to give unequivocal instructions on the subject and while Macready publicly denounced unauthorised reprisals, he admitted in their early stages that they could be defended and could have a positive effect.[8]

Greenwood's half-truths and evasions when tackled about reprisals in parliament confirm the ambivalent approach taken by politicians. Under aggressive questioning, he would play for time by saying he was awaiting further information, would place the blame on those committing the original atrocity and point out that Irish towns amounted to little more than villages. Only as late as April 1921, long after the storm of unauthorised activity had abated, did Lloyd George express to Greenwood his concern about lack of discipline amongst the Auxiliary police.[9] The failure to condemn and to charge more miscreants demonstrates sympathy at best, complicity at worst. It was not until the political consequences had become apparent at home and abroad that there was even an admission that appalling incidents had occurred. The authorisation of official reprisals in December only confirms the long-held sympathy with police actions. Once the dreadful saga of atrocity and revenge developed, events took on a logic and momentum of their own. Reprisal in one place stimulated reprisals in others: there was a strong element of copycat violence.

The most notorious of unauthorised reprisals took place just before the decision to authorise official ones. On the night of 11 December 1920, following a successful ambush by the IRA at Dillons Cross, most of Patrick Street — the central shopping area in Cork — was burned down and looted: a few hours later the City Hall and Carnegie Library were also in flames. Two military enquiries, one led by General Strickland, the O/C Sixth Division, placed the responsibility on members of K Division of the Auxiliaries and the failure of their commanding officer to control them. The police member of the enquiry dissented from the verdict and Sturgis was correct to point out that the same men could not have been responsible for a series of burnings in the preceding weeks.

Nonetheless a letter from one of the Auxiliaries to his mother after their expulsion to Dunmanway confirms guilt: 'I contracted a chill on Saturday night during the burning and looting of Cork in all of which I took perforce a reluctant part. We did it all right never mind how much the well-intentioned Hamar Greenwood would excuse us. In all my life . . . and in all the tales of fiction I have read I have never experienced such orgies of murder, arson and looting as I have witnessed during the past 16 days with the RIC Auxiliaries. It baffles description. And we are supposed to be ex-officers and gentlemen. There are quite a number of decent fellows and likewise a lot of ruffians . . . The houses in the vicinity of the ambush were set alight and from there the various parties set out on their mission of destruction. Many who witnessed similar scenes in France and Flanders say that nothing they have experienced ever compared to the punishment meted out to Cork.'[10]

In the Commons, Greenwood embarrassingly sought to minimise and excuse the action and just as controversially the government refused publication of General Strickland's enquiry report. To cap it all, on 15 December near Dunmanway one of the expelled Auxiliaries, Cadet Harte, killed a retarded youth and an aged priest, Canon Magner, as they walked peacefully on a rural road. Harte was soon after declared to be insane by the British authorities, leaving Sturgis to comment: 'Still this murder of an old inoffensive priest in broad daylight with no possibility of mistake, or excuse of any kind is so ghastly that unless he be proved raving mad he should hang — and if he gets off on the plea of insanity surely those responsible for leaving him loose on the world in charge of a party armed to the teeth should take his place in the dock.' The Auxiliary earlier quoted testified: 'We were very kindly received by the people but the consequences of the cold-blooded murder is that no-one will come within a-mile of us now and all the shops are closed. The brute who did it has been sodden with drink for some time and has been sent to Cork under arrest for examination by experts in lunacy.'[11]

The reprisals issue is more complex than it is usually depicted. Irish contemporaries often criticised the IRA for the original provocation and for failing to protect the community from all but inevitable retaliation. The IRA's defence of Ballinalee, County Longford, in November 1920 is a rare example of a successful, if short-term, protection of the community. Father Patrick Gaynor, who was an active Sinn Féin supporter, later wrote: 'Volunteers who carried out the initial raid should have taken some measures to protect the town from attack and to attack the British . . . instead of slinking away to safety and regarding themselves as heroes for having fired a few shots at no risk.' The military inactivity of many areas may in part be explained by the fear of reprisals.

It remains true that what mattered most was the perception of British responsibility and guilt. Criticism of the original atrocity was often forgotten in the midst of the horrors of retaliation. The reprisal was most often against the whole community, the provoking action against the individual. The *Galway Express* wrote after the first reprisals at Tuam: 'When they throw petrol on a Sinn Féiner's house, they are merely pouring paraffin on the flames of Irish nationality.'[12] It is remarkable that the British government did not realise from the start that such measures were counter-productive. Reprisals may have been a deterrent in their early stages; they had, however, disastrous wider and long-term implications.

While the level of physical conflict considerably escalated during the last five months of 1920, the period is most notable for the number of spectacular and gruesome incidents that occurred — the constant stream of accounts about reprisal and counter-reprisal; the widespread shootings; the first large-scale IRA ambushes; the best-remembered of all hunger strikes and the execution of the first prisoner under court-martial powers. The headline-making events followed each other rapidly. The last stages of Terence MacSwiney's hunger strike coincided with Kevin Barry's incarceration, Bloody Sunday and the Kilmichael ambush happened within a week of each other and were soon followed by the burning of part of Cork city. In August, Art O'Brien commented that news of MacSwiney had relegated the coverage of Archbishop Mannix' ban from visiting Ireland to the back pages.[13]

The most significant events in the War of Independence should be judged on the effect they had on public opinion and the headlines they generated rather than on the scale of the military conflict. The historian Charles Townshend has commented: 'The purely military effect of guerrilla warfare will usually be seen as subordinate to its political and psychological effect.'[14]

Hamar Greenwood's constant reassurances to parliament and the press that the security forces had events under control were consistently belied by the publicity. The space devoted to Irish events in the British and foreign press greatly increased during these months with large photographs of burning buildings and homeless people. The Sinn Féin publicity machine may not have been as efficient as British sources at the time, and many historians since, have maintained but did not need to be; the sheer power of the events themselves, their volume and frequent coincidence in timing guaranteed interest. The British gift for creating martyrs went hand in hand with the Irish talent for dramatising death into sacrifice for the Cause. 'No war', said Anderson, 'can be carried on effectively in the full glare of public criticism.'[15] The sight of Southern Ireland's second city in flames and the spilling out of the Intelligence war into the centre of Dublin struck at the heart of Britain's imperial pride and sensitivity. For the first time the public could see on newsreels incidents like the shooting affray resulting in Seán Treacy's death. A mighty imperial power was seen to be humbled by mere guerrilla fighters and liberal consciences were aroused.

Two strong and very different personalities made the headlines during July and August 1920. The *Freeman's Journal* reported a speech to police recruits at Listowel on 19 June by Colonel Gerald Smyth, District Commissioner for Munster and a native of Banbridge, County Down, in which it was alleged that a carte blanche was given for reprisals. The accuracy of the report was denied in the Commons but the claim was widely circulated. On 17 July, Smyth was assassinated by the IRA. The Cork IRA had struggled to get information on Smyth but he was easily identified as he had lost an arm in the Great War. With the help of a waiter, a party of the First Brigade's most experienced gunmen entered the County Club in the city centre and shot him. The raiders spent no more than three minutes in the building. The event provoked major violence in the North and struck terror into the heart of the British establishment. This, unlike Lucas' kidnapping, was not a joking matter.[16]

Meanwhile Archbishop Daniel Mannix of Melbourne was prevented from visiting Ireland. The boat bringing him from the United States was intercepted on government orders on 8 August and Mannix forced to disembark at Penzance. A former President of Maynooth College and frontline opponent of conscription in Australia, Mannix had made many speeches in the US enthusiastically supporting Sinn Féin. He stayed on in Britain for several months, providing a long-running irritant for British politicians.[17]

Such episodes were dwarfed in the public consciousness by the imprisonment and subsequent hunger strike of Terence MacSwiney, Lord Mayor of Cork. In a kind of apostolic succession, MacSwiney had succeeded Tomás MacCurtain after the latter's murder in March 1920. MacSwiney's words in his inaugural address anticipated the cause of his later fame. He declared: 'It is not those who can inflict the most, but those who can suffer the most who will conquer.' A writer, teacher and leading figure within Gaelic revivalist circles, MacSwiney had a nominally commanding position in the Cork IRA. On 12 August, as a result of intercepted correspondence, he was arrested with many others at an IRA meeting in the City Hall in Cork. Ironically, Liam Lynch and Seán O'Hegarty, two far more important figures in the IRA, were released by the British.

The British claimed that a police code was discovered on MacSwiney's person, a fact later denied by IRA sources. Ten fellow Cork prisoners joined MacSwiney on hunger strike. The Lord Mayor was transferred to Brixton

Prison on 17 August; whatever the reason behind that move, the tactic hugely misfired due to the attention of the world's press and to the emotional support of Irish sympathisers. An editorial in *The Times* of 2 September 1920 commented: 'Alderman MacSwiney, a man whose name was unknown outside his own city, will, if he dies, take rank with Fitzgerald, with Emmet, and with Tone in the martyrology of Ireland.' Liam de Róiste wrote in his diary on 27 August: 'If released alive he will have won. If released in death he shall still win . . . MacSwiney in Brixton, Lloyd George on the Swiss Mountains — was there ever material for an epic such as this?'[18]

All wondered at the apparent miracle of MacSwiney's 74-day endurance, which coincided almost exactly with the American Presidential campaign, a point of great concern to Lloyd George. On 25 September, Michael Collins wrote: 'The prolongation of life seems to be absolutely wonderful — in fact, little short of miraculous.' A considerable range of opinion at home and abroad clamoured for the prisoner's release. Many feared appalling consequences if MacSwiney was allowed to die; the Irish Lord Chancellor recommended a retrial.

Although there was some anguished debate in church circles as to whether MacSwiney's strike amounted to suicide, there was a powerful spiritual element of sacrifice and atonement. MacSwiney was accompanied throughout his slow slide to death by the strongly republican Capuchin Father Dominic. One of the Cork hunger strikers, Michael Fitzgerald, died on 17 October and MacSwiney succumbed eight days later. In a final message to Cathal Brugha, MacSwiney wrote of 'the pain of Easter Week' being finally expunged in reference to his feelings of responsibility for the failure of Cork to come out in 1916.

For all their concern about the consequences of MacSwiney's sacrifice, the British authorities completely bungled his burial arrangements. At the last moment permission was withdrawn for the body to go home via Dublin. This only increased the size of the services and processions in Southwark Cathedral, London en route to Euston and Cork. Another of the Cork hunger strikers, Joseph Murray, died a few hours after MacSwiney. At that point Arthur Griffith issued a statement calling off further hunger strikes.[19]

The traditional view of MacSwiney's martyrdom tells of a publicity triumph for the republican cause and of an inept, insensitive British government playing into its hands. The psychological impact of the protest was extremely potent, yet many different aspects of the whole situation call for examination. Many within the Sinn Féin leadership, including Michael Collins, had considerable reservations about the hunger-strike tactic. They were against the sacrificial 1916 culture and preferred active resistance. Ernest Blythe regarded the many earlier hunger strikes as a kind of game between the two sides under which rules no actual death would take place. He had been disturbed that MacSwiney's declarations ruled out any compromise and felt that MacSwiney was a terrible loss to the Sinn Féin leadership. Naturally, any doubters were honour bound to support the protest. The strike forced a fundamental reappraisal of the whole strategy and the realisation that the deaths represented, as Art O'Brien put it, 'the end of the hunger-strike as a weapon'.[20]

The implications were just as great for the British government. Memories were vivid of the consequences for military and police morale of the hunger-strike releases of March. From his Lucerne retreat, Lloyd George told Bonar Law: 'If we released him we might as well give up again attempting to maintain law and order in Ireland.' With characteristic bluntness, Mark Sturgis wrote: 'If he is let out we do not see how we can ever hold another hunger striker again . . . it would convince everybody that (the Government) had been bluffing again and would make our job impossible.' The Lord Chancellor was the only member of the Castle administration to advocate release. It seems that the example of Thomas Ashe prevented the authorities from trying force-feeding. Police and military sources viewed the subsequent IRA ban on hunger striking as a British victory.[21]

The sheer length of MacSwiney's fast had led to progressively less publicity being devoted to it. As bulletins from Brixton Prison became increasingly repetitive and suspicion of covert feeding grew, reprisals were attracting more publicity. Sturgis waspishly reported that 'peasant opinion' was outraged at the Lord Mayor's fast blasphemously outlasting that of Christ's forty days and nights in the desert. There was some surprise at the time that MacSwiney's death did not provoke a more dramatic violent response. Some planned operations did not take place and it is difficult to connect conclusively specific incidents to MacSwiney's death.[22]

Though undistinguished academically, Kevin Barry was to become the most famous student in the history of University College, Dublin. The fourth of seven children of a dairy-owning family, Barry had been a pupil at the elite Belvedere College. While at school, he joined what became H Company of the 1st Battalion Dublin IRA Brigade and participated in the successful King's Inns arms raid of 1 June 1920. On the morning of his medical re-sit examination of 20 September 1920, the same day as the Balbriggan and Rineen reprisals, Barry was involved in an ambush of a troop convoy collecting bread from Monk's Bakery in Church Street, in the north of the city. In this first Dublin IRA attack on troops of the War, three soldiers were shot, later to die of their wounds. Barry was found hiding under a lorry clutching a rifle. Subsequent investigations proved the link between Barry's rifle and the bullets which killed Private Whitehead. A court martial held on 2 October inevitably found Barry guilty. At that time evidence of torture was revealed in the early stages of Barry's imprisonment before he was sentenced. Under powers given by the Restoration of Order in Ireland Act, Barry was sentenced to be hanged, the first to be so since Fenian days.[23]

It was soon apparent that Barry had all the necessary qualifications for martyrdom, most notably his youth: he was only eighteen. Liberal opinion in Ireland and Britain, including Archbishop Walsh, demanded remission of the death sentence. As in the MacSwiney case, the Lord Chancellor urged mercy at this time on grounds of the prisoner's youth and out of fear as to public reaction if the sentence was carried out. In response, Lord French commented: 'It is most unfortunate that a man who can take such views should be the chief Law Officer.' With chronic insensitivity, the British set the execution day as 1 November, All Saints Day. As Donal O'Donovan has written: 'Quite apart from the outcry against hanging a man on a church holiday, the British forgot, or perhaps simply ignored, the effect of executing a young man on a day when every church in the country would be full to the doors several times over. The saying of Masses would be continued for six hours and more, creating a groundswell of public protest where the Catholic Irish were at their most susceptible, in church.'[24]

Again it was inconceivable that the British government would change its stance and risk the wrath of the military authorities. Macready was keen to contrast the army's adherence to official procedures with unauthorised police methods. Mark Sturgis pointed out that: 'the 3 soldiers he (Barry) and his party killed were all under 19.' The Dublin Castle officials admitted that Barry died bravely, Ernest Clark, the Head of Propaganda, issuing the sickest of compliments: 'he went to the drop with callous composure.'[25]

The *Irish Independent* reported on 4 November that virtually all boy babies born on the two days before had been named Kevin. At the time and since, a number of ballads were composed commemorating 'the lad of eighteen summers' and numerous clubs and societies have been named after him. For all the apparent logic of the British position, it is difficult to avoid the force of a comment at the time: 'When people have to hang young boys like that, their cause is lost, their day is over.'[26]

The events of Sunday, 21 November 1920 were the most dramatic of the War of Independence: they represented a microcosm of the whole conflict in respect of the role of Intelligence, the appalling violence, the thirst for revenge and the inextricable link with propaganda.[27] The total number of casualties involved — twenty-six killed — hardly constituted an Irish version of the Massacre of Saint Bartholomew or comparison with even a few hours of the French Great Terror of 1793/94, but the ghastliness of the events had a massive contemporary and historical effect.

No set of incidents was so decisive in changing British attitudes to the war. The corpses of the assassinated British officers were taken in procession through the streets of London to a massive funeral in Westminster Abbey: as a result of these events and the Kilmichael ambush a week later, barriers were placed at the end of Downing Street. With the recent news of IRA attacks on Britain the Irish situation could no longer be taken lightly. The case for both coercion and conciliation was heightened with the application of martial law for part of Ireland, and the subsequent Clune peace initiative.

For the IRA leadership, there must have been a realisation that the British military and Intelligence effort would be immensely stepped up as a consequence of Bloody Sunday. In sum, the importance of the events of 21

November ranks on a par with that of the next Bloody Sunday, 30 January 1972 in Derry. Meanwhile, the debate will continue as to whether the killings of the morning can be justified as a necessary part of a just war or whether they amounted to callous murders; likewise as to whether the Croke Park shootings of the afternoon constituted a reprisal or were the product of chaos and confusion.

For some time the IRA leadership in Dublin had been aware that British Intelligence was becoming much more effective and that the net was closing in around them. A week before, Mulcahy's papers giving details of IRA membership and plans had been seized. Mulcahy testified in his convoluted writing style: 'What we struck against was a scheme that we had definite information was, in a considered and deliberate way, planned as an espionage system for the definite purpose of destroying the Directing Corps of the Volunteer activity . . . a very dangerous and cleverly placed spy organisation.' A network of spies operated throughout the city linking up with informers and touts. Collins made it clear, as he put it, that it had become a prime necessity to get their blow in first, before they were all annihilated.[28]

For weeks before Bloody Sunday, plans were laid to deal with the Intelligence and security menace and to discover the addresses and movements of the British agents. Information was gleaned from housemaids, from wastepaper baskets, from the drunken boasts of one of the killers of the Sinn Féin official, John Lynch, in the Exchange Hotel a few weeks before and from Sergeant Mannix of the Donnybrook RIC. Parties of men were briefed by Collins and McKee on the evening of 20 November as to their targets.

Those chosen for the raids were a mixture of Squad and Dublin Brigade men; most often the Squad men led the parties. Some showed a reluctance to participate and members of the First Battalion were to be disciplined for failing to carry out their instructions. Matty MacDonald recalled: 'Charlie Dalton couldn't sleep that night of Bloody Sunday. He thought he could hear the gurgling of the Officer's blood and he kept awake in fright until we told him a tap was running somewhere.'[29]

Twenty agents were targeted in eight sites. The actions all took place from 9 a.m., through the front doors, in the heart of gracious and salubrious south Dublin, with the exception of the Gresham Hotel in O'Connell Street. The Intelligence information seems to have been generally accurate, although a party which entered the Eastwood Hotel in Leeson Street found their quarry had left. Todd Andrews was relieved to find that his target in Rathfarnham was out.

The attack on the main centre of the spies at 28 Upper Pembroke Street saw four killed but two major targets escaped. At 22 Lower Mount Street, one was killed and one escaped; the cries of the maids resulted in Auxiliaries surrounding the building. In the exchange of fire, two Auxiliaries were killed and Frank Teeling wounded and arrested escaping from the back of the house. Captain Bagelly, a courts martial officer rumoured to have taken part in the torture of Kevin Barry, was killed by a three-man group including Mick White, who stayed on to eat the dead man's breakfast, and the future Taoiseach, Seán Lemass. Sixty years later viewers of Robert Kee's series 'A Television History of Ireland' saw Vinnie Byrne, a veteran of the Squad, give a disturbingly humorous account of his 'plugging' one of the two victims in 38 Upper Mount Street. In another Mount Street killing, a man lying in bed with his wife was shot by Tom Ennis.

In all fourteen of the British forces died, six were wounded: four of the killed were military Intelligence officers and four were either Secret Service or MI5 agents. The only Irish casualties were Teeling, as mentioned, and Billy Maclean who escaped with an injured hand.[30]

A boat was laid on to expedite the return of the IRA parties to North Dublin. Pat MacCrea reminisced on his going to midday Mass after taking part in the shootings; in the afternoon his wife quizzed him about his supposed morning fishing trip. 'Seeing that there was no use in concealing things any longer from her, I said "Yes, and don't you see we had a good catch," . . . She then said "I don't care what you think about it I think it's murder". I said: "No, that's nonsense: I'd feel like going to the altar after that job this morning," . . . I don't think she put out any lights in the house during the following winter. I did not stay at home then for about a week.'

In the months following, several members of three of the shooting parties were convicted by courts martial. Patrick Moran and Thomas Whelan were executed and Teeling escaped from Kilmainham Gaol after being sentenced to death.[31]

That day crowds had gathered for a Gaelic football match between Dublin and Tipperary at Dublin's largest stadium, Croke Park, a mile north-east of the city centre. It is possible that the shootings of the morning were timed to take advantage of the crowds thus occasioned: however it was, the British authorities felt that the IRA would use the event as a cover for their activities. By lunchtime Seán Russell, a key figure within the Dublin IRA, was sufficiently alarmed by the increased security presence to urge that the game be postponed. Though backed by Michael Collins, the request was turned down by Frank Shouldice, a leading GAA official. RIC authorities had drawn up a plan to search fans and an announcement was to be made by megaphone to the assembled crowd.

The police action, however, began before the troop cordon surrounding the ground was completed and firing broke out, followed by a stampede. Some testified that shooting came from armoured cars across the nearby canal. Eleven of the crowd and Michael Hogan, a Tipperary player, were killed and many injured. The British authorities reported that thirty revolvers were found on the ground.

The inevitable and inconclusive debate followed as to who fired the first shot: what was not denied was that the RIC had fired a considerable number of shots into the crowd. It is scarcely surprising that the events, even in the

Daily Mail, were depicted as a straightforward reprisal. At best, the British plans were impractical and insensitive. The afternoon's incidents shifted some attention away from those of the morning. They served for all time to intensify the link between the GAA and advanced nationalism: the largest stand in Croke Park is still known as the Hogan Stand.[32]

This was not the only violence that weekend. On the Saturday night, Dick McKee, O/C Dublin Brigade, and his deputy, the engineering expert Peadar Clancy, had been arrested in a raid in Lower Gloucester Street. Captured with them was Conor Clune, a nephew of Archbishop Clune of Perth, Western Australia, apparently on a business trip from County Clare. All three were interrogated, tortured and killed on the Sunday night in Dublin Castle by British agents, led by the notoriously sadistic Captain Hardy. The British authorities claimed in time-honoured fashion that the prisoners were shot while trying to escape.

The informer responsible for these arrests was soon tracked down by the IRA and killed. Collins was devastated by the loss of McKee and came out of hiding to carry the coffin at the large public funeral. He commented: 'Yes, it was very sad about Dick and Peter . . . Something occurs in the Brigade, for instance, and it is so much harder to put it right without Dick. Some other disaster occurs like the discovery of the factory, and it is so much more difficult to start again without Peter.' Mulcahy was frequently to comment that the Dublin Brigade never recovered from the loss.[33]

The British authorities immediately responded to the events of Bloody Sunday by imposing roadblocks and steamer searches: the curfew was extended and as far as possible British personnel were rehoused in secure accommodation: internment powers were applied with the opening of Ballykinlar Camp. Five hundred arrests were made in the week after and a widespread raiding policy carried out. On 25 November, Arthur Griffith and Eoin MacNeill were arrested on the flimsiest of grounds and without political sanction.[34]

The historian Ronan Fanning has argued that Bloody Sunday was the defining moment in changing British attitudes to Irish independence: the violence used opened the way to negotiation. Therefore the end had seemingly justified the means. In the short term, however, the hawks on the British side were encouraged and any moves towards a settlement would have been political suicide. The IRA had been forced into their high-risk assault by the threat to their very existence. As Barère, a member of the Committee of Public Safety during the French Revolution, had put it: 'We had but one sentiment, that of self-preservation, but one desire, to preserve our existence, which each of us thought to be threatened. One had one's neighbour guillotined to prevent oneself being guillotined by one's neighbour.'[35]

10

FROM THE IMPOSITION OF MARTIAL LAW TO THE TRUCE: THE BRITISH PERSPECTIVE

The possibility of martial law had been frequently raised since the beginning of 1919. It was turned down because of concern by the military over insufficient troop numbers, political awareness of legal complications and, most significantly, because it was realised that to implement it would mean acknowledgment that something larger than a rebellion was happening. The calamities of Bloody Sunday and the Kilmichael ambush, which took place on successive weekends, caused a sudden change of attitude.

At the beginning of December, the Cabinet conferred with Greenwood and with the military leadership in Ireland about whether or not to impose martial law. At this of all times, Macready was holidaying on the French Riviera and was absurdly slow in returning. The army commanders were all in favour of martial law being applied to the whole of the twenty-six counties, although Major-General Boyd, of the General Command in Dublin District, was concerned about the effect it would have on Irish public opinion and that the action would appear the policy of last resort. It was concluded that the most beneficial aspects of martial law would lie in the achievement of unity of command and in increased speed and efficiency of action.

The Cabinet insisted, however, on limiting the area covered to Cork, Kerry, Limerick and Tipperary. Later, Macready did his best to reassure his colleagues by saying the area could be extended at his own request, but the military leadership were all too aware of the difficulties of the Proclamation applying only to a part of the country, and were particularly worried at the exclusion of Dublin.[1] Such fears were only partly assuaged by the inclusion of the remaining Munster counties in a proclamation of 5 January 1921.

Not only was martial law limited geographically, but the particular form adopted amounted to what Macready later called a half-hearted measure.

Military recommendations for passport controls, identity cards and press censorship were disregarded. The provisions, announced on 10 December, insisted that arms be handed in by 27 December, and that the death penalty be enforced for carrying arms or ammunition and for the civilian use of British uniforms. The public statement to all intents and purposes admitted a state of war: 'A state of armed insurrection was declared to exist . . . The forces of the Crown in Ireland were also declared to be on active service.' Separate proclamations sanctioned official reprisals and the use of hostages in military convoys.[2]

The first official reprisal occurred at Midleton, County Cork, on 29 December 1920, when six houses were destroyed as a response to an earlier ambush that day. Late in September Major-General Radcliffe told Wilson: 'I think the only solution to this problem is to institute a system of "official" reprisals . . . If there is a definite scheme of reprisals in force, and made known beforehand, it should be easy to get the troops to restrain their unofficial efforts, while the deterrent effect on Sinn Féin cannot but be inconsiderable.'

For the first five months of 1921 attacks on property of supposed Sinn Féin sympathisers, or those allegedly complicit in guerrilla activity, became a regular occurrence. War Office official files document thirty-three of these official reprisals and the 'History of the Sixth Division' lists the destruction of 191 houses as official punishments, but there were clearly far more. It was hardly surprising that this policy caused IRA attacks on loyalist houses, a point belatedly acknowledged when the government ended it on 6 June 1921. These official actions further heightened community alienation from the British authorities and, if anything, encouraged rather than discouraged IRA retaliation.[3]

Despite the appointment of officers commanding as military governors, there was still confusion as to military authority over the police and the relationship of martial law to civil law. From the start, there was the expectation that the powers should be applied more severely in some locations than others. Macready commented that: 'There are various little points on which we have to give way to the politicians . . . Strickland will have to watch the police very carefully, because certainly Prescott-Decie (the 6th Division police adviser) will think that martial law means that he can kill anybody he sees walking along the road whose appearance may be distasteful to him . . . I fully realise the difficulty this partial application of martial law means, but the "Frocks" were firm not to impose it all over. We must begin slowly and I have no doubt will be able to fit in a workable scheme as time goes on.' Anderson could see no military justification for the action taken and concluded: 'The limited application of martial law has no doubt political reasons.' The 'History of the Fifth Division' saw it as another demonstration of how reactive and confused British policy was.[4]

In a memorandum of 18 February 1921, Macready was forced to admit that the declaration of martial law had not changed anything very much. He concluded that: 'the actual enforcement of martial law in Munster is by no means the martial law that is understood by military men.' He bewailed the fact that the police in the martial law area continued to be independent of the army in disciplinary matters and he remained harshly critical of Tudor. He warned of major clashes between military and police if matters were not taken in hand. In April, such an incident was to occur at the Shannon Hotel, Castleconnell, County Clare. An Auxiliary raiding party, some in civilian clothes, mistook some off-duty RIC men for rebels and attacked. One on each side was killed and even after the mistake was realised, the Auxiliaries killed another RIC man and the hotel landlord. The full truth only came out because Lord Parmoor, the brother of one of the hotel's residents, relayed the grisly story to the House of Lords. Even then, the military court found no evidence of Auxiliaries running amok, despite Macready's unease about the whole affair.[5]

Up to and beyond the Truce, Macready despaired of legal appeals being allowed to the civil courts, and even to the House of Lords, on judgments made by the military courts. Attempts were made to prosecute Army personnel for committing official reprisals: just before the cessation of hostilities in the case of *Egan v Macready*, the Irish Master of the Rolls ruled that the declaration of martial law had been illegal. Macready argued that, originally, one of the main reasons for martial law was to speed up the punishment process, but by the spring several cases were being held in abeyance. Military opinion up to the end of the War continued to point out the absurdity of Dublin being exempt from military law, and their first recommendation for improving the efficiency of the military effort was always the implementation of martial law over the whole twenty-six counties.[6]

The 'History of the Sixth Division' commented: 'Martial law, in the fully accepted sense, never existed at all, and, although it caused a considerable amount of alarm amongst the rebels when it was first imposed, they soon found that its "bark was worse than its bite" . . . it cannot be argued too strongly that the half-hearted measure used in the 6th Divisional Area was absolutely no test of what martial law could, or could not, achieve.' Warren Fisher summed up: 'Martial law everywhere is an intelligible policy, or martial law nowhere . . . Unity of command as a condition of success is surely a common-place.'[7]

The Dublin Castle junta and Macready continued to press for the imposition of unity of command. On 6 March 1921, Sturgis wrote in his diary: 'It isn't enough to restore discipline in the police — that might have done the trick two months ago — now we want a united command. We are ready to make a good peace but if we are to fight we must fight properly which we aren't doing — everybody agrees to this yet we don't seem to get down to the root of the evil and put it right.' For Lloyd George to have acted on this issue would have been to concede explicitly that it was not a rebellion but a war.[8]

In a purely military sense, there was much to encourage the British side in the first six months of 1921. A massive number of IRA men were arrested, including key men like Seán MacEoin and Seán Moylan. Numbers interned rose from 1,478 for the week ending 17 January to 2,569 for the week ending 21 March, and 4,454 for the week ending 16 July. The Intelligence services had

had some major successes, notably in the capture of Richard Mulcahy's papers in November 1920 and in February 1921, and Eileen McGrane's papers at the end of December 1920. The passive resistance techniques of the hunger strikes and the rail protest had been officially called off. The counter-state had been pushed back on the defensive and struggled for its very survival — the republican courts continued to meet in only a few areas. Much more effective methods to deal with guerrilla warfare were being implemented and the discipline of the Black and Tans had somewhat improved. On 8 June 1921, Sturgis records: 'Wylie spoke of the vast improvement in the manner and discipline of the "Black and Tans", now a first-class force which everybody can respect. He said that if they had behaved all through as they behave now the result would in his opinion be very different and the enormous bulk of popular opinion would be now on their side versus the gunmen.'[9]

Such cautious reasons for British hope did not offset the harsh reality that any military victory was far from imminent. Towards the end of 1920 there was unease in the Cabinet about military resources: there was a scarcity of armoured cars and drivers for them, and also of armour plating for lorries. Fifty Peerless and sixteen Rolls Royce armoured cars were sent to Ireland in December 1920 and their numbers had risen to seventy and thirty-four respectively by the end of March 1921. Armoured protection for lorries was also increased at this time; the character of the terrain and of the whole fighting did not suit these clumsy vehicles, and to use them in country lanes was to invite trouble. The greatest threat to the IRA proved to be the foot patrols used in the last two months of the conflict.

Both at the time and since, the limited use of planes has been questioned. Churchill stated that only eighteen serviceable machines were available for use in Ireland in September 1920 and their use was restricted before April 1921. In the Fifth Division, the official history cited the scarcity of landing strips. There was hardly any radio equipment nor were there other essential resources for them, like fuel. In addition there were huge problems of identifying the flying columns from the air; indeed it was extremely difficult even at ground level.[10]

In February, Macready admitted: 'I cannot say that I see any grounds for optimism in regard to anything like a permanent settlement of the country outside Ulster.' On his return to Ireland in the same month, Warren Fisher also painted the blackest of pictures: 'the gunmen did exactly what any ordinarily intelligent fellow would do — they concentrated in the martial law area ... most of their best organisers and most of their best trained fighters in order to make martial law look silly. The police (as gallant and stupid as the Six Hundred at Balaclava) have given the gunmen every opportunity of practice — and the rest of Ireland (outside Dublin where the Court Martial trials have needed a counter) has been comparatively quiet.'[11]

Hugh Elles, an Army commander, on a visit to Dublin in June 1921, concluded that the British army in Ireland was besieged: 'If you pour in more troops on the present lines, you are simply throwing good money after bad.' He held that unless extreme measures were taken, including an economic blockade, political pressure would 'cause us to abandon the country, and we shall be beaten'. Elles realised that they had been fighting without a defined front and that large-scale sweeps were ineffective unless there was a target. The fundamental problem was one of combating guerrilla warfare. During the Truce, Sir John Anderson came to similar conclusions about the British forces having been hopelessly over-extended and concluded that if the War was restarted it would have to be prosecuted on completely different lines involving economic blockade and intense military occupation of only a few strategically important areas.

The last two months of the War saw easily the worst casualty figures for the British army: there were forty-eight deaths between the start of May and the Truce. Only in June, after the threat of troops being removed from Ireland to Britain to deal with a General Strike had been removed, was a serious attempt made to raise the army's numbers, but by that time there was a strong realisation of how elusive any long-term victory would be. The 'History of the Fifth Division' notes that 'We were never fully prepared for the next rebel move, and . . . while they were progressing from sporadic murder and intimidation to a well organized guerrilla campaign, supported and shielded by systematic frightfulness, our measures always fell short of what the situation at the moment demanded.'

General Strickland believed that the politicians intervened in the form of a Truce just when the army was getting on top of the IRA.[12] From a narrowly military perspective, this view had some justification, but in guerrilla warfare a volunteer army can melt away and return at will. Other aspects relating to politics and shifting perspectives, both nationally and internationally, came to matter more than the state of the fighting and the strengths of the two sides.

11

GUERRILLA WARFARE IN DUBLIN

The War of Independence was primarily a Dublin and Munster affair and there were considerable tensions as to which of the two was most important. The Easter Rising had been overwhelmingly associated with Dublin, and Cork was uneasy about its performance in 1916. Two memoranda from Mulcahy emphasised that Dublin should be given the greatest priority by GHQ. The Chief of Staff wrote: 'This is the first Irish War in which Dublin has been in National hands . . . (it) places at our disposal all the resources of a capital city . . . Dublin (is) by far the most important Military Area in Ireland — an importance to which people are partly blinded by reason of the outstanding military successes of our troops in the South-west. If we had to start the present War without initial possession of Dublin where would we be now?' On another occasion, Mulcahy stressed: 'The grip of our forces in Dublin must be maintained and strengthened at all costs . . . it cannot be too clearly stated that no number nor any magnitude of victories in any distant provincial areas have any value if Dublin is lost in a military sense.' Ned Broy declared: 'Cork could be wiped out and Kerry but as long as Dublin was there surely it meant a guarantee of safety.'[1]

Cork IRA men were hardly likely to be impressed by such references to parts of Munster as ' distant provincial areas' but there was much force in Mulcahy's logic. It was essential to the credibility of the Dáil government that the IRA kept an effective presence in the capital city and actions in Dublin gained the biggest publicity in the British and international press. Between 1919 and 1921 guerrilla warfare tactics were adopted with great success. First, however, the Volunteer movement in Dublin had to reorganise after 1916 and this was achieved more speedily in Dublin than anywhere else.

Reorganisation had begun even before the great boost of the release of internees and prisoners in the following winter and spring. The restructuring started at the battalion rather than at the brigade level. It was the Dublin Brigade's organisation of the massive procession following Thomas Ashe's funeral in September 1917 which both raised the profile of the movement and led to its renaissance.[2]

As in the countryside, much depended on leadership within localities. Revival began in specific areas in the city, for instance Fairview and Inchicore. A network of close colleagues with similar backgrounds and cultural influences, so often the Gaelic League, the GAA and the Christian Brothers' schools, emerged. Almost all had come out in 1916.

In Fairview the triumvirate of Dick McKee, Oscar Traynor and Frank Henderson had been good friends before 1916; Traynor and McKee were printers by trade, and Henderson came from a similar lower middle class background. All had been interned and on release became the dominant men in the Second Battalion, McKee becoming O/C Dublin in 1918 with Traynor succeeding him on his death in 1920. The youthful Paddy O'Connor, whose father was a Gaelic language teacher, had travelled from post to post during the Easter Rising striving to find a commander who would take him on. During the War of Independence he became the leading figure in an IRA company consisting mainly of friends and relations in Inchicore, in the south-west of the city.[3]

Mulcahy, who lived in the suburb of Clontarf, had a rather different upbringing but a similar swift rise to command. A university student in 1916, Mulcahy had been associated with Thomas Ashe in the Ashbourne raid, the one successful military operation of the Rising, and had been prominent in Frongoch. Just as importantly, his experience as a Post Office worker gave him administrative competence. He took over as Brigade O/C in 1917 and Chief of Staff in March 1918.[4] This pattern of local involvement did not apply to the most significant and charismatic figure in Dublin's fighting story, Michael Collins.

Harry Colley recorded his dislike of Collins pre-1916, regarding him as an abrasive, overbearing intruder, and such feelings were widely reflected in the preference shown for Mulcahy rather than Collins as Chief of Staff in 1918. Nevertheless, Collins' charisma and his work in Frongoch signalled him out as a natural leader and brilliant organiser. It was he who delivered the swift rhetorical blast at Ashe's funeral after the rifle salute. Collins declared: 'Nothing additional remains to be said. That volley which we have just heard is the only speech which it is proper to make above the grave of a dead Fenian.' It was Collins also who first saw the relevance of parliamentary elections for Volunteer development.

Through 1917 and 1918, the various companies drilled in public and in uniform and so were frequently arrested. Again the prison experience strengthened the bonds within and without the capital. By the end of 1918, McKee was in command of a training camp in West Cork. The Volunteer Convention in Dublin in October 1917 unified the disparate elements and, coming immediately after the Sinn Féin Convention, related the movement to the political side. A spectacular growth in Volunteer numbers resulted from the conscription crisis of 1918, and McKee then drew up a complex blockhouse system for resistance should the legislation for implementation be enforced. By the time of the December 1918 election, many of the Volunteer leadership were well known nationally and locally.[5]

The Volunteer renaissance, of course, depended most on the acquisition of arms. In this respect the Dublin Brigade was more fortunate than others in the size and number of nearby barracks. Some of the Howth gun-running material of 1914 was still available and some arms and ammunition was taken from the old National Volunteers. A considerable amount of war material was stolen, handed over or purchased from British soldiers before and during the War. Archie Doyle recalled purchasing arms from soldiers at Richmond and Island Bridge Barracks at £4 per rifle, and Brian Holman got arms out of a British officers' mess where he worked. The biggest arms raid took place in March 1919 when twenty-five men in five cars raided Collinstown Aerodrome. The action was expedited by building workers there and seventeen rifles were taken without resistance. Amiens Street Station saw another lucrative raid by the Volunteers.[6]

As early as 1917, Patrick McHugh and Michael Lynch had set up a munitions factory in the basement of a cycle shop at 198 Parnell Street. To start with one hundred grenades were produced in a week. Meanwhile Tom Keogh of the Squad was making detonators in Dominick Street. Crucially, during the next three years the firing time was lowered from seven seconds to three. By October 1920, experiments were being made, sometimes with disastrous results, on the production of trench mortars. On 10 December 1920, the British captured the bomb factory. The staff, however, escaped, soon establishing another factory in other premises.[7]

The transformation of a part-time volunteer army in the city into an efficient guerrilla fighting force by 1920 was the product of the attack on the DMP and the development of Collins' Intelligence system. Regular IRA work, whether mundane drilling or limited raids, faded into insignificance compared with the attacks on the 'G' men and British Intelligence agents. For this work, Collins established his notorious Squad.

The Squad was formed at a meeting in July 1919. Its members took orders from Collins, independently of GHQ and the Brigade. It appears that the initial membership was five and through various changes built up to over twelve by 1921. The description of them as the twelve apostles is therefore somewhat inaccurate. At the time and since, there has been much confusion as to who was or was not in the Squad. Members came from an intimate working class background and were paid £4. 10s a week from Dáil funds; many were friends and some were related. Squad composition was looser than had been traditionally accepted: Breen and Treacy, for instance, acted with them in the second half of 1919. It was made clear from the start that there was no room in the unit for anyone having moral scruples about the use of violence: the Squad operated a shoot-to-kill policy. Information was supplied mostly by Collins' Intelligence unit, who sometimes joined in with shootings themselves.[8]

The first target was the G Division DMP, which was effectively wiped out by the beginning of 1920. D/I Smith was the first detective to be killed by Squad men at the end of July 1919 in Drumcondra, and on 12 September D/O Hoey was shot dead near police headquarters in Brunswick Street in the city centre. D/O Johnny Barton was eliminated at the end of November and a double agent, Molloy, killed in March 1920. As a consequence of the shattering of the DMP's morale, D/I Redmond was summoned from Belfast to reorganise Intelligence and with the specific brief to find Collins. Within a few weeks of his arrival in Dublin, he was assassinated in Harcourt Street by a mixture of Squad and Intelligence unit gunmen. Squad members participated in the abortive attempt on Lord French's life at Ashtown in December 1919. This was not the only botched operation: Detectives Revelly and Wharton were wounded but not killed.

During 1920 the targets widened to include Intelligence officers acting out with the police force. In March, Alan Bell, an old Land League detective, was brought in to investigate Sinn Féin bank accounts and also the French and Redmond shootings. After careful clocking of his regular movements, Bell was ordered off a bus in Ballsbridge and shot dead on the street. Jim Slattery, a member of the Squad, criticised the fact that Bell was shot in a quiet residential area, which made escape more difficult. On 30 July 1920, Paddy Daly, the Squad leader, and Slattery entered the office of Frank Brooke, Director of the Great Southern and Eastern Railway Company and member of French's Advisory Council, and killed him. Bloody Sunday saw the apotheosis of this killing spree.[9]

This policy of assassinations was very high risk. It might easily have led to accidental shootings of passers-by and may have alienated public opinion. The shootings came out of the blue, in busy streets, no doubt shocking and frightening young and old alike; the men targeted were regular Irish policemen, often well known and liked in their locality. Attitudes were very different by the latter half of 1920, when the targets were Black and Tans and Auxiliaries. The British administration singularly failed to capitalise on such potential tensions. Ned Broy argued that Collins left a long gap between the first and second killings of 'G' men for fear of antagonising the public. Up to then Collins had argued that men should only shoot in self-defence.[10]

As in Cork, a divide grew up between the gunmen and those with distinct reservations over the use of violence. Frank Henderson told McKee in early 1920 that shooting police would lie on his conscience and testified that 'some sincere men' refused to take part in street ambushes. Henceforward, Henderson was sidelined to administrative tasks. Todd Andrews recorded that when Volunteers realised that shooting was involved 'quite a few of them decided, on grounds of conscience, that they could not continue.' The days of easy camaraderie and good times were being replaced by a kind of Terror.[11]

For much of 1920, there was little regular Dublin IRA action apart from a continuation of arms raids, stealing of mail and assistance to the Intelligence effort. The most dramatic event was on 1 June when the King's Inns, situated close to the British military base in the North Dublin Union, was raided and twenty-five rifles, two Lewis guns and a quantity of ammunition taken. The Church Street bakery attack in October, in which Kevin Barry was arrested, was the first on British troops in Dublin since the Rising. Bloody Sunday abruptly changed matters, with the enormous stepping-up of raids by British military causing the IRA to re-assess its strategy.[12]

At the very end of the year, the Dublin active service unit was formed. It consisted of fifty men, picked from the elite of the four battalions and divided into sections corresponding to the geographical areas of the battalions. Each section was to operate independently although occasionally they united for a large operation. As in the countryside, knowledge of the locality was invaluable — earlier in the conflict, Joe O'Connor, the O/C Third Battalion, recorded that men were prohibited from operating outside their own areas. These men worked full time and were also paid £4. 10s a week. The order that all actions had to be cleared at Brigade level before being implemented soon proved impractical.[13]

As a consequence of these developments, regular attacks on the enemy, transport and military supplies began. Revolvers and hand guns were the order of the day in a city context. A target of three actions a day was aimed for and often achieved. Regular patrols were set up and small parties of gunmen frequently harassed troops coming and going from their military barracks. The Aungier Street and Camden Street area, which runs down into the city centre from Portobello Barracks, became a particular focus for street ambushes, aided by the plethora of side streets and alleyways. It came to be nicknamed the Dardanelles. Any such actions had to be small-scale and swift. There was no possibility of road cutting to delay troop movements, and no point in the city was far away from a barracks. There was also the huge problem of avoiding civilian casualties. Cathal Brugha was particularly sensitive about this. Often, however, the populace lent support; Madge Clifford remembered how the flower sellers in Moore Street helped to spirit away arms and ammunition. The horse and cart became the most useful means of conveying arms.[14]

With connivance from prison warders, the IRA brought about the escape of Frank Teeling, Ernie O'Malley and Simon Donnelly from Kilmainham on 14 February 1921. Teeling had been convicted and sentenced to hang for participation in the Bloody Sunday killings. General Macready's reaction well demonstrates the effect of such coups: 'We have had a real disaster. The man Teeling and two other important men escaped last night from Kilmainham Prison and got clear away. It is about the worst blow I have had for a very long time, and I am naturally furious.'[15]

On 14 May members of GHQ and the Squad attempted the most daring of all the prison rescues. By dint of careful observation and planning, an armoured car was seized from an abattoir near the North Circular Road where the Army regularly picked up meat. Two members of the British forces were killed and the car was driven into Mountjoy Prison with Emmet Dalton and Joe Leonard wearing stolen British army uniforms. Dalton's experience in the British army no doubt gave him the confidence to carry this off. The aim was to meet the Governor and bring about Seán MacEoin's release by the elaborate ruse of requiring him for interview elsewhere. The plan only failed because of a change in MacEoin's movements for the day; the raiding party had to shoot their way out of the prison in the armoured car. This vehicle was ditched in Clontarf after it broke down. No incident better demonstrated to British eyes the cavalier spirit of the IRA and the risks Collins was prepared to run to rescue key men and close friends.[16]

Todd Andrews recorded how clumsily some of the ambushes were laid and detailed testimony shows how many attacks had to be aborted. A major setback for the IRA occurred when British forces got wind of an ambush near Drumcondra Bridge on 21 January 1921: five IRA men were captured, one died and four of the prisoners were later hanged.

One of the few confrontations of any size and length was in Brunswick Street in March with two Auxiliaries and three IRA killed. A planned attack by all sections on Auxiliaries in June in Grafton Street had limited success for only one section. Attacks on trains were also disappointing. An ambush on the Belfast to Dublin express bringing troops back from the opening of the Northern parliament, also in June, collapsed when two men fired by mistake at the Howth suburban train. Soon after an attack on another troop train at Ballyfermot was partially pulled off.

By 1921, British safety procedures had improved; armoured cars were reinforced with steel. The foot patrols of the Igoe gang, consisting of non-uniformed men brought in from the west under their Sergeant Igoe, put considerable pressure on the IRA. In addition, the cordoning off of specific parts of the city for intensive searches produced few concrete results but added to the siege-like conditions. In January, the streets around the Four Courts, in February those around Mountjoy Square and shortly after, the areas around Nassau Street and Kildare Street were surrounded and searched. While this produced few results, in separate activities the British made major discoveries of IRA arms dumps.[17]

ASU activity often concentrated on the shooting down of Auxiliaries, agents and spies. In June, Paddy O'Connor and three colleagues burst into the Mayfair Hotel in Baggot Street, shooting dead one Auxiliary and wounding another in front of their wives. A British military report commented that the assailants were 'young (17 to 24), very badly dressed and altogether of poor appearance'. O'Connor's and Jim McGuiness' attack in the same month on a cricket match between the army and the Gentlemen of Ireland at Trinity College resulted in the death of a girl spectator who got in the line of fire.

Oscar Traynor considered that while actions did not bring about spectacular losses for the enemy, they did weaken their morale. The IRA recorded fifty-three operations in March 1921, sixty-seven in April, one hundred and seven in May and ninety-three in June.[18]

The spectacular exception to the generally small-scale character of IRA actions in the city came on 25 May 1921 with the burning of the Custom House. This was planned by the Second Brigade and used the Squad and the ASU only for protection outside the premises. Entry into the building and the burning of the local government offices went according to plan, but before evacuation started an armoured car full of Auxiliaries arrived and a shoot-out occurred. A large number of IRA, estimated at between eighty and 130, were captured and Tom Ennis, O/C Second Battalion, was amongst those seriously wounded. While the IRA's official verdict was to hail the destruction of Dublin's finest building as a triumph, obviously the loss of manpower was a huge blow. Harry Colley said that the Second Battalion thereafter was 'a wash-out'. Considerable criticism of Traynor's leadership of the Dublin Brigade followed. Members of the Squad and ASU pointed to the inadequate preparations for a getaway. Mulcahy and Collins had been unhappy about the wisdom of such a large mobilisation in the centre of Dublin, Collins feeling that it savoured too much of an insurrection. The implication was that the planning had gone beyond the authority of Mulcahy and Collins and was related to de Valera's desire for big gestures.[19]

After this disastrous episode, the ASU and the Squad were merged and called the Dublin Guard. Many, however, resigned from the new body, refusing to serve under Paddy Daly, who had replaced Paddy Flanagan as O/C. The latter had been reprimanded severely by Collins for the clumsy shooting of a spy in Jervis Street Hospital and for failing to carry out instructions to attack a British cordon. Early in June, the National Shell Depot in Phoenix Park was raided and during that month there were plans for a series of major attacks in the city. A particularly big offensive against Auxiliaries in Grafton Street was called off because of the impending Truce. Such plans, though, could not cover up the weakened state of the Dublin units.[20]

12

THE WAR IN CORK

As befitted the largest of the Irish counties with a strong nationalist history, Cork played a leading role in the development of the Irish Volunteers. In common with the rest of the country there had been a steep dip in membership of advanced nationalist organisations in pre-Rising days. Describing his work as an IRB organiser in the county in 1915, Ernest Blythe gave a withering account of the state of Volunteer organisation with the single exception of that at Mitchelstown. He depicted Volunteer meetings in Mallow as little more than opportunities for drinking cheap liquor and he poured scorn on the training methods used by the Hales brothers around Bandon.[1]

Cork's failure to participate in the Easter Rising, and the surrender of arms in that week, had created many divisions and rankled for long afterwards. During 1917 the Volunteer leaders, Tomás MacCurtain and Terence MacSwiney were summoned to explain their actions to the membership. MacCurtain and MacSwiney agreed with de Valera and Brugha that the IRB should end and that in the future activity should be centred on public organisations, while Seán O'Hegarty and Florrie O'Donoghue continued to stress the importance of the IRB as a revolutionary elite.[2]

The reorganisation of the Irish Volunteers in the county in 1917 and 1918 was gradual but successful. As elsewhere, much depended on the release of the internees; the fact that hardly any of the leadership had been lost in 1916 aided the recovery. O'Donoghue records that at the time of the Rising there were only forty-six organised companies, with none exceeding 120 men. At the end of 1916, he commented that those that remained were: '. . . a handful of the population . . . poor, untrained, almost unarmed, a lot of frothy patriotic sentiment, . . . apparently futile and without a policy'. However, by mid-1918 the Cork Brigade consisted of twenty battalions with around eight companies each and a total strength of 8,000 men. Cork did not experience any of the crucial by-elections which acted as a focus elsewhere for Volunteer, as well as Sinn Féin, revival. Cork men, though, did help in elections in other areas and Seán Moylan emphasised how such activity liberated individuals and brought

them into touch with other leaders. While the principle of election of officers
was adhered to, a hard revolutionary leadership surfaced, a combination of
pre-1916 officers and new blood.[3]

The election system according to O'Donoghue sometimes favoured 'the
plausible talker rather than the capable worker'. Moylan shared with
O'Donoghue a contempt for those who loved bands and public parades. Men
like O'Donoghue, Donnchadha MacNeilus, Frank Busteed, Liam Deasy and
Tom Barry were wary of political influences and convinced of the need for
physical force. Other men, usually associated with cultural movements, faded
from the scene when rhetoric changed to action. When Fred Murray, the O/C
of O'Donoghue's battalion, objected to the use of arms in MacNeilus' escape
from Cork Jail in 1918, he was 'allowed to fade out later without comment'.
The same applied to Seán O'Sullivan, the O/C Second Battalion. While personally sympathetic to Terence MacSwiney, O'Donoghue regarded him as 'a
gentle soul . . . it was part of our tragedy that he had to be a soldier. He never
looked well in uniform.' MacSwiney only took part in one action: a failed
ambush.[4]

The new militants were usually IRB members and strongly attached to Seán
O'Hegarty. When, in the summer of 1919, Harry Varies shot an RIC man,
MacCurtain felt that the incident undermined his authority as an officer
commanding a brigade. Nobody accepted responsibility for the action and
O'Hegarty resigned as MacCurtain's deputy over the matter.

O'Hegarty had been dismissed from his local government post because of
his Volunteer work. An abrasive, puritanical character, O'Hegarty was particularly intolerant of political interference. He was a fiercely proud Cork city man
and often took part in county guerrilla activity. He was determined to produce
a more efficient fighting force and a sober one, as he demonstrated by his vigorous campaign against poteen in his Cork First Brigade. Moylan described
him as wearing home-spun trousers and a bowler hat. 'He looked like an old
time music hall artist' but was 'a serious man of keen intellect. If he had a sense
of humour, it was of that sardonic and devastating type peculiar to Cork.'[5]

The Volunteer resurgence was locally based. Regular activity and strong
IRA/Volunteer organisation were confined to particular areas of the county,
notably around Bandon, Newmarket, Mallow and Midleton in addition to the
city. Skibbereen and the area west of it was not fertile ground for guerrilla fighters, its population being mainly poor farmers and fishermen. The active areas
were most often associated with a strong, popular leadership, for instance, the
Hales brothers and Liam Deasy around Bandon, Moylan in Newmarket and
Liam Lynch in Fermoy. It is clear that many joined because they were related to
the officers or due to employment or Gaelic Athletic Association (GAA) contacts. Among members of the Macroom Battalion traced by the census, 50 per
cent were brothers. The figures were 58 per cent for the Lisgoold Company and
49 per cent for the Mourne Abbey Company. Liam Deasy recorded that 80 per
cent of his Valley Rovers Gaelic Football team joined up and the Hales brothers

had strong GAA links. Recently, Peter Hart's research has highlighted the eclectic background of IRA men; they were far from being the scum of society portrayed in British propaganda. Membership was strong in town and countryside: weakest amongst the well-off and the poor.[6]

The archetypal IRA man was aged between eighteen and twenty-five, came from the lower middle class and was well educated, often by the Christian Brothers. Men joined the Volunteers/IRA for recreational and social reasons as well as political ones. It provided a colourful alternative to the monotony of small-town life: many veterans were to look back on these years as the happiest of their lives. Liam Deasy reminisced: 'Even now, after a lapse of more than fifty years, I can recall the thrill of those early parades — the feeling of high adventure, the sense of dedicated service to the cause of Irish freedom, the secret rendezvous and the gay comradeship — all were to me and my companions like signs of the return of the Golden Age of Ireland's ancient chivalry.' To become a Volunteer was to enhance social prestige; a kind of tribal loyalty developed with the column leaders resembling medieval chieftains.[7]

The biographies of Florrie O'Donoghue, Liam Lynch, Seán Moylan and Tom Barry provide fine examples of this new type of Volunteer. Born in Rathmore, County Kerry in 1894, O'Donoghue moved to Cork city at the age of sixteen to work in a shop. He joined the Volunteers after the Easter Rising and soon became a key figure in the Cork Brigade, setting up the Intelligence system which independently grew to resemble Michael Collins' in Dublin. His rapid advancement owed much to his closeness to Seán O'Hegarty, who was the most sympathetic of the old order to an aggressive policy. O'Donoghue thought O'Hegarty regarded him as a surrogate son. He also rose because of his IRB membership which helped to ensure that he became a confidant of Michael Collins. Following MacCurtain's death in March 1920, O'Donoghue left his employment and became a full-time Brigade officer using an assumed name, George Egan, with the front of the Dripsey Woollen Mills. At the time, O'Donoghue feared that the rise of Sinn Féin would detract from military matters and cause the loss of important men but he came to realise that the relationship was mutually advantageous. He admitted that he hated guns but justified violence by the paramount need to remove the historic invader — in contrast to some others, he stressed he felt no personal hatred towards British forces.[8]

O'Donoghue was to write the biography of Liam Lynch who came from the Limerick/Cork border, also served in a shop and also owed much to IRB links. Lynch had opted for membership of the National Volunteers rather than the Irish Volunteers in 1914 and again the Rising was instrumental in his move to republicanism. Lynch was an effective administrator who rose quickly through the ranks to leadership of the First Brigade by 1918.[9]

Originally from Kilmallock in County Limerick, Seán Moylan was a builder by trade and had been steeped in the Fenian tradition from birth. After moving to Newmarket, Moylan ran one of the most successful and disciplined flying columns. He always stressed that his men were effective only in their own areas. Moylan had notoriously frosty relations with his brigade leadership and regarded Lynch, whom he could not bring himself to name in his Statement to the Bureau of Military History, as a mere pen-pusher.[10]

The well-educated Barry, the son of a policeman turned shop owner, was a shop assistant before enlisting in the British army, claiming in retrospect to have experienced a Damascene conversion to the nationalist cause on hearing the news of the Easter Rising in Mesopotamia. His application to join the IRA was only granted after a considerable delay, any doubts eventually overcome by appreciation of his military prowess and his potential as a training officer. He remained a maverick figure, capable of inspiring both huge loyalty and bitter enmity.[11]

The rapid growth of the Cork organisation was also due to the early development of an Intelligence network which, under O'Donoghue's direction, rivalled in scope and effect Collins' one. Siobhan Lankford (née Creedon), who worked in the Post Office in Mallow, became Liam Lynch's chief Intelligence source, supplying information on troop movements and intercepting police and military correspondence. It was her warnings that prevented the Mourne Abbey debacle of February 1921 from being even worse. The prize Intelligence coup, however, has been hidden from historians until recently.[12]

During 1919, O'Donoghue had been put in touch with Josephine Marchmont, a typist working within the British Army 6th Division Headquarters. Through Father Dominic, she agreed to supply Intelligence, subsequently becoming known as Agent G. She was the daughter of an RIC man and had married a Catholic convert in Wales. Widowed in 1917, she had lost custody of her youngest son to the paternal grandparents who kept him in Wales. Mrs Marchmont constantly urged the IRA leadership for help, only narrowly avoiding British detection on the day MacSwiney was arrested in the City Hall. Eventually in October, with Collins' support, O'Donoghue and a driver successfully abducted the child, Reggie Brown, from his school in Barry and reunited him secretly with his mother in Ireland. The British press reported the strange incident while of course unaware of its massive implications. Josephine Marchmont carried on supplying crucial information right up to the time of the Truce, and later married Florrie O'Donoghue.[13]

In terms of organisation and arms, Cork was in advance of all IRA brigades outside Dublin. By the end of 1918, the county had been split into three brigades: the First covering the east, the city and mid-Cork, the Second the north and the Third the west. A sound communication system had been established. Specific incidents, usually involving arms captures, while provoking British reaction and the imprisonment of Volunteers, accelerated recruitment and raised morale. The culmination of this came with the conscription crisis of 1918.

As in all other areas, the conscription crisis produced a considerable rise in Volunteer membership. On the plans to take the fight to the hills if conscription was enforced, O'Donoghue commented: 'It is certain that resistance would have been determined and sustained; whether it would have been successful is another question.' Much of the new membership evaporated after the crisis had passed and, despite Volunteer involvement in the General Election, many felt that a mistaken priority was being given to political issues.[14] Up to this stage, Volunteer activity in the form of drilling, processions and prison protests was public. The whole character of the movement would dramatically change in the months following.

For all its fighting reputation in these years, Cork conforms to the limited, small scale and erratic pattern of the conflict generally. Isolated attacks on the RIC in 1919 were followed by intensified attacks on police barracks in the first half of 1920 and the appearance of flying columns from the late summer. Even Tom Barry's famous column was involved in comparatively few major operations. It is not surprising that the memoirs of contemporaries have told a story of successful ambushes and heroic resistance. They have, however, given a misleading impression of widespread and fairly continuous action which was hardly the case.

The number of failed ambushes far exceeded the successful ones, Seán Moylan admitting: 'the number of attacks we had made . . . up to the end bore no relation to the number of attempts made to organise such attacks.' One IRA man commented: 'Hundreds of key battles would have taken place in all areas but the enemy used never turn up — often after 4 or 5 days waiting on ambush.' Tom Barry was driven to distraction by the failure of mines and all were restricted by ammunition shortages. Co-operation between battalions and columns was often faulty as a consequence of local particularism and tensions between leaders. Moylan commented that 'the Brigade area was sacrosanct.' In North Cork, Moylan and Lynch barely spoke to each other. On top of this there was deep resentment as to what was perceived to be the refusal of GHQ to support them adequately: Cork men often commented that no one from Dublin visited them after December 1919.[15]

Volunteers became progressively disenchanted during 1919 by the lack of action. The fact that it was Tipperary and not Cork that fired the first shots in the War of Independence was a little against the odds, as there were numerous cases of RIC men being disarmed in Cork. The county, however, did make the first attack on a military target: on 7 September 1919, twenty-five Volunteers of the 2nd Brigade under Liam Lynch attacked a party of fourteen soldiers attending the Wesleyan church in Fermoy. One soldier was killed, three wounded and fifteen rifles captured. The town was sacked by troops that night, a foretaste of things to come in the next year.[16]

By the autumn of 1919, MacCurtain and MacSwiney, in response to the urgings of their more militant officers, were asking GHQ for permission to stage attacks on police barracks. MacSwiney at that time had plans for widespread assaults, a kind of rolling Rising from area to area. This went against Mulcahy's determination to avoid large confrontations. In rejecting such requests, GHQ cited the need to concentrate on plans to assassinate Lord French. Eventually, in January, approval was granted for three barracks attacks on the same day: that at Carrigtwohill was successful, the first such success in the country since Ashbourne in 1916; one failed, one was aborted. Other barracks attacks took place with variable success before the general destruction of evacuated buildings following British evacuation from rural areas in April 1920. This phase of the conflict had greater significance in raising morale than in purely military terms. In one case, after a protracted failure to capture a barracks, the RIC evacuated it the very next day anyway.[17]

The transformation from episodic conflict to bitter tit-for-tat violence involving massive increases in troop and police numbers was less the product of regular organised IRA activity than the response to specific events and legislation. Early on 20 March, massed gunmen broke into Lord Mayor MacCurtain's house in the suburb of Blackpool and killed him in front of his wife. Ignorant of this, a military patrol raided the house that same day. Some British sources imaginatively suggested that MacCurtain had been the victim of IRA men critical of his relative moderation, but the considerable likelihood is that an RIC squad was responsible for his murder. The jury at the coroner's inquest attached guilt to Lloyd George and D/I Swanzy. The latter was killed in retaliation in Lisburn, County Antrim in August 1920.[18]

Terence MacSwiney replaced MacCurtain as Lord Mayor and O'Donoghue prevailed upon O'Hegarty to return as O/C Cork One. While a few months later attention centred on MacSwiney's hunger strike, the IRA militants had won control. British Intelligence had no idea who the really important men were, as shown by their release of Lynch and O'Hegarty when they were arrested with MacSwiney in August. The killing of Colonel Smyth in the County Club in July and the botched assassination attempt on General Strickland in the city centre in September were amongst incidents contributing, together with the hunger strikes, to a sharp rise in tension. The fasting prisoners in particular day by day increased emotional feelings and there was much talk of vengeance if MacSwiney was allowed to die. The Lord Mayor finally expired at a time of massive crisis in Cork city.

The dirty war character of the violence in Cork city at this time is graphically illustrated by the tit-for-tat killings in the densely populated Barrack Street area in the west of the city on the night of 17–18 November 1920. The shooting of the popular Sergeant James O'Donoghue in Winter Street was followed by instant retaliation in the form of two gangs of masked men killing three men in Broad Street, Broad Lane and the North Mall. Those murdered were not the targets of the raids, but died because of their association with the O'Brien family, members of whom were connected with the O'Donoghue shooting. Later, three men were killed on suspicion of giving information to the RIC which provided the basis for the raids.[19]

The Restoration of Order in Ireland Act and the introduction of the Auxiliaries had a speedier impact in Cork than it had in the rest of the twenty-six counties. A number of flying columns were formed throughout the county, demonstrating that the conflict was no longer a part-time affair for the IRA's elite. A wave of shootings and reprisals began in the city, a strict curfew was imposed and a series of arson attacks occurred.[20] Against this background, the first and best-remembered major ambush took place at Kilmichael, on 28 November.

The ambush started at 4.05 p.m. after a long wait by Barry's column of thirty-six men. Two lorries containing an Auxiliary patrol approached the site at a remote, boggy place on the Macroom to Dunmanway road, one and a half miles from the village of Kilmichael. In order to enable the lorries to be trapped within the range of the scattered men, Barry stood in the road signalling the first lorry to stop. A brief successful attack was made against this vehicle and vicious hand-to-hand fighting ensued when the second lorry drew up and was engaged by another section of Barry's column. Barry maintained that a brutal assault on the remaining Auxiliaries occurred after they had pretended to surrender. Seventeen Auxiliaries were killed, the only survivor left in a coma, while the IRA lost three men.[21]

Kilmichael is the best known of all the ambushes in the War of Independence; today signposts point just towards 'the ambush'. It is also the most controversial, with the debate still going on as to whether a false surrender did happen or not. The Macroom IRA battalion was annoyed that the presence of Barry's column had scuppered their own plans for an attack on Macroom Castle. What cannot be doubted is that by travelling along a regular route in just two vehicles, the Auxiliaries had made themselves very vulnerable. There were larger ambushes later but none had the same impact.[22] Within two weeks, most of Munster had been placed under martial law and much of the centre of Cork city had been burnt down.

The establishment of martial law resulted in a further considerable increase in the intensity and scale of the conflict in Cork. On the IRA side, there was a determination to demonstrate that they were in no way cowed by military rule: the British, as stressed by General Strickland to the Cabinet, saw the next few months as vital. Official reprisals began, with the first in response to a successful ambush in Midleton at the end of December, and soon the IRA retaliated by attacks on loyalist properties.[23]

At this time the priority given by the IRA to large flying columns posed enormous risks. With large numbers of men concentrated in specific areas there was a real danger that whole units could be annihilated. In a series of disasters for the IRA between late January and March, this almost happened.

On 28 January 1921, the flying column of the 6th Battalion Cork One laid an ambush some half a mile west from Dripsey Bridge on the main Macroom to Cork road. Mrs Lindsay, an elderly loyalist widow from nearby Coachford and a personal friend of General Strickland, journeyed to Ballincollig to report the IRA presence. The local priest warned the column of the breach in security but was disregarded as an IRA man commented: 'he is against the cause.' Troops converged on the site in two large companies. Last-minute awareness of the threat allowed fifty men to flee but two died and five were cap-tured together with arms, ammunition and incriminating documents. The five were court martialled and then executed; the IRA, which had seized Mrs Lindsay and her chauffeur as hostages, later executed them without consulting or even informing Dublin GHQ.[24]

Two weeks later an IRA informer, Dan Shields, gave away details of a con-centration of columns at Mourne Abbey, 2nd Brigade Headquarters, in hilly country south of Mallow. Again troop parties enveloped the area: some escaped, thanks to Siobhan Lankford's warning, but four were killed and five wounded and captured. Of these, two were executed. In early March, Shields was again responsible for a raid on two IRA columns at Nadd, in mountains south of Banteer. Three IRA were killed; Congo Maloney and Joe Morgan were badly wounded but got away after a series of desperate adventures helped by Liam Lynch who was himself nearly captured.

An even more serious reverse was suffered on 20 February 1921 at Clonmult, five miles north of Midleton, where another betrayal resulted in a house full of IRA men being surrounded. In the ensuing gun battle which the British claimed involved a false IRA surrender, twelve IRA soldiers were killed, four wounded and four captured. Mick Leahy commented that after Clonmult: 'Things went to hell in the battalion.'

These and other setbacks emphasised the need to root out informers and led to a big rise in the execution of so-called spies. Loyalists, masons, ex-servicemen and tramps became particular targets. The war in Cork, far more than elsewhere apart from the North, took on the nature of a vendetta. There was a lot of criticism of Lyons, the Kanturk O/C, for allowing the despised Shields into his ranks.[25] The other lesson generally learned was to scale down the size of columns and to prevent large-scale gatherings. However, there was to be one significant exception.

The nearest approximation to a conventional battle in the whole War hap-pened at Crossbarry, between Bandon and Cork city, on 19 March 1921. With considerable justice, Crossbarry is regarded as a victory for the IRA but can also be seen as a missed opportunity for the British. As a result of information gleaned from a prisoner captured in the Upton train ambush, the British learned of a major gathering of IRA columns. Barry's men had recently returned to the area after days waiting for an ambush on the Kinsale to Bandon road. A massive sweep was organised from all directions, descending on a site just north of Crossbarry with lorries dropping police and military off at a distance, these men then proceeding stealthily on foot or cycle.

Before the British columns reached their intended destination, Charlie Hurley, the Cork Three O/C, was trapped in a house and killed. At the last moment the IRA leaders became aware of the danger and, sensing there was no safe recourse, Barry decided that they would fight their way out. British casual-ties vastly exceeded those of the IRA, who made a long retreat successfully. Republican sources claimed over thirty British were killed: the official British figures were ten killed and three wounded, with six IRA men killed. The British had made key mistakes in timing and mapwork while the IRA resistance had been courageous.[26]

While there were a large number of IRA successes, they were periodic and rarely amounted to unqualified victories. On 28 September 1920, the military barracks in Mallow was successfully raided for arms, acting on information passed on by Dick Willis, a painter, and Jack Bolster, a carpenter, who had been working there. Thirty-seven rifles were taken and prisoners held there released. The troops staged a reprisal that night. The arms captures made possible much of the Cork Two Brigade's actions in the months following. In the north of the county, Moylan led a successful ambush at Tureengariff on 28 February in which D/C Hoban was killed and one other, with six rifles taken.[27] The British suffered two other major reverses in ambushes at Coolavokig, near Ballyvorney, on 25 February 1921, and at Clonbannin, a few miles west of Kanturk, on 5 March.

In the former case, a large convoy of Auxiliaries drove into an ambush which had been waiting for four days. Three Auxiliaries, including the O/C Major Grant, were killed and eight wounded. The IRA column retreated when British reinforcements arrived. 'The History of the Sixth Division' concluded that 'an excellent opportunity of defeating the enemy was missed owing to bad tactics, and failure to work out a proper plan of operations based on information received.' IRA sources were just as critical about the performance of their men, citing: 'bad scouting, bad inter-communication between units, bad control of the units, lack of initiative and sense of responsibility on the part of subordinate Commanders'. It concluded 'A critical examination of this action shows that it might easily have been a disaster only for bold and steady action of small groups.'

At Clonbannin, troops going between Killarney and Buttevant had been forewarned of a trap, but were confused by a last-minute change in the ambush position. Their armoured car was accidentally ditched at the start of the fighting. Colonel-Commandant Cumming, the head of the British Kerry command, and three others were killed. The official British report found that 'this was undoubtedly one of the worst reverses suffered by the Army.'[28] The IRA, however, were concerned about the failure of many mines to detonate.

The end of the railway workers' strike in December and the movement of troops by train thereafter provided fresh targets. The IRA had only limited success in attacking troop trains. On 11 February a successful attack was made at Drishanebeg, near Millstreet on the Killarney to Cork line, in which a sergeant was killed and five others wounded. The British learned from this that troops should not be concentrated in designated carriages and that train movements should be less predictable. Four days later, a major ambush was planned on the branch line between Cork and Bantry at Upton station. It was expected that British troops would travel in the central carriage of the train. What had not been allowed for was that more than fifty troops would board the train at Kinsale Junction and mingle with civilians throughout the train. A shorter than usual stop at the junction prevented IRA scouts warning the raiding party in time. As a consequence six civilian passengers were killed and ten wounded; three IRA men also died.[29]

At the very end of March, Barry's column of thirty men and two officers staged an attack on the police barracks at Rosscarbery, the only example in 1921 of such an action against by then well-fortified buildings. This followed the occupation of a large house belonging to a leading loyalist family and an inept British attempt to dislodge them. There was a major lull before any other sizeable attacks. O'Donoghue recorded that it was impossible to sustain a fight which required the expenditure of more than twenty or thirty rounds.[30]

On 31 May the military band of the Hampshire Regiment was ambushed at Youghal: seven were killed and twenty-one wounded. Because of the youth of those involved there was massive publicity in Britain. On 16 June at Rathcoole, between Millstreet and Banteer, a party of Auxiliaries travelling in four lorries was attacked by a large column brought together from the various West Cork battalions. This time the mines laid did explode, wrecking three lorries, killing at least twelve soldiers and wounding many besides.[31]

In the first six months of 1921, the British military applied their minds to the best methods to combat guerrilla warfare. Planes were used for reconnaissance only rarely. Recourse was made to the use of small columns travelling on foot or by cycle, mimicking IRA tactics, and also to large-scale sweeps across country, as used in the Boer Wars. Both methods yielded some limited gains, and by May and June the IRA had been forced to disband many columns and men spent much time on the run. Seán Moylan, who was captured in one of the sweeps, said that his ASU was 'harried from pillar to post' and that 'the net was irrevocably closing on the base of those who were regarded as the main core of the resistance.' O'Donoghue reports that he spent May and June travelling around the west of Cork and Kerry, relying on his network of friends to remain one step ahead of the British, admiring the scenery and reading De Wet's *Three Years War*.[32]

An estimated 800 British troops converged on the Macroom area from 4 June. O'Donoghue commented on 14 June: 'The recent attempted round-up . . . was a huge fiasco. Fourteen different parties, converging from every point of the compass took part; all working towards Claydagh, where 1000 armed rebels were popularly supposed to be encamped. The enemy had between 2 and 3000 men, of all arms, with aeroplanes etc.' By mid-June, O'Donoghue was reporting that 8000 troops were being sent to Ballincollig to carry out a large drive of the Millstreet area from 23 June. British sources admitted that the results were disappointing. The distances involved were too great to maintain a level of surprise and the lengthy marches put a huge strain on the troops. The IRA cutting of roads rendered mechanical transport ineffective. Because of the IRA's use of very small mobile units, every area had to be trawled separately, a task that proved impossible in the time allotted. Local knowledge was insufficient for accurate identification of suspects; the choice was either to intern massive numbers or to release many already imprisoned. The IRA were well aware that sweeps could only be undertaken in summertime.[33]

For all the limitations of the British methods, the IRA had been placed on the defensive by the end of June. Leading Cork sources subsequently denied Beaslai's claim, in his biography of Collins, that Liam Lynch had journeyed to Dublin in May to press the desperate need for a truce. No one denied though that the arms and ammunition situation had become dire, particularly after the collapse of the Italian arms deal (see pages 77–8). Cork leaders felt that they were having to carry too much of the fight on their own, which goes some way to accounting for the formation of the First Southern Division in the spring. The British had applied a huge proportion of their resources to Cork but the outcome of guerrilla warfare cannot be determined by military considerations alone.[34]

13

THE WAR IN TIPPERARY, LIMERICK, WATERFORD, WEXFORD AND KILKENNY

~

TIPPERARY AND LIMERICK

Of all counties, Tipperary, and particularly south Tipperary, has been most strongly identified with the War of Independence. The Soloheadbeg ambush of 21 January 1919 is generally accepted as the beginning of the armed conflict. The fact that the South Tipperary Brigade was the first to go to war meant that events there have been better recorded and more graphically described than those in most other places. The actions in early 1919 anticipated what occurred in the rest of the country from mid-1920. However, in the localised and patchy character of the guerrilla resistance this, the largest of Ireland's inland counties, resembled many others.

Before Christmas 1918, the Brigade leaders had decided to attack an RIC patrol carrying gelignite from Tipperary town to a quarry at Soloheadbeg. Dan Breen's brother took a job in the quarry to supply them with information. The eleven chosen men had to hang around waiting for several weeks; three of them had to return to their jobs. The plan was, if possible, to take the gelignite without any violence, but the RIC men refused to surrender the explosive and were shot and killed.

Both the men appear to have been popular in the locality and the action was widely criticised in pulpits and press. At the subsequent inquest, the coroner said of Constable McDonnell 'a more quiet inoffensive man he had never met' and of Constable O'Connell that he was 'quiet and decent'. The Volunteer GHQ had not authorised the action and Richard Mulcahy later declared that it was tantamount to murder. The gelignite was smuggled away to be used in several barracks attacks months later and Seán Treacy, Dan Breen, Seamus Robinson and Seán Hogan, the leaders of the attack, spent the next months as outlaws.[1]

Many have argued that by their action the South Tipperary Brigade had shown the way to the rest of the country and triggered the move away from the tactics of passive resistance. Such an argument underlay Dan Breen's best-selling and highly influential *My Fight for Irish Freedom*, one of the bibles of the traditional nationalist interpretation. The fact that Soloheadbeg assumed such importance was accidental. There had been numerous attempts to disarm RIC men during 1918 but this was the first to cause fatalities and took place on the same day as the first sitting of the Dáil. Ironically, considering Breen's contempt for politicians, it was the link with them which gave the ambush such signifi-cance. Militarily, the ambush appears out of context and counter-productive in the short term, causing loss of leadership and a subsequent decline in activity for some months. From the detached vantage point of old age, Todd Andrews pointed out that Soloheadbeg simply amounted to an operation which went wrong, its importance being retrospective.[2]

Despite Tipperary's Fenian and Land League tradition, the Irish Volunteers before 1916 were sparse in number and poorly trained. The post-Rising revival focused on specific localities, notably villages surrounding Tipperary town, and particular individuals. The ascetic Seán Treacy came from a poor small farmer background, left school at fourteen and was a keen Gaelic League member. Treacy's was an unbending physical force nationalism, heavy with religious conviction. From Dundalk Gaol in May 1918 he advised a Tipperary colleague; 'Deport all in favour of the enemy out of the district. Deal sternly with those who try to resist. Maintain the strictest discipline. There must be no running to kiss mothers goodbye . . . Get the men to go to confession and com-munion and remember Sarsfield, the men of '48 and '67 and the men of 1916.' Breen, his rough-hewn school friend, became a lineman on the railway. Treacy's frequent spells in prison in 1917 and 1918 involving hunger strikes gave him prominence among the revolutionary elite, and he formed close rela-tionships with other local Volunteer leaders. Michael Brennan in Clare, a very close friend, vowed with him never to land in prison again.

Perhaps due to his peripatetic role organising the Volunteers throughout the county, Treacy chose not to become O/C of the Brigade on its establish-ment in 1918. Surprisingly, Seamus Robinson was invited to take that position. Robinson, a Belfast man, was for several years active in Gaelic League and Volunteer circles in Glasgow, returning to participate in the Easter Rising. As an outsider he was to have problems with the close, clannish world of South Tipperary. In later years, Robinson would bitterly contest Breen's account of the War, pointing out that Breen spent most of the time out of the county, took part in few actions and held no senior rank for years.[3]

Of central importance in explaining the peculiar development of the South Tipperary Brigade was its estrangement from the IRB. This stemmed from the Supreme Council's refusal to grant permission for an attack on a policeman in 1917. In contrast with Cork, in Tipperary the secret society was associated with caution and moderation. Notwithstanding Breen's and Treacy's good relations with Collins, the arch-IRB man, this independence from IRB leadership extended to independence also from the Volunteer GHQ in Dublin. In his reminiscences, Mulcahy frequently despaired of South Tipperary's failure to respond to his efforts to control and regulate them. Long before Soloheadbeg, no approval was sought for actions and from late 1918 the Brigade became increasingly critical of what they regarded as the pussy-footing caution in Dublin. Whereas in Cork, MacSwiney and MacCurtain came into line despite similar reservations, South Tipperary never did.[4]

Following Soloheadbeg, some within the Dublin GHQ thought that the South Tipperary Brigade leaders should be spirited away to the United States. Breen, Treacy and Robinson took refuge in safe houses in Limerick and Clare before Seán Hogan was captured at a dance on an ill-advised trip home. This provided the opportunity for what Robinson was later to call 'the follow-through of Soloheadbeg'. It was decided that the only realistic hope of rescuing Hogan would be on his transfer by train, on 13 May, from Thurles to Cork. Originally the dramatic train rescue was to have taken place at Emly but due to faulty Intelligence had to be switched at the last minute to Knocklong, the next station down the line. Some Volunteers travelling on the train gave the signal for Treacy and Breen to overpower the guard and in the fight that followed two RIC men were killed and Hogan rescued. Breen and Treacy were both wounded and forced to take refuge in Dublin after further stays in Clare and North Tipperary. At this stage the British authorities declared Tipperary a military area.[5]

The immediate consequence of these dramatic events was to disrupt Volunteer organisation and activities and enhance the British military/police presence in the county. Other policemen were killed in the south of the county in 1919: especially notorious was the assassination of D/I Hunt at Thurles on 23 June. He was shot in the town centre by Jim Stapleton, who had been involved in several shootings, amidst a throng of people returning from the local races. No-one attempted to come to his aid: locally unpopular, he was thought to have vital information on the Knocklong killings.[6]

While acknowledging the need for the Brigade leadership to go on the run in the immediate aftermath of both Soloheadbeg and Knocklong, many have questioned why Breen and Treacy took so long to return from Dublin. Collins gave them some work attached to the Squad, notably in the attempted assassination of Lord French at Ashtown. While Treacy was involved in attacks on barracks in 1920, he and Breen had returned to Dublin by the autumn. On 11 October they were tracked down by Intelligence agents and escaped after a celebrated shoot-out at the house of Professor Carolan in Drumcondra. Carolan was killed and Breen seriously injured. Nine days later, Treacy was shot dead in an exchange of fire outside the republican outfitters in Talbot Street in the city centre. The aftermath of the affair was filmed. Thereafter the action in south Tipperary conformed to the general pattern of flying column formation and isolated ambushes.[7]

There was some criticism within the Tipperary IRA of Treacy's and Breen's unauthorised activities. In 1919, Frank Drohan, the O/C Clonmel Battalion, had complained to GHQ about unnecessary actions; in a letter found on Treacy's body, Éamon O'Dwyer detailed similar objections. While Breen soon complained that there was too little fighting, many of his colleagues thought the opposite.[8]

Comparatively little attention has been paid to the guerrilla activity in the north of the county which, after a slow start, was equally widespread and as significant as that of the south. The Volunteers here it appears were slow to recover after 1916 because of the failings of the local leadership. Seán Gaynor was amazed at how quickly he rose to dominance in the local brigade, considering his lack of military experience up to 1919. It was only after the old guard leadership, elected for their social prominence, was replaced by younger, more determined, men, chosen rather than elected, that the IRA resistance really took off.

The Volunteer commanders were just as legendary in their own areas and as cynical of GHQ interference as Treacy and Breen. In the fiercely independent mountainous area south of Newport, Paddy Ryan Lacken ploughed his own furrow. Mick Kennedy commented: 'he had a good opinion of himself . . . he was a difficult man. . . and he did what he pleased.' A tall, handsome figure, Ryan inspired awe in his followers and hatred in the British, who burnt the family home early in 1921, and then carried his father around as a hostage. Ryan's revenge was in the savage killing of D/I Biggs and Miss Barrington, a local loyalist, on 15 May 1921.[9] Two ambush parties had targeted Biggs at this time; the one that succeeded was under the command of Seán Gaynor. It appears that Miss Barrington, who was sitting in the passenger seat of a car alongside Biggs, was unrecognised as a woman because of her riding uniform. Ryan evidently fired the shots.

County boundaries often counted for little as the conflict developed. Men from Tipperary frequently took part in guerrilla actions in Limerick, where city and county vividly demonstrate how local divisions could determine the level of Volunteer activity. Post-1916 the Limerick City Battalion became hopelessly split over the Rising and the IRB. Supporters of Donnachadha O'Hannigan remained true to their IRB membership while those of Liam Manahan preferred independence from secret society control. There were attempts in 1917 to discipline Manahan for dumping arms at the time of the Rising and for failing to come out in support of Dublin. GHQ tried unsuccessfully to resolve differences by forming a second battalion. There appears to have been a class barrier between the two battalions: the first was associated with white-collar workers, the second was more working class.

Limerick saw some dramatic events during the conflict. After the IRA attempt on 6 April 1919 to free a prisoner in the prison workhouse, two RIC men and the prisoner were killed. On 6 March 1920 the Lord Mayor, George

Cleary, and his predecessor in office, Michael O'Callaghan, were murdered in separate raids on their homes by armed gangs, very probably of RIC.

In the early stages of the War, Tomás MacCurtain tried mediation between the contending Volunteer elements in the county. Later Tomás Malone was sent to the east of the county with instructions from Collins to initiate military action, thereby distracting from local feuding. Malone arrived under the cover of a position as Dáil Loan Organiser and the assumed name Seán Forde. While taking no official position in the local Volunteer movement, Malone planned a series of barracks attacks involving both sets of men and taking control from Seán Wall, the local O/C, who had little military experience or ability. Malone's claim, however, that his actions spelled the end of internecine feuds was not borne out by the testimony of many insiders and by the continuation of the same divisions during the Civil War. Malone linked up effectively with neighbouring battalions in Tipperary and with Ernie O'Malley, who was performing a similar organising role there. The East Limerick Brigade was responsible for some of the most successful attacks of the War and saw the formation of the first flying column in the country.[10]

Many of the most famous raids on barracks in 1920 took place in Tipperary and Limerick. For all the extensive and colourful literature and the considerable amount of planning involved, not discounting the use of hundreds of men in road blocking, the end product of these raids was very limited. A high proportion were aborted or had little success and many targets were evacuated shortly after anyway. Indeed, most destruction of British barracks occurred once the premises had been safely evacuated. Such attacks did, however, have symbolic importance underlining the collapse of British administration, and in some cases, the central purpose of capture of arms and ammunition was achieved.

The first successful barracks attack in Limerick was led by Tomás Malone on Ballylanders RIC station on 27 April 1920. Thirty men were employed and, as was customary, the occupation of neighbouring buildings enabled men to smash holes in the roof so as to throw in petrol bombs. Once the station was burning, it was promptly surrendered. As was so often the case, the Volunteers exhausted all their ammunition during the fight.[11]

The big prize came with the attack on Kilmallock Barracks which started on the morning of 28 May 1920. For this men came to assist from neighbouring brigades; Seán Treacy, Michael Brennan from Clare, and Seán Wall at the head of men from West Limerick. Malone thought it 'about the biggest' such attack during the whole war. It lasted several hours and this time the two sergeants and eight constables inside refused to surrender. Two RIC men were killed and eight wounded, one IRA man was killed and one wounded before the insurgents prevailed. Malone, however, admitted that so much ammunition had been expended that East Limerick was 'a bit disorganised after it'. Malone's column moved on to West Limerick and Clare where plans for a large-scale attack on Sixmilebridge Barracks did not come off.[12]

The first major attack on a barracks in north Tipperary occurred on 26 June 1920 at Borrisokane. For this, supplies were collected from Dublin and about two hundred men were involved. After two hours and what seemed imminent surrender by the RIC inside, the Brigade O/C, Frank McGrath, suddenly ordered withdrawal. Additional distress was caused by the fact that two wounded comrades were abandoned. Seán Gaynor, the key figure in implementing the action, commented: 'it was in a very disappointed frame of mind that I carried out these orders and withdrew from the attack when we were on the verge of success. We discovered later that, half an hour after we had left, the garrison were forced to leave the burning building.' Andy Cooney, later Chief of Staff in the post-Civil War IRA, who participated in the attack while on holiday from his medical studies in Dublin, was just as critical of the local leadership. McGrath was to claim that the safety of his men had been uppermost in his mind but Gaynor's step-brother, Father Patrick, pointed out that McGrath feared reprisal on his commercial interests.[13]

McGrath was seemingly compromised by his dependence on local businessman and fixer Frank Maloney, who had fallen out with Sinn Féin over a by-election nomination. Father Gaynor further implied that McGrath was unsuited to physical force: he had been chosen because of his prominence on the hurling field and in Gaelic revivalist circles. Seán Gaynor's resignation in protest as Brigade Adjutant after this and McGrath's refusal to permit Ernie O'Malley to proceed with an attack on Rearcross Barracks at the beginning of July forced McGrath's replacement by Gaynor himself. The eventual big attack on Rearcross Barracks again resulted in destruction without capture of arms. A similar story was enacted at Hollyford Barracks in south Tipperary on 11 May 1920 and at Drangan Barracks on the Tipperary/Kilkenny border on 7 June.[14]

The wave of barracks attacks came to an end in the late summer of 1920. Before the establishment of flying columns, they had given the IRA crucial experience under fire. Michael J. Costello recalled, from his Tipperary background, how large numbers of men were used when hardly necessary in order to gain fighting experience for them.[15] The men that mattered — Malone, Treacy, Gaynor, O'Malley — were remarkably few in number.

The switch from raids on police stations to ambushes on police and military convoys and patrols was particularly rapid in Limerick and Tipperary — a reflection of the number of British forces in the area. The formation of the first flying column in East Limerick was a direct consequence of Malone's men being forced to go on the move away from home. Because of limitations in arms and ammunition, the successes were comparatively rare. Many attacks had to be aborted and there were some notable failures. By 1921, the British had become much more adept at avoiding likely ambushes and, under pressure from large-scale sweeps, the IRA was forced to break up its battalion columns, usually consisting of about thirty men, into much smaller units.

On 28 July at Oola, near Limerick Junction, two soldiers were killed and two wounded in an ambush in which General Lucas, who had recently escaped from the IRA, was coincidentally involved. The newly-formed South Tipperary Brigade Column under Dinny Lacey was responsible for two successful ambushes at Thomastown, on the road between Tipperary and Cashel, where six of the British forces were killed, and in the Glen of Aherlow, where four Tans were fatally shot.

On 8 November 1920, an ambush was prepared at Grange, on the main road between Bruff and Limerick. The IRA was anticipating that only two lorries would arrive but was forced to retreat when confronted by eight. Although the attackers had success against the first lorry, Malone admitted that they had somewhat the worse of the overall fight. The opposite occurred in the next major ambush, at Glenacurrane, between Galbally and Mitchelstown, where a much larger British force was expected than actually arrived and was easily overcome. Four of the British forces were killed and several badly wounded. On 3 February 1921 at Dromkeen, near Pallas, in another successful attack, eleven police were killed, some, it was claimed, after surrendering.[16]

One of the worst reverses in the whole war for the IRA happened at Lackelly on 2 May 1921. A mixed bicycle patrol of police and military from Galbally was attacked by a large IRA column. Five IRA men were killed; on the return journey the patrol was ambushed on three further occasions equally unsuccessfully. The whole affair lasted five and a half hours. British sources thought fourteen of their enemy were killed and at least thirty wounded: IRA sources made no attempt to deny the severity of the setback. They had vastly outnumbered the British forces and seemingly had had much in their favour. While a British military source concluded: 'The whole action is a fine example of what a "leader" in command of "soldiers" can do', the IRA Command strove to distribute the blame, citing poor preparation and communication.[17]

North Tipperary was different from many other active areas in that little Intelligence information came from enemy sources. As usual, the main post offices were the crucial source for British movements where sympathisers intercepted mail and eavesdropped on telephone conversations. The formation of flying columns went on simultaneously with the development of the Brigade's administrative efficiency. It was the work of the Black and Tans and the Auxiliaries, however, which did most to stimulate IRA reaction. While a large ambush at Letteragh, between Nenagh and Templemore, in the second half of November 1920 was aborted, on 16 December, at Kilcommon Cross, four British forces were killed and three wounded in a successful attack.

The largest confrontation in the area came on 3 June 1921 at Modreeny, between Borrisokane and Cloughjordan, in which an IRA column of seventeen, divided into three sections, occupied an excellent ambush site and attacked a joint military and police patrol consisting of cyclists, four cars and a military lorry. The British force of forty was far bigger than the thirteen expected. The action was largely successful despite the lorry escaping the encirclement and one of the IRA sections fleeing, feeling outnumbered by the military. Four of the British were killed and fourteen wounded, two rifles were captured and an amount of ammunition. There were no IRA casualties.[18]

While the formation of flying columns initially increased the level of violence, it became difficult in 1921 to sustain any success. The second column formed in South Tipperary, under Seán Hogan, was not involved in any ambushes. One member, in urging a change of leadership, declared that they had something better to do than hang around waiting for suitable targets which never arrived. There was an increasing intolerance of those who issued orders from offices, with particular virulence directed against Seamus Robinson's distant command. By May 1921, the brigade columns were forced to subdivide for safety. In the amount of fighting and the number of incidents, Tipperary and Limerick were amongst the most important of the counties subject to martial law. They provide excellent examples of the successes and limitations of guerrilla warfare in small town/rural settings.[19]

WATERFORD, WEXFORD AND KILKENNY

The war in Cork and Tipperary put the contribution of the neighbouring counties in the shade. The record of Waterford was particularly heavily criticised. There were major difficulties relating to leadership and organisation and the guerrilla action was very much sporadic in nature and often unsuccessful. During 1921 the major energies of the leadership were directed towards gun-running from the Continent, which did not come to fruition until the Truce. Victorious attacks in the county were confined to the end of 1920. On 1 November 1920 the Piltown ambush was staged, and there were simultaneous assaults on the RIC barracks and Marine Station at Ardmore.

At Piltown a British military patrol from Youghal suffered two killed and six wounded with thirty captured. An attack on military reinforcements at Tramore went badly wrong and two IRA men were killed and two wounded. It was alleged that three of the column were drunk and that several rifle shots were fired long before the enemy's arrival. The enquiry into the ambush concluded that such a large-scale operation should not have been attempted because many of the men had never fired a shot before and had 'neither discipline, morale or arms for such a fight, especially night fighting'.[20]

This added to the widespread criticism of Commandant Paddy Paul's leadership of the brigade. Paul was not allowed to forget that he was an ex-British Army soldier and that he had voted for Captain Redmond in the 1918 Waterford City by-election. For his part Paul claimed that he had never wanted the job and 'All I did was to try and make an inactive B'de become active and eliminate those who tried to impede or hold up operations. There was also a certain amount of jealousy to overcome.' Matters came to such a pitch that the Waterford IRA was amalgamated into one brigade in June 1921.

The Divisional Commandant complained that some areas had been completely neglected, including the Lismore Battalion, and concluded that 'Cork can easily push in over 30 riflemen and Machine Guns at any time and in general make it hot for enemy there.' As was to be the case in the Civil War, the Cork IRA were frustrated by their Waterford neighbours. On 29 June, another engagement at Piltown resulted in an IRA section surrendering, and then being court-martialled.[21]

A similar story of disunity and ineffectiveness applied to the North and South Brigades of Wexford. The county did not live up to its strongly republican fighting tradition, a reputation gained in 1798 and to an extent in 1916. Geographical problems were offered as an explanation. Commandant W.J. Brennan-Whitmore, in a handbook on guerrilla tactics published before 1916, wrote that: 'As far as guerilla warfare is concerned, Wexford is a cul-de-sac.' A GHQ report on the North Wexford Brigade on 20 March 1921 said that: 'Wexford . . . must overcome the geographical isolation that was so fatal to its own effort in 1798. For this purpose you must be in close touch with Sth Carlow and through there with Kilkenny: also you must develop your area towards Arklow and be in touch with the men there.'

As in other quiet areas it was concluded that the emphasis should be on harassing the enemy and on breaking British communications. The South Wexford Brigade did not even form a flying column. Men were brought in from Dublin to assassinate RIC targets. It is difficult to identify one major success against the British in the county. Underlying this passivity was the continued support for parliamentarianism and labour in the county, indicating that support for advanced nationalism was far less than in most other areas.[22]

The reputations of the brigades and columns of the IRA in Kilkenny have suffered by comparison with nearby Tipperary. The Seventh Battalion area around Callan was particularly active and frequently linked up with the South Tipperary Brigade. The Hugginstown RIC barracks attack in March 1920 was the third victory of that kind for the IRA. The joint attack on Drangan Barracks in May 1920 lasted seven hours and almost amounted to a pitched battle, with the IRA emerging largely successful. The West Kilkenny Brigade, however, suffered a major reverse when Ernie O'Malley was captured at Inistioge in December 1920. His notebook revealed the names of all the members of the Seventh Battalion and many arrests followed. Ironically, O'Malley had been a harsh critic of slovenly organisation in the county; he never lived down this embarrassment.

Nevertheless, a successful ambush was carried out on a joint military and police patrol on 20 December 1920 at Nine-Mile-House, near the county border between Clonmel and Kilkenny. Two further attacks were carried out on reinforcements from Clonmel and in all eight soldiers were killed and an RIC sergeant, with several wounded, the IRA suffering no casualties. One of the IRA men there, Jackie Brett, had played for the Tipperary football team a month before at Croke Park, on Bloody Sunday.

On 21 February 1921 the IRA carried out a daring ambush in the centre of Kilkenny town, in Friary Street: the attack misfired and two Volunteers were killed and two wounded. On 12 March 1921, the column of the Seventh Brigade was surrounded by British forces at Garryricken House, off the main Kilkenny/Clonmel road, but some managed to shoot their way out, killing one Black and Tan. Following this and other incidents in April, a larger column was formed linking the Seventh Battalion flying column with the Second column of the South Tipperary Brigade, which continued with a little success until the Truce.[23]

14

THE WAR IN KERRY AND CLARE

For all its republican tradition, many observers feel that Kerry made a disappointing contribution to the War of Independence. It was absurd, though, for Eoin O'Duffy to claim in 1933 that: 'Kerry's entire record in the Black and Tan struggle consisted in shooting an unfortunate soldier the day of the Truce.' There were more killings of RIC men in Kerry than in any county outside Dublin and Tipperary. The animosities of the Civil War period distorted judgment of Kerry's role in the preceding conflict. Attacks on the RIC and British reprisals were particularly widespread and brutal in the county. It had one of the highest figures for overall casualties in the conflict, fifteen dead or injured per 10,000 residents, but compared with neighbouring west and north Cork, its guerrilla activity was much less successful.[1]

Kerry claimed the first attack on a police barracks since 1916 at Gortatlea, near Tralee, in April 1918, though it was unsuccessful. In the rest of 1918 and in 1919 raids and attacks on police were few and far between. The transition from barracks attacks to ambushes was swifter in Kerry than in most other counties, and flying columns were formed before the autumn of 1920. The Kerry One flying column on 13 July 1920 killed two constables in an ambush near Dingle. A spate of murderous attacks on RIC men at the end of October and beginning of November 1920, coinciding with Terence MacSwiney's death and funeral, resulted in what became known internationally as 'the Siege of Tralee', a series of reprisals and burnings by the RIC on public buildings and business premises. While talk of famine conditions was an exaggeration, the town was effectively closed for business in the first ten days of November.[2]

At the same time as Hamar Greenwood was ducking questions about the Tralee situation in the Commons, the famous journalist Hugh Martin was being threatened on the streets of Tralee by police. Martin's articles in the *Daily News* had become known for exposing Black and Tan atrocities and these threats only caused Martin to emphasise Tralee's notoriety. He reported that Tralee 'is like a town with the plague. Not a shop is open and people remain behind closed doors and shuttered windows from morning to nightfall. An hour before darkness sets in, women and children leave their homes and go anywhere they can for the night.'[3] The town suffered many more reprisals in the months to come.

The British made matters even worse by false propaganda concerning the so-called 'Battle of Tralee'. A confrontation between the IRA and Black and Tans and Auxiliaries at Ballymacelligott on 12 November in which two IRA men were killed, was blown up by Dublin Castle officials as 'the fiercest and probably the largest-scale of any fight between Crown forces and the Volunteers'. A Pathe Gazette film of the affray which faked a scene, including clear footage of the Vico Road in Dalkey, County Dublin, was easily exposed by the IRA. In the days following, a company of Auxiliaries under Major B.A. McKinnon arrived in Tralee and heightened tensions even further. On Christmas Day 1920 McKinnon led a patrol which shot and killed two men. McKinnon then ordered that their homes be burned.[4]

The first months of 1921 saw an escalation in column activity and increased co-operation with neighbouring Cork brigades, most notably at Clonbannin on 5 March. On 21 March the ambush at Headford Railway Junction, near Killarney, lays claim to being one of the largest single engagements of the whole conflict. IRA columns engaged troops leaving a train from Mallow in a protracted and vicious gun battle. Civilians were caught up in the shooting; three died and several were wounded. Two IRA officers were killed and the number of British casualties, probably at least twenty, has been heavily questioned. Headford was obviously not an unqualified success for the IRA — allowance had not been made for the arrival of another train — but the psychological effect on British morale in the county was considerable.[5]

April 1921 was notable in Kerry for its assassinations. On 14 April Sir Arthur Vicars was killed at his Kilmorna House home in the north of the county, and a day later the loathed Major McKinnon, O/C H Auxiliary Company, was shot dead while putting on the third green of Tralee golf course, which had just increased its fire insurance cover from £786 to £2,900. The popular story that McKinnon died saying 'Burn Ballymac . . .' was no doubt apocryphal. Reprisals and retaliatory killings predictably followed.[6]

Early in May the body of a suspected spy placed on the roadside at Rathmore was used to lure the police to the spot, where eight constables were then killed. On the first day of June, five RIC men were killed at an ambush near Castlemaine and in the last major confrontation of the conflict on 10 July at Castleisland four British soldiers were killed and three wounded. Ironically, amongst the five IRA dead was John Flynn who had participated in the first confrontation in the county at Gortatlea in 1918.[7]

The flat, fertile north of the county was ill-suited to guerrilla warfare but more would have been expected of the mountains and glens of the south and west, and particularly of Tralee, one of the most republican of Ireland's small towns. Kerry is a rare example of a county where the majority of Volunteers at the time of the split in 1914 sided with MacNeill and the provisional committee. These areas were to be the centre of republican resistance in the Civil War. The explanation for the relatively poor performance lies in the personal antipathies and clannish feuding within the IRA and the tense relationship between GHQ and the local commands. Mulcahy had divided Kerry into three brigades in 1918: Kerry One covering the north and the Dingle peninsula, Kerry Two the south and Kerry Three the east. GHQ was never to establish effective communication with them.[8]

As was so often the case, the problems dated back to the Easter Rising. The Kerry Volunteers, and in particular Austin Stack, were heavily criticised for the confusion concerning the projected arms landing at Fenit and for their failure to prevent Casement's arrest. Stack's closest associate in the Tralee area, Paddy Cahill, was the dominant figure in the Volunteers in Tralee and the Dingle peninsula and became Brigadier of the Kerry One Brigade. Cahill was a businessman and owned a local newspaper; he was much older than the majority of IRA men. Denis Daly, an IRA officer in Cahirciveen, commented on Cahill's personal popularity with the poorer classes in Tralee. He owed his position to his local reputation rather than to any military ability. The situation assumed far more than Kerry significance because of Cahill's friendship with Stack and Cathal Brugha. Mulcahy's and Collins' criticism of Cahill and his brigade became associated with the personal tensions and struggles between GHQ and Brugha and Stack in Dublin.

Cahill's control led to charges of cronyism and criticisms of his over-cautious approach. Daly described him as 'a shade careful' and Tadhg Kennedy dismissed him as too old. A wealth of testimony points to Cahill avoiding military confrontation and retiring with his column to a hut, their base, on the Dingle peninsula between Castlemaine and Inch. Little contact was made with GHQ or with neighbouring commands. There was a bitter dispute between Cahill and Tom McEllistrim, the leader in the active Ballymacelligott region, stemming it seems from Cahill's refusal to share out arms and resulting in McEllistrim's men switching allegiance to Kerry Two.[9]

The problems were not confined to Cahill's area. J.J. Rice, later O/C in Kerry Two, recorded that the few key IRB men in Kenmare were determined to avoid physical confrontation. Killorglin had a reputation for being particularly ineffective, as did Listowel. Tom O'Connor said that his brigade column in the south was at last ready for action as the Truce came.[10]

The First and Second Kerry Brigades played no part in the formation of the First Southern Division in the spring of 1921 and were to be heavily criticised by the Division's leadership for organisational failings. Liam Lynch wrote of the Intelligence Officer for Kerry One during the Truce that he 'is grossly incapable of filling the position and his conduct in Tralee town in dealing with enemy was nothing more than laughable'. Lynch went on to say that the

Lixnaw Battalion area 'is simply a mob' and that in the Dingle region 'the enemy had and have a shocking free hand'.[11]

It was only in the first half of 1921 that GHQ felt confident enough to send out two organisers to deal with the problems in Kerry. Andy Cooney was sent down to the south of the county to reorganise Kerry Two. He felt such a mission had been so long delayed that this in itself was a criticism of GHQ. Cooney was obliged to travel under an assumed name to Castleisland and was largely ostracised by IRA members in the area. He was told that IRB membership was crucial for penetrating the intimate, incestuous world of the Kerry Volunteers. Cooney had not been given permission to transfer his IRB status to Kerry. He undertook a complete reorganisation of the brigade, appointing Humphrey Murphy as O/C, and established a flying column, based in the Gap of Dunloe, under Danny Allmann and Tom McEllistrim. This column participated in the Headford Junction attack and joined with the North Cork Brigade for the successful Clonbannin ambush in the spring of 1921.[12]

Cooney was transferred in June 1921 to Kerry One where he faced an even more difficult task. GHQ had suspended Paddy Cahill and the majority of the brigade there had refused to serve under anyone else; Cooney's presence was resented as outside interference. Billy Mullins, QM of Kerry One and an intimate of Cahill, wrote of Cooney: 'I will be charitable and say no more about him other than that all of us known as "Cahill's men" absolutely refused to serve under the new man.' Cooney's stern personality seems to have exacerbated matters: the local Cumann na mBan regarded him as a male chauvinist, with some justification. GHQ had previously attempted to appoint Tadhg Brosnan, the O/C of the active Castlegregory Company, as Cahill's replacement, but Brosnan refused the job. Brosnan was harshly described as a 'very good fighting man but a bit slow perhaps from an educational point of view'.[13]

In June 1921 another GHQ Inspecting Officer had written in the bleakest terms of the Brigade. Battalions had been working independently of each other, there had been no systematic training, hardly 10 per cent of the men could use a rifle and he recommended removal of almost half of the officers. He reported that the Brigade column, based on the Dingle peninsula, had devoted its energies 'to eating, sleeping and general amusements'. He advised that the Brigade HQ be transferred to the north of the county where Cahill's influence was less directly felt. Eventually Cooney was placed in command against his wishes. In retrospect, Cooney thought that GHQ had mishandled the affair and that Cahill's suspension had compounded the problems. A messy compromise was resorted to during the Truce, whereby Cahill was allowed to form his own independent battalion. Given the failure of Kerry to punch at its full weight during the war, it is ironic that the final shots of the conflict were fired on the night of 10/11 July in Castleisland.[14]

CLARE

For many reasons Clare has been one of the counties most strongly associated with the War of Independence. Éamon de Valera was elected MP in the East Clare by-election of 1917 and Michael Brennan is one of the best remembered of IRA leaders. In many respects Clare led the way in militant resistance to the British authorities. Nonetheless, in the uneven, highly localised and limited character of the fighting, the county conformed to developments elsewhere.[15]

The Volunteers in Clare were among the first to reorganise after the Easter Rising: in February 1918 the county was declared a Special Military Area following attacks on the RIC. Attacks on police barracks in Clare began as early as August 1919. Along with Tipperary, Clare was the first county to enforce the police boycott.

Much of the initiative came from the Volunteer company in Meelick, a small village near Limerick; it was led by the three Brennan brothers, Michael, Paddy and Austin. Michael Brennan when aged fifteen in 1911 was sworn into the IRB and used sporting clubs, notably the tug-of-war team, for recruitment purposes. Throughout 1915 he 'practically lived on a bicycle' as he formed companies in lots of villages. He was dismayed by 'the cock-eyed schemes' surrounding Easter 1916. Interned after the Rising and released in December 1916, Brennan used public drilling to reorganise the Volunteers which led to regular bouts of imprisonment and the formation of close ties with other IRA leaders, notably Seán Treacy.[16]

As in south Tipperary, the restructuring of the Volunteers in Clare preceded the formation of a national GHQ and this made any control from Dublin difficult to achieve. In addition to the crucial Volunteer assistance for de Valera's election campaign, one hundred Clare Volunteers travelled to Armagh to help in the by-election there in early 1918. Originally formed as one brigade, the Clare Volunteers were divided into three in 1918: west, mid and east. The change was dictated by the tense relationship between the three key families in the respective sections — the O'Donnells in West Clare, the Barretts in Mid-Clare and the Brennans in East Clare. Hostile relations between the Brennans and the Barretts appear to stem from complaints of men being poached from the Barretts' area. The three brigades never effectively coalesced during the War and when the First Western Division was formed in 1921, Frank Barrett only agreed to serve under Michael Brennan with extreme reluctance.[17]

By 1917, Michael Brennan had become a powerbroker in political as well as military affairs. During the war he was to become the leading figure in local government. From early 1919, Brennan sought to force the pace of the resistance, aware of the fall-off in Volunteer numbers since the conscription crisis, together with the chronic need for arms. His plan for a general onslaught on RIC barracks throughout his brigade area was rejected by Richard Mulcahy, who told Brennan that 'the people had to be educated and led gently into open war.' Following this, Brennan travelled to Dublin to procure arms. His efforts there were resented by Oscar Traynor who felt that Brennan was inter-fering with Dublin Brigade sources. Brennan commented: 'Neither then nor later did I ever succeed in extracting even one rifle from GHQ,' and he was to accuse Collins of favouring Cork in the supply of arms.[18]

The strained relations with GHQ reached new depths when, just before Christmas 1919, Brennan leading a party of twenty Volunteers raided the Limerick GPO and took £1,500. GHQ removed Brennan from his rank as O/C East Clare; he was replaced by his brother Austin but the Brigade was allowed to keep the money. At this time some of the men called for the Brigade to be run independently of Dublin, but Michael Brennan warned of the consequences. Thereafter a kind of stand-off existed between local initiative and central control: the vague outline of GHQ policy was accepted but spontaneous developments on the ground continued to be the rule.[19]

RIC evacuation of police barracks started in the autumn of 1919, earlier than in most other places. This, rather than isolated successful raids on RIC stations, explains the IRA control of rural areas. The most significant and dra-matic events in the county occurred on 22 September 1920 with the killing of R/M Lendrum and the Rineen ambush. Lendrum was travelling to a local assize and stopped at a level crossing which had been closed by Volunteers, near Doonbeg; he drew a revolver and was then shot. It is unclear whether he died at once, but his body was buried secretly in the sands nearby. Father Patrick Gaynor, a local Sinn Féin priest, commented that 'the incident was not to our credit.'

That same day a military patrol was attacked at Rineen, between Miltown Malbay and Ennistymon, by a column led by Seán Liddy. Six British troops were killed and seven wounded but a disappointing amount of eight rifles and sixty rounds of ammunition was all that was gained. Michael Brennan was still firm: 'The be-all and end-all of every proposed operation was arms and ammu-nition, but particularly ammunition.' There was no follow-up and thereafter West Clare was quiet. The immediate aftermath was brutal reprisals in Ennistymon, Lahinch and Miltown Malbay.[20]

The memoirs of Father Gaynor, curate at Mullagh, record how quiet west Clare was during much of the war. Gaynor was republican police chief for the area and a member of the Sinn Féin Supreme Executive; his colleague, Father Michael McKenna, was commandant of the local Volunteers. Far from record-ing an account of terror in the region, Gaynor recalled that 'gaiety was the order of the day — and of the night' in their house where Ignatius O'Neill, the local IRA leader, and other Volunteers enjoyed their generous hospitality. Of the fighting, Gaynor said that there was 'little glamour' and outside a limited number of places 'little heroism' . He wrote: 'Apart from the well armed flying columns very few men ever fired a shot in the Sinn Féin War.'

Gaynor put much of this down to the failures of the local leadership in his area. He concluded: 'Seán Liddy, whom I really liked, had plenty of courage, but had ill-luck when he planned an operation. He would have been an ideal adjutant, but as a brigadier, he did not inspire the confidence and enthusiasm which would have been needed among his badly armed and untrained followers, in order to make them an efficient fighting force. A few successes might have given him the repute which Michael Brennan had in East Clare, but the chance did not come his way. He had to reckon too with a survival of the clan spirit which is more noticeable in Corcabaiscinn than in other parts of the county and which led many of the Volunteers to take sides in local feuds. Then again, he had no organised Flying Column to harass the enemy.'[21]

Gaynor's cool, critical view of the IRA in the north-west of the county is mirrored by the testimony of the old American soldier turned IRA leader, Bill Haugh, in the south-west. Haugh talked of the 'miserable fiasco' of one ambush and physically assaulted one of his men who had fired precipitately during the IRA occupation of Kilrush in the spring of 1921. In a desperate attempt to stimulate action, Seán Liddy had asked Michael Brennan to bring his column to the west, where partially successful attempts were made to attack the occupants of the Kilrush coastguard station and police barracks.[22]

Between November 1920 and June 1921 the Mid Clare Brigade attempted 144 ambushes, 130 of which did not even result in any sight of the enemy. Michael Brennan recalled that a number of traps were laid near Tulla, on the Scariff/Killaloe road, but the enemy failed to appear. He concluded: 'As our armament usually consisted of two rifles, four shotguns and revolvers, it may have been just as well.' Successful attacks as at Glenwood, between Sixmilebridge and Broadfoot, in which a D/I and five of his men were killed, two wounded and ten rifles captured, were rare. The Chief of Staff was particularly critical of the Mid Clare Brigade, saying that their activities 'indicate the absence of practically any military intelligence or technique . . . it shows constant watching for the Enemy in a district in which there is almost daily activity on the part of the latter, yet contact with the Enemy is only established on three days in the month.' The conclusion was that checks should be imposed to ensure that the best men surfaced as officers.[23]

After a promising start to the war, Clare proved something of a disappointment to GHQ. A report just before the Truce on the West Clare Brigade declared that: 'I found West Clare to be a district of great possibilities, there are fine men, very few capable Officers and practically no arms . . . the O/C 1st Battalion is entirely inefficient and should be scrapped immediately. The 5th Battalion should be wiped out and a few of the alleged Officers shot if possible.'[24]

15

THE WAR IN THE WEST AND NORTH-WEST COUNTIES

The western and north-western counties, with the partial exception of Mayo and Sligo, saw very little action during the war. In Galway and Donegal especially, it was very difficult to distinguish agrarian disorder from politically motivated actions, and Leitrim and Roscommon were heavily criticised by GHQ for their failure to organise. The moderate amount of fighting in Sligo contrasted with the intense conflict there in the early stages of the forthcoming Civil War. Only near the end of the War of Independence did Mayo, and then mainly the western part of the county, stage ambushes. The concentration in much of the writing about the conflict in the Westport and Castlebar areas reflects the number of local veterans making available their accounts, as well as the fact that that region suffered the most casualties. The later dominance of the Fourth Western Division by West Mayo men also helps to explain this. To talk of the west awakening in 1921 was decidedly premature.[1]

MAYO

Mayo has a long nationalist tradition. The county had seen a high degree of United Irish League organisation in the early years of the century, and a division between the Ancient Order of Hibernians and the more radical American Alliance. Castlebar Urban District Council controversially criticised the Easter Rising. Ned Moane, the adjutant of the Westport Battalion IRA, said that Westport men never forgave Castlebar for surrendering arms in 1916. While this accusation is unproven, the Castlebar Council was to be heavily criticised for passing a resolution condemning the Rising. Divisions between the small towns of the west of the county were to remain a continuing theme in the history of the Volunteers there.

The Volunteers in East Mayo had been first organised during 1917 by Sean Corcoran, O/C of the Swinford Battalion. The fact that few of the local leaders were arrested after the Rising, and thus missed out on the bonding and networking experienced by other areas, may go some way to explaining the slowness of Volunteer development after May 1917. Matters were further hindered by a split, dating back to the time of Parnell's fall, between activists in Swinford and Meelick. The region was, however, particularly involved in the early organisation of republican courts from May 1920. A major row within the local IRA occurred in 1920 when the Brigade's Vice O/C Tom Ruane refused to obey Corcoran's order to return petrol he had stolen. Ruane was dismissed following a courtmartial. Tom Carney commented: 'Both sides went on the run with a greater hatred of each other than they had of the Tans. Then there was an official and an unofficial gang on the run and nothing happened in the Brigade as a result.' On 22 August 1920 a column under Sean Corcoran and Sean Walsh, the Captain of the Bohala Company, captured Ballyvarey Barracks with arms and ammunition. This was the only occupied police barracks taken in the whole county. The East Mayo Brigade was formed in September 1920. Major divisions continued to plague the organisation for the rest of the conflict. Corcoran was killed on 1 April 1921 near Ballyhaunis. The area saw no successful completion during 1921 of plans for barrack attacks and ambushes.

Activity in North Mayo was similarly patchy. In July 1920, RIC patrols were twice ambushed in Ballina, with one RIC man killed in the attack on the 29th and one wounded. Ballina men participated in August in the capture and burning of the coastguard station in Enniscrone, County Sligo. In the months following, the area was a special target of RIC and military raids. In November numerous local leaders, including Tom Ruane, the Company Captain, were arrested in Ballina. On 23 June 1921 a column waiting to attack a patrol from Ballycastle was itself attacked by British forces from three directions. Seven of the column were captured and one killed. The column was struggling to reorganise itself at the time of the Truce.

At the end of March, the resident magistrate J.C. Milling was shot dead in Westport while putting his clock forward to British Summertime. This was probably carried out by the 'young Turks' in the IRB and meant to pressurise senior Volunteer officers to initiate action in West Mayo. The secrecy concerning the incident both at the time and since seems to confirm the impression of IRB involvement. Immediately the region was declared a Special Military Area. Despite this, Mayo did not join in the wave of barracks attacks and became a frequent butt of GHQ criticism; the level of organisation up to mid-1920 was way behind that in Munster.

The success of republican courts in Mayo, the Sinn Féin triumph in the local government elections in the summer of 1920 and the arrival of the Black and Tans and Auxiliaries provoked a reorganisation of the Volunteers in late 1920. In September 1920 a GHQ organiser journeyed to Castlebar and split Mayo into four separate brigades: north, south, east and west. Soon a change in leadership emerged in the localities with the rise of a younger element not afraid of physical force. In the Western Brigade, Tom Ketterick replaced a previously inactive Quartermaster-General and became legendary for getting and retaining arms supplies. Local businessmen in Westport supplied the funds for the war material.[2]

In January 1921, Tom Derrig, who had been a part-time O/C of the West Brigade while retaining his teaching job in Ballina, was arrested and replaced by the much more active Michael Kilroy from Newport, a puritanical and ascetic blacksmith. Sixteen-year-old Tommy Heavey commented that he was sick of sitting around doing nothing and in the spring of 1921 was reprimanded for extra-curricular shooting activities. By that time the Brigade leadership had considerable problems enforcing discipline and soon the impatience of the younger set stimulated action. The establishment of small flying columns based on the main towns had had little effect and it was only when the larger Brigade column was formed that meaningful activities ensued.[3]

The West Mayo Brigade's confrontations with British forces had mixed results. After a short exchange of fire near Carrowkennedy in April, a major ambush laid on 6 May at the Big Wall at Islandeady, between Westport and Castlebar, went horribly wrong. While Westport and Castlebar units waited for a party of RIC to arrive, the British patrol turned off the main road in search of Michael Staunton, a Sinn Féin officer and a republican court judge, and then returned to Castlebar, surprising a unit who were cutting the road. Two of the IRA were killed and two captured. One man in the main ambush party was shot dead later in a separate incident.[4] The major setback, however, occurred at Kilmeena, between Newport and Westport, on 19 May 1921.

This was meant to be the first large-scale attack on British forces in the area. On 18 May two small units attacked police in Westport and Newport as a means of luring the British from their well-defended garrison. One RIC sergeant was killed in Newport. The next day forty-one IRA men took up their position at Kilmeena and commenced a long wait. After two false alarms Kilroy was about to disperse the column when the British patrol of one Ford car and two Crossley tenders came in sight. The first lorry burst through the ambush position and the other vehicles stopped and counter-attacked, using a Lewis gun. During a two-hour fight, five IRA men were killed at the time, including Seamus MacEvilly, clerk of the District Court, and Paddy Jordan, Vice-Commandant of the Castlebar Battalion, who was wounded and died later. Seven others were injured. A desperate retreat followed northwards across the mountains, carrying some of the wounded to Skerdagh, where there were safe houses. The column included Dr John A. Madden, probably the only qualified doctor to serve in a column during the war. He tended the wounded at Skerdagh. The British tracked them there and in a brief affray killed another Volunteer.

Back in Westport, both dead and wounded were thrown onto the street, which cruel and callous action aroused the ire even of the Marquis of Sligo. At the funeral of Seamus MacEvilly in Castlebar, a British officer forbade mourners to drape the coffin in the tricolour, and ordered the removal of a wreath of national flowers shaped in a cross. Only twelve of the relatives were allowed to attend, including two brothers of Seamus from other brigades, Jerry from Cork Two Brigade and Tom from the Sligo Brigade.

Ernie O'Malley recalled how reluctant Mayo IRA veterans were to talk about Kilmeena over twenty years later. There was talk of some men fleeing from the action and there had been an appalling failure to block the road. Many criticised the Westport men's non appearance. The retrospective criticism was related to the fact that the Westport men's leader, Joe Ring, was later, in contrast to the vast majority of the West Mayo men, to take the pro-Treaty side in the Civil War. There was also a general feeling that the ambush site had been badly chosen. It seems that Kilroy had been under strong pressure from GHQ to take action which would compensate for a string of failed ambushes. The British were left to praise the successful application of their new methods to counter guerrilla warfare.[5] The horror of Kilmeena was soon to be avenged in the largest engagement during the War in the west at Carrowkennedy, on the Westport/Leenane road, on 3 June. An IRA column of twenty-five, divided into small sections, killed six of the British forces, including the local D/I RIC, and captured a Lewis gun, eighteen rifles and a great amount of ammunition. A massive sweep of the whole area from Connemara to North Mayo followed, involving a sea blockade and planes, which captured nobody.[6]

1921 also saw the first significant action in south Mayo. A British patrol was attacked and surrendered on 7 March on the road between Ballinrobe and Castlebar at Kilfall. On 3 May Tom Maguire's South Mayo column ambushed a patrol supplying the isolated police barracks at Derrypark. This was a rare example of an attack taking place in the centre of a village, Tourmakeady, in which five of the British forces were killed. A large round-up followed as the column retreated — 600 Crown forces from Galway, Claremorris and Ballinrobe to the south, Castlebar to the north, and Westport to the west. Maguire was wounded during a gunfight in the Partry Hills, and his adjutant, Michael O'Brien, was killed. Lieutenant Ibberson who led the pursuit was also wounded. The rest of the column escaped in the darkness and managed to smuggle Maguire away with them. The West Mayo Brigade had arrived too late to help in the ambush.

Richard Mulcahy overreacted to the success of Tourmakeady by saying that it 'helps to confirm us more and more in the conviction that . . . we have the intelligence and the courage and the military skill to bring the present struggle to very definite victory'. Nonetheless, he warned against any further long-drawn-out engagements and concluded, in terms reminiscent of his reaction to planned operations in Cork and Clare in 1919: 'What we want at the moment is to harass the enemy as much as possible, while providing our own forces with just sufficient activity to get them used to active service and to let them gain confidence in themselves and get the best possible use out of their weapons.'[7]

Just before the Truce Mulcahy commented: 'It has not been established who the Brigade Commandant in North Mayo actually is.' A GHQ report on east Mayo in August 1921 talks of only one man attempting to carry out 'active operations' and of there being 'very few arms and very little ammunition'. The reputation of Mayo as a fighting county rests properly with the west, and even there local and personal animosity limited the effectiveness of the IRA.[8]

SLIGO

As was true of the other Connacht counties, Sligo saw a moderate degree of military action in the conflict. Only nineteen deaths can be attributed to the war. Of these fourteen were RIC and three British military; one IRA man was killed and one alleged spy. These figures lag appreciably behind those in Mayo and Clare. In early 1919, 1.2 per cent Catholic males in the county were members of the IRA, compared with 2.6 per cent in Mayo and Tipperary: by late 1920 the figure had risen to 4.7 per cent but dropped in 1921. This corresponds with the fact that the huge majority of military incidents in the county took place in the second half of 1920. The Sligo Brigades had particularly low armament resources and were slow to organise flying columns. This late development is a major reason for the lack of activity: by mid-1920 it was much more difficult to stage arms raids than it had been earlier.[9]

The first capture of an RIC barracks in Sligo did not take place until June 1920, and the first successful ambush on 26 July at Ballyrush was on the soft target of an RIC cycling patrol. A month later, West Sligo companies joined with the North Mayo Brigade to destroy Enniscrone coastguard station. After the dramatic escape from Sligo Gaol of Frank Carty, the O/C in the south of the county, the area round Tubbercurry hit national headlines after a series of attacks. A patrol which included the new D/I, Brady, was attacked at Chaffpool, about three miles from Tubbercurry. Brady died and two other RIC men were wounded. Carty's plans to protect the town from reprisals were described by an IRA veteran as 'a complete fiasco' and Jack Brennan, of the local company, commented that 'this wasn't good for our reputation.'[10]

The best-remembered ambush in Sligo took place on 25 October 1920 at Moneygold, on the main road between Grange and Cliffony. Three RIC were killed, three wounded and arms and ammunition taken. One of the ambush party immediately went on to fulfil his duty of ringing the church bells in Grange. This attack was particularly notable for its postscript: the captured arms were intercepted en route to the south of the county by the British, who had been tipped off, at Lough Gill. Linda Kearns, the IRA car driver, was taken prisoner, together with three leading IRA men who were subsequently beaten up, Seamus Devins, Andrew Conway and Eugene Gilbride. Kearns had been since 1916 a key figure in Collins' communication network with the west and had been regularly transferring arms between the various columns. She was sentenced to ten years, remaining in prison until after the Truce. The incident caused a sharp downturn in morale and organisation was slow to recover in north Sligo.[11]

In contrast to west Mayo, there was a dropping off in major incidents in 1921. The only successful ambush occurred at Culleens on 1 June when two

RIC men were captured and shot dead. *The Irish Bulletin* falsely claimed that these men were killed in action. Throughout the first half of 1921, GHQ in Dublin was berating the Sligo IRA, and particularly Liam Pilkington its O/C, for failures in organisation and lack of action. In response Pilkington pleaded their shortage of arms. It appears that he staged an attack on Collooney police barracks in March, which failed disastrously, as an attempt to prove his worth.

Eventually Pilkington was forced to write to Mulcahy: 'My faults, my short-comings, my incapacities, you have emphasised and depicted very vividly and admittedly correctly . . . for the future all that can possibly be done to remedy and put right my many faults as O/C of this area I shall do. Concluding, with the hope that our future dealings will be productive of the more successful prosecution of the war in the North West.' Because of later Civil War animosi-ties, Pilkington's inadequacies were probably exaggerated. The Sligo IRA was to be famous only for Carty's various jail escapes.[12]

GALWAY

County Galway took little significant part in either the War of Independence or the Civil War. This can mostly be explained by the remoteness and poverty of the area and its sparse and widely scattered population. The poorest of farmers and fishermen were rarely IRA members, as was true in west Cork and west Clare. Peter Joe McDonnell (Petie Joe), a Leenane coach builder and the leader of the West Connemara IRA, argued that the bleak, bare and unfenced land offered no cover for ambushes and pointed out that British patrols care-fully avoided the Kylemore Pass, between Leenane and Clifden, the one likely spot in the area.

The Connemara Volunteers had a chronic lack of arms and ammunition and suffered badly from emigration. The membership consisted entirely of labourers, cottiers and tradesmen. McDonnell recorded that at the time of the formation of the brigade column in early 1921 none of them, except for the QM and himself, had ever fired a rifle. Pikes had been used for training. The column could only be formed when a small amount of arms and ammunition was supplied from Dublin.[13]

The county remained as one IRA brigade until mid-1920, when it was re-organised by Mulcahy, the last one to be divided up. Ernie O'Malley com-mented that Galway's size made it very difficult to administer, but the situation was made infinitely worse by the excesses of local particularism.[14]

In Galway city, the British army HQ in the west, the only physical force ini-tiatives appear to have been taken by the University Battalion. They were rep-rimanded for their independent action by the local brigadier whom Mulcahy described as averse to fighting. In Connemara rival battalions clashed with each other. Peter Joe McDonnell was reluctant to accept his appointment by Mulcahy as O/C of the new West Galway Brigade because of local differences. Mulcahy had stressed that he wanted teachers and Gaelic League organisers to retire from IRA leadership.[15]

The West Connemara column staged an attack on Clifden on the night of 16 March 1921, in which two RIC men were killed and one Volunteer ran away from the action. While buildings in Clifden were set ablaze by the police as a reprisal, the column retreated to the Maam valley where an attack was repelled at Munterowen and an ambush at Screebe spoilt by premature firing. On receiving reports of this action, a GHQ officer commented: 'They show a decided improvement on the part of a few of our officers in the west. I think this man (McDonnell) deserves the greatest credit and we should do something to help him in his attempt to get the men in Galway fighting.' McDonnell concluded: 'Every man on the column was anxious to have a really good fight and justify our existence as a fighting unit.'

By the final stages of the War, it was clear that the Connemara IRA's most useful work would be in association with West Mayo. McDonnell's men played a key role in the successful ambush at Carrowkennedy in June 1921 by destroying communications. Before that, at the height of the conflict in West Mayo, McDonnell had travelled to the Newport area to wed Michael Kilroy's sister, Matilda. Both the groom and his best man and QM John Feehan carried grenades and ammunition during the ceremony. At the end of the War the column had less than two hundred rounds of ammunition for its twelve rifles.[16]

In the north of the county, the O/C of the Tuam Brigade complained in June 1921 that they had six ambushes prepared but the British 'would not come out'. He attributed blame to the flatness of the countryside and the impossibility of holding a position for longer than two days without the enemy hearing of it. The chronic shortage of arms and ammunition applied as always. During the Truce, the O/C of the South-east Galway Brigade reported that not more than 120 of his men knew how to use a rifle.[17]

In the spring of 1921, Michael Brennan saw the necessity of reorganising the south of Galway as a means of taking the pressure off his Clare Brigade. A member of his East Clare column, James Hogan, future leading Free State Army officer and professor of history at University College, Cork, said of this area: 'Although there were active individuals and small groups, these parts of the country — one of the most disturbed parts of Ireland — as, for example, Craughwell was on the eve of 1914 — were now dormant.'

A number of Galway men had approached Brennan complaining of the collapse of the Volunteer organisation there and begging for his column to visit their area. Brennan had the most damning views of the Galway leadership and appointed a new brigade staff. Of the Galway city leadership, Brennan commented: 'No responsible City would put some of these alleged Officers in charge of a dust-bin.' He found the South West Galway Brigade 'by far and away the toughest proposition in practically the whole West'. It was the assistance from Clare which was responsible for a dramatic ambush at Ballyturin House, near Gort, on 15 May 1921. D/I Blake, his wife and two soldiers were shot dead returning with friends from a tennis party at the very gates of the estate.[18] Despite the general inactivity there were some headline-making events in

Galway. On 1 November 1920, the day of Kevin Barry's execution, Black and Tans shot Mrs Ellen Quinn dead as she sat on a wall in Kiltartan cradling her child; the police were driving around the village firing wildly. The small town of Tuam was sacked in July and September 1920. In November a local priest and Sinn Féin sympathiser, Father Michael Griffin, was killed by the Black and Tans and found in a bog near Barna. Afterwards, the body of an informer was discovered, following his execution by IRA men. The mystery surrounding these events is symptomatic of the internecine feuding endemic in this region.[19]

DONEGAL

Out in the north-west, the Donegal IRA had to contend with many difficulties. Geographically, the county is remote and all but cut off from the rest of the twenty-six counties. Its natural urban centre should be Derry, from which it was separated by the Government of Ireland Act halfway through the conflict in 1920. There was inevitably much confusion as to the western or northern relevance of IRA actions in Donegal.

The poverty-stricken barren countryside and the perennial loss of a high proportion of the youth to Scotland crop-picking made recruitment and training extremely problematic. The O/C of the First Northern Brigade reported that 'difficulties are arising . . . through most of (his) best officers and men having notified him that they are migrating to Scotland. You are probably aware that up here the holdings are all uneconomic and every year the young men migrate to the mines and other works in Scotland while the older men and young boys and girls go to the potato digging in the same country. The end of summer and all the autumn is for us a bad time of the year as during that period the numbers of the organisation are very small and generally the best men are absent.'[20]

The survival of acute land grievances meant that IRA and Sinn Féin members did not support the conservative work of the Dáil courts and so republican unity between the county and Dublin was never fully achieved. On top of all this was the sheer size of the county, together with the great sectarian and cultural differences between the Gaelic-speaking Catholic west and the mixture of Protestant and Catholic in the east.

Despite these seemingly insuperable problems, small columns were formed in the county in 1921 and small-scale ambushes attempted. The redoubtable Peadar O'Donnell, later to fictionalise his war experiences, set up a column in the Bogside in Derry and led them to his native Rosses. They linked up with a column led by Joe Sweeney in the east of the county to attack troop trains; O'Donnell's column in March killed an RIC man while attacking Falcarragh police barracks. O'Donnell's independent attempts to stage attacks on British forces in Derry were frowned upon by the rest of the county leadership and there were acute problems of geographical demarcation between each column.

In the spring of 1921 a thousand British troops launched an offensive against the Donegal IRA, perhaps overestimating their potential threat, and

GHQ set up the First Northern Division in recognition of the special problems in that region. The Divisional Commander Frank Carney soon had a major row with O'Donnell before being arrested and imprisoned in May. Liam Archer was sent by GHQ to examine the poor relations between the senior commanders in the county. On the basis of his report, Collins kept O'Donnell as Brigade O/C but ruled that he should not operate in Derry. Internecine tensions in Donegal, therefore, long preceded the Treaty.[21]

16

THE IRISH MIDLANDS, SOME SURROUNDING COUNTIES AND IRA ACTIVITY IN BRITAIN

Encircled by inactive areas in the Irish Midlands, Longford appears like a lonely outpost in the struggle for Irish independence. When the Longford IRA leader Seán MacEoin was arrested in the spring of 1921, Liam Lynch commented 'Cork will be fighting alone now.'[1] However, the fighting fame of the county only applied to its northern half: the south saw comparatively little activity and was far less organised. Even in the north, Longford town lived up to its garrison reputation, and virtually all the fabled IRA activity centred on the village of Ballinalee, the home of both Seán MacEoin and Seán Connolly. The majority of the fighting in the county was limited to a period between the autumn of 1920 and the following spring: there was a sudden falling off after MacEoin's arrest and Connolly's death, which underlines the significance of individuals.

Longford's important role in the War relates to its swift mobilisation in 1917. Various factors were at play here. Firstly the Longford by-election in 1917 attracted a wealth of support from Volunteers throughout the country. Subsequently, a significant proportion of the 406 military service pension applicants stated that they joined the Volunteers in April, during the election campaign. Michael Collins and Harry Boland now began their special relationship with the county through their rivalrous courting of Kitty Kiernan, who lived in Granard. At this early time MacEoin and Connolly surfaced as effective and popular leaders.

MacEoin had inherited the local blacksmith's business from his father and was prevailed upon by Collins to become a full-time Volunteer. Connolly came from a small farmer background, linked through his antecedents with the

United Irish movement. An amateur engineer and keen hurler, Connolly was popular and intensely practical. MacEoin and Connolly were IRB men with close links to Dublin and thus developed excellent relations with GHQ. At the time of the Volunteer split in 1914, all ten men who formed the Irish Volunteers in the county were IRB members. Nothing demonstrates better the personal and institutional closeness than the desperate efforts made by Collins to rescue MacEoin from Mountjoy in 1921.[2]

In April 1919 a failed attempt to disarm two RIC constables at Aughnacliffe, resulting in the wounding of two Volunteers, stimulated Volunteer organisation. Longford was one of the first counties to stage a GHQ-approved attack on an RIC barracks, which failed due to non-detonation of bombs, at Drumlish on 6 January 1920. After the burning of evacuated RIC posts in April 1920, an attack in June forced the abandonment of Ballinamuck police station. On 18 August, MacEoin and Connolly led a daring raid for arms on the Upper Military Barracks in Longford town, with the help of Jordy, an army deserter who provided inside information. Soon after, Connolly at the head of his men raided the Ballymahon Barracks capturing ten rifles, four revolvers and twelve grenades with ammunition. The foundations had been well laid for more dramatic deeds in the following months.[3]

The British counter-offensive, stemming from The Restoration of Order in Ireland Act, served to reduce Volunteer activity in Longford as Black and Tans and Auxiliaries were heavily deployed. The situation abruptly changed at the end of October with the assassination of two RIC men. On 31 October the new D/I, Kelleher, was shot dead in the bar of the Greville Arms in Granard, while drinking with republicans. The next day an RIC constable called Cooney, notorious for cross-dressing, was killed between Ballinalee and Granard. GHQ ordered both shootings, it seems as a response to Terence MacSwiney's death. After initial opposition from MacEoin's flying column, the Black and Tans set fire to much of Granard.[4]

Following this, MacEoin staged a dramatic defence of Ballinalee against superior British forces: a convoy of eleven lorries retreated when surrounded by sections of MacEoin's column. Virtually all the villagers left before the shooting began. The British forces fought for two and a half hours, under the impression that they were engaging a much larger number of Volunteers than was actually the case, and then retreated, just when the IRA units were running out of ammunition. MacEoin had to admit that luck had been on their side, and criticised the inept performance of one of his sections.

In the early morning, a whole array of material looted from Granard by the British was found littering the roads, including a melodeon, bottles of whiskey and provisions. The defence of the village continued for over a week before the column moved out. Subsequently they continued to harry for some months the British forces who had occupied some of the buildings and had burnt out the Connolly family home. In January 1921, MacEoin shot dead D/I McGrath while escaping from a cottage in the village which his mother was visiting.

With the enormous British pressure on the small towns of north Longford, attempts were made to spread the conflict to the south of the county. The column's projected ambush at Terlicken, near Ballymahon, failed, again due to faulty armaments.[5]

While the Longford IRA was forced to concentrate on smaller actions for most of 1921, on 1 February it had its greatest triumph. At Clonfin, on the road between Granard and Ballinalee, eighteen Auxiliaries in two Crossley tenders were ambushed. A mine exploded under the first lorry, killing the driver instantly, and a two-hour gun battle with the occupants of the second lorry ensued before the British surrendered. Four Auxiliaries were killed and eight wounded, and eighteen rifles, twenty revolvers, a Lewis gun and a substantial amount of ammunition captured. While the British had to acknowledge that the ambush site had been skilfully chosen, MacEoin was concerned that insufficient cover had allowed an Auxiliary to escape and summon help. MacEoin was later to be applauded by the British authorities for allowing the wounded medical treatment despite the fear that reinforcements were imminent. In 1954, T.J. Wilford, one of the Auxiliaries ambushed at Clonfin, revisited the site and sent MacEoin his account of the event, emphasising MacEoin's chivalry.[6]

At the beginning of March, MacEoin was arrested at Mullingar railway station and charged with the murder of D/I McGrath. Connolly was immediately recalled to the county from his work in Leitrim, but was killed in an ambush before he could leave. From then on, little was achieved in the county by the IRA. This can partly be explained by intense British military sweeping tactics but was also due to tensions within the Brigade resulting from the new leadership and from shortage of arms. In June 1921, in a protracted correspondence with the Longford leadership about the taking of hostages as an insurance against the likelihood of MacEoin's execution, Mulcahy commented: 'Longford is frightfully unsatisfactory now. There is an indefiniteness about it that is absolutely appalling.'[7]

ROSCOMMON AND LEITRIM

By late 1920, GHQ regarded the neighbouring counties of Roscommon and Leitrim as problem cases. Collins commented: 'There are a lot of good lads in Roscommon but there is nobody to lead them.' Frank Davis of the Longford Brigade 'found South Leitrim terrible' and Tom Reilly described his county as full of Ancient Order of Hibernians (AOH) men and Orangemen. Some of the problems were put down to the failings of the local leadership while others drew attention to the flatness of the North Roscommon countryside. Nonetheless a successful ambush was staged on 12 October 1920 at Ballinderry, where four RIC men were killed.[8]

With a view to taking the pressure off North Longford, Seán Connolly was sent in the autumn to Roscommon and then to Leitrim to reorganise the Volunteers there and to initiate actions. In effect, Connolly was a GHQ organiser and did not take over the headship of the Brigade. He was particularly keen to root out poteen distilleries on the hilly borders of the counties. Connolly instructed the Roscommon men on how to make and use mines but had little success in sundry attacks on police barracks. He was transferred to Leitrim in February 1921, having been warned by Collins that it was the most treacherous county in Ireland. It was reported that Mitchell, the brigadier in Leitrim, 'was neither active in mind nor in intention, nor would he normally go out of his way to look for fight'. Connolly was killed together with five others at Selton Hill, near Mohill, on 11 March 1921 when the location of his column was given away by a local Orangeman and doctor.[9]

A fortnight later, on 23 March, the South Roscommon flying column brought off its most successful action at Scramogue, on the Strokestown/Longford road, at a site Connolly had suggested. A joint military and police patrol travelling in a Crossley tender was ambushed. One army officer and the police driver were killed at the time and one constable died later from wounds. In addition, two Black and Tans were captured and executed after the fighting and all arms and ammunition, including a Hotchkiss gun, taken. GHQ could reflect that major successes could be achieved in hitherto backward areas and the British authorities were left to question why a lorry had travelled unescorted.[10]

WESTMEATH AND MEATH

Both these counties conform to the pattern in the Irish Midlands of intermittent and extremely small-scale military action. In 1921 GHQ saw their role primarily as hindering British communications to the west by blocking roads and interfering with transport. Even in such a superficially quiet area, the Black and Tan and Auxiliary presence resulted in burnings and lootings, most notably in Trim in late September 1920. There were no major attacks on police barracks in Westmeath, the historian of the conflict in that area writing that 'while some men were willing to act, they did not like the fight to be near their own houses.'[11] The flat terrain was unsuited to ambushes. Athlone, the only sizeable town in Westmeath, was dominated by the British garrison.

Seamus Finn, a leading Volunteer in Meath, testified that 'at no time were we . . . in possession of sufficient arms, ammunition or other war materials to engage any large sized force of the enemy . . . I have known men go into ambush positions with shotguns and cartridges packed with buckshot and crude home-made grenades.' During three years in the Navan Company of the IRA, Bobby Byrne only once handled a gun. When the Brigade O/C Seán Boylan transmitted GHQ's instructions for ambushes to be carried out in all battalion areas, some refused on the grounds of insufficient arms and were then court-martialled.

Six men were killed as spies in the county between 1919 and 1921 in contrast to the three IRA men killed in action or by mistake; three police fatalities, including again one accidental killing, and no military deaths point to the general lack of action. Peter O'Connell, one of the Meath Volunteers, commented 'just because we were an army didn't mean we had to go round shooting people all the time. We could get our way by other means. We didn't want to kill anyone.'[12]

KILDARE, CARLOW, WICKLOW, OFFALY (KING'S COUNTY) AND LAOIS (QUEEN'S COUNTY)

A letter from the IRA Chief of Staff to the O/C First Eastern Division at the end of April 1921 emphasised the importance of his region in suppressing the British forces. 'Very many times' he commented, 'the military domination of Ireland has turned on the results of battles fought in this region. Its importance is no less today than at any earlier time.' He thought, however, that the emphasis should be less on military confrontation than on containing the enemy by the destruction of communications. He argued: 'The underlying strategic idea of all operations in this area would be to hem back the Enemy against the Wicklow Mountains, the hostile city of Dublin and the sea . . . in Dublin — Curragh region English have permanently quartered between ⅓ and ½ of their total armed strength in Ireland, and all their vital lines of communication have to pass through the narrow bottle-neck between Celbridge and Brittas. This is a sufficient reason to bring all possible pressure to bear on them in the area — despite poor quality of units immediately available there.'

The implication was that this area had under-performed up to that time in the crucial disruption of communications, the activity to which it was best suited. The containment policy was never fully acted upon and it is obvious that it had never been explained adequately to the actual fighting units concerned.

Accounts of the conflict in these counties adopt an almost apologetic air as excuses are sought for their minimal involvement. Wicklow and Carlow had a distinguished 1798 republican pedigree and the former appears topographically well-suited to guerrilla warfare, with its rolling hills and deep glens. Andie MacDonnell remembered saying to a colleague: 'Wicklow will never be any good until we burn the town of Wicklow and blame it on the Tans, then the bastards will fight there.' A historian of Carlow in that period commented that it 'does not have a very active fighting story. This may sometimes have been alluded to by way of implied reproach.' The usual alibis were trotted out, the Brigade-Adjutant writing: 'The changing state of organisation, the lack of rifles and ammunition, and the state of the terrain over half the brigade area made the selection of activities very limited.'

Both Carlow and Kildare were reasonably prosperous with easy access to Dublin; the southern plain of Kildare was dominated by the Curragh Camp, the foremost British military centre outside the capital. As late as April 1921, GHQ was warning Kildare units against becoming involved in confrontation with the enemy before the necessary training had been undergone. There appear to have been no more than twenty-five rifles in the Carlow Brigade early in 1921. A rare attempt at an ambush by the belatedly-organised flying column at Mullinaglown on 9 April 1921 resulted in the capture of the O/C.

The Kildare flying column at the end of 1920 operated mostly in the county of Wicklow and two of the West Wicklow companies transferred to the South Dublin Brigade. Lar Brady, the IRA leader in Laois, became noted in republican circles for his determination to avoid military confrontation. He theorized that IRA sections from North Tipperary should strike there and retreat into Offaly, and that Offaly men strike at home and then retreat into Laois; it seems that these ideas never bore fruit.[13]

Offaly saw more action but on a small scale: for instance, two RIC constables were killed at Kinnity on 19 May 1921. The Offaly Second Brigade in 1921 came under particularly heavy criticism from GHQ. In April, Mulcahy commented: 'Unless each individual officer in Offaly No 2 shows that he appreciates his responsibilities he shall have to go,' and in July a report said that the 'enemy has contempt for the Brigade in general'.[14]

FINGAL

The Fingal area, north of Dublin City, was particularly heavily criticised by GHQ for its lack of activity and poor organisation. In September 1920 this area had seen the most notorious of reprisals at Balbriggan after Head Constable Peter Burke was killed in a pub. Two Sinn Féin sympathisers were shot dead by the Black and Tans in retaliation, and then Balbriggan itself was systematically sacked. The international publicity which followed this, together with the military and police presence in a place so close to the capital, may well have militated against further IRA hostilities. The last thing the local population needed as they rebuilt their lives was a repetition of that violence.

Gormanstown was the chief base for the Black and Tans in the country. The flatness of the countryside, no doubt, did not help matters for the IRA and much of the IRA membership, as in Wicklow, gravitated towards the city. As a means of transforming the region GHQ even advocated large-scale immigration from Southern Italy. In April 1921, Mulcahy wrote of the Fingal IRA : 'The total loss inflicted on the enemy in three months in this Black-and-Tan infested area, is apparently 5 killed and 13 wounded. No damage to enemy war material has occurred, except bullet marks on a few lorries . . . From the standpoint of the war as a whole this can be described as negligible.'[15]

CAVAN, MONAGHAN AND LOUTH

Much of the significance of the border counties of Cavan, Monaghan and Louth lies in the fact that they posed a potential threat to the Northern government. Their participation in the War of Independence was minimal and the strong Unionist minority, particularly in Cavan and Monaghan, made organisation awkward. Much of the action had sectarian overtones. The IRA work in the Dundalk area cannot be divorced from that across the border around Newry, as demonstrated by the Fourth Northern Division, set up in the spring of 1921, incorporating Louth and South Armagh. In August 1920 and June 1921 there were killings of RIC men in Dundalk.[16]

Under the charismatic leadership of Eoin O'Duffy, then in local government, the Monaghan IRA made one of the first successful police barracks attacks at Ballytrain in February 1920. There was, however, little follow-up to this in the rest of the year. Two Brigade columns were formed but could claim only three notable actions. On 1 January 1921, one policeman and one civilian were killed and three Auxiliaries were wounded in the main street of Ballybay. An attack on Carrickmacross RIC station was aborted when a mine failed to detonate. A necessarily brief account of the war in Monaghan concluded that many ambushes were planned 'but something always prevented their being undertaken. Unlike the army in the West and South of Ireland the Monaghan Volunteers were working in an area that was not solidly behind them. The Unionist minority could at times be very dangerous'.[17]

As a means of escaping the perils of Belfast and with the aim of training their men, one of the two Belfast flying columns on GHQ orders moved to the Cootehill area in northern Cavan in May 1921. The column consisted of thirteen men with eleven rifles, 800 rounds of ammunition and ten grenades. An engagement on the Lappinduff mountains on 8 May after British troops had surrounded the area ended with one IRA man killed, two wounded and eleven captured. Recriminations followed. The O/C of the flying column reported: 'Local Volunteers were very slow and do not seem to grasp anything at all. They are just typical of the sleepy place, and seem to hold enemy forces in great dread.' Another report to GHQ concluded of the affair that it showed 'a most appalling lack of training or negligence which, in view of the fact that it involves the lives of men and the morale of the country generally, is criminal'.[18]

IRISH ACTIVITY IN BRITAIN

Both in terms of political mobilisation and physical force, Irish activity in Britain between 1919 and 1921 did not realise its potential. The Irish Self-Determination League, the main exile nationalist society, founded as late as 1919, had a disappointingly small membership of around 27,000 at its peak and had little influence beyond propaganda.[19] During the conscription crisis of 1918 and at the height of the War of Independence there were grandiose plans to assassinate leading political figures but in the end only small-scale attacks on property and arson occurred.

The British government's fear of IRA outrages and the extent of press coverage of incidents was out of proportion to the actual scale of the threat. The large Irish community in Britain, both resident and transitory, and almost exclusively urban-based, appeared all too easily as the enemy within. The proximity of Ireland itself added to this very real fear. Apart from this the chief importance of the Irish in Britain during the conflict was as a key supplier of arms and ammunition, through Collins' IRB smuggling network. IRB men were well placed in the crew of ships belonging to the transatlantic Cunard and White Star lines.

The IRA in Britain was organised during 1919 and was dominated by old Fenians. The important men were remarkably few: in Liverpool, Neil Kerr, Steve Lanigan, Paddy Daly and a few others; in Manchester, Paddy O'Donoghue and William McManus; and in London, Seán McGrath, Reggie Dunne (the future assassin of Sir Henry Wilson), Denis Kelleher, Sam Maguire and Art O'Brien, the London envoy of Sinn Féin. The surrounding mining areas of Liverpool and Glasgow particularly were good sources of explosives, detonators and so on; St Helens, near Liverpool, and Motherwell, near Glasgow, are prime examples of this. The Glasgow area was a valuable supplier of war materials but riven by personal divisions, and the situation there was complicated by the continuing appeal of the Marxist Citizen Army. The firm of J. Corbett in Glasgow was a large supplier of gelignite and detonators.

Many men in Liverpool had migrated back to Ireland for the Easter Rising, which goes some way to explaining the age profile there. Controversy over participation in 1916 appears to have been a major factor in the Glasgow discord as in so many Irish areas. Between 11 June 1919 and 23 June 1920, Collins sent over £2,000 for arms to Scotland. Birmingham and Newcastle were organised later. The IRA membership of forty in Liverpool in 1919 had expanded to 150 by November 1920. Manchester together with Salford had 100 members and Glasgow 600. In London IRB membership was virtually interchangeable with that of the IRA and the Self-Determination League.[20]

In November 1920, plans were laid for attacks on Liverpool Docks and the Stuart Street Power Station in Manchester. Rory O'Connor, Director of Engineering at Dublin GHQ, came across to run operations. The capture of Richard Mulcahy's papers gave away details of the proposed raid and resulted in a spate of arrests of key men, particularly in Liverpool. To prove that the rump of the organisation was still capable of action, nineteen warehouses out of twenty-three targeted were burnt in Liverpool and Bootle, causing around £250,000 damage. The operations in Manchester never got off the ground. In December, de Valera was taken to the safe house of Mrs McCarthy, the widow of an IRB man in Liverpool, after arriving as a stowaway from the United States en route for Dublin.[21]

Between February 1921 and the Truce a series of incendiary attacks took place around London and in other towns. IRA sources described these as mere pinpricks but they did have a profound psychological effect on British opinion. They apparently stemmed from a retaliatory urge within the Irish community in Britain rather than as a result of orders from Dublin. Information was gathered on the location of the residences of Black and Tans and Auxiliaries in Britain; there were some reprisal attacks but they were not as widespread as might have been expected. The scheme by the London IRA to assassinate the new Lord Lieutenant, Lord Fitzalan, in the spring collapsed farcically when a car broke down on Hampstead Heath. Evidently the unit had only one car driver in their ranks, an indication of how unprepared they were generally.[22]

Other plots which went awry involved poisoning horses at Knightsbridge Barracks before the State Opening of Parliament in 1921, and Brugha's favourite scheme of liquidating the entire British cabinet. GHQ in Dublin refused to sanction an attack on the village of Upton in Cheshire, chosen for its analogous size and for its proximity to Liverpool, as a counter-reprisal to Balbriggan. From the end of November 1920 to the beginning of July 1921 there were eleven shootings in Britain and 149 buildings were attacked; six targets were killed and nineteen wounded in total. A wave of arrests seems to have been particularly effective in clamping down on the developing insurgency around Glasgow, where four senior officers of the Glasgow Battalion were lifted in May 1921. In London, Art O'Brien became a fugitive and lost most of his staff, curtailing his operation. At the time of the Truce, sporadic raids and burnings were still going on.[23]

PART IV

~

CONSEQUENCES

17

THE NORTH-EAST AND THE WAR OF INDEPENDENCE

The most important consequences of the War of Independence related to the six counties of the north-east, despite the fact that little of the fighting occurred in Ulster and that the existence of the Dáil government applied only in theory to the whole island. Ulster Unionist resistance, by preventing a settlement along Home Rule lines and by radicalising opinion in the south and west, was the most significant cause of the War. The Truce terminating the conflict followed soon on the establishment of Partition: hence the Northern Question had been the key factor in dictating the fighting's duration.

The existence of a Conservative-dominated British Coalition government at the end of the First World War made it inconceivable, even if the desire had been there, for an attempt to be made to impose an all-Ireland settlement on the north-east. The Government of Ireland Bill had been drafted with the need to appease Ulster Unionist opinion as its priority, for all the talk by the government of the eventual desirability of achieving Irish unity through the Council of Ireland. It was well appreciated that there was no hope of Sinn Féin agreeing in the South to implement the Act.

In a brutally frank manner Lord Birkenhead explained the motivation behind the Bill, saying it afforded: '. . . an ingenious strengthening of our tactical position before the world. I am absolutely satisfied that the Sinn Féiners will refuse it. Otherwise in the present state of Ireland I could not even be a party to making the offer . . .'[1] To confirm Ulster Unionist acceptance of the Bill it was necessary to agree to a six- rather than nine-county partitioned area and thus to depart from the historic province of Ulster. Inclusion of Donegal, Cavan and Monaghan would have endangered a built-in Protestant majority in the prospective province, and the exclusion of Tyrone and Fermanagh, which had Catholic majorities, would, it was felt, have made the province appear too small on the map. Conciliating Northern loyalists, therefore, outweighed any attempt at rapprochement with Southern nationalism.[2]

On the surface, the Sinn Féin leadership continued to stress the preservation of Irish unity alongside their demand for recognition of the Republic, oblivious to the mutual incompatibility of these aims. Most Irish nationalists, of whatever shade, traditionally saw no problems in reconciling their demands with the continuance of Irish unity. *The Kilkenny People* commented: 'It is a truism amongst Irish Nationalists that the differences between North and South are largely, if not entirely, the creation of English interference, and then if that interference were once withdrawn such differences as exist would be amicably adjusted' (28 January 1922).

Blinkered Southern nationalist attitudes demonstrated a failure to appreciate the depth and volume of Northern Unionist feeling even after the Ulster Crisis of 1912-14. Sinn Féin had found the threat of Partition to be an extremely useful issue with which to berate the Parliamentary Party, but after their victory in the 1918 general election it soon became apparent that the new party had no effective or coherent Northern policy. The Sinn Féin boycott of Westminster and their necessary concentration on developments in the South made it easier for the British government to pass the Government of Ireland Act. Indeed, J.J. Walsh, a Sinn Féin TD, admitted that they had been striving for a Republic for only three-quarters of Ireland.[3]

It was tacitly admitted by the IRA leadership that an aggressive physical force policy in the north-east would be counter-productive. The advantages accruing from a sympathetic population (which guerrilla fighters had had in the South) did not apply where the minority Catholic population was fairly equally divided between the Nationalist Party and Sinn Féin supporters and was, moreover, geographically dispersed. Up to the Truce, membership of the two battalions of the IRA in Belfast never rose much above 1000, and of those a comparatively small proportion was active. In country areas particularly, the Volunteers were much slower to organise than in most of the twenty-six counties. Even in the strongly nationalist South Armagh, it took the by-election of early 1918 to produce much recruitment, and the Ancient Order of Hibernians continued to win a large measure of support.

The interests of Catholics living in Belfast enclaves surrounded by hostile Loyalist communities did not relate easily to the interests of strong Catholic-dominated areas, often on the fringes of the six counties.[4] In Belfast the vulnerable geographical position of so many of the Catholic areas meant that the Volunteers/IRA function was primarily defensive. Only in May and June 1921 were city ambushes attempted; before that most violence was tit-for-tat against Specials and Protestant paramilitary groups, as well as targeting of Black and Tans and Auxiliaries. Most casualties on both sides occurred as a consequence of spontaneous riots relating to specific events rather than planned actions.[5]

The small-scale activity of the War's course during 1919 had little direct relevance to Ulster. For many reasons as the fighting intensified in 1920, Ulster could not remain unaffected. The summer of 1920 saw a level of violence in the six counties, particularly in Belfast and Derry, on a scale greater than anything which had occurred in the nineteenth century or was to occur again until the late 1960s. Between 21 July 1920 and the end of that year seventy-four people were killed in Belfast alone, of whom thirty-six were Catholics.[6] The effects of the War and the imminence of Partition interacted with sectarian and labour tensions to produce a major crisis.

The Government of Ireland Act created a Northern Irish Catholic minority who were bound to have different priorities from their co-religionists in the south and west. For their part Northern Unionists were obsessed with the danger of IRA activity spreading on a large scale to the north-east, and were deeply concerned about the British government's commitment to their cause, fearing that the Government of Ireland Bill would be amended during its tortuous passage through parliament. They decided, therefore, that the apparatus of government and security should be placed in their hands long before Northern Ireland was formally established. As the reality of Partition became apparent together with sectarian violence, nationalists in the South could not avoid involvement.

The IRA extended action to the north-east in the spring of 1920; attacks were made on many police barracks, mostly previously evacuated, and on tax offices throughout the six counties. In June, an RIC man was killed in an ambush in South Armagh.[7] Patrick Loughran, killed in an attack on Cookstown police barracks on 16 June, became the first IRA man to lose his life in the north-east.[8] The first major confrontations, however, took place in May and June in the city of Derry and, as with the later Belfast disturbances, can be ascribed to both long- and short-term factors.

There had been concern that Protestant ex-serviceman shipyard workers had been replaced in their jobs by migrant Catholics. Nationalist victory in the January local government elections had resulted in the election of the first Catholic mayor of the city for over three centuries, followed by the prompt retraction of the offer of the freedom of the city to Lord French. Clashes between the communities in the Waterside and, across the river, Bishop Street areas in mid-June resulted in the intervention of the Ulster Volunteers and the IRA, and what amounted to the siege of St Columb's College by loyalists. The British Army and Dublin Castle authorities only intervened when the violence had petered out and a peace commission of local notables established.[9] A month after the termination of the Derry crisis, Belfast erupted.

The traditional 12 July celebrations took place in particularly unfortunate circumstances that year; Sir Edward Carson, the Ulster Unionist leader, stirred emotions in an address warning of the Sinn Féin threat and saying that if necessary: '. . . we will take the matter into our own hands.'[10] In the next few days a series of anonymous letters were published in the *Belfast Newsletter* warning, in one case, that: '. . . the Protestants of Ulster are asleep while the Sinn Féiners, who are pouring into our province, are wide-awake; they are busy organising, while we prate of the deeds of our forefathers and do nothing ourselves.'[11] As in Derry, there was concern in the shipyards about the loss of ex-servicemen's jobs, exacerbated by the effects of depression in the industry itself.[12]

At that time of all times, 17 July, RIC D/C Colonel Smyth was killed by IRA gunmen in the County Club in Cork city. Smyth was a native of Banbridge, County Down and had been reported in June as giving an inflammatory address to RIC men in Listowel.[13] Railwaymen prevented Smyth's remains being returned to the North by train, further straining tensions. Riots and expulsions of Catholic workers occurred in Banbridge and Dromore.[14] On 21 July, the first day back at work after the holiday of 12 July, a meeting in Workman Clark's shipyard in East Belfast brought about the expulsion of Catholics and some 'rotten Prods', and soon spread to the bigger Harland and Wolff yard. The expulsions extended to other industries very quickly and a total of 7,000 Catholics and labour activists became unemployed.[15]

In the days following the shipyard expulsions, violent clashes occurred in habitual centres of sectarian tension, the Newtownards Road/Short Strand, Shankill/Falls, New Lodge/Old Park and York Street/Docks areas. What would today be called ethnic cleansing occurred in large parts of the city.[16] In press and historical accounts conclusions have been unsurprisingly partisan: nonetheless the greatest number of casualties and the worst affected areas were Catholic.

Tensions broke out again a month later and this time the immediate cause was much clearer. On 22 August D/I Swanzy was shot dead leaving church in the centre of Lisburn. Again the Cork IRA were responsible. Swanzy had been the D/I in Cork at the time of the murder of Lord Mayor MacCurtain in March and had been blamed by the inquest jury for the crime.[17] After Swanzy was transferred to Lisburn, Michael Collins' Intelligence network tracked him down: Seán Culhane, who had been one of the assassins of Colonel Smyth, along with others of his column, travelled north by train to wreak vengeance. Joe McKelvey, of the Belfast Brigade, gave information on Swanzy's movements and Joe Leonard, a taxi driver from County Sligo, was employed to drive the Cork men to the scene of the attack. Roger McCorley of the Belfast IRA joined in the shooting. Culhane used MacCurtain's personal revolver to shoot Swanzy, although the testimony from Cork and Belfast IRA veterans contested who fired the fatal shots. While returning to Dublin, in first class rail carriages to avoid detection, the Cork men saw Lisburn in flames.[18]

The assassination immediately resulted — and no attempt has been made to contradict this — in the reprisal burning of large areas of the Catholic part of Lisburn.[19] A deputation from Lisburn in October, seeking to reduce the sentences of those prosecuted for the reprisals, commented: 'Swanzy was murdered on a Sunday morning as people were leaving their place of worship, the feelings of all right thinking persons (which had already been deeply stirred by the murders of soldiers and police . . . daily reported in the press and in particular by the murder of Major Smyth) could no longer be restrained and reprisals took place . . . under the circumstances it is not to be wondered that a virile population, deeply stirred by a dreadful crime, should decide on the spot to make it abundantly clear that practices which had been sympathised with or at any rate tolerated in other parts of Ireland would not be tolerated in Lisburn, and in consequence took stern measures with all whom suspected to be guilty of connivance at the crime, or sympathy with the political party to whom they attributed the crime.' Three days later the reprisals and riots spread to many parts of Belfast.

From then on up to the Truce, regular bouts of sectarian violence took place. In September and October, flashpoints included the removal of furniture from a Catholic house in a frontier area, violence directed against football supporters returning home through an alien North Belfast region, and RIC shootings of three Catholic men in their homes. In April 1921, Donegall Place in the Belfast city centre was the scene of shooting in which two Auxiliaries were killed: that night two brothers were the victims of reprisal killings in the Falls Road area. There were sundry isolated incidents, involving IRA and Specials, in the rest of the six counties.[20]

The loyalist resistance was confined to the six counties, although Lieutenant-Colonel Fred Crawford, the old UVF gunrunner of 1914, was involved in clandestine debate about infiltrating IRA ranks in Dublin and abortive plans to kidnap Arthur Griffith. He decided he could be of most use to the cause by remaining at home; a Belfast accent, he realised, would not help in penetrating IRA Intelligence.[21] This is the only extant example of suggested Ulster Unionist direct involvement in the southern fighting.

The response to the disturbances of June and August by the loyalist leadership vastly inflated the threat posed by the IRA and resulted in the reorganisation at a local level, both in country and city areas, of the Ulster Volunteer Force (UVF). Colonel Wilfrid Spender, another veteran of the Ulster Crisis, was brought across from England to run the force.[22] On 9 September 1920, Spender told Craig: 'The UVF except in Co Antrim, S. Belfast and one or two other parts is about as far advanced at the present time as I now wish, the numbers being fairly satisfactory and the proportion of ex-servicemen very large. I have no doubt we could give useful help to the Government for any recognised force in the districts where the Protestants predominate . . .' Spender was concerned, however, that 'some of the Orange Lodges have decided to raise a special force of their own, they saying that the UVF is too slow.'[23] By late July, joint patrols of police and these Specials were being used experimentally on a temporary basis, demonstrating tacit British government approval of the UVF's reorganisation.[24] By September, in Derry and some other areas, the army was communicating directly on matters of Intelligence with the UVF, bypassing the RIC.[25]

Unionist feeling that RIC numbers were insufficient, and that its membership was dominated by Catholics, fuelled demands for the government to recognise a new force. A memorandum of June 1921 expressed alarm that the Glenravel RIC barracks was manned by only twenty-four Protestants out of eighty-one and that its D/I McConnell had 'alleged . . . strong Sinn Féin sympathies'. Wilfrid Spender claimed that it was Macready's policy to send RIC men with such leanings to the North. Further, he claimed that some of the RIC were showing 'marked bias' towards 'the rebels'.[26]

There was a justified conviction that troop numbers were inadequate and that the military was too inexperienced. Fred Crawford commented, 'the Schoolboys over here in uniform and called soldiers will be useless.'[27] With this went a fear that industrial troubles in Britain would result in troop withdrawals.[28] On 23 July 1920, in a Cabinet discussion with the Irish authorities, Winston Churchill asked: 'What . . . would happen if the Protestants in the six counties were given weapons and . . . charged with maintaining law and order and policing the country.'[29] Churchill appeared to approve of the idea that such a force be used to supplement British forces throughout the thirty-two counties.

In early September Sir James Craig, by this time the leading spokesman for Ulster Unionism and future Northern Irish Prime Minister, was adopting a harsh tone in demanding that the British government accept what amounted to an officially approved UVF. He also demanded the appointment of an Assistant Under-Secretary to deal solely with matters in the north-east, and increased autonomy for the police and military forces there.[30]

After attending a meeting of the Ulster Unionist Council, Craig circulated a memorandum among the Cabinet saying: 'The Loyalists in Ulster believe that the Rebel plans are definitely directed towards the establishment of a Republic hostile to the British Empire, and that they are working in conjunction with Bolshevik Forces elsewhere towards that end . . . In the North they are gradually extending their influence partly by causing the withdrawal of the Constabulary, who have to be concentrated for reasons of self-defence, and partly by the intimidation of the Loyalists who find themselves deprived of the ordinary Government protection which they have hitherto enjoyed.' Craig concluded: 'The present situation in Ulster is that Sinn Féin is already the predominant factor over a considerable proportion of the Province . . . The Loyalist rank and file have determined to take action . . . they now feel that the situation is becoming so desperate that unless the Government will take immediate action, it may be advisable for them to see what steps can be taken towards a system of "organised" reprisals against the Rebels, mainly in order to defeat them, but partly to restrain their own followers from acts which are regrettable, and in a large measure ineffective.'[31]

The British Cabinet went virtually the whole way in satisfying Craig's demands. The establishment of A, full-time, B, part-time, and C, reserve, elements of a Special Constabulary was agreed to: the force was recruited largely from the UVF and the Orange Lodges and the talk of encouraging Catholics to apply very quickly became a sick joke. Sir Ernest Clark became the first Assistant Under-Secretary to be based in Belfast, quickly proving himself sympathetic to Northern Unionism.[32]

By failing to act over the shipyard expulsions and by the establishment of the Specials, the British government had alienated itself completely from the Catholic minority in the North. The consequences of its actions were even less defensible than its establishment of the Black and Tans a few months before had been. Both General Sir Nevil Macready and Sir John Anderson warned the government in the strongest possible terms of the consequences.

Macready commented: 'It is well to analyse the expression "Loyalist" as applied to Ulster. The Force it is now proposed to mobilise is the same force who, for their own opinions, armed against the Government of the day in the early part of 1914, and I am firmly convinced that they would take up arms again tomorrow if they thought that they could gain their own ends, even against the Constitution of the Empire, by so doing.'[33] On 2 September 1920, Anderson wrote to Bonar Law: 'We have . . . tried the experiment of setting up an unarmed body of Special Constabulary in Belfast and even that has not been an unqualified success. On the first night three of the Special Constables were arrested for looting . . . you cannot in the middle of a faction fight recognise one of the contending parties and expect it to deal with disorder in the spirit of impartiality and fairness essential in those who have to carry out the Orders of the Government.'[34]

These developments defined the long-term character of loyalist government of the six counties even before the Government of Ireland Bill was passed. A memorandum laying down the essential points for the new administration can leave no-one in any doubt as to what was to be expected. The Northern government, it promised, 'will, undoubtedly, be formed from the Protestant majority. Consequently the steps now taken should be in accordance with the views of that majority. It should not be a Government in which both sides are treated as being equally entitled to a voice in whatever measures are taken . . . The essential point to remember is that the Unionists hold that no rebel who wishes to set up a Republic can be regarded merely as a "political opponent" but must be repressed.'[35]

Remarkably, not even the British government's major concessions to Ulster Unionists satisfied hardline opinion. Throughout September, Spender in Belfast conveyed to Craig in London criticism from the grassroots.[36] They were irritated at the delay in setting up the Specials and were obsessed by what they regarded as Sinn Féin influences in Dublin Castle. They demanded that Clark be accountable directly to the Chief Secretary and that he should not communicate first with the Joint Under-Secretaries, as was usual. The Chief Secretary, Sir Hamar Greenwood, and Sir John Anderson journeyed, no doubt reluctantly, to Belfast to meet a deputation of the Ulster Unionist Council's Standing Committee on 13 October 1920. H.L. Garrett started proceedings by bluntly stating: 'If anyone wants to start terrorism to-day in the north of Ireland they will soon find two can play at that game.' He felt that: 'The time has come when Belfast and the north of Ireland should not be associated with the rest of Ireland in any sort of way' and went on to declare: 'We have not the smallest confidence in the officials in Dublin Castle.' Suspicion was targeted particularly on the Catholic Joint Under-Secretary James MacMahon, who was quite unjustifiably looked upon as being in league with Sinn Féin.

Loyalist distrust had not been assuaged and continued throughout the War of Independence, the Treaty negotiations, long beyond and up to the present day. Spender wrote: 'The manoeuvres of the British Government during this period resembled those of a yacht trying to take advantage of every variety of breeze on an almost windless day. I well recollect a memorable interview which some of our Cabinet Ministers had with Mr Lloyd George . . . when he expressed views which, as they said, were more vigorous than those of the most extreme Orangeman, but I must admit that I thought Lord Craigavon looked rather thoughtful after the interview and that he was well aware that a strong puff of wind on the starboard tack too often foreshadowed an early change to port.'[37]

Advanced nationalists, both north and south, were well aware that a counter-offensive in the north-east to the events of June-September 1920 was impractical. Roger McCorley, a prominent figure in the Belfast Brigade, admitted that the pogrom of July disrupted their plans, forcing them to concentrate on defending nationalist areas, and testified that they lost contact with Dublin for supplies of arms and ammunition.[38] Seamus Woods, future O/C 3rd Northern Division, described the Belfast IRA as a 'close circle' and added : '. . . for we had to be very careful'.[39] John McCoy, second in command of the Newry Brigade, recalled that they had no more than a dozen rifles and recorded the difficulty of staging successful ambushes in mixed areas.

The IRA GHQ in Dublin was well aware of communication problems with Northern units, and that was a major reason why Divisions were formed during 1921 to replace the old Brigade/Battalion system. There was bound, however, to be a feeling that Northern interests were being neglected. The historian Éamon Phoenix writes that the Northern Sinn Féiner Louis J. Walsh 'seems to have perceived at an early stage that, whilst the Sinn Féin movement had made great play with "the naked deformity of Partition" in its campaign to displace the Irish Party, it had tended to rank the Ulster Question as a poor second to "Independence" in its scale of priorities'.[40]

The direct response from the South came in the traditional form of a boycott. As early as December 1919, traders in Galway had staged a boycott of Ulster Unionist businesses; this spread to some extent in the first half of 1920.[41] Soon after the shipyard expulsions, a Belfast Expelled Workers' Fund was organised and on 6 August Seán MacEntee, one of the few Northerners in the Dáil, introduced a motion supporting a ban on financial and trade dealings with Unionist companies, initially only in Belfast.[42]

In August, somewhat reluctantly, the Dáil government supported a limited boycott and by the end of the year a general policy was being implemented. Despite MacEntee's claim that: 'They could not reduce Belfast by force of arms, but they could bring her to reason by economic force',[43] many argued with considerable justification that the tactic would harden partitionist attitudes. Michael Collins was to admit that the boycott was only partly successful, reinforcing the already strong north-eastern business attachment to British markets and increasing Northern Unionist antagonism to the southern government.[44]

The boycott policy amounted to little more than gesture politics: it was an example of the often counter-productive Sinn Féin policy regarding the North. Sandy Lindsay, an old Oxford friend of Erskine Childers, commented: 'Absolutely everything that de Valera has said to the NE he has with the best intentions said the thing most calculated to put their backs up. I think that now you are preserving the unity of the South and West at the expense of making impossible or delaying for a long time the unity of the whole of Ireland'.[45]

Until the beginning of 1921 the Northern question did not feature in the sundry attempts to negotiate a truce or a settlement during the War of Independence. Lloyd George and his Deputy Bonar Law, made it clear that separate treatment for the six counties, and hence Partition, was non-negotiable. After de Valera's return from the United States in late December 1920, British and Irish intermediaries frequently sought to arrange a meeting between him and Carson or Craig.[46] It was hoped that any such meetings would be preparatory to a full-scale conference with the British government, although it was not clear how this could be reconciled with loyalist insistence on the precise terms of the Government of Ireland Act.

On 4 May 1921 James Craig, recently elected Leader of the Ulster Unionist Party, left Belfast for Dublin apparently with the sole purpose of paying his respects to the new Lord Lieutenant, Lord Fitzalan. This was two weeks before the election which gave authority for the establishment of Northern Ireland. The day following, Craig met de Valera secretly in circumstances which would have done justice to a second-rate detective novel. Craig was spirited away by various middlemen to a rendezvous in the North Dublin suburbs. Surprisingly little attention has been paid by historians to the meeting: it tends to be quickly dismissed as a failure and in retrospect both participants had their reasons for belittling it. In fact, though, contemporary evidence suggests it had great potential significance.

According to Hamar Greenwood's testimony, de Valera did most of the talking, going over 'the story of 1798 and every trouble since'. Craig, for his part, '. . . explored the Council of the Act (Government of Ireland) as the hope of the future'.[47] At the end they agreed that they should meet again after the elections, Craig suggesting that the return match should take place in an Orange Hall.[48] Even the stern de Valera was amused by this. Long after, both the participants gave negative accounts of the meeting, concluding that they had drawn up a bland communiqué with nothing concrete achieved. They, however, had vested interests in giving such a slant on events.

The British and Southern Irish press gave a generally enthusiastic reception to the news that Craig and de Valera had met. Northern Unionist alarm was

dealt with by faith in Craig's integrity and by Craig's emphasis at election meetings that he was in no way compromising Ulster's position.[49]

What were the two leaders trying to achieve? Both were to claim that misleading assurances by the British government had brought them together. It is
difficult to believe, however, that this alone could have led them to take such
a gamble. Craig was obviously aware of the considerable risks he was running
with regard to his own support; he was quick to emphasise on his return to
Belfast that he had gone at de Valera's request, and was only interested in
achieving a better understanding with the South as a means to urge them to
operate the Government of Ireland Act. He was surely sincere in stressing that
there could be no change to Northern Ireland's future constitutional position.
For his part, de Valera had little to say in public about the meeting, not wishing
to increase Craig's difficulties. Right through to the Anglo-Irish Treaty, Craig
was to play no further rôle in negotiations.

It is clear that it was Dublin Castle, and especially the undercover work of
the Assistant Under-Secretary Andy Cope, which brought Craig and de Valera
together.[50] It follows that the British were using Craig to find out more about
de Valera's position. Craig, it appears, was interested in discussing with de
Valera the financial provisions of devolution and the prospect of finding some
common ground over the Council of Ireland. Mark Sturgis recorded on 31
March that Craig had told Anderson 'exactly how far he is prepared to go' and
Anderson commented 'it is very far indeed.'[51] On 2 April, Craig told Anderson
that he was willing to help de Valera 'to get anything short of a Republic which
does not take away from Ulster anything she has already got'. He was also
agreeable to an amnesty for prisoners if a truce was arranged.[52]

In the weeks following the meeting it was provisionally arranged that Cope
would present Craig's terms to de Valera. Greenwood was optimistic that Craig
and de Valera 'will ask for cessation in order to discuss settlement, and by that
time, the terms of settlement will be more or less definite'.[53] Craig's agenda consisted of: no republic for the South; no change in Ulster's status; an Exchequer
Board 'for all Ireland under the Council of the Act to make certain the South
pays its quota of taxation as well as the North'; consideration of fiscal autonomy but insistence on free trade with Britain; continued Irish payment to an
Imperial contribution and the National Debt. If all this was agreed, Craig and
de Valera were to ask for a truce and then were to meet Lloyd George.[54]

These terms may have been attractive to de Valera in potentially freeing him
from what he described as 'the straitjacket of the Republic' and also to Craig
in improving Northern Ireland's financial basis. De Valera frequently pointed
out that autonomy for Ulster could be granted within a federal Ireland settlement. Ironically Mark Sturgis observed that Craig's agenda may well have been
in advance of anything the British government was willing to concede.[55] In any
case the terms were not offered and by June British attention turned to different strategies which in the end produced a more direct peace initiative.
Evidently time could not afford to wait for the conclusion of Craig and de

Valera's ritualistic sparring. This study of an historical might-have-been illustrates how pragmatic de Valera and Craig could be despite their apparently inflexibly dogmatic public stances.

For all the debate during and after the Paris Peace Conference about self-determination and the rights of minorities, there had been no coherent plan setting out any rational concept behind the Partition of Ireland. In a tortuous, often confused, way the British government implemented it in an ad hoc fashion with a view to preventing the Ulster Question from blocking Home Rule. They seemed unaware of the acute irony that the only part of Ireland that accepted a devolved government was the north-east. Ulster Unionists had initially been reluctant to form their own government and parliament, preferring the status quo of government from Westminster. They soon saw the advantages in devolution once they had ensured that it would be for six not nine counties and that there was little safeguard for minority rights. The Northern Ireland Prime Minister's brother, Charles Craig, a Westminster MP, put it well: 'They had got a parliament of their own . . . if, with that majority, they could not maintain a parliament according to their views and aspirations, they would not be . . . business-like . . . people.'[56]

The early stages of the Northern Irish government assumed a kind of appalling inevitability. Ulster Unionists won an extremely comfortable victory in the election establishing the parliament in 1921: all their candidates were elected and the nationalist cause was not aided by divisions between constitutionalists and Sinn Féiners. No seat was won by Sinn Féin in Belfast, where Joe Devlin's influence still counted for much. All nationalists boycotted the new parliament and Cardinal Logue refused to attend its opening, claiming a prior engagement.[57]

The new government waited only just over a year to remove the safeguard for Catholics of proportional representation in local government elections. A heavy emphasis was placed on security with the Specials soon becoming involved in revenge killings and reprisals. The Truce which ended the War in the South coincided with the worst violence yet in Belfast: the week between 10 and 17 July saw sixteen Catholics killed and 216 Catholic homes destroyed.[58] A protracted loyalist reprisal had followed an ambush in Raglan Street. It took another year for the British government to realise the need to appoint an enquiry into security in the province and the actions of the Specials.[59]

For all the harsh realities of developments in the north-east, Southern nationalists retained their irredentist beliefs. In July 1921 de Valera told the South African leader Jan Smuts: 'An Ireland in fragments nobody cares about. A united Ireland alone can be happy or prosperous.'[60] De Valera was to tell Lloyd George that the Ulster Question 'must remain . . . for the Irish people themselves to settle. We cannot admit the right of the British Government to mutilate our country, either in its own interest or at the call of any section of our population. We do not contemplate the use of force. If your Government stands aside, we can effect a complete reconciliation.'[61]

Southern nationalists had failed to make a priority of the Northern Question and, for all their protestations on the subject, to defend minority interests in the North effectively. A large measure of independence for the twenty-six counties would be won at the expense of their compatriots. Patrick Baxter, a Sinn Féin TD, observed: 'It struck me . . . many of the Southern, Midland and Western Deputies are not as interested in the North as they might be and should be.'[62] Despite the time-honoured rhetorical emphasis placed on Irish unity at some ill-defined time, the main strands of Southern political opinion repeatedly failed to confront the issue realistically. It was only from the 1970s that some Southern nationalists were to examine the limitations of their traditional attitudes towards the North.

18

THE AMERICAN DIMENSION

Since Fenian times, Irish nationalists of all shades had had enormous faith in the value of Irish-American support. For their part, British governments had a great fear of the Irish question proving to be a considerable complicating factor in Anglo-American relations. At no time was this more true than in the period between the end of the First World War and the Anglo-Irish Treaty. From their different perspectives both de Valera and Lloyd George were almost obsessed by Irish-America.[1]

Before the First World War, the US was chiefly important as a supplier of funds for Irish nationalist institutions; from the end of that War, Wilson's self-determination doctrine and the association of the Irish cause with the controversy over American membership of the League of Nations made the Irish question, for a short time, a central issue in American politics. The actual significance, however, of America to Irish developments was less than it appeared to be.

While the War of Independence was at its peak in late 1920 and the first six months of 1921, the scale and effectiveness of Irish-American assistance was dwindling. The exile nationalist organisations were plagued with personal and ideological divisions, and tensions between the American leaders and Irish envoys to the States. Nevertheless, perceptions themselves were significant: Lloyd George felt that no official support for reprisals could be given until the 1920 Presidential election was over, and in the heart of the conflict, de Valera chose to spend eighteen months in the US, raising funds and chasing the hopeless dream of US recognition of the Dáil government.

The end of the First World War saw something amounting to a renaissance in Irish-American ranks. From 1916, and particularly after American entry into the war, the pro-German associations of the exile nationalist leadership had marginalised Irish activity. Wilson's stress on the rights of small nations allowed the Irish cause to regain respectability and relevance and also held out the hope that pressure could be put on the British government internationally at the Paris Peace Conference, which began in January 1919. The US

Consul in Queenstown, Charles M. Hathaway, recorded the views of a Sinn Féiner who 'expressed great confidence in the President and was hopeful that a League of Nations would be set up which would by its very nature make inevitable an Irish solution sooner or later'.[2] *The Boston Pilot*, the chief organ of the Catholic Church in Massachusetts, wrote on 30 November 1918: 'The war has been won for democracy. The world awaits the practical application to small nations of the principles for which it has been waged. Its vision is especially focused on Ireland. Ireland's sorrows and demands must reach the conference room. Ireland is the great test, without it victory will prove to be shadow and not substance.'

The outward sign of the Irish-American revival came in the form of mass meetings. On 10 December 1918, Cardinal O'Connell of Boston addressed a gathering in Madison Square Garden in New York. Shane Leslie, the writer and critic, commented that O'Connell's speech 'got into the Irish press and aroused the country like a trumpet call. They felt that they had the intellectual and moral force of America working in their favour and they have begun to hope again.' In December and January, through the cities of the East Coast, rallies were used as the central means of Irish-American propaganda. They were linked to the resurgence of The Friends of Irish Freedom organisation (FOIF), under the leadership of the veteran Fenian John Devoy and Judge Daniel F. Cohalan, an intimate of Tammany Hall, the Democratic Party's notorious headquarters in New York City. The FOIF was the public front of the Clan na Gael, the American wing of the IRB.[3]

The Philadelphia Race Convention, which met in mid-February 1919, was the culmination of the Irish-American revival. Five thousand delegates crammed into the music auditorium to listen to two days of oratory on Ireland's sufferings, England's sins and the hopes that Wilson had aroused. A Victory Fund was established, a delegation chosen to pressure the President on his imminent return from Paris during a break in the Conference, and three representatives nominated to present the Irish-American cause in Paris. Behind the scenes, however, there were strains within the movement.

While Irish representatives in Philadelphia, notably Patrick McCartan, felt that the Convention should recognise the existence of an Irish Republic, Devoy and Cohalan insisted on the use of the term 'self-determination' in Convention resolutions. Cohalan was a fierce isolationist and opponent of the League of Nations and a long-term subject of the President's ire. This division mirrored a personal one between the New York leadership and that based in Philadelphia, around local businessman and long-term Clan activist Joseph McGarrity. It was possible to achieve an appearance of unity in public at the Convention, with the moderate Cardinal Gibbons of Baltimore presenting the main resolution, but soon all the tensions would be revealed.[4]

President Wilson met extremely reluctantly with the delegation from the Philadelphia Convention following his speech at the Metropolitan Opera House in New York on 4 March, but he insisted that Cohalan be excluded. By this time it was realised that there was little hope of the Irish cause being heard at the Paris Peace Conference.

The American Commission's Press Officer in Paris, Ray Stannard Baker, recorded Wilson's views of the meeting. 'He said that he refused to receive the Committee if Judge Cohalan was on it and that he told the representatives who came to him, and in language so plain and loud that it could be heard by the Tammany policemen who stood about, that he regarded Judge Cohalan as a traitor . . . When the representatives eventually came in "they were so insistent" said the President, "that I had hard work keeping my temper".' Baker summed up: 'The Irish question is now a domestic affair of the British Empire and that neither he nor any other foreign leader has any right to interfere or to advocate any policy. He said he did not tell them so but he believed that when the League of Nations Covenant was adopted and the League came into being a foreign nation — America if you like — might suggest, under one of its provisions, that the Irish question might become a cause of war and that therefore it became the concern of the League — but that time had not yet arrived.'[5]

There was never any realistic hope that the Irish cause would be heard in Paris. To have raised the issue publicly would have imperilled Anglo-American relations and the Conference could only be concerned with territories directly affected by the First World War. In private, Wilson did remind Lloyd George of the importance of a speedy resolution of the Irish question, pointing out his problems with the sizeable and influential Irish-American lobby within his own Democratic Party. Moreover the President told Lloyd George 'that there was nothing which would be so influential in strengthening the prejudice against the League as the failure to settle the Irish question'.[6]

The Irish-American delegation in Paris had two testy interviews with Wilson and caused major embarrassment over their visit to Ireland in May. During the second of those meetings in June, Wilson lectured the delegation on the realities of diplomacy, emphasising that he could only apply unofficial pressure and concluding: 'Of course Ireland's case from the point of view of population, from the point of view of the struggle they have made, from the point of interest that it has excited in the world, and especially among our own people . . . is the outstanding case of a small nationality. You do not know and cannot appreciate the anxieties that I have experienced as the result of the many millions of people having their hopes raised by what I have said.'[7]

Soon after, the delegation was officially told that the Irish case was not to be considered. The failure in Paris drove Irish-American opinion into the arms of the opposition to the League of Nations in the US, and the Irish-American delegation's work promoted the view in Ireland that the US was the key to any aspirations of international recognition for the Dáil. De Valera had arrived in New York over two weeks before the delegation returned home.

The limitations of American support are well demonstrated by the history of resolutions in Congress on the Irish question. The declarations of mere sympathy for the Irish cause in either House did not merit the enthusiastic reception they received in Ireland. From the end of the First World War to the Anglo-Irish Treaty there was scarcely a time when some Irish resolution was not before the Committee on Foreign Affairs of the House of Representatives or the Senate Foreign Relations Committee. This was more, however, a product of the politicians' desire to appease a large Irish constituency within their own localities or to embarrass the Presidential administration than a serious attempt to affect Irish policy. The power to recognise a foreign government lay with the Executive. It was the President's initiative alone which determined the course of foreign policy and which could influence British policy towards Ireland. The British Government and press, when faced with such resolutions, were able to dismiss them as episodes in American domestic politics.

The Flood Resolution in the House of Representatives in March 1919 was the result of complex manoeuvring between the parties and was so mildly phrased as to produce little opposition. Greater significance attached to the passage of the Borah Resolution in the Senate in June. This went so far as to express the Senate's 'sympathy with the aspirations of the Irish people for a government of their own choice'. Its passage was dependent on an unholy alliance between Republican opponents of the League, and Democratic critics of Wilson's administration. The resolution reflected the rapidly increasing anti-League sentiment in the Senate and did not correspond to significant events in Ireland.

Senator Henry Cabot Lodge, the arch-opponent of Irish interests in Boston, suddenly began to support the Irish nationalist cause, consumed by his personal detestation of President Wilson. Senator Phelan of California, a leading Irish-American Democratic Party politician, commented that 'the Republicans had been animated by the motive of embarrassing President Wilson in his stand for the self-determination of nations . . . It is unfortunate that so great a cause should be so crudely used as a vulgar means of winning votes by men whose previous actions would indicate that they had no real sympathy with Ireland.'[8]

Judge Cohalan and Senator Borah exchanged triumphant telegrams once the resolution had been passed and Frank P. Walsh, one of the Irish-American delegation in Paris, saw it as 'easily the most important and significant action taken by America in opposition to England since our forefathers declared against the rule of George III'. Consul-General Hathaway reported from Queenstown in early July that 'the leading subject of the period under review in the press and in the minds of the people has been the American activities with respect to the Irish question . . . culminating in the Resolution of the Senate.' The Dublin correspondent of *The Times* wrote that the Irish nationalist press was telling the country 'that the whole American people stands behind the Irish claim for self-determination and will not rest till it has been conceded. Undoubtedly this belief, ill founded though it probably is, will stimulate agitation in Ireland and will magnify the difficulties of the Irish.'[9]

British government sources, however, noted the superficial character of the Senate support for Ireland. Sir William Wiseman, a British diplomat, wrote:

'Several of the Senators, Republicans and Democrats, with whom I talked, admit that they do not regard a separate Irish Republic as either feasible or desirable and all they meant by the Resolution was to register their conviction that something ought to be done. Those who will discuss the matter frankly admit that it is not practical politics for them to oppose any Irish Resolution however extreme.' More acidly, the owner of *The Philadelphia Public Ledger* declared that 'the attitude of the typical American, as apart from the Irish-American, on the Irish question is one of complete lack of interest. Irish-Americans are never satisfied. They are the most sensitive people in the world. The typical Yankee does not understand what the Irish want and he does not care.' The progressive journalist William Allen Wright concluded: 'Ireland is a football in American politics. It must be taken out of American politics for the good of Ireland and the future peace of the world.'[10]

From June until March 1920, the Irish issue became part of the means by which American membership of the League of Nations was defeated in the US Senate. One of the reservations which destroyed Wilson's mission concerned the Irish question. At no time was it explained how rejection of the League would aid the Irish cause. To be anti-League and anti-Wilson was to adopt an advantageous political position, but solved nothing as far as Ireland was concerned; Irish considerations had become supplementary to American party politics.[11]

Following the collapse of both Wilson's health and his administration from the autumn of 1919, the prospect of a Republican administration did not hold out any hopes for Ireland. Opposition to Article X of the League Covenant, which sought to 'respect and preserve against external aggression the territorial integrity and existing political independence of other nations', could never explain how and in what circumstances America could directly interfere in the Irish situation. *The New York Times* declared on 19 July 1919 that only if the Irish were prepared to implicate the United States in war with Britain was their opposition to the League explicable. Irish opposition to the League, however, was an important element in the wave of anti-English feeling at this time. In Wilson's own words, the Irish question was 'the political dynamite of the whole English speaking world'.[12]

Just before the party conventions of 1920, there was a battle over the long-delayed Mason Resolution in the House of Representatives which provided salaries 'for a minister and consuls to the Republic of Ireland' when a watered-down version was blocked by the administration. *The New York Tribune* stressed: 'Congressmen are fond of playing comedies and even melodrama in Presidential years.'[13]

Developments in Irish-America had meanwhile been enormously intensified by the arrival of Éamon de Valera in New York City on 11 June 1919. He personified the Irish cause in the US at the same time as that cause reached its height in terms of political influence. De Valera had stowed away on a cargo ship and arrived in filthy, lice-ridden clothes; before staging a press conference at the Waldorf Astoria Hotel on 23 June he lay low for a while, avoiding both American and British authorities. De Valera's presence took the State Department completely by surprise: the British government swore that he would not be allowed to return. The situation was an acute embarrassment for both governments.[14]

The timing of the visit coincided with the final stage of the Peace Conference. De Valera's faith in politics as a means by which to achieve independence had long switched from Paris to the US. With this went an awareness of the financial support and publicity the US could give to the cause. De Valera's own background (he was born in Manhattan) also had much to do with his decision to visit the US. The stay suited his essentially diplomatic and political talents; he had neither the stomach nor the aptitude for guerrilla warfare. In contrast to Parnell and Redmond, de Valera was not well known to general American audiences. His advent caused great problems within the exile nationalist movement: Cohalan and Devoy saw their leadership challenged.

De Valera's mission implied an over-estimation of the rôle the US could play in the Irish question. Recognition proved a futile call and de Valera was to be disappointed with the amount of money raised. From his eighteen months' stay, de Valera learned that the Irish question had to be settled in London and Dublin, rather than by means of mass meetings in the US.

The arch wheeler-dealer in Sinn Féin ranks, Harry Boland, had arrived sometime ahead of de Valera. He soon identified himself with the Philadelphia wing of the Clan and de Valera's first stop was at the home in that city of Joe McGarrity. Contemporaries record that at their first meeting, de Valera and Cohalan took an immediate dislike to each other. De Valera soon announced the plan to raise a $5,000,000 bond issue and the closing of the FOIF's Victory Fund and took a much less hostile line on the League of Nations than the American leadership.[15]

From the publicity aspect, de Valera's visit started well. The first mass meeting took place at Fenway Park Baseball Stadium in Boston where a crowd of over fifty thousand listened to speeches from local politicians, including Senator David I. Walsh, the first Irish-American US Senator for Massachusetts, who depicted de Valera as Ireland's answer to Abraham Lincoln. De Valera began his speech in Gaelic, which confused many, but it was the occasion which mattered. He then returned to New York for four overflow meetings in Madison Square Garden before commencing a tour west.

De Valera's missionary zeal took him three times to the West Coast, as well as the Mid-West and the South. His peripatetic activity became a familiar part of the American environment and the novelty of it wore off fairly quickly. The New York correspondent of *The Times* wrote that: 'undoubtedly the doings of de Valera in the US have given fresh impetus to his followers in Ireland. Sinn Féin newspapers publish eagerly glowing reports of the progress, of the enthusiasm of his meetings and the success of the loan . . . it is, however, possible to exaggerate the influence of the American tour. Ultimately de Valera will be

Refugees escaping from Balbriggan following its destruction by the Black and Tans

*Seán MacEoin and
Seán Moylan*

Éamon de Valera

Members of Cumann na mBan recite the rosary outside Mountjoy Jail on 25 April 1921, the morning that Thomas Traynor was hanged.

A troop raid

Terence MacSwiney

David Lloyd George

Forces of the Crown: a member of the DMP, a regular soldier and two Black and Tans

*Black and Tans con-
fiscate property taken
from Liberty Hall, the
headquarters of the
Irish Transport &
General Workers'
Union.*

Sir Hamar Greenwood

Irish delegates at the Treaty negotiations in London: Arthur Griffith is on the extreme left with Robert Barton next to him. Desmond FitzGerald is standing left. Erskine Childers is seated right.

British troops on parade on the great square of the Royal Barracks (now Collins Barracks)

Seán T. O'Kelly left, Eoin MacNeill second from left, and Éamon de Valera second from right.

W.T. Cosgrave

judged not by his triumphs in America, but by the merits of his policy in purely Irish affairs.'[16]

Like Parnell, Redmond and Davitt, de Valera was always strongly aware of the
value of American financial support. The monied Sinn Féiner was a rare man
and the potential represented by Irish-American millionaires was shown by the
Californian oil magnate Edward L. Doheny, who became de Valera's nominee
as the first National President of the American Association for the Recognition
of the Irish Republic. The question of who was to hold the pursestrings of the
Irish-American movement was central to the split between the FOIF and de
Valera. Supporters of de Valera alleged that an insufficient proportion of the
one million dollars raised by the Victory Fund had been used for Irish purposes. Despite complications over its legality, de Valera pressed ahead with a
Bond Drive aiming at a target of five million dollars. James O'Mara and Seán
Nunan came over from Ireland to help run the drive and by the time it started
in December 1919, Devoy and Cohalan had been pushed aside.[17]

While the $5,300,000 raised by the Drive was well in advance of earlier
efforts, its success was largely dependent on a few states. Nearly half of the
amount was contributed by New York City and Massachusetts alone. The five
hundred thousand subscribers were mainly working class and the average sub-
scription only seven dollars. De Valera was dissatisfied by the result and in
future strove even more strongly to cultivate millionaires. Only around one
half of the sum was to leave American banks by the time of the Anglo-Irish
Treaty. After the Truce ending the War of Independence, a second Bond Drive
was organised with a very ambitious target of twenty million dollars, but by that
time there were strong signs of donor fatigue and the project faded.[18]

Between the autumn of 1919 and the summer of 1920, the divisions sepa-
rating de Valera from the FOIF and Clan leadership widened dramatically and
became a complete split, with the formation of public and secret separate
organisations. To some extent the split was a personal one. For Devoy, de Valera
was 'the most impossible man who ever came to America to speak for Ireland
. . . his malignity is almost phenomenal', while Dr William Maloney, a de Valera
supporter, claimed that 'Cohalan was essentially an American factionist.' As de
Valera was stressing that his first responsibility was to the Irish people, his
opponents were holding that they were the best judges of what should be done
in their own country. There was some justice on both sides: de Valera was tact-
less and overbearing, the old leadership was cliquish and arrogant.[19]

De Valera's interview with *The Westminster Gazette* of February 1920 gave an
opportunity for the divisions to harden. He argued that an independent
Ireland should have a relationship with Britain regarding foreign policy akin
to that of the contemporary US and Cuba. On 10 February, Devoy's newspaper
The Gaelic American immediately portrayed this as a hauling down of the Irish
Republican flag, and a vicious correspondence ensued between Cohalan and
de Valera. An attempted peace meeting in March resulted in a public slanging
match in the Park Avenue Hotel, New York City. De Valera then stated that he

had not been in America a month when he concluded that 'there wasn't room in the country for Judge Cohalan and himself.'[20] Soon the dissension amongst Irish-Americans over the drafting of the Mason Resolution and the tactics to be followed at the two national party conventions finalised the split.

Rival Irish-American delegations attended the Republican Party Convention at Chicago in June 1920. With a supreme disregard for diplomatic niceties, de Valera set up a committee which sought to win a resolution recognising the Irish Republic. Cohalan and his supporters meanwhile limited their hopes to a vague expression that the Irish people 'have the right to determine freely, without dictation from outside, their own governmental institutions and their international relations with other states and peoples'. The de Valera Resolution was rejected almost unanimously by the Platform Committee. There never had been the remotest possibility that the Republican party would show any genuine commitment to the Irish cause. Meanwhile Devoy accused de Valera of misappropriating three thousand dollars of Bond Drive money by using it for his activities in Chicago.[21]

De Valera soon transferred his attentions to the seemingly more promising territory of the Democratic Convention at San Francisco. This time the Cohalan supporters did not attend but again a recognition resolution was impractical; the Convention showed itself far more concerned with the Prohibition issue. Eventually the usual weak sympathy resolution was passed. Patronisingly de Valera declared: 'Ireland has learned how to face defeat, the lesson of the refusal . . . is that the American public need to be more systematically educated in the noble principles of Sinn Féin.' He announced his plan to spend incredible sums in an attempt to capture the intellect of America. For Ireland itself, in the throes of guerrilla warfare, the proceedings at the Conventions had little or no significance.[22]

Harry Boland was sent to Ireland in the summer of 1920 to win support for de Valera's position and while in Ireland took steps to cut the Clan na Gael off from its IRB ties, a process complete on 18 October. An attempted purge of the Clan membership failed before a Reorganised Clan was established. McGarrity admitted that they found it necessary to burgle *The Gaelic American* offices in December 1920 to gain the list of Clan members.[23]

Meanwhile attempts to reform the FOIF from within finally collapsed in September and de Valera announced to the press on 16 November the launching of The American Association for the Recognition of the Irish Republic (AARIR). The awkward name, as convoluted in an acronym as when given in full, encumbered the organisation from the beginning. There was also a marked lack of definition about the organisation's policy. Though de Valera remarked after a month back in Ireland that if he were Woodrow Wilson he would not recognise the Irish Republic, the AARIR persisted with a futile search for its recognition.[24]

It was conceded even in FOIF circles that the AARIR membership soon vastly outnumbered that of its rival. It seems, however, to have been less closely organised. The FOIF's regular membership fell from 100,000 in 1919 to 20,000 after the split, and by May 1921 the AARIR was claiming 965,000 members. Faction fighting and argument between the Irish and American wings of the movement quickly spread to the new organisation.[25]

With the split completed in December 1920, de Valera decided to return to Ireland. Signing a document which entrusted Joe McGarrity on the event of his death with the funds in America, de Valera left, as secretively as he had arrived, on 10 December 1920. While he had successfully publicised the Sinn Féin movement and could claim to have raised more funds than ever before, his contribution to heightening dissension within exile nationalist ranks was to resemble, as many enemies were later to point out, his contribution to divisions over the Anglo-Irish Treaty and the resulting Civil War.[26]

In the summer and autumn of 1920, the Irish cause gained more from the publicity connected with Archbishop Mannix' visit and Terence MacSwiney's hunger strike than it did from all de Valera's machinations. Mannix had frequently denounced English imperialism during his two-month stay in the US from June 1920 and when he left New York, *The Times* reported that 'Over 2,000 rowdy singing Irish men and women invaded the White Star quay.' As a response to the British refusal to let him land in Ireland, longshoremen on the White Star lines pleaded that work be tied up on every British ship in New York. MacSwiney's death became a day of exile nationalist mourning. A memorial meeting attended by 75,000 was held at the Polo Grounds in New York. Soon MacSwiney's widow Muriel and his sister Mary visited America to testify before *The Nation* Committee.[27]

Between the sacking of Balbriggan and the burning of Cork, *The Nation* Committee of One Hundred was established to enquire into the need for relief in Ireland. By January 1921, this committee had metamorphosed into the American Committee on Relief in Ireland (ACOMRI). The money raised by the latter organisation amounted to approximately half of the eleven million dollars raised for the Irish cause from June 1919 until the time of the Anglo-Irish Treaty.[28]

The original idea for the Committee was Dr William Maloney, an Irish-American propagandist and close colleague of McGarrity. He told Patrick McCartan in early September 1920 that 'what we need is an American Commission sitting in Washington to investigate the British atrocities in Ireland as they occur.' Maloney appears to have had a great faith in the appeal to public opinion rather than to the Executive or the legislature. The liberal *Nation* journal sponsored the setting up of the Committee and the hearings held in Washington to examine evidence from both sides of the conflict. The Committee, soon expanded to 150, included church leaders, progressives and labour leaders. *The Times* commented that the membership was 'a strange mixture of Anglophobes, idealists and radicals'.[29]

By refusing visas for the sub-committee to visit Ireland and by preventing any British witnesses from testifying, the British government ended any hope of the Committee reaching objective findings. The hearings began on 19

November 1920 and the testimony from witnesses, particularly John Durham (Balbriggan town councillor) and Mary and Muriel MacSwiney, produced widespread publicity. The clandestine arrival of the new Mayor of Cork, Donal O'Callaghan, provided a further source of embarrassment for the British Foreign Office and the American State Department.[30]

The ACOMRI was soon attached to the Irish White Cross which was hastily set up in order to distribute funds in Ireland. The membership of its committee consisted of wealthy businessmen and lawyers, influential Irish-American politicians and experienced Quaker relief workers. The endorsement of President Harding, William MacAdoo, all the American cardinals and Herbert Hoover was won. The money raised came largely from the wealthy, unlike that raised by the Bond Drive. Big donations came from the Ancient Order of Hibernians and church dioceses and from dinners and concerts, some given by John McCormack, the popular tenor.[31]

Once raised, the problem was how the money should be distributed in Ireland and for what purpose. In February 1921, Clement France and John McCoy, with six other Quakers, arrived in Dublin to administer the fund. Their presence appeared as firm proof of American sympathy and President Harding's endorsement was blown up to appear as American administration approval for Sinn Féin. The Committee's report gave a baleful and exaggerated picture of the social and economic conditions currently prevalent in Ireland. France admitted to Dumont, the US Consul in Dublin: 'You can appreciate . . . that those wanting publicity for a committee like ours . . . are prone to overstate rather than understate the case.'[32]

The Committee was plagued by administrative problems and by the time of the Anglo-Irish Treaty around one half of the money raised had still to be given out. Dumont was cynical about how the money was used, writing that: 'the IRA would have to quit operations in three months if it were not supported by American money . . . it is not the intention of this organisation to do more with these funds than to put them at the disposal of the opponents of the British Government in Ireland.' To supply relief funds on an apolitical basis in Ireland in 1921 was inconceivable.[33]

1921 saw a decline in the effectiveness of Irish-American organisations. The main reason for this was the lack of any relevant American issue, after the League of Nations dispute and the Presidential election, with which they could be associated. The main aspects of Irish-American activity were not concerned with mainstream American politics any longer. Any expectation that the Harding administration would back the Irish cause was soon dashed. James O'Mara, soon to resign as the chief Irish fundraiser in America, told Mary MacSwiney that 'Nothing is being done at Washington because there is nothing to do and no one to do it with. Neither de Valera, nor you, nor Ireland makes the least impression on Washington, any more than on Paris or Berlin.'[34]

Unlike Wilson, Harding could well afford to ignore the question: the Republican administration was in no way indebted to Irish politicians and there was no longer the confusing issue of the League of Nations. Irish affairs had been little mentioned during the election campaign. Harding's Presidency exerted no pressure on the British government over Ireland. *The Irish World*, published in New York, asked on 30 April 1921: 'What have we gained by the change? President Harding is a simple-minded man, ignorant of world affairs and easily misled by those in whom he trusts . . . the whole Cabinet is English and imperialistic.' Strongly-worded resolutions on Ireland from Senators Norris and La Follette were held up in the Senate. Of La Follette's resolution, Senator Lodge commented: 'It is being referred to the Foreign Relations Committee and it will stay in the Committee a damn long time.'[35]

In May 1921 the *Montreal Daily Star* wrote: 'The Irish cause against England does not today enjoy the well-nigh universal support it once did in America . . . the resentment at the war abstention has somewhat passed but there has been no recovery of the old American automatic sympathy with the Irish cause.' Senator David I. Walsh told Maloney that 'for some reason or other I feel that there has been a slump in American sentiment on the Irish question. I do not know how to account for it. It seems to me that it is time for us to move slowly and cautiously and give serious thought to the cause for the present widespread indifference of the American people toward the Irish struggle.'[36]

There seems little correlation, therefore, between the heightening of guerrilla warfare in Ireland from the autumn of 1920 until the summer of 1921 and the level and effectiveness of exile nationalist activity. The lack of effective American leadership, the ongoing divisions and the want of realism in much of the policy followed must all be taken into account in explaining this, but the basic cause must be that they had an infertile field to plant during 1921. On hearing of the Truce, Edward L. Doheny declared that 'the affair is after all for the people of Ireland to settle among themselves.'[37]

The greatest significance of Irish America during 1921 was in the supply of arms and ammunition as well as financial support. In May, the American Embassy in London reported a conversation between the British Home Secretary and the Director of Intelligence indicating that de Valera's appeals to the US for more financial aid proved the exhaustion of the Dáil government's fiscal resources. Evidence for direct American aid came in the supply of guns across the Atlantic. In February there were State Department reports of the storage of machine guns and rifles for use in Ireland in Roxbury, a suburb of Boston, and Pawtucket, Rhode Island. In June, 495 Thompson machine guns bound for Ireland were found concealed aboard the SS *East Side*, moored at Hoboken, and there was soon similar information from Boston. According to official statements in the House of Commons, 16,388 rounds of American ammunition had been captured in the Dublin District since March 1921.[38]

It has proved easy to exaggerate the importance of American backing for Irish independence and to talk of the common wishes of supposedly twenty million people of Irish descent. There was a considerable degree of opposition to the Irish cause in the country, exacerbated by dislike of Irish-American machine politicians. However, the Irish question tapped into a widespread distrust of British imperialism and made it impossible for there to be close Anglo-American relations during the Paris Peace Conference. It was so important simply because it was believed to be so by the principal players.

19

THE PEACE PROCESS

Political historians overwhelmingly concern themselves with achievement, with what was brought to a conclusion, rather than with failure
and consideration of what might have happened. There has, therefore,
been a massive amount of writing on the negotiations which resulted
in the signing of the Anglo-Irish Treaty of December 1921, but comparatively
little interest has been shown in the sundry peace initiatives which occurred
during the War of Independence at regular intervals between June 1920 and
the Truce.

Detailed study of these peace moves throws light on the eventual settlement
and involves consideration of how necessary the latter, most violent, stages of
the conflict were. Terms put forward were similar to those eventually agreed in
the early hours of 6 December 1921 — safeguards on defence and Ulster, the
granting of fiscal autonomy and a form of Dominion Status to the twenty-six
counties. Concentration on the immediate context of the Treaty obscures the
fact that a settlement could, and perhaps should, have been achieved much
earlier. When welcoming the Treaty, Warren Fisher wrote: 'Better late than
never, but I can't get out of mind the unnecessary number of graves.'[1]

The implication of Fisher's rueful observation is that there had been more
than twelve months of background machinations and that a wide range of
opinion in Ireland and Britain had long seen the necessity for compromise.
Nonetheless a failure of political will on the part of the British government had
prevented any realistic peace terms being offered openly. That period saw the
most violent part of the war, which soured Anglo-Irish relations for many
decades subsequently. Responsibility for this must be placed squarely on Lloyd
George, who has not merited the favourable press he has generally received on
the Irish Question.

A.J.P. Taylor claimed that Lloyd George 'solved the Irish question or at any
rate came nearer than any other man to doing so'. In somewhat more meas-
ured terms, George Boyce wrote of Lloyd George that 'few would deny his
achievement in disposing of one of the most distracting problems in British

politics — the Irish question.'[2] Significantly, these judgments were made just as the six counties exploded into violence in the late 1960s. Any achievement of Lloyd George's on Irish policy between 1919 and 1923 was in the British political context. Taylor's and Boyce's views imply that Partition was a success, ignoring the disastrous consequences of the War of Independence and the general ineptitude with which policy was conducted.

Admittedly, party political considerations must be taken into account when examining Lloyd George's record on Ireland. Of the 484 MPs supporting the Coalition following the 1918 General Election, 338 were Conservatives. Within the twenty-two-strong Cabinet itself, seven were Liberals and all the rest were Tories. In March 1918 Lloyd George told Lord Riddell: 'It is no use being Prime Minister unless you can do what you want to do. It is useless for me to say that I can, because I can't. I have to make compromises all the time in order to conciliate different sections . . . take the Irish question. If I had a clear majority in the House of Commons I could soon settle it, but I have not.'[3]

It is true also that the pressures of the time often prevented the Prime Minister from paying sufficient attention to the matter. At a delicate moment during his peace initiative, Mark Sturgis was warned by Frances Stevenson that it was important to seize and hold Lloyd George's attention before some other crisis intervened.[4] Nonetheless it is impossible to defend Lloyd George's appointment of Lord French as Irish supremo and his allowing Walter Long to dominate the Cabinet's Irish policy for so long. The appointments of Macready and Anderson and the commissioning of Warren Fisher's report virtually amounted to a volte-face. By that time, however, much of the damage had been done. The use of the Black and Tans and Auxiliaries was ultimately Lloyd George's responsibility and ran counter to so much of the advice he was receiving at a time of much less distraction, long after the Paris Peace Conference and when Irish affairs were taking up a large portion of the Cabinet's time.

It can be claimed that the offer of Dominion Status was not an option until events forced Lloyd George's hand by late June/July 1921. Certainly the Tory party reacted unfavourably to any suggestion of it and Lloyd George himself said that Dominion Status 'was really a demand for the right of secession, since the Dominions were virtually independent States and could secede at any time if they chose'. The Prime Minister argued, when the subject was raised in early 1921, that any offer of such terms would leave them with no further ground to negotiate on if talks with Sinn Féin broke down: it had to be made clear that the Irish leadership would accept such a compromise before an offer could be made. Paul Bew argues that it was Sinn Féin's failure to clarify their negotiating position which was responsible for the breakdown of earlier peace talks.[5]

This, however, is to ignore how close a settlement was in December 1920 and how Lloyd George was to blame for the collapse of the Clune initiative then (see pages 182–5). Leading Tories, notably Lord Curzon and Austen Chamberlain, were supportive of conciliation and it is insufficient to explain Lloyd George's caution by reference to Irish republican intransigence or to confusion as to whether negotiations should be with Collins or with de Valera. Leaders of advanced nationalism, political and military, were more receptive of Dominion Status compromise than they could ever admit publicly at the time or, indeed, since.

Throughout the peace initiatives the Prime Minister acted deviously and inconsistently. Lloyd George's failure to act on the advice offered by so many prolonged the war. In contrast to his skilful handling of the Treaty negotiations, he made no attempt to isolate die-hard opinion. The Prime Minister's ambiguous response to their urgings made his advisers in Dublin Castle increasingly uneasy. This is scarcely surprising as Lloyd George had little sympathy for the Irish and, apart from considerations of his own political advantage, was chiefly motivated by the implications the question had for international, and especially American, relations.

In the late spring and early summer of 1920, against the background of increasing alarm in Whitehall and Dublin Castle about the security situation in Ireland and the virtual collapse of British administration, various tentative suggestions were made about the need for some kind of accommodation with Sinn Féin. In March the Conservative MP Alfred T. Davies had told Art O'Brien, the Sinn Féin representative in London, that the majority of the House of Commons favoured a peaceful settlement and that he was desirous of bringing about a meeting between Griffith and Lloyd George.

In July the labour lawyer Sir Charles Russell testified that he had been approached by Lloyd George to contact Sinn Féin 'to see if anything could be done in the way of a settlement'. Lloyd George indicated to Russell that he would enable Cabinet Ministers to meet with representatives of the Dáil but insisted that the latter would not include Collins and Gallagher (evidently meaning Brugha).[6]

In July also Thomas Jones recorded a meeting of a friend of his with Desmond FitzGerald, the Dáil's Minister of Publicity. FitzGerald related that the Dáil's leadership was willing to accept defence safeguards for Britain and constitutional safeguards for Ulster. 'As regards Dominion Home Rule, the name itself with its past associations might imply to the popular mind a compromise . . . which is anathema, but any bona fide scheme of real self-determination would be earnestly considered.' FitzGerald concluded: 'to refuse to recognise the Dáil is as futile as to refuse to recognise the Soviet.' Contact was also made with the Irish diplomat James MacNeill from which Jones gathered that MacNeill's brother Eoin would be willing to accept a Dominion Home Rule Settlement.[7]

Sympathy for some kind of rapprochement came from some unlikely quarters. On 23 July Lord Curzon asserted that he was 'in favour of getting into touch with the responsible leaders of Sinn Féin' with a view to 'remodelling' the Government of Ireland Bill. Meanwhile James MacMahon, in Dublin Castle, was assuring his colleagues of the certainty of the Catholic hierarchy's support if Dominion Status was offered.

A long-running saga in the peace process was triggered by a letter in *The Times* of 8 October 1920 from Brigadier-General George Cockerill, Conservative MP for Reigate. The letter had originally been written in September and had been held back from publication because of its coincidence with the final stages of Terence MacSwiney's hunger strike. Cockerill suggested that an immediate truce should precede a British-approved meeting of the Dáil. At that time also Cockerill wrote to the Prime Minister concluding: 'for pity's sake, let the troops have either peace or war.'[8]

Cockerill's initiative produced an immediate response from Sinn Féin in the form of frequent visits made to London by Patrick Moylett, a Mayo and Galway businessman and IRB member, who was to act as a middleman on behalf of Arthur Griffith. John Steele, the London editor of the *Chicago Tribune*, put Moylett in touch with leading figures in the Foreign Office and particularly C.J. Phillips. Moylett's frequent meetings with Phillips were attended by H.A.L. Fisher, the Minister of Education, one of the leading critics within the government of unauthorised reprisals.[9]

Fisher strove to get Moylett to help win Sinn Féin acceptance of the need for compromise on demands for a Republic. The implication from the British side was that the Government of Ireland Bill could be modified on financial matters. In terms later approved in a letter of Griffith's of 18 November it was laid down that the Dáil should be allowed to meet with the sole purpose of electing representatives to a conference.

It was stated that: 'Sinn Féin's idea of the conference is that it would consist of one or two members representing Ulster, one or two representing Sinn Féin and (say) five others representing England, Scotland, Wales and possibly the two Dominions specially interested in the Irish Question, viz. Canada and Australia.' The memorandum concluded: 'Sinn Féin professes confidence in the success of such a conference.' Again there seemed agreement on the need to recognise British security interests and for some Irish liability for contribution to imperial finance. In his letter, Griffith sought fiscal autonomy and consular representation but accepted a degree of autonomy for Ulster and that there should be no separate Irish army or navy.[10]

As was the case in all the peace initiatives the talks dragged on in a confused manner, often affected by developments on the ground in Ireland, most notably the Bloody Sunday killings of 21 November. At that time Phillips advised Moylett to tell Griffith not to break 'the slender link which has been established'. He quoted the Prime Minister as saying that a week of quiet was necessary to create an atmosphere for peace and continued: 'tragic as the events in Dublin were, they were of no importance. These men were soldiers and took a soldier's risk.'[11]

It seems that the death knell for any hopes of these discussions came with the arrest of Griffith on 25 November which, much to Phillips' annoyance, was done without government authority. There appears little credence to Moylett's claim that Dublin Castle was responsible for wrecking his initiative. Moylett was to admit that his leaking of details of his activities to the *Irish Independent* killed off any lingering hopes. For the next six months Moylett continued to use his links in London but was no longer trusted by the Sinn Féin leadership, including Griffith. Collins said of Moylett: 'I fancy him to be a man who thinks nobody can tell him anything.'[12]

While the Moylett peace move stuttered on, General Macready acted as the link between Dublin and London in efforts at reconciliation made by two Southern Unionists, General O'Gowan and Doctor Crofton, at the end of October. Macready reported to Sir John Anderson that the two intermediaries had been assured that a substantial section of the Dáil were prepared to accept an amended Government of Ireland Bill but would require definite assurances of the Prime Minister's position. Anderson thought their original proposal too vague but a meeting was arranged between the intermediaries and Lloyd George, Greenwood and Bonar Law on 7 November.

At that meeting Lloyd George was told that the Dáil would accept the exclusion of the six counties provided that fiscal autonomy was granted to the twenty-six; Lloyd George indicated that that was not too high a price to pay. Even the normally pessimistic Law was moved to tell Anderson that: 'it looked more like a reality than anything I have heard of before.' Despite Griffith's doubts about Lloyd George's trustworthiness, Griffith and Collins initially appeared positive to these developments. Soon, however, Bloody Sunday and Griffith's arrest intervened. At a particularly sensitive time, neither side could give definite assurances which would provide the basis for firm negotiations. Cockerill told Moylett on 10 December: 'Neither country ready for an honourable peace at the same time.'[13]

In September an attempt had been made to bring Griffith together with Sir John Anderson. For once a direct approach was adopted. Wylie assured Sturgis that the moderate wing of the Dáil wanted a 'secret confab' and a meeting was arranged between Griffith and Anderson in the solicitor Corrigan's office in St Andrew's Street in the centre of Dublin. Wylie had defended Corrigan when the latter was prosecuted for involvement in the Easter Rising, and regarded this as the payback on the favour. Corrigan was the legal adviser for the Irish National Aid and Dependants' Fund and Michael Collins often used a room above his office.

There is conflicting testimony as to whether Griffith and Anderson actually met on 26 September, but Sturgis can most likely be relied upon when he reported that Griffith backed away at the last moment by insisting that Anderson recognise the equal status of the Dáil. Nonetheless Sturgis could conclude that: 'It looks as if the pressure on the Quiet Side of SF to break away from the Gunmen was increasing.'[14]

At the end of November the poet and mystic George Russell (AE) and Winston Churchill's American cousin Shane Leslie put themselves forward as potential intermediaries. AE met Lloyd George and was reputedly told that the British government 'will not tolerate a Republic but anything short of that'. In late November/early December the British Labour Party's Commission on Ireland was seen as a potential bridge but was soon overtaken by a new and more important intervention.[15]

Of all the numerous abortive peace initiatives during the War that of Archbishop Patrick Joseph Clune, of Perth, Western Australia, came closest to success. It was brought about at Lloyd George's own behest and provoked a serious response from the Sinn Féin and IRA leadership. Beginning in the immediate aftermath of Bloody Sunday and the Kilmichael ambush and co-inciding with the declaration of martial law for most of Munster, it could not have happened at a more sensitive time. Clune's mission took place when the policy options were clearer than ever before and when emotions were at their rawest. As the bodies of those killed at Kilmichael were ceremonially laid to rest in Westminster Abbey, Clune embarked on his complex manoeuvring.

While Lloyd George and Collins were to distance themselves from associa-tion with the mission's failure, they had both invested considerable hope in Clune's activities. At an early stage Art O'Brien told Griffith: 'The three inter-views, none of which have been sought by us, all seem to me to exhibit a greater anxiety for peace than they have previously exhibited.' Welcoming the possibility of a truce, Collins relayed the view on 2 December: 'It is too much to expect that Irish physical force could combat successfully English physical force for any length of time if the directors of the latter could get a free hand for ruthlessness.' Collins told Griffith: 'My view is that a Truce on the terms specified cannot possibly do us any harm. It appears to me that it is distinctly an advance.' When Clune's efforts foundered, Collins was quick to dissociate himself and to talk of the dangers of British espionage, but that should not hide his original interest in a possible truce.[16]

Many were to look back on Clune's efforts as what Asquith called the 'big missed opportunity'. Tim Healy told Lord Beaverbrook: 'the silly Cabinet turned him (Clune) down, believing they can crush the Shinns, and that their acceptance of a Truce spelled weakness. No worse incident has occurred for 100 years.'[17]

Born in County Clare, Clune had been a Redemptorist missionary in New Zealand and Australia. Appointed Bishop of Perth in 1910, he became its first Archbishop in 1913. He had been principally noted for his administrative ability, helping to restore the finances of a bankrupt diocese, and for his prowess as a giver of grandiloquent sermons, most famously on Edward VII's death. He was a moderate Home Ruler and a monarchist who supported con-scription in Australia during the First World War and had been Catholic Chaplain-General to the Australian forces from 1916.[18] By late 1920 Clune had been in England and Ireland for several months following his *ad limina* visit to the Vatican. At the time of the Lahinch reprisal on 21 September, he had been staying with Bishop Fogarty in Ennis. His nephew Conor had been killed, along with Dick McKee and Peadar Clancy, in Dublin Castle during the Bloody Sunday weekend.

On 30 November 1920, at a farewell dinner for the Archbishop hosted by Sir J.D. Connelly, the Agent-General for Western Australia, and attended by Lord Morris, T.P. O'Connor and Joe Devlin, two remnants of the IPP at Westminster, Clune was prevailed upon to postpone his departure. Devlin arranged an interview with Lloyd George on 1 December. Clune related to Lloyd George his experience of conditions in Clare and, following an expression of regret about reprisals, Lloyd George asked him to interview the Sinn Féin leaders in Dublin, arranging safe conduct for Clune to visit Griffith and other leaders in Mountjoy Prison. Before leaving for Dublin, Clune visited Art O'Brien who set up contacts with Collins. He also sought the advice of Archbishop Mannix, a considerably less popular Australian prelate as far as the British government was concerned.[19]

During the next three weeks Clune practised shuttle diplomacy. In Dublin he stayed in the home of the prominent Dublin solicitor Sir John O'Connell in the beautiful seaside suburb of Killiney, under the pseudonym Reverend Doctor Walsh. He was soon escorted by Andy Cope into Mountjoy to meet Griffith and Eoin MacNeill. Joseph O'Reilly, Collins' faithful lieutenant, cycled out to Killiney to arrange a meeting with Collins at Doctor Robert Farnan's house in Merrion Square. Bishop Fogarty accompanied Clune on his various interviews.[20]

The early stages of Clune's mission went well. The Archbishop established good relations with the Dublin Castle junta of Anderson, Cope and Sturgis. Negotiations concentrated on achieving a truce followed by a meeting of the Dáil. The British originally insisted that Collins and Mulcahy not attend this and that church and labour representatives be added to the membership.[21]

In the days following Clune's first meeting with Griffith a series of external developments served to complicate matters. On 3 and 4 December resolutions of the Galway County and Urban District Councils called for truce negotiations and a meeting of the Dáil. A day later Father Michael O'Flanagan, Acting President of Sinn Féin, sent a telegram to Lloyd George asking him for his peace terms. This followed on appeals for peace from Roger Sweetman, a TD, and the Bishop of Tuam.

On 6 December, the American Consul in Dublin, Frederick Dumont, reported that he had been approached by IRA men to act as a middleman with the British Army — a shadowy reference confirmed by a comment in Sir Henry Wilson's diary. A later comment by O'Flanagan suggests that his cable was a deliberate attempt to sabotage Clune's efforts, which he held to be too much influenced by Dublin Castle.

These developments encouraged many within the British military and political establishment to believe that Sinn Féin was desperate for peace. Greenwood told Lloyd George: 'The SF Cause and organisation is breaking up. Clune and everyone else admits this . . . there is no need of hurry in settlement. We can in due course and on our own and fair terms settle this Irish Question for good.' Military opinion held that it was particularly inapposite to talk of truce when martial law had been partially established.[22]

By the time that Lloyd George met Clune again in London on 8 December, he was stressing that his freedom of action was curtailed by military and political considerations. He observed that the period following Bloody Sunday and Kilmichael was not the most favourable for truce discussions. In his report on this meeting Clune accepted that there was a distinction between the military perspective and that of Lloyd George; Griffith concluded that the Prime Minister 'apparently wants peace but is afraid of his Militarists'. Collins, however, took a more cynical line on Lloyd George's motivation, telling Art O'Brien: 'there is far too much a tendency to believe that LG is wishful for Peace, and it is only his own wild men prevent him from accomplishing his desires . . . I am not convinced that he is the peace-maker.'

At his meeting with the Prime Minister, Clune had stressed that any insistence on arms surrender would be fatal to the negotiations. By the time Clune returned to Dublin, however, Lloyd George was insisting that IRA weapons be given up prior to a formal truce. In the Commons on 9 December the Prime Minister affirmed that the government 'have no option but to continue and indeed to intensify their campaign'.[23]

It was virtually inevitable that Griffith and Collins would reject the revised terms when Clune next visited them. Griffith feared that the British were using Clune's visits for espionage purposes and Art O'Brien was opposed to the continuation of the mission, believing that the Archbishop was too naive and trusting to deal with Lloyd George.[24]

Until the end of the year the British still remained in contact with Clune. The Cabinet together with military advisers reviewed the truce issue on 29 December. Macready then emphasised the danger of IRA reorganisation during a truce and Sir Henry Wilson argued that to halt the conflict 'would be absolutely fatal'. While the Liberal critics of a hard-line policy still argued for compromise, the comfortable majority supported the continuation of the war. It was left to Philip Kerr, a member of Lloyd George's kitchen cabinet, to interview Clune, to point out to him the South African precedent for arms surrender preparatory to the end of the war and to thank the Archbishop for his efforts. Clune was at last free to return to Australia via Rome.[25]

On 3 January 1921, Cope wrote to Sturgis: 'Just back from tea with the Archbishop. He wishes to be remembered to you and Jonathan. He is very disappointed . . . he is satisfied that if the business had been left to the three of us in the Castle, a settlement would be a few days off — a final settlement he means. He says he felt sure that Jonathan and himself had arranged a truce commencing Xmas.' Sturgis confirmed the accuracy of the Sinn Féin claim that Lloyd George had belatedly imposed terms which did not exist at the beginning of Clune's mission. Sturgis writes in his diary of 18 February 1921: 'Speaking last night on the Clune peace talk the PM said that all his advisers said Truce without the surrender of arms was impossible — this is contrary to my recollection and back pages bear me out.'

Clune broke his silence when interviewed in Paris by 'La Liberté' where he declared that the Irish leaders were not assassins but were the 'cream of their race'. Clune went on to warn Pope Benedict XV of the depth of the crisis in Ireland and played an important rôle in preventing the Papacy from agreeing to British pressure to condemn Sinn Féin outrages.[26]

Prior to Clune's return to Perth, the Western Australian Governor-General Sir Francis Newdegate denounced the Paris interview and urged the British Home Office to detain Clune in Britain, fearing that his homecoming would exacerbate labour disturbances, but this advice was ignored by the British authorities. Addressing a large crowd gathered to welcome him home outside St Mary's Cathedral in Perth, Clune castigated British policy in Ireland and compared Black and Tan atrocities to those in Belgium during the First World War. Following his few months of fame, Clune was to have little to say publicly about Irish affairs though he supported the Anglo-Irish Treaty.[27]

Responsibility for the abortive initiative and its consequences lies squarely with Lloyd George himself. He had backed away from interest in a truce when faced with military and Conservative opposition. His actions and words were a disastrous mixture of private manoeuvring and public inflexibility. He must have been aware that it was inconceivable that the Irish leadership would agree to arms surrender and that the initiative would provoke the reaction it did in British military and political circles. Not for the first or last time Dublin Castle was bemused by the policy vacillations in London. The affair strikingly resembles Lloyd George's morally dubious and politically inept handling of the Irish-American delegation's visit to Ireland in the spring of 1919.

It was no defence for Lloyd George to plead the political restraints on him, for they only made it the more important that he did not become involved in risky projects which he did not have the necessary commitment to sustain. The affair was to strongly increase Sinn Féin suspicions concerning Lloyd George's integrity and to make them more reluctant to open fresh negotiations. During his peace efforts with labour leaders in March 1921, Sturgis reported being told that: 'the Shins regard themselves as tricked and sold over Clune. Clune saw them all and went to London with terms in his pocket and was led on and then turned down . . . of course I said "not so" but that's their reading of it.'

Collins and Griffith were keen to play down the importance of the Clune visits but it was not any lack of commitment on their part which resulted in the breakdown of the talks. It suited Collins meanwhile to put the blame on Father O'Flanagan and the Galway Councils. 'It seems to me,' he wrote, 'that something might have been done . . . were it not for the ill-timed actions of (a) Galway Council (b) Father O'Flanagan's wire. To them must be added R.M. Sweetman's very futile and very foolish letter.'[28]

The failure of the Clune mission, the final passage of the Government of Ireland Bill and the extension of martial law somewhat surprisingly did not signal the end of peace moves. Mark Sturgis commented on 1 January 1921: 'The side to the whole thing which is most cheering is that it seems only necessary for one, two or three Peace Balloons to bust for another to take its place in the sky. There *must* be a very real anxiety to settle.' Despite the poor reception of his letters in the press in December, Father O'Flanagan, together with Lord Justice O'Connor, met with Lloyd George in early January in Downing Street.

The meeting came about on O'Connor's initiative and immediately followed on de Valera's return to Ireland. As shown by the orders to the police and military that de Valera should not be arrested, the British regarded the President as the moderate in Sinn Féin ranks and the best hope for peace. Greenwood later described de Valera as: 'the one man who can deliver the goods'. Sturgis and Cope were assured by O'Connor that de Valera was 'most anxious to stop bloodshed'. De Valera responded to the sundry peace feelers with extreme caution. He was determined not to publicly lower republican demands and to avoid being drawn into indirect negotiations.

Cope and Sturgis arranged the meeting with O'Connor and O'Flanagan, Sturgis remarking, 'It is very pleasant to be "in the know" but a bit embarrassing for the Under-Secretary to be asked in so many words to arrange for an interview with the PM and not to tell the Chief Secretary about it.'[29] O'Connor created a disastrous impression. Lady Greenwood said that at an earlier meeting with Lloyd George, O'Connor 'had talked great nonsense and . . . the PM thought nothing of him'. Since O'Flanagan's clumsy intervention in December there was no hope that any effort by him could win general acceptance within Sinn Féin. Collins stressed that O'Flanagan's audience with Lloyd George was not 'at my wish nor with my sanction and I can positively say the same for President de Valera. Very likely LG and Co are making a fool of Father Michael.'[30]

O'Flanagan and O'Connor stayed at the Hotel Russell; their movements tracked by the Secret Service. Their meeting with Lloyd George took place on the 6 January after a preliminary meeting with Cope, Sturgis and Greenwood in the Treasury. O'Flanagan made a favourable impression despite his refusal to shake hands on meeting Greenwood. Sturgis recorded: 'O'Connor talks too much with great vehemence. O'Flanagan spoke little except when directly addressed and then with great simplicity and great force and clearness. I am sure he is a man with whom one could do business.'

Discussion was on settlement terms this time and not on a truce. The Irishmen argued for amendment of the Government of Ireland Act by the granting of fiscal autonomy and suggested that the Irish contribute to the War Debt indirectly by re-allocation of the American Loan. Lloyd George, however, offered little hope for a settlement. Lady Greenwood wrote: 'The PM's great difficulty is to add anything to the Home Rule Act now that it *is* an Act and that the Shinns should have made their proposal before it passed into law.' By the time that Lloyd George made his opposition to their proposals clear in correspondence with O'Connor he was aware that they were not official representatives of the Dáil. Later developments, however, showed that Lloyd George had only agreed to the meeting in order to set up communication with de Valera.[31]

Anderson at this time told O'Connor and O'Flanagan to sound de Valera out, and de Valera agreed to talks if no preconditions were attached. A preparatory meeting between de Valera and Sir Edward Carson was to be arranged. O'Connor visited his old legal colleague Carson in London and together with O'Flanagan had a surprisingly positive meeting, with Carson suggesting reduction of Ireland's debt rather than fiscal autonomy and showing a willingness to meet de Valera.[32] Coinciding with this, Lady Greenwood and Mark Sturgis were involved in an elaborate correspondence aimed at bringing Carson and de Valera together before a possible meeting with the Prime Minister.

In late January, at a meeting with Cabinet members, Lloyd George was totally confused about whether de Valera had been in direct communication with him regarding possible negotiations. His secretary Frances Stevenson was sent out to check correspondence in the Prime Minister's pockets and came back with a letter from Lady Greenwood supporting a meeting with de Valera and giving her assurance that what de Valera 'wanted was a face-saver, that he was willing to drop the republic and even fiscal autonomy if it could be done'. Hamar Greenwood expressed opposition to any such contacts and Bonar Law stated: 'Coercion was the only policy . . . in the past it had been followed by periods of quiet for about 10 years' and that he had come to the conclusion 'that the Irish were an inferior race'. Lloyd George expressed the desirability of a settlement in the context of Anglo-American relations and cited General Jeudwine's gloom about military prospects.[33] It was apparent, therefore, that Lloyd George was tempted to compromise, but still hesitated to make any final commitment.

It was at this time that Lady Greenwood became the crucial figure in trying to bring de Valera and Lloyd George together. In a series of cryptic letters to Sturgis she acted as a go-between, her efforts aided by her close relationship to Frances Stevenson. The role of women in high politics was usually an obscure one and Lady Greenwood used a pseudonym in most of her correspondence. Sturgis commented that in discussions with O'Connor and O'Flanagan 'I gave no hint of the writer about whom I only said that *he* was *not* a Member of Parliament and *not* a Civil Servant; but a friend of mine and an intimate and trusted friend of the PM's.'[34]

Lady Greenwood played a much more central part in the peace plotting than her husband did: she was in a position to act more independently and was much more highly regarded in Dublin Castle and Downing Street than Sir Hamar. She obviously relished political intrigue and moving outside her social and domestic sphere.

For all Lady Greenwood's and Sturgis' efforts, it was to prove impossible to set up a meeting between Carson and de Valera, primarily it appears because de Valera insisted that he be told what the British terms were prior to any conference. Sturgis told Lady Greenwood that he had it on good authority that de Valera would meet Lloyd George if he could be assured that something definite would result. Lady Greenwood stressed that the Prime Minister would have to be convinced of de Valera's willingness to do business. Using the code-names of Violet for de Valera, Carrie for Carson and Bishop for Lloyd George, Lady Greenwood and Sturgis strove unsuccessfully to bring de Valera and Carson together in London. Their efforts broke down on the unwillingness of either side to make the first offer. By 23 February Lady Greenwood reported that Lloyd George had become aloof on the issue and that his mind had turned to international matters.[35] Sturgis was left to despair at the lack of polit-ical courage.

The three most obvious intermediary sources were organised labour, the church and Southern Unionists. Each in turn came into play during the first six months of 1921. Different members of the Dublin Castle administration acted as links and Sturgis saw their efforts as almost competitive. MacMahon had close relations with the Catholic hierarchy, Cope had a variety of contacts with Sinn Féin and Sturgis' primary contacts in March and April were with union leaders. Much more is known about Sturgis' efforts than those of the others because of his diaries and letters. Cope had to operate in an under-world and MacMahon left no private papers.

It was Sturgis' close friend, Richard Wyndham Quin — Keeper of the Horse for the Governor-General — who put Sturgis in touch with labour figures, ini-tially through J.J. Parkinson, coal-mine and racehorse owner. In March the Irish Railway Executive had set up a meeting of William O'Brien, General Treasurer of the Irish Transport and General Workers' Union (ITGWU), and Thomas Foran, General President of that union, with Edward Shortt, the British Home Secretary. Shortt had been optimistic that a Dominion Home Rule settlement would be offered with the usual restrictions, and the union leaders appeared agreeable to this provided it involved fiscal autonomy. On their return Foran and O'Brien saw de Valera. In late March Sturgis took over the role as mid-dleman, his activity helped by a shared interest in horse-racing.[36]

Sturgis had heard from Shortt via Anderson that 'the PM is in a much more yielding mood and is prepared . . . not only to make big fiscal concessions but to take the initiative and say — of course after preliminary discussion into which the Ulster people would be brought — what price he is willing to pay for peace.' Sturgis urged his labour contacts to take advantage of this opportunity. He concluded: 'I have got very good personal relations with the people I've met so far — swapping racing tips etc and if there is a hitch from the SF side I'd make a push to see others.' Despite these hopes and the fact that these efforts took place during a stay in executions, Sinn Féin soon vetoed any direct dealings between labour and the British government. Sturgis concluded: 'It really is all rather like a nightmare, isn't it — one cannot see that there is really any material thing at all between us if only this fencing for position could stop and we could get round a table.'[37]

The church was always cautious with regard to becoming too closely identi-fied with peace moves. Individual members of its hierarchy, however, were often active behind the scenes. Bishops had a variety of views about Sinn Féin and Anglo-Irish relations. Bishop Fogarty had strong advanced nationalist sympathies, Bishop Cohalan became a harsh critic of IRA methods and Cardinal Logue had moderate views better suited to the Home Rule era. There remained a gulf between the views of the hierarchy and much of the younger clergy. These, however, were not the primary reasons for the church's reluctance to become publicly involved.

The institution was always hesitant to attack established government, to risk disturbing Anglo-Irish relations or to embarrass the Papacy. Collins understood that it would be inept to try and get the church to publicly express support for Sinn Féin. It was clear, however, that a Dominion Status settlement was supported by the bishops as would be shown when they enthusiastically welcomed the Anglo-Irish Treaty. Following a meeting of bishops at Maynooth in early April, MacMahon set up various discussions with individual church leaders. There were obviously hopes that Fogarty in particular would provide the bridge to de Valera but again nothing concrete emerged.[38]

In the first half of 1921 frequent efforts were made by Southern Unionists to put pressure on the British government. They saw themselves as representing business as well as minority interests and often had audiences with Lloyd George. It was not until June that they were able to have any demonstrable effect. These months also saw sundry individual initiatives. In February the Killarney landowner Arthur Vincent wrote to *The Times* advocating arms surrender, fiscal autonomy and a meeting of de Valera with Ulster leaders. He was in touch with Basil Thomson, the Head of British Intelligence, but confusion blocked any hope of direct discussions.[39]

In April attention switched to a direct initiative by Lord Derby, and then to attempts to set up direct relations between Craig and de Valera and consideration of whether a truce should be arranged for the elections to the projected Southern parliament.

Lord Derby's peace mission to Ireland in April had many of the elements of a genteel farce: for some newspapers and for Mark Sturgis it became the subject of hilarious anecdote and apocryphal stories. It was not the product of any initiative by the British government or by Dublin Castle. The Sturgis Diaries reveal that surprisingly little was known in the Irish administration about Derby's movements and purpose. Derby was an intermediary of some social and political stature. One of the most powerful of landed aristocrats, he was an important figure within the Tory party and had been War Minister between 1916 and 1918. On urging Derby to become involved, Edward Saunderson quoted Arthur Balfour as saying: 'that the Irish will trust no one except a gentleman'.

Derby was approached in the first instance by two Catholic Liverpool MPs, Sir James Reynolds and Colonel John Shute. To prepare the ground Father Hughes, a parish priest in Liverpool, visited Cardinal Logue several times and accompanied Derby on his mission. Before they left, not only was Logue's approval gained but also de Valera's agreement to meet with Derby. His

Lordship journeyed to the North on 18 April, visiting the Cardinal in Armagh before staying at the Gresham Hotel in Dublin from 21 April.[40]

It had been decided to place a heavy emphasis on secrecy, although Lloyd George and Greenwood were put in the picture. Derby travelled under the name 'Mr Edwards' and de Valera was referred to in all correspondence as 'administrator'. Apart, however, from the difficulty of the well-known Derby and his large figure avoiding recognition, several amateurish slips were made: Derby left a coat with his name on in his hotel room, subsequently being taken aback at the chambermaid respectfully addressing him as 'Me Lord', and later was given an inappropriately ostentatious welcome when meeting Cardinal Logue at a railway station. Sturgis had a fund of Derby stories and recorded gleefully on 2 May:

I have just made MacMahon tell me again the best of the Derby stories, and true, so help me . . . Derby and Hughes were walking in the Cardinal's grounds at Armagh when a curate who had been officiating in the Cathedral and knew Father Hughes, came across to speak to him and was introduced to 'Mr Edwards'.

Father H: 'Let me introduce you to Mr Edwards.'

Lord Derby: 'This is an extremely fertile part of the country — I see that it is an orchard country.'

Curate: 'It is indeed, we grow a great quantity of apples.'

Lord D. : 'What's the best apple in this part of the country?'

Curate: 'Well, Sir, the best apple we grow is the "Lord Derby"; it's a big apple, and an ugly apple, and it seldom ripens entirely but 'tis a good marketable baking apple for all that and the best we grow in these parts.'

When he turned away Lord Derby insisted that he was discovered; Hughes that it was a pure coincidence. Father Hughes pursued the Curate and by dint of judicious questioning satisfied himself that he was right. Coincidence it was. The Curate had no idea of Mr Edwards' identity.

Such stories soon broke in the press. *The Daily Express* commented: 'the sombre tragedy of Sinn Féin has been relieved before now by a few touches of comedy' and referred to 'Lord Derby, of all men, masquerading as Mr Edwards at an Irish Commercial Hotel'.[41]

Derby met de Valera at the wealthy Sinn Féiner James O'Mara's house in Fitzwilliam Street. Derby evidently offered concessions on fiscal independence and on removing reserved services for the whole of Ireland. De Valera naturally testified that he held firm to his republican commitment. It was agreed that the Irish leader would state his terms in a letter to Derby which would be conveyed to Lloyd George before his next statement in the House. Again, however, confusion reigned. After Derby left, Father Hughes failed to get possession of de Valera's statement in time and resorted to opening the letter himself. De Valera's answer amounted to a question of his own: whether Lloyd

George would agree to see him without any assurances on Irish willingness to be flexible. By meeting Griffith and MacNeill in Mountjoy Prison, Hughes again took too much on himself and was reprimanded by Derby. The initiative fizzled out.[42]

In 1954 de Valera told Derby's biographer, Randolph Churchill, that Derby's visit had broken the ice and had some significance in preparing the way for the Truce. That, however, seems over-respectful to Derby's historical significance and to the biographer's needs. The visit produced little other than amusing stories, although it is noteworthy that de Valera agreed to see Derby. It all underlined the absurdity of avoiding a direct approach and the unwillingness on both sides to make the first move.[43]

20

THE PATH TO THE TRUCE

The imminence of the 22 May elections for the Northern and Southern parliaments led to often confused debates in the British Cabinet about whether the polls should be postponed or a truce negotiated for the election period. This provided the background to the semi-official peace moves of the time. At this stage also there were rumours of changes in the Dublin Castle administration and in particular of Greenwood's transfer back to London. The Chief Secretary, however, scarcely merited promotion and to have replaced him at that time would have been a distinctly negative comment on the British administration. One change that did occur was French's retirement from the Lord Lieutenancy.

The old general had long ceased to have any relevance and even Sturgis, who had considerable affection for him, found it impossible to hide the pathetic nature of his departure in mid-April. French was replaced by Edmund Talbot, Lord Fitzalan, the first Catholic to be appointed to the post. Fitzalan's high Tory credentials did not indicate any radical hopes for his tenure; his appointment was pure tokenism. Sir John Ross, the future Lord Chancellor, and Anderson saw Fitzalan's arrival as an opportunity for an appeal for truce and negotiations to be made. A memorandum was drawn up but never acted upon.[1]

At a meeting on 8 March, Lord Midleton told members of the Cabinet of Southern Unionist fears about the consequences of the election going ahead. It was argued that the poll should be held at a later time in the South than in the North to allow the military situation to improve, though Lloyd George expressed cynicism about any such hopes. Even Greenwood admitted that he had been over-optimistic in December and joined in the general consensus that any military solution was a long way from fulfilment. It was remarkable that Lloyd George had to point out how bad postponement of the elections would look overseas.[2]

In early April, encouraged by the seemingly flexible attitudes which de Valera had shown in various foreign press interviews, Greenwood and Lloyd George became hopeful of a truce being negotiated, but by the time of lengthy Cabinet discussions on the matter in late April and May, attitudes had changed. During the final debate on the issue on 12 May, confidence in the Cabinet's judgment is undermined by Thomas Jones' comment: 'The fact that the nominations were on the following day came as a surprise to several Ministers whose idea had been to have a truce over the period of the elections (13–14th) but had not realised that the period was upon us.'

Opinions in the Cabinet divided straightforwardly along Liberal/Conservative lines and the vote went 9:5 against a truce being offered. The outcome had clearly been influenced by the almost universal opposition of the Dublin authorities to any cessation of hostilities, with Macready and Winter stressing the negative consequences for Intelligence and the opportunity a truce would offer for IRA reorganisation. Anderson, however, thought the time ripe for a *beau geste* and concluded: 'It would be a thousand pities to let it slip.'

Significantly, Lloyd George spelt out his staunch opposition to any further concessions in terms of deep antipathy to the Irish in general. When H.A.L. Fisher urged the Prime Minister 'to seize the first opportunity', Lloyd George replied: 'I've taken part in two or three acts of this kind. We sent back deportees and they laughed at us. Did the same at the Convention and after the Easter Rebellion. Every one a failure; there was no response from the Irish and they took full advantage of us . . . Every war has its squalid side and every crime and every prosecution of crime. Dartmoor is squalid. All crime is squalid. You've got to face that. But I can't see myself signing away right to levy tariffs on Great Britain. That means war. We'd have to re-conquer Ireland. Give them Army and Navy and they'd intrigue in U.S.A. And all this in order to save one, two or three years of an unpleasant business of this kind . . . I gravely urge that we should not be in a hurry. I've given tremendous thought to this. We've been generous in the Home Rule Act. Anything beyond that would contain germs of trouble . . . you have had these phases before. Now you've deprived them of every legitimate grievance.'

Lloyd George was also keen to point out that Intelligence information indicated that Collins' intransigence would prevail over de Valera's supposedly more moderate attitudes in Sinn Féin circles. The debate, however, was only put aside until the elections were over.[3]

No election took place in the twenty-six counties. All 124 seats were filled by Sinn Féiners: apart from the four University constituencies, no other candidates put themselves forward. The first Dáil became the second Dáil by kind permission of British policy and advanced nationalist control was consolidated at the expense of wide-ranging minority opinion, including farming and labour interests, which were thus effectively stifled. Meanwhile the election in the North copperfastened Unionist control.

The consequences of the elections landed the British government with a choice of unpalatable alternatives. The timetable for implementation of the Government of Ireland Act meant that the Southern parliament had to be established by 12 July. Failing that, a decision had to be made between declaring Crown Colony government, and with that the imposition of martial law for all of the twenty-six counties with a considerable increase in the military effort, or truce and negotiation. There was no more scope for prevarication and delay. The Irish Situation Committee on 27 May set out the practical advantages of martial law in unifying military and police control and a Cabinet meeting on 2 June saw it as a means to end authorised reprisals. The target date was postponed to 14 July when Jones whispered to the Prime Minister that the anniversary of the Battle of the Boyne was an unfortunate date.[4]

The British Cabinet and its sub-committees weighed up the options during the first half of June, going into some detail about the precise military strategy to be applied if the hawkish option was decided upon. There never seems to have been any possibility that such a course would be followed. It was Macready who made the most effective case against coercion. In a letter to Frances Stevenson he argued that even if military action should succeed, he saw no prospect of a stable government emerging and did not see the necessary support in Britain for an escalation of the conflict. He was also very concerned about the morale and fitness of the troops.

The C-in-C concluded: 'There are, of course, one or two wild people about who still hold the absurd idea that if you go on killing long enough peace will ensue. I do not believe it for one moment, but I do believe that the more people that are killed, the more difficult will be the final solution, unless while killing is going on a body of opinion is growing up embued (sic) with a strong sense that the Government have made a generous and definite offer to Ireland. It must be remembered that every Irish man and woman distrusts any British Government, and will not be content with anything less than a public pledge, which they consider cannot be afterwards bargained away.'

Anderson fully agreed and warned of the difficulties of waging war in the modern glare of publicity. Of public opinion he commented: 'I think . . . they are war-weary, tired of strife, and that the instinctive desire in relation to Ireland is to forget.' Macready and Anderson felt that half-hearted martial law had failed and had no expectations that full martial law would succeed. Anderson quoted Macready as saying: 'It is a case of "all out or get out".'[5] It is Lloyd George's extremely belated acceptance of these views which explains the U-turn in British policy, from outright rejection of any truce and unconditional offer of negotiations in May to the offer of virtual Dominion Status in early July. This cannot be put down to any greater willingness by Sinn Féin to negotiate nor to any changes in the military situation, nor to any rumoured threat to Lloyd George's leadership of the Coalition. The constitutional and military realities had clarified the issues and the establishment of the Northern government cleared away the major block to negotiations with the Southern government. The King's address when opening the Northern Ireland parliament on 22 June was the great opportunity for indicating a shift in policy (Appendix H).

There remained the problem of finding out whether the Dáil government would respond positively to any direct peace initiative. Sturgis commented in his diary of 13 June: 'I cannot but believe that the Shinn reluctance to come out and play the statesman is due to the simple fact that they are to a certain extent all to pieces. If we want to deal with England there's L.G. — if we want to talk to Ulster there's Craig or Carson, but when we want to talk to SF it's a heterogeneous "collection" of individuals who thanks largely to our activities are not even "collected' — all over the place, and they severally if they know their own minds, which I doubt they certainly don't, know each others and all fear to act off their own bat.'

While Cope was ever active in tracking down Sinn Féin sources, notably Éamon Duggan, de Valera himself remained elusive and conclusions had to be drawn from his interviews with the foreign press. There were many offers to act as intermediaries but General Jan Smuts, the South African Premier, turned out to be the key player. The meeting of colonial Prime Ministers in London in early July gave an obvious opportunity. Colonel Maurice Moore, former Inspector-General of the Irish Volunteers, had been sent to South Africa by the Dáil government in April and May to enlist Smuts' assistance. From their own recent experience it was inconceivable that the South Africans would advocate dogmatic insistence on the preservation of the Republic.[6]

After his arrival in London on 11 June, Smuts put pressure on Lloyd George to make a public offer of Dominion Status to de Valera. He pointed out: 'In the first place the establishment of the Northern Parliament definitely eliminates the coercion of Ulster, and the road is now clear to deal on the most statesmanlike lines with the rest of Ireland.' Smuts composed a draft of the King's Belfast speech which was amended from what Balfour and Chamberlain described as 'gush' to generalities about peace and reconciliation. A predictably favourable press response followed and on 24 June invitations were sent out to de Valera and Craig to negotiate in London. Embarrassingly de Valera had been arrested on 22 June and was hastily released on Cope's orders a day later; since his return from the United States, there had been a prohibition on de Valera being arrested.[7]

At this time also Tom Casement, brother of the executed Sir Roger, who had known Smuts in South Africa, journeyed to Dublin to bring about contact between de Valera and Smuts. Casement related in his diary that de Valera had told him that he was not going to insist on a republic and impressed on Smuts the importance of a truce before negotiations could begin. Seán T. O'Kelly commented: 'The L.G. letter is interesting. Dev and Co will have to act very warily. The invitation cannot be flatly refused but cannot be accepted unconditionally.' Art O'Brien reported from London: 'I find the opinion strongly expressed by several leading people in the political world that Lloyd George's letter was due more to general public uneasiness than to any action taken by the Dominion Premiers, although this latter may have been the final weight in the balance.' De Valera made clear that he would only meet with Lloyd George without Craig's presence, regarding the latter only as a spokesman of an Irish minority. He suggested first a meeting with representatives of Southern and Northern Unionist opinion. Predictably Craig refused to attend any such conference.[8]

Smuts and Casement went to Dublin and through Cope were instrumental in gaining the release of Griffith and MacNeill, and later Desmond FitzGerald, to assist in the projected negotiations. On 1 July the King expressed his delight that Midleton was meeting de Valera. The Sinn Féin and Southern Unionist representatives met on 4 and 8 July; between those dates Midleton visited London to gain 'with some difficulty' Lloyd George's agreement to a truce to be arranged by the military authorities.

The British insisted that de Valera be accompanied at any London negotiations by other Sinn Féin leaders, Midleton saying of de Valera: 'He requires inexhaustible patience.' Under pressure from the Southern Unionists, de Valera agreed to release the kidnapped Lord Bandon, who had been held captive during the previous few weeks. As long as the British government were willing to do the same, de Valera was willing to abide by the truce terms agreed with Archbishop Clune in the previous December. At this stage Macready joined the talks and agreed truce terms with Barton and Duggan, representing the IRA. The agreement was signed on 9 July and came into force on 11 July. De Valera and Lloyd George agreed to meet on 14 July in London.[9]

The announcements from British Military Headquarters and in the *Irish Bulletin* differed in some respects over the agreed terms. The Irish version was explicit on the restrictions placed on the British army, and particularly the use of secret agents. Both accounts agreed that the IRA should cease all attacks and that the British should end military manoeuvres, raids and searches. There were to be no troop reinforcements and curfew restrictions were lifted. The issue of whether or not the IRA was allowed to import arms was avoided. The terms applied to the six north-eastern counties as well as the South.[10]

It is a final ironic commentary on the British administration in Ireland during the War of Independence that the military and civil authorities immediately claimed individual credit for the Truce. Macready stated that Cope was acting way beyond his authority and was over-trusting of the Irish: the civil servants in the Castle suspected that Macready was at the last moment milking the situation for his own ends. Macready told Anderson: 'Cope is very excellent, no doubt, in carrying out negotiations with people like Valera and Co, but to put it not too strongly, I consider it a perfect scandal that he should be the only representative of the Civil Government over here . . . he has not a large enough mind and has apparently no idea whatever of the dignity of the Empire. I am quite prepared to swallow a good deal, and have already done so, in order that no obstacle may be placed in the way of the possibility of an agreement — but there is a limit, and my difficulty is that I do not think poor Andy Cope is mentally capable of seeing when that limit is reached.'

Sturgis was told that Cope: 'is having an "awful" time with Macready and Brind . . . Macready said to him "Of course you're looking for a peerage out of this" . . . that from Macready!!' Sturgis' correspondent concluded: 'The military . . . have no idea of loyal co-operation. They seem bent on driving Andy (and with him the Civil Govt) out of any participation in any credit that may be going, and (what is far more important) are likely to hitch the whole show in doing it.'[11]

For IRA column men fighting in the most active areas, news of the Truce came like a bolt from the blue. They resented the fact that the Dublin leadership had failed to consult them and in some quarters claimed that their military prospects were favourable. From the vantage point of Treaty and Civil War divisions, it was hardly surprising that pro-Treaty sources stressed the necessity for a truce, and the pessimistic outlook for the IRA, while republican veterans argued the reverse. The British order of a cessation of hostilities and unconditional negotiations called for a pragmatic response amongst the IRA leadership at GHQ, and the revival of the Sinn Féin movement's political relevance. While de Valera had been a marginal figure during much of the war, it was he who led the negotiating team to London in July. These implications behind the Truce had much to do with the later Treaty split.

The British decision to negotiate a truce represented an uncomfortable acknowledgment of realities and also the dominance of political over purely military considerations. The option of martial law for the whole of Ireland and a vast stepping-up of troop numbers had proved unpalatable.

From both Irish and British perspectives, the logic behind a cessation of hostilities meant that the achievement of a settlement became imperative. Any successful compromise was to be on the lines suggested in the earlier peace initiatives.[12]

CONCLUSION

MOTIVATION

Neither at the time nor since was there much call for complex analysis of motivation behind IRA membership and action. Many veterans related their reasons for joining the IRA to hearing stories of the United Irishmen and the Fenians, or to the immediate effect of the Easter Rising. Todd Andrews wrote of Wexford, Wicklow and Carlow: 'It was curious how the memory of the 1798 rebellion persisted in this part of the country . . . hardly a day passed that some reference was not made to the heroes and villains of the period.' Men like Andrews, Seán O'Faolain and Frank O'Connor, who looked back after successful careers in the civil service and literature, depicted their involvement in the IRA as naive idealism. O'Faolain wrote: 'I had nothing to guide me but those flickering lights before the golden ikons of the past.' Andrews declared: 'I was in thrall to Pearse; to the standards of Cuchulainn and Fionn.'[1]

A high proportion of many IRA units consisted of close friends and kith and kin. This applied to women as well: in local areas a substantial proportion of Cumann na mBan activists were relatives of IRA members. A sense of thrill and adventure plus the camaraderie involved attracted the young and idealistic from their dull, provincial and highly controlled home environments. Later they recalled the revolutionary years as the highlight of their lives, to be commemorated in reunions, anniversaries and memorial projects. The traditional nationalist songbook of ballads and laments swelled to include Kilmichael, Kevin Barry and many more. While campaigning for Sinn Féin in the June 1922 election, Con Collins complained that he had never heard of the Labour candidate Dan Morrissey as he had never encountered him in prison or at an ambush. To have been 'out' in 1916 was to ensure status and often employment for many decades after.[2]

RÔLE OF WOMEN

The exclusive, macho world of the IRA columns is reflected in the patronising tone of so many memoirs regarding women's contribution to the War. There are obligatory references in IRA reminiscences to the valuable role women played as nurses, couriers, cooks, cleaners and providers of safe houses. The

Cumann na mBan training emphasised first aid and medicine. The movement came to embody separate spheres: there appeared to be no possibility of women fighting alongside men as they occasionally had during the Easter Rising, nor of them taking direct command. Eithne Coyle reminisced: 'We were more or less auxiliaries to the men, to the fighting men of the country. It wasn't a case of taking orders because we had our own executive and we made our own decisions, but if there were any jobs or anything to be done, the men — they didn't order us — but they asked us to help them, which we did.'[3]

The Countess Markievicz was the first and only woman elected in December 1918 to both the Westminster parliament and the Dáil. The extension of the suffrage to women over thirty had heightened the potential for female involvement but only five further female deputies were elected to the Second Dáil in May 1921 and of these, four were either widows or mothers of republican martyrs. The strong republican beliefs of such formidable women had been formed before the loss of their kin. Kathleen Clarke and Mary MacSwiney led the majority of Cumann na mBan in taking an extremely hard anti-Treaty line before, during and long after the Civil War. Throughout their very long lives Maire Comerford and Sheila Humphreys maintained their pure republican convictions and were held in awe by pragmatic compromising men who both feared and admired them.

Women were often the car drivers who transported arms and ammunition as well as chauffeuring IRA men. Todd Andrews wrote that meeting Kay Brady during the Civil War 'led me to a concatenation of minor surprises. I had never known anyone who owned a car except a taxi driver. A car owned and driven by a woman was a complete novelty. Miss Brady and (Ernie) O'Malley indulged in much mutual leg-pulling. I had never seen men and women in that relationship before and was impressed by the fact that her mental agility was much greater than his. My education in the qualities of women had begun and it continued as we drove to Carrickmacross.'[4]

However, it was in the field of Intelligence and propaganda that women really excelled and played a most crucial role. The information, for instance, that Lily Merrin supplied from within Dublin Castle and Josephine Brown from within the British Sixth Division Headquarters ranked with any espionage success during the conflict. These women faced and endured a permanent risk to their personal safety rather than the intermittent risks faced by the fighters. Kathleen MacKenna had a dual role in espionage as well as compiling the *Irish Bulletin*. Better known was the female contribution to the various campaigns for prison releases and humanitarian issues, and in the formation of the fundraising for the Irish White Cross in 1921.

At the head of these protest and humanitarian movements were the exotic figures of Maud Gonne, legendary beauty and republican, and Charlotte Despard, amazingly enough the sister of Lord French. Constance Markievicz, founder of the Fianna, member of the Citizen Army and Minister of Labour in the Dáil government was the best-known and most unmanageable of these female revolutionaries. For a long time these rare creatures were the only women studied as part of the Irish Revolution, and the dangerous and vital work carried out by legions of others was largely underplayed.[5]

It seems that comparatively few women were imprisoned during the War. In April 1921 twenty-six were in jail compared to about 4,000 men. Individuals however, received harsh sentences: Linda Kearns and Eileen McGrane were sentenced to ten years each for arms and Intelligence offences. There was great sensitivity on the whole subject of imprisoned women, connected to the recent history of suffragette hunger strikers. Any maltreatment discovered was a propaganda godsend for the IRA.[6]

GEOGRAPHICAL SPREAD

The county by county review of the war reveals how uneven IRA activity was. This applies not only to the disparity between, for instance, Cork and Wicklow, but also within counties; for instance, the strong fighting area round Bandon contrasted with the relative inactivity west of Skibbereen, and North and South Longford are another obvious contrast. Particular parishes, as around Tipperary town and Westport, had disproportionately high levels of IRA action.

It remains true that the conflict was predominantly confined to Dublin city and Munster. Methods of quantifying the numbers of incidents and outrages are notoriously unreliable, but it is clear that Ulster, Connacht and Leinster, outside Dublin, made a comparatively small contribution to the War effort. IRA membership was overwhelmingly youthful, and based in urban and rural areas. The relationship between the fighters and the community was more complex than traditional accounts suggest. Overall, though, a surprisingly small proportion of the young were IRA members and the actual fighting was done by relatively few.[7] The targets of compulsory IRA levies could not have been critical only under the Truce; criticism of reprisals often extended beyond the auxiliary police to those who had provoked the British response.

There has been considerable debate as to why particular areas were more active or inactive than others. Many at the time and since have sought explanations in the suitability of the countryside for guerrilla fighting — the hills of North Tipperary and West Kerry were ideal for ambushes and column work, while the flat open land of Kildare militated against it. The Wicklow hills, however, saw little fighting and there are few high places in Longford.

The importance of charismatic and effective leadership was considerable — the rôles of Newmarket (North Cork) and Bandon in the War can never be divorced from Seán Moylan and the Hales family. It is true that Barry and MacEoin would in all probability have found it impossible to stimulate much action in Wicklow or Westmeath, but there is a clear link between the falling off in activity in particular areas after the arrest of key figures there.

The remoteness and poverty of areas such as Connemara and Donegal provides a ready explanation for limited involvement in the struggle. These impoverished areas had high migration and emigration amongst the young. A very different disadvantage was faced by Kildare and the Fingal area where proximity to Dublin inhibited IRA work. Broadly speaking, the IRA received most support in districts of middling prosperity.

Munster's strong nationalist tradition was a precondition for the IRA's strength there. Many IRA veterans had been members of the United Irish League and in parts of West Mayo IRA members had been in the American Alliance. The massive Sinn Féin membership in the West, the greatest proportionately in the country, was not reflected in IRA membership figures there. This has been ascribed to the IRA's failure to support agrarian protest and to the lack of middle-class leadership in that region.

The importance of speedy Volunteer reorganisation after 1916 has been another popular explanation for the variation in IRA activity. It became progressively more difficult to obtain arms once the British had tightened security at barracks and in convoys, and GHQ tended to distribute its limited military supplies to areas already active. Some localities, however, notably West Mayo, did join the fighting late and the availability of arms and ammunition was not necessary for many tasks in the War.

The nature and extent of the police presence and local sectarian tensions may have contributed also to the amount of guerrilla activity in some areas. A strong police/military presence could either provoke or deter, and was often a response to guerrilla activity. Much of the killing can be put down to retaliatory violence on both sides.

Single-cause explanations about the geographical distribution of revolution do not convince. Too many conclusions have been drawn from work on limited regions and too many generalisations made about the contribution of whole counties. The more important question is how such a part-time, untrained, under-resourced force could succeed to the extent it did. The answer to that lies in the nature of guerrilla warfare and the weakness of British policy.

IRA fighting did not need to be that widespread or that continuous: individual actions on a comparatively small scale had profound effects on British opinion and morale. The British military had a far higher opinion of IRA Intelligence in the provinces than the IRA's own GHQ did. The success of a guerrilla force is partly built on myth: from a British perspective it was a sinister, shadowy, intangible and ubiquitous presence threatening them anywhere and at any time. For Irish nationalists, the IRA were their own heroic freedom fighters.[8]

CASUALTIES

It appears that total casualties in the war amounted to around 1,400, of which 624 were members of the British security services and 752 were IRA and civilians. The fact that the major part of the fighting occurred in the last twelve months of the conflict is strikingly demonstrated by the figures: police and army deaths rose from forty-four in the first six months of 1920 to 171 in the second half of the year, and 324 in the next six months. Meanwhile deaths on the Irish side were thirty-two, then 228 and 182 for the same periods. Official figures suggest that about 200 civilians were killed and some 150 of these were in 1921. The relatively small proportion of civilian casualties is in sharp contrast to the figures for the Northern Ireland crisis since 1969, where these deaths have considerably outnumbered military and paramilitary deaths.[9]

Conventional military fatalities were not the norm. In Cork, which saw a high level of violence, most deaths could be attributed to assassinations or reprisal killings. Broadly speaking, the same holds for Dublin. The number of official executions, 14, was just under one-sixth of those carried out by the Free State government in the Civil War. In the First World War, the Irish casualties were between 25–30,000 deaths.[10] Much of normal life, even in the martial law areas, carried on; there was little interruption for instance to race meetings and the economy seemingly was little damaged. The War's effects, however, went far beyond statistics. In many ways the conflict resembled a civil war, and shared responsibility with the later conflict for many of the divisions within Irish society which persisted for the rest of the century.

The fruits of the War were bitter. Large elements of Irish society were effectively excluded from Irish politics; Sinn Féin represented only a part of the Irish nation. The virtual ban on the commemoration of the Irish dead of the First World War dramatically demonstrates this. Novelists have been the only ones, until recently, to examine the effects of the revolution on minorities.[11] Historians have tended to offer accounts of that time which suit the views of the political rulers. The memory of the events between 1919 and 1921 plays a crucial part in the make-up of the Irish Republic's opinion of itself, and has long continued to hinder Anglo-Irish relations. Now that the Government of Ireland Act has at last been replaced, a change of perspective should be possible.

It remains true that the War achieved for the twenty-six counties a measure of independence undreamed of in 1910. For the British government in July 1921 to agree to negotiate with those whom they had called gunmen for so long was a triumph for the IRA and, to a lesser extent, its political wing, Sinn Féin. The guerrilla warfare had often been effective and courageous. Nevertheless, a Republic could not be won by arms and no effective resistance was offered to Partition and the establishment of the Northern Irish government. Any sense of victory was soon lost in the depressing internecine conflict of the years following.

There lingered in some parts of Irish society an unease about the methods used to win this limited independence and the question has been asked whether a similar result could have been gained without violence.[12] Passive resistance tactics had shown no signs of achieving their object by 1920 and IRA actions had been instrumental in causing the collapse of British administration as well as impressing the British government. Without IRA actions, the likelihood is that any substantial British concessions would have been delayed for much longer. The primary reason for the abrupt slide to widespread violence in the second half of 1920 was the British government's refusal to offer settlement terms which could have proved at least as acceptable then as they did a year later. Lloyd George's other disastrous decision was to establish Partition before attempting a settlement with the South. The short-term fix had dire long-term consequences.

APPENDICES

APPENDIX A

Proclamation of the Republic of Ireland, 1916
Source: National Museum of Ireland, EW 21

POBLACHT NA HEIREANN

The Provisional Government of the Irish Republic to the people of Ireland
IRISHMEN AND IRISHWOMEN: In the name of God and of the dead generations from which she receives her old tradition of nationhood, Ireland, through us, summons her children to her flag and strikes for her freedom.

Having organized and trained her manhood through her secret revolutionary organization, the Irish Republican Brotherhood, and through her open military organizations, the Irish Volunteers, and the Irish Citizen Army, having patiently perfected her discipline, having resolutely waited for the right moment to reveal itself, she now seizes that moment, and, supported by her exiled children in America and by gallant allies in Europe, but relying in the first on her own strength, she strikes in full confidence of victory.

We declare the right of the people of Ireland to the ownership of Ireland, and to the unfettered control of Irish destinies, to be sovereign and indefeasible. The long usurpation of that right by a foreign people and government has not extinguished the right, nor can it ever be extinguished except by the destruction of the Irish people. In every generation the Irish people have asserted their right to national freedom and sovereignty; six times during the past three hundred years they have asserted it in arms. Standing on that fundamental right and again asserting it in arms in the face of the world, we hereby proclaim the Irish Republic as a sovereign independent state, and we pledge our lives and the lives of our comrades-in-arms to the cause of its freedom, of its welfare, and of its exaltation among the nations.

The Irish Republic is entitled to, and hereby claims, the allegiance of every Irishman and Irishwoman. The Republic guarantees religious and civil liberty, equal rights and equal opportunities to all its citizens, and declares its resolve to pursue the happiness and prosperity of the whole nation and of all its parts, cherishing all the children of the nation equally, and oblivious of the differences carefully fostered by an alien government, which have divided a minority from the majority in the past.

Until our arms have brought the opportune moment for the establishment of a permanent national government, representative of the whole people of Ireland, and elected by the suffrages of all her men and women, the Provisional Government, hereby constituted, will administer the civil and military affairs of the republic in trust for the people. We place the cause of the Irish Republic under the protection of the Most High God, whose blessings we invoke upon our arms, and we pray that no one who serves that cause will dishonour it by cowardice, inhumanity, or rapine. In this supreme hour the Irish nation must, by its valour and discipline, and by the readiness of its children to sacrifice themselves for the common good, prove itself worthy of the august destiny to which it is called.

Signed on behalf of the provisional government,
Thomas J. Clarke, Seán MacDiarmada, Thomas MacDonagh, P.H. Pearse, Éamonn Ceannt, James Connolly, Joseph Plunkett.

APPENDIX B

1918 election manifesto of Sinn Féin
Source: National Museum of Ireland, EW 129

GENERAL ELECTION
MANIFESTO TO THE IRISH PEOPLE
THE coming General Election is fraught with vital possibilities for the future of our nation. Ireland is faced with the question whether this generation wills it that she is to march out into the full sunlight of freedom, or is to remain in the shadow of a base imperialism that has brought and ever will bring in its train naught but evil for our race.

Sinn Féin gives Ireland the opportunity of vindicating her honour and pursuing with renewed confidence the path of national salvation by rallying to the flag of the Irish Republic.

Sinn Féin aims at securing the establishment of that Republic
1. By withdrawing the Irish Representation from the British Parliament and by denying the right and opposing the will of the British Government or any other foreign Government to legislate for Ireland.
2. By making use of any and every means available to render impotent the power of England to hold Ireland in subjection by military force or otherwise.
3. By the establishment of a constituent assembly comprising persons chosen by Irish constituencies as the supreme national authority to speak and

act in the name of the Irish people, and to develop Ireland's social, political and industrial life, for the welfare of the whole people of Ireland.

4. By appealing to the Peace Conference for the establishment of Ireland as an independent nation. At that conference the future of the nations of the world will be settled on the principle of government by consent of the governed. Ireland's claim to the application of that principle in her favour is not based on any accidental situation arising from the war. It is older than many if not all of the present belligerents. It is based on our unbroken tradition of nationhood, on a unity in a national name which has never been challenged, on our possession of a distinct national culture and social order, on the moral courage and dignity of our people in the face of alien aggression, on the fact that in nearly every generation, and five times within the past 120 years our people have challenged in arms the right of England to rule this country. On these incontrovertible facts is based the claim that our people have beyond question established the right to be accorded all the power of a free nation.

Sinn Féin stands less for a political party than for the Nation; it represents the old tradition of nationhood handed on from dead generations; it stands by the Proclamation of the Provisional Government of Easter, 1916 reasserting the inalienable right of the Irish Nation to sovereign independence, reaffirming the determination of the Irish people to achieve it, and guaranteeing within the independent nation equal rights and equal opportunities to all its citizens. Believing that the time has arrived when Ireland's voice for the principle of untrammelled national self-determination should be heard above every interest of party or class, Sinn Féin will oppose at the polls every individual candidate who does not accept this principle. The policy of our opponents stands condemned on any test, whether of principle or expediency. The right of a nation to sovereign independence rests upon immutable natural law and cannot be made the subject of a compromise. Any attempt to barter away the sacred and inviolate rights of nationhood begins in dishonour and is bound to end in disaster. The enforced exodus of millions of our people, the decay of our industrial life, the ever-increasing financial plunder of our country, the whittling down of the demand for the 'Repeal of the Union', voiced by the first Irish Leader to plead in the Hall of the Conqueror to that of Home Rule on the Statute Book, and finally the contemplated mutilation of our country by partition, are some of the ghastly results of a policy that leads to national ruin. Those who have endeavoured to harness the people of Ireland to England's war-chariot, ignoring the fact that only a freely-elected government in a free Ireland has power to decide for Ireland the question of peace and war, have forfeited the right to speak for the Irish people. The Green Flag turned red in the hands of the Leaders, but that shame is not to be laid at the doors of the Irish people unless they continue a policy of sending their representatives to an alien and hostile assembly, whose powerful influence has been sufficient to destroy the integrity and sap the independence of their representatives. Ireland must repudiate the men who, in a supreme crisis for the nation, attempted to sell her birthright for the vague promises of English Ministers, and who showed their incompetence by failing to have even these promises fulfilled.

The present Irish members of the English Parliament constitute an obstacle to be removed from the path that leads to the Peace Conference. By declaring their will to accept the status of a province instead of boldly taking their stand upon the right of the nation they supply England with the only subterfuge at her disposal for obscuring the issue in the eyes of the world. By their persistent endeavours to induce the young manhood of Ireland to don the uniform of our seven-century-old oppressor, and place their lives at the disposal of the military machine that hold our nation in bondage, they endeavour to barter away and even to use against itself the one great asset still left to our Nation after the havoc of centuries.

Sinn Féin goes to the polls handicapped by all the arts and contrivances that a powerful and unscrupulous enemy can use against us. Conscious of the power of Sinn Féin to secure the freedom of Ireland the British Government would destroy it. Sinn Féin, however, goes to the polls confident that the people of this ancient nation will be true to the old cause and will vote for the men who stand by the principles of Tone, Emmet, Mitchel, Pearse and Connolly, the men who disdain to whine to the enemy for favours, the men who hold that Ireland must be as free as England or Holland, or Switzerland or France, and whose demand is that the only status befitting this ancient realm is the status of a free nation.

ISSUED BY THE STANDING COMMITTEE OF SINN FEIN

APPENDIX C

Declaration of Independence
Minutes of the proceedings of the first parliament of the republic of Ireland, 1919–1921, official record (hereinafter 'Dáil Eireann proceedings, 1919–1921') (Dublin Stationery Office, n.d.) 14–16
English Translation

DECLARATION OF INDEPENDENCE
Whereas the Irish people is by right a free people:

And Whereas for seven hundred years the Irish people has never ceased to repudiate and has repeatedly protested in arms against foreign usurpation:

And Whereas English rule in this country is, and has always been, based upon force and fraud and maintained by military occupation against the declared will of the people:

And Whereas the Irish Republic was proclaimed in Dublin on Easter Monday, 1916 by the Irish Republican Army acting on behalf of the Irish people:

And Whereas the Irish people is resolved to secure and maintain its complete independence in order to promote the common weal, to re-establish justice, to provide for future defence, to insure peace at home and goodwill with all nations and to constitute a national policy based upon the people's will with equal right and equal opportunity for every citizen:

And Whereas at the threshold of a new era in history the Irish electorate has in the General Election of December, 1918, seized the first occasion to declare by an overwhelming majority its firm allegiance to the Irish Republic:

Now, therefore, we, the elected Representatives of the ancient Irish people in National Parliament assembled, do, in the name of the Irish nation, ratify the establishment of the Irish Republic and pledge ourselves and our people to make this declaration effective by every means at our command:

We ordain that the elected Representatives of the Irish people alone have power to make laws binding on the people of Ireland, and that the Irish Parliament is the only Parliament to which that people will give its allegiance:

We solemnly declare foreign government in Ireland to be an invasion of our national right which we will never tolerate, and we demand the evacuation of our country by the English Garrison:

We claim for our national independence the recognition and support of every free nation in the world, and we proclaim that independence to be a condition precedent to international peace hereafter:

In the name of the Irish people we humbly commit our destiny to Almighty God who gave our fathers the courage and determination to persevere through long centuries of a ruthless tyranny, and strong in the justice of the cause which they have handed down to us, we ask His divine blessing on this the last stage of the struggle we have pledged ourselves to carry through to Freedom.

APPENDIX D

Dáil Eireann address to the free nations of the world, 21 January 1919
Dáil Eireann proceedings, 1919–21, 20

MESSAGE TO THE FREE NATIONS OF THE WORLD
To the Nations of the World! Greeting.
The Nation of Ireland having proclaimed her national independence, calls through her elected representatives in Parliament assembled in the Irish Capital on January 21st, 1919 upon every free nation to support the Irish

Republic by recognising Ireland's national status and her right to its vindication at the Peace Congress.

Nationally, the race, the language, the customs and traditions of Ireland are radically different from the English. Ireland is one of the most ancient nations in Europe, and she has preserved her national integrity, vigorous and intact, through seven centuries of foreign oppression: she has never relinquished her national rights, and throughout the long era of English usurpation she has in every generation defiantly proclaimed her inalienable right to nationhood down to her last glorious resort to arms in 1916.

Internationally, Ireland is the gateway of the Atlantic. Ireland is the last outpost of Europe towards the West: Ireland is the point upon which great trade routes between East and West converge: her great harbours must be open to all nations, instead of being the monopoly of England. To-day these harbours are empty and idle solely because English policy is determined to retain Ireland as a barren bulwark for English aggrandisement, and the unique geographical position of this island, far from being a benefit and safeguard to Europe and America, is subjected to the purposes of England's policy of world domination.

Ireland to-day reasserts her historic nationhood the more confidently before the new world emerging from the War, because she believes in freedom and justice as the fundamental principles of international law, because she believes in a frank co-operation between the peoples for equal rights against the vested privileges of ancient tyrannies, because the permanent peace of Europe can never be secured by perpetuating military dominion for the profit of empire but only by establishing the control of government in every land upon the basis of the free will of a free people, and the existing state of war, between Ireland and England, can never be ended until Ireland is definitely evacuated by the armed forces of England.

For these among other reasons, Ireland — resolutely and irrevocably determined at the dawn of the promised era of self-determination and liberty that she will suffer foreign dominion no longer — calls upon every free nation to uphold her national claim to complete independence as an Irish Republic against the arrogant pretensions of England founded in fraud and sustained only by an overwhelming military occupation, and demands to be confronted publicly with England at the Congress of the Nations, in order that the civilised world having judged between English wrong and Irish right may guarantee to Ireland its permanent support for the maintenance of her national independence.

APPENDIX E

Democratic programme of Dáil Eireann
Dáil Eireann proceedings, 1919–21, 22–23

DEMOCRATIC PROGRAMME

We declare in the words of the Irish Republican Proclamation the right of the people of Ireland to the ownership of Ireland, and to the unfettered control of Irish destinies to be indefeasible, and in the language of our first President, Pádraig Mac Phiarais, we declare that the Nation's sovereignty extends not only to all men and women of the Nation, but to all its material possessions, the Nation's soil and all its resources, all the wealth and all the wealth-producing processes within the Nation, and with him we reaffirm that all right to private property must be subordinated to the public right and welfare.

We declare that we desire our country to be ruled in accordance with the principles of Liberty, Equality, and Justice for all, which alone can secure permanence of government in the willing adhesion of the people.

We affirm the duty of every man and women to give allegiance and service to the Commonwealth, and declare it is the duty of the Nation to assure that every citizen shall have opportunity to spend his or her strength and faculties in the services of the people. In return for willing service, we, in the name of the Republic, declare the right of every citizen to an adequate share of the produce of the Nation's labour.

It shall be the first duty of the Government of the Republic to make provision for the physical, mental and spiritual well-being of the children, to secure that no child shall suffer hunger or cold from lack of food, clothing, or shelter, but that all shall be provided with the means and facilities requisite for their proper education and training as Citizens of a Free and Gaelic Ireland.

The Irish Republic fully realises the necessity of abolishing the present odious, degrading and foreign Poor Law System, substituting therefore a sympathetic native scheme for the care of the Nation's aged and infirm, who shall not be regarded as a burden, but rather entitled to the Nation's gratitude and consideration. Likewise it shall be the duty of the Republic to take such measures as will safeguard the health of the people and ensure the physical as well as the moral well-being of the Nation.

It shall be our duty to promote the development of the Nation's resources, to increase the productivity of its soil, to exploit its mineral deposits, peat bogs, and fisheries, its waterways and harbours, in the interests and for the benefit of the Irish people.

It shall be the duty of the Republic to adopt all measures necessary for the recreation and invigoration of our Industries, and to ensure their being developed on the most beneficial and progressive co-operative and industrial lines. With the adoption of an extensive Irish Consular Service, trade with foreign Nations shall be revived on terms of mutual advantage and goodwill, and while undertaking the organisation of the Nation's trade, import and export, it shall be the duty of the Republic to prevent the shipment from Ireland of food and other necessaries until the wants of the Irish people are fully satisfied and the future provided for.

It shall also devolve upon the National Government to seek co-operation of the Governments of other countries in determining a standard of Social and Industrial Legislation with a view to a general and lasting improvement in the conditions under which the working classes live and labour.

APPENDIX **F**

Martial law in four southern counties
Dublin Gazette, 10 December 1920

PROCLAMATION
WHEREAS certain evilly disposed persons and associations with the intent to subvert the supremacy of the Crown in Ireland have committed divers acts of violence whereby many persons, including members of the Forces of the Crown and other servants of His Majesty, have been murdered and many others have suffered grievous injuries and much destruction of property has been caused; And WHEREAS in certain parts of Ireland disaffection and unrest have been especially prevalent and repeated murderous attacks have been made upon members of His Majesty's Forces culminating in the ambush, massacre, and mutilation with axes, of sixteen Cadets of the Auxiliary Division, all of whom had served in the late War, by a large body of men who were wearing trench helmets and were disguised in the uniform of British soldiers, and who are still at large.

Now, I, JOHN DENTON PINKSTONE, VISCOUNT FRENCH, Lord Lieutenant-General and General Governor of Ireland, do hereby proclaim by virtue of all the powers me thereunto enabling that the following counties, namely: — The County of Cork (East Riding and West Riding); The County of the City of Cork; The County of Tipperary (North Riding); The County of Tipperary (South Riding); The County of Kerry; The County of Limerick; The County of the City of Limerick; are, and until further order, shall continue to be under and subject to

MARTIAL LAW
And I do hereby call on all loyal and well-affected subjects of the Crown to aid in upholding and maintaining the peace of this Realm and the supremacy and authority of the Crown and to obey and conform to all orders and regulations of the Military Authority issued by virtue of this Proclamation.

Given at His Majesty's Castle of Dublin, this 10th day of December, 1920.
FRENCH
GOD save the KING.

APPENDIX G

Government of Ireland Act, 1920
Acts parl. U.K., 1920, (10 & 11 Geo V, Cap. 67)

Extracts

An Act to provide for the Better Government of Ireland. 23rd December 1920.

Be it enacted by the King's most Excellent Majesty, by and with the advice and consent of the Lords Spiritual and Temporal, and Commons, in this present Parliament assembled . . .

1.–(1) On and after the appointed day there shall be established for Southern Ireland a Parliament to be called the Parliament of Southern Ireland consisting of His Majesty, the Senate of Southern Ireland, and the House of Commons of Southern Ireland, and there shall be established for Northern Ireland a Parliament to be called the Parliament of Northern Ireland consisting of His Majesty, the Senate of Northern Ireland, and the House of Commons of Northern Ireland.

(2) For the purposes of this Act, Northern Ireland shall consist of the parliamentary counties of Antrim, Armagh, Down, Fermanagh, Londonderry and Tyrone, and the parliamentary boroughs of Belfast and Londonderry, and Southern Ireland shall consist of so much of Ireland as is not comprised within the said parliamentary counties and boroughs.

2.–(1) With a view to the eventual establishment of a Parliament for the whole of Ireland, and to bringing about harmonious action between the parliaments and governments of Southern Ireland and Northern Ireland, and to the promotion of mutual intercourse and uniformity in relation to matters affecting the whole of Ireland, and to providing for the administration of services which the two parliaments mutually agree should be administered uniformly throughout the whole of Ireland, or which by virtue of this Act are to be so administered, there shall be constituted, as soon as may be after the appointed day, a Council to be called the Council of Ireland.

(2) Subject as hereinafter provided, the Council of Ireland shall consist of a person nominated by the Lord Lieutenant acting in accordance with instructions from His Majesty who shall be President and forty other persons, of whom seven shall be members of the Senate of Southern Ireland, thirteen shall be members of the House of Commons of Southern Ireland, seven shall be members of the Senate of Northern Ireland, and thirteen shall be members of the House of Commons of Northern Ireland.

The members of the Council of Ireland shall be elected in each case by the members of that House of the Parliament of Southern Ireland or Northern Ireland of which they are members . . .

3.–(1) The Parliaments of Southern Ireland and Northern Ireland may, by identical Acts agreed to by an absolute majority of members of the House of Commons of each Parliament at the third reading... establish, in lieu of the Council of Ireland, a Parliament for the whole of Ireland consisting of His Majesty and two Houses . . .
(2) On the date of Irish union the Council of Ireland shall cease to exist and there shall be transferred to the Parliament and Government of Ireland all powers then exercisable by the Council of Ireland, and .. the matters which under this Act cease to be reserved matters at the date of Irish union, and any other powers for the joint exercise of which by the Parliaments or Governments of Southern and Northern Ireland provision has been made under this Act . . .

4.–(1) Subject to the provisions of this Act, the Parliament of Southern Ireland and the Parliament of Northern Ireland shall respectively have power to make laws for the peace, order, and good government of Southern Ireland and Northern Ireland with the following limitations . . .

(1) The Crown . . . or the Lord Lieutenant, except as respects the exercise of his executive power in relation to Irish services as defined for the purposes of this Act . . .
(2) The making of peace or war, or matters arising from a state of war . . .
(3) The navy, the army, the air force, the territorial force . . .
(4) Treaties, or any relations with foreign states, or relations with other parts of His Majesty's dominions . . .
(5) Dignities or titles of honour . . .
(6) Treason, treason felony, alienage, naturalization, or aliens as such, or domicile . . .
(7) Trade with any place out of the part of Ireland within their jurisdiction, except so far as trade may be affected by the exercise of the powers of taxation given to the said parliaments, or by regulations . . .
(8) Submarine cables;
(9) Wireless telegraphy;
(10) Aerial navigation; . . .
(11) Lighthouses, buoys or beacons; . . .
(12) Coinage; legal tender; negotiable instruments . . .
(13) Trademarks, designs, merchandise marks, copyright, or patent rights . . .
(14) Any matter which by this Act is declared to be a reserved matter, so long as it remains reserved. Any law made in contravention of the limitations imposed by this section shall, so far as it contravenes those limitations, be void.

8.–(1) The executive power in Southern Ireland and in Northern Ireland shall continue vested in His Majesty the King, and nothing in this Act shall affect the exercise of that power . . .

APPENDIX H

Speech of King George V opening Northern Ireland parliament

Northern Ireland Parliamentary debates, House of Commons, vol. 1, 19–22,22 June 1921

Extracts.

For all who love Ireland, as I do with all my heart, this is a profoundly moving occasion in Irish history . . .

This is a great and critical occasion in the history of the Six Counties, but not for the Six Counties alone, for everything which interests them touches Ireland, and everything which touches Ireland finds an echo in the remotest parts of the Empire . . .

Most certainly there is no wish nearer My own heart than that every man of Irish birth, whatever be his creed and wherever be his home, should work in loyal co-operation with the free communities on which the British Empire is based . . .

Full partnership in the United Kingdom and religious freedom Ireland has long enjoyed. She now has conferred upon her the duty of dealing with all the essential tasks of domestic legislation and government . . .

I speak from a full heart when I pray that My coming to Ireland to-day may prove to be the first step towards an end of strife amongst her people, whatever their race or creed. In that hope, I appeal to all Irishmen to pause, to stretch out the hand of forbearance and conciliation, to forgive and to forget, and to join in making for the land which they love a new era of peace, contentment, and goodwill.

It is My earnest desire that in Southern Ireland, too, there may ere long take place a parallel to what is now passing in this Hall . . .

May this historic gathering be the prelude of a day in which the Irish people, North and South, under one Parliament or two, as those Parliaments may themselves decide, shall work together in common love for Ireland upon the sure foundations of mutual justice and respect.

APPENDIX I

ARTICLES OF AGREEMENT
For a
TREATY BETWEEN GREAT BRITAIN AND IRELAND
Signed in London on the 6th December, 1921.
Source: National Museum of Ireland

Extract:

1. Ireland shall have the same constitutional status in the Community of Nations known as the British Empire as the Dominion of Canada, the

Commonwealth of Australia, the Dominion of New Zealand, and the Union of South Africa, with a Parliament having powers to make laws for the peace order and good government of Ireland and an Executive responsible to that Parliament, and shall be styled and known as the Irish Free State . . .

4. The oath to be taken by Members of the Parliament of the Irish Free State shall be in the following form:–

I . . . do solemnly swear true faith and allegiance to the Constitution of the Irish Free State as by law established and that I will be faithful to H.M. King George V, his heirs and successors by law, in virtue of the common citizenship of Ireland with Great Britain and her adherence to and membership of the group of nations forming the British Commonwealth of Nations.

5. The Irish Free State shall assume liability for the service of the Public Debt of the United Kingdom as existing at the date hereof and towards the payment of war pensions as existing at that date in such proportion as may be fair and equitable . . .

7. The Government of the Irish Free State shall afford to His Majesty's Imperial Forces:–

(a) In time of peace such harbour and other facilities as are indicated in the Annex hereto, or such other facilities as may from time to time be agreed between the British Government and the Government of the Irish Free State; and

(b) In time of war or of strained relations with a Foreign Power such harbour and other facilities as the British Government may require for the purposes of such defence as aforesaid.

8. . . . If the Government of the Irish Free State establishes and maintains a military defence force, the establishments thereof shall not exceed in size such proportion of the military establishments maintained in Great Britain as that which the population of Ireland bears to the population of Great Britain . . .

10. The Government of the Irish Free State agrees to pay fair compensation on terms not less favourable than those accorded by the Act of 1920 to judges, officials, members of Police Forces and other Public Servants who are discharged by it or who retire in consequence of the change of government effected in pursuance hereof.

Provided that this agreement shall not apply to members of the Auxiliary Police Force or to persons recruited in Great Britain for the Royal Irish Constabulary during the two years next preceding the date hereof. The British Government will assume responsibility for such compensation or pensions as may be payable to any of these excepted persons.

11. Until the expiration of one month from the passage of the Act of Parliament for the ratification of this instrument, the powers of the Parliament and the government of the Irish Free State shall not be exercisable as respects Northern

Ireland and the provisions of the Government of Ireland Act, 1920, shall, so far as they relate to Northern Ireland, remain of full force and effect . . .

12. If before the expiration of the said month, an address is presented to His Majesty by both Houses of the Parliament of Northern Ireland to that effect, the powers of the Parliament and Government of the Irish Free State shall no longer extend to Northern Ireland, and the provisions of the Government of Ireland Act, 1920, (including those relating to the Council of Ireland) shall so far as they relate to Northern Ireland, continue to be of full force and effect, and this instrument shall have effect subject to the necessary modifications. Provided that if such an address is so presented a Commission consisting of three persons, one to be appointed by the Government of the Irish Free State, one to be appointed by the Government of Northern Ireland and one who shall be Chairman to be appointed by the British Government shall determine in accordance with the wishes of the inhabitants, so far as may be compatible with economic and geographic conditions, the boundaries between Northern Ireland and the rest of Ireland, and for the purposes of the Government of Ireland Act, 1920, and of this instrument, the boundary of Northern Ireland shall be such as may be determined by such Commission . . .

On behalf of the Irish Delegation
ART O GRIOBHTHA (ARTHUR GRIFFITH)
MICHEAL O COILEAIN
RIOBARD BARTUN
EUDHMONN S. O DUGAIN
SEORSA GHABHAIN UI DHUBHTHAIGH

On behalf of the British Delegation
D. LLOYD GEORGE
AUSTEN CHAMBERLAIN
BIRKENHEAD
WINSTON S. CHURCHILL

December 6th, 1921 . . .

NOTES

Introduction (pages xvii–xxi)

1. Barry, Tom, *Guerilla Days in Ireland* (Dublin 1949); Breen, Dan, *My Fight for Irish Freedom* (Dublin 1924); O'Malley, Ernie, *On Another Man's Wound* (London 1936). Amongst the biographies of Collins: Coogan, Tim Pat, *Michael Collins: A Biography* (London 1990); Forester, Margery, *Michael Collins: The Lost Leader* (London 1971); Taylor, Rex, *Michael Collins* (London 1958); O'Connor, Frank, *The Big Fellow* (Dublin 1965); Dwyer, T. Ryle, *Michael Collins: The Man who Won the War* (Cork 1990). For a traditional narrative approach see Macardle, Dorothy, *The Irish Republic 1911–1925: A Documented Chronicle* (London 1937).

2. See de Valera's involvement in the writing of his official biography: Longford, Earl of, and O'Neill, T.P., *Eamon de Valera* (London 1970).

3. Foster, R.F., 'History and the Irish Question' in *Paddy and Mr Punch: Connections in Irish and English History* (London 1993) pp. 18–20.

4. The records of the Bureau of Military History consist of a massive number of testimonies from IRA veterans together with documentary material.

5. Bradshaw, Brendan, 'Nationalism and Historical Scholarship in Modern Ireland' in *Irish Historical Studies*, xxvi, 1988–9.

6. Three recent books relating to the revisionist controversy contain little or nothing on the War: Boyce, D. George (ed.), *The Revolution in Ireland, 1879–1923* (Dublin 1988); Boyce, D. George and O'Day, Alan (eds), *The Making of Modern Irish History: Revisionism and the Revisionist Controversy* (London 1996); Brady, Ciaran (ed.), *Interpreting Irish History: The Debate on Historical Revisionism* (Dublin 1994).

7. Garvin, Tom, *1922: The Birth of Irish Democracy* (Dublin 1996); Laffan, Michael, *The Resurrection of Ireland: The Sinn Féin Party, 1916–1923* (Cambridge 1999) p. xi.

8. Townshend, Charles, *The British Campaign in Ireland, 1919–1921* (Oxford 1975); Fitzpatrick, David, *Politics and Irish Life, 1913–21: Provincial Experience of War and Revolution* (Dublin 1977); O'Halpin, Eunan, *The Decline of the Union: British Government in Ireland, 1892–1920* (Dublin 1987); McColgan, John, *British Policy and the Irish Administration, 1920–22* (London 1983).

9. Fitzpatrick, op. cit.; Augusteijn, Joost, *From Public Defiance to Guerrilla Warfare: The Experience of Ordinary Volunteers in the Irish War of Independence, 1916–1921* (Dublin 1996); Hart, Peter, *The IRA and its Enemies: Violence and Community in Cork, 1916–1923* (Oxford 1998); Farry, Michael, *The Aftermath of Revolution: Sligo 1921–23* (Dublin 2000); Coleman, Marie, 'County Longford 1910–1923: A Regional Study of the Irish Revolution', Ph.D. thesis, University College, Dublin, 1998.

10. Hart, op. cit.

11.   Murray, Patrick, *Oracles of God: The Roman Catholic Church and Irish Politics. 1922–37* (Dublin 2000) pp. 7–8.
12.   Mitchell, Arthur, *Revolutionary Government in Ireland: Dáil Éireann 1919–22* (Dublin 1995); Kotsonouris, Mary, *Retreat from Revolution: The Dáil Courts, 1920–24* (Dublin 1994).
13.   Fanning, Ronan, 'Michael Collins: An Overview' in Doherty, Gabriel and Keogh, Dermot (eds), *Michael Collins and the Making of the Irish State* (Cork 1998) pp. 204–7.
14.   Foster, R.F., *Modern Ireland 1600–1972* (London 1988) p. 506.
15.   Keogh, Dermot, *Twentieth-Century Ireland: Nation and State* (Dublin 1994).
16.   Follis, Brian, *A State under Siege* (Oxford 1995); Stewart, A.T.Q., *The Narrow Ground: Aspects of Ulster, 1609–1969* (London 1977).
17.   Augusteijn, Joost (ed.), *The Revolution in Ireland* (London 2002).
18.   See a series of perceptive observations in: Jeffery, Keith, 'British Security Policy in Ireland, 1919–21' in Collins, Peter (ed.), *Nationalism and Unionism: Conflict in Ireland, 1885–1921* (Belfast 1994) pp. 163–75.

Chapter 1 British Rule in Ireland (pages 3–10)
1.   National Library of Ireland, Cockerill Papers, MS 10606.
2.   Mansergh, Nicholas, *The Unresolved Question. The Anglo-Irish Settlement and its Undoing, 1912–72* (New Haven 1991). For an interesting examination of hypothetical outcomes see Jackson, Alvin, 'What if Irish Home Rule had been enacted in 1912?' in Ferguson, Niall (ed.), *Virtual History: Alternatives and Counterfactuals* (London 1997) pp. 175–227.
3.   Bew, Paul, *Ideology and the Irish Question: Ulster Unionism and Irish Nationalism, 1912–1916* (Oxford 1994).
4.   Laffan, Michael, *The Partition of Ireland, 1911–25* (Dublin 1983); Kendle, John, *Walter Long, Ireland, and the Union, 1905–1920* (Montreal 1992) p. 105 onwards.
5.   McDowell, R.B., *The Irish Convention, 1917–1918* (London 1970).
6.   Quoted in Boyce, D.G., 'How to Settle the Irish Question: Lloyd George and Ireland, 1916–21' in Taylor, A.J.P. (ed.), *Lloyd George: Twelve Essays* (London 1971).
7.   For Dublin Castle see: McDowell, R.B., *The Irish Administration, 1801–1914* (London 1964); Ward, Alan J., *The Irish Constitutional Tradition: Responsible Government and Modern Ireland, 1782–1992* (Dublin 1994); MacBride, Lawrence W., *The Greening of Dublin Castle: The Transformation of Bureaucratic and Judicial Personnel in Dublin Castle in Ireland, 1892–1922* (Washington 1991); O'Halpin, Eunan, op. cit.; Paul-Dubois and Morley quoted in Flanagan, Kieran, 'The Chief Secretary's Office 1853–1914: A Bureaucratic Enigma', *Irish Historical Studies*, xxiv, 1984–5.
8.   The MP John Roebuck speaking in the Commons 25 March 1858, quoted in Flanagan, op. cit.; Flanagan, op. cit.
9.   McDowell, op. cit.; MacBride, op. cit.
10.   Quoted in McDowell, op. cit., p. 67 and Ward, op. cit., p. 35.
11.   Quoted in MacBride, op. cit., p. 123.
12.   Kendle, op. cit., pp. 76, 77.
13.   MacBride, op. cit.
14.   Jalland, Patricia, 'A Liberal Chief Secretary and the Irish Question: Augustine Birrell, 1907–14', *Historical Journal*, 19 June 1976; Boyce, D.G. and Hazelhurst,

Cameron, 'The Unknown Chief Secretary: H.E. Duke and Ireland, 1916–17', *Irish Historical Studies*, xx, 1976–7; O'Halpin, Eunan, 'Historical Revisions: H.E. Duke and the Irish Administration', *Irish Historical Studies*, xxii, 1980–1.

15. O'Halpin, *The Decline of the Union*, p. 157.
16. Ó Broin, Leon, *Dublin Castle and the 1916 Rising* (Dublin 1966).
17. MacBride, op. cit., p. 15.
18. Hammond, J.L., *Gladstone and the Irish Nation* (London 1938); O'Day, Alan, *Irish Home Rule 1867–1921* (Manchester 1998); Cooke, A.B. and Vincent, J., *The Governing Passion: Cabinet Government and Party Politics in Britain, 1885–6* (Brighton 1974).
19. Long to Sir Matthew Nathan, 10 and 18 December 1914, quoted in Kendle, op. cit., pp. 90–91; Spender to C.P. Scott, 23 August 1919, *Political Diaries of C.P. Scott*, edited by Wilson, Trevor (London 1970), p. 377.
20. Winston Churchill to Clementine Churchill, 31 March 1920 in Gilbert, Martin, *Winston S. Churchill*, Companion Volume IV, Part 2: *July 1919–March 1921* (London 1977); Bonar Law quoted in Thomas Jones Diary for 30 January 1921 in Jones, Thomas, *Whitehall Diary*, volume III: *Ireland 1919–1925*, edited by Middlemass, Keith (London 1971) p. 50; Macready to Macpherson 11 January 1919, Strathcarron Papers, Bodleian Library.
21. Morgan, Kenneth O., *Consensus and Disunity: The Lloyd George Coalition Government, 1918–1922* (London 1979); Cowling, Maurice, *The Impact of Labour, 1920–24* (Cambridge 1971).
22. Lord Oranmore Diary for 16 May 1918: Butler, John (ed.), 'Lord Oranmore's Journal, 1913–27', *Irish Historical Studies*, xxix, 1994–5; Duke at War Cabinet, 3 April 1918, 31A. CAB 23/6.
23. For French see Holmes, Richard, *The Little Field Marshal: Sir John French* (London 1981); French to Lloyd George, 12 October 1918, French Papers, Imperial War Museum, 75/46/11, and Lloyd George Papers, House of Lords Record Office, F/48/61/10.
24. Ross to Long, 14 February 1920, Long Papers, Wiltshire Record Office 947/334; Wylie Memoir, PRO 30/89–1; French, 9 October 1918, Long Papers, 947/230.
25. For the Saunderson family see Jackson, Alvin, *Colonel Edward Saunderson: Land and Loyalty in Victorian Ireland* (Oxford 1995); Saunderson to Long, 28 January 1919, Long Papers, 947/347.
26. Kendle, op. cit.
27. O'Halpin, *The Decline of the Union*, pp. 53–66; Long Memorandum, Lloyd George Papers, F/33/2/73.
28. *Dictionary of National Biography, 1931–40* (Oxford 1949) p. 810.
29. French to Lloyd George, 2 September 1918, French Papers, 75/46/117.
30. French to Long, 28 June 1918, Long Papers, 947/229; French to Lloyd George, 12 October 1918, French Papers, 75/46/13.
31. O'Halpin, *The Decline of the Union*, pp. 159–63. For material published in 1921: O'Halpin, op. cit., p. 162.
32. Townshend, Charles, *Political Violence in Ireland* (Oxford 1983) pp. 207–21.
33. Memorandum by Long, 9 October 1918, French Papers, 75/46/13.
34. O'Halpin, *The Decline of the Union*, pp. 181–4; Townshend, *British Campaign*, p. 22; Long in Jones, *Whitehall Diary*, volume I, p. 83.

Chapter 2 Background to the Irish Revolution (pages 11–21)

 1. Hobson, Bulmer, *Ireland Yesterday and Tomorrow* (Tralee 1968). Joyce quoted in O'Brien, Conor Cruise, '1891–1916' in his (ed.) *The Shaping of Modern Ireland* (London 1960), p. 13.

 2. Mandle, G.F., *The Gaelic Athletic Association and Irish Nationalist Politics, 1884–1924* (Dublin 1987); de Burca, Marcus, *The GAA: A History* (Dublin 1980); Hutchinson, John, *The Dynamics of Cultural Nationalism: The Gaelic Revival and the Creation of the Irish Nation State* (London 1987); Garvin, Tom, *Nationalist Revolutionaries in Ireland, 1858–1928* (Oxford 1987).

 3. Maye, Brian, *Arthur Griffith* (Dublin 1997); Davis, Richard, *Arthur Griffith and Non-Violent Sinn Féin* (Dublin 1974).

 4. Garvin, *Nationalist Revolutionaries*; Gailey, Andrew, *Ireland and the Death of Kindness: The Experience of Constructive Unionism, 1890–1905* (Cork 1987).

 5. Foster, R.F., *Modern Ireland*, pp. 431–3. See sundry interviews in O'Malley Notebooks, O'Malley Papers, UCD Archives.

 6. Ward, Margaret, *Unmanageable Revolutionaries: Women and Irish Nationalism* (Dingle 1983); Murphy, Cliona, *The Women's Suffrage Movement and Irish Society in the Early Twentieth Century* (Hemel Hempstead 1989).

 7. Ward, op. cit., pp. 88–118. MacNeill quote, p. 91. For Proclamation of Irish Republic see Appendix A.

 8. Townshend, *Political Violence in Ireland*, pp. 277–303.

 9. Coogan, *Michael Collins*, pp. 53–4; Greaves, C. Desmond, *The Life and Times of James Connolly* (London 1961); O'Donoghue, Florence, *Tomás MacCurtain: Soldier and Patriot* (Tralee 1971); Dwyer, T. Ryle, *Tans, Terror and Troubles: Kerry's Real Fighting Story, 1913–23* (Cork 2001) pp. 73–90.

10. O'Donoghue Reminiscences, O'Donoghue Papers, NLI P31/24 (1) (2); Fitzpatrick, *Politics and Irish Life*, pp. 127–32.

11. Laffan, *The Resurrection of Ireland*, pp. 77–90.

12. Ibid., pp. 96–103; Monsignor Michael J. Curran, Bureau Statement, NLI MS 27728 in 3 volumes.

13. Laffan, op. cit., pp. 108–12, 112–13, 122–8.

14. Ibid., pp. 116–21.

15. Collins, Michael, *The Path to Irish Freedom* (Dublin 1922), p. 67.

16. Fogarty, L. (ed.), *Collected Writings of James Fintan Lalor* (Dublin 1918); Hobson, Bulmer, *Defensive Warfare: A Handbook for Irish Nationalists* (Belfast 1909).

17. Townshend, op. cit., pp. 238–45.

18. McCoy, Bureau Statement.

19. Mulcahy Memoir, Mulcahy Papers, P7b/139.

20. Coleman, 'County Longford, 1910–1923'; McCoy, Bureau Statement, op. cit.

21. Mulcahy Memoir, Mulcahy Papers, P7b/139.

22. O'Donoghue, 'Guerilla Warfare in Ireland, 1919–1921', Mulcahy Papers P7/D/1.

23. Monsignor Curran, Bureau Statement, op. cit.

24. Murray, *Oracles of God*, pp. 4–8.

25. De Róiste Diaries, Cork City Archives, U271/A.

26. Ó Broin, Leon, *Revolutionary Underground: The Story of the Irish Republican Brotherhood, 1858–1924* (Dublin 1976), pp. 175–205.

27. Hopkinson, Michael (ed.), *Frank Henderson's Easter Rising: Recollections of a Dublin Volunteer* (Cork 1998), pp. 25, 26.

28. Cooney, O'Malley Notebooks, P17b/107; Mulcahy Notes on proposed book, Mulcahy Papers P7b/134(1).

29. Coogan, Tim Pat, *De Valera: Long Fellow, Long Shadow* (London 1993).

30. 'A Report of the Intelligence Branch of the Chief of Police from May 1920–July 1921', CO 904/156 B.

31. Army Enquiry 1924, Mulcahy Papers, P7/C/29; Thornton, Bureau Statement.

32. Coogan, *Michael Collins*, pp. 58–93.

33. Mulcahy Memoir, Mulcahy Papers, P17b/139.

34. Coogan, *Michael Collins*, pp. 106–8.

35. Maye, *Arthur Griffith*, p. 152.

36. O'Donoghue, Florence, *Cathal Brugha*, O'Donoghue Papers, NLI MS 24913; Gaughan, J Anthony, *Austin Stack: Portrait of a Separatist* (Dublin 1977).

37. Michael Brennan, Bureau Statement; Laffan, *The Resurrection of Ireland*, pp. 157–9.

38. Hart, op. cit., pp. 134–64; Fitzpatrick, op. cit., pp. 200–15, for analysis of IRA membership. Campbell, Fergus, 'Land and Politics in Connacht, 1898–1920', Ph.D. thesis, University of Bristol, 1997.

39. Hopkinson, Michael, 'President Woodrow Wilson and the Irish Question', *Studia Hibernica*, no. 27 1993, pp. 89–111.

40. O'Halpin, *The Decline of the Union*, pp. 159–63.

41. Laffan, *The Resurrection of Ireland*, pp. 162–8.

Chapter 3 The War, January 1919–June 1920 (pages 25–9)
NB   no references

Chapter 4 British Administration 1919–April 1920 (pages 30–37)

1. Fisher Diary, 8 January 1919, Fisher Papers, Bodleian Library, MS 14.

2. *Dictionary of National Biography, 1930–40* (Oxford 1949) pp. 593–4; Fisher Diary, 27 January 1919, op. cit.; Note by Macpherson, 20 December 1919, Strathcarron Papers, 490.

3. Long to French, Long Papers, 947/231; Long to Lloyd George, 21 May 1919, ibid., 947/292.

4. French to Lord Londonderry, 3 January 1920, French Papers, 75/46/12; Ross to Long, Long Papers, 947/334.

5. French Memorandum, 17 December 1919, French Papers, 75/46/12.

6. French to Long, 14 January 1919, Long Papers, 947/231; Long to French, 16 January 1919, ibid.; French Memorandum, 17 December 1919, op. cit.

7. Periscope (G.C. Duggan), 'The Last Days of Dublin Castle', *Blackwood's Magazine*, August 1922; Wylie Memoir, PRO 30/89–1.

8. Long to French, 4 July 1918, French Papers, 75/46/3; French to Londonderry, 3 January 1920, ibid., 75/46/12; French to Macpherson, 11 December 1919, ibid., 75/46/13.

9. Long to Lloyd George, 21 May 1919, Long Papers, 947/292; French to Long, 11 January 1920, ibid., 947/232.

10. Long to French, 8 January 1920, ibid., 947/232; Lloyd George to French, 30 December 1919, French Papers, 75/46/11; Saunderson to Long, 12 January 1919, Long Papers, 947/347; Warren Fisher to Austen Chamberlain, 9 November 1921, Austen Chamberlain Papers, University of Birmingham, 23/2/147.

11. Macpherson to Lloyd George, ibid., 23/21/18; Fisher to Austen Chamberlain and Lloyd George, 18 November 1921, ibid., 23/2/16; *The Times*, 19, 20 December 1919.
12. See Carroll, Francis M., *American Opinion and the Irish Question, 1910–23* (Dublin 1978); Hopkinson, 'President Woodrow Wilson and the Irish Question'.
13. Frank P. Walsh Papers, New York Public Library, Box 124, Walsh's Diary for 18 April 1919.
14. American Commission on Irish Independence (Frank P. Walsh and Edward F. Dunne), *Report on Conditions in Ireland with a Demand for Investigation by the Peace Conference* (Paris 1919).
15. *The Times*, 5 May 1919.
16. Macpherson to Prime Minister, 8 May 1919, Lloyd George Papers, F/46/1/3; Frank P. Walsh Diary, 17 May 1919, Frank P. Walsh Papers, Box 124, op. cit.
17. Committee's First Report, 4 November 1919, CP 56 CAB 77/68.
18. CAB 12 (19) 10 December 1919, CAB 10 (19) 31 December 1919; CAB 23/18-19.
19. Butler (ed.), 'Lord Oranmore's Journal', 17 March 1920; Fisher to C.P. Scott, 16 March 1920, in Wilson, Trevor (ed.), *The Political Diaries of C.P. Scott, 1911–1918* (London 1970), p. 382.
20. Kendle, *Walter Long, Ireland, and the Union*, pp. 190, 191.
21. For January swoops see: Bonar Law to Lloyd George, Bonar Law Papers, 103/2/4; Wylie Memoir, op. cit.; French to Bonar Law, 16 April 1920, Bonar Law Papers, 103/2/9.
22. Churchill to King George V, 26 March 1920, Royal Archives; Gilbert, *Winston Churchill*, Companion Volume IV, Part 2, op. cit., pp. 1056, 1057.
23. Macready, General Sir Nevil, *Annals of an Active Life*, 2 volumes (London 1924).
24. Macready Memorandum, 24 May 1920, Lloyd George Papers, F/36/2/14; Churchill to Sir Henry Wilson, 31 July 1920, WO 32/9520.
25. Macpherson to French, 2 April 1920, French Papers, 75/46/11; French to Bonar Law, 16 April 1920, French Papers, 75/46/13.
26. Riddell Diary, 14 December 1920, British Library.
27. *Dictionary of National Biography, 1940–1950* (Oxford 1957) pp. 324, 325; Duggan, op. cit.; Butler (ed.), 'Lord Oranmore's Journal', 16 May 1920.

Chapter 5 The Dáil and the Dáil Government (pages 38–46)

1. For the two meetings in January see Mitchell, *Revolutionary Government*, pp. 11–12; *Dáil Proceedings*, 22 January 1919.
2. Blythe Papers, UCD Archives, P124/1958–9.
3. Hayes in *Capuchin Annual* 1972, pp. 251–85.
4. *Dáil Proceedings*, 7 April 1919.
5. Béaslaí, Piaras, *Michael Collins and the Making of a New Ireland* (Dublin 1926) volume I, p. 241; Monsignor Curran, Bureau Statement.
6. Collins to Austin Stack, 26 March 1919, Collins Papers, NLI MS 17090.
7. Bric, Deaglan, 'Pierce McCann, MP (1882–1918)' Part II, *Tipperary Historical Journal*, 1989.
8. Mitchell, Arthur, *Revolutionary Government*, p. 37.
9. *Irish Times*, 10 May 1919.
10. Mitchell, *Revolutionary Government*, pp. 147–54.
11. 'Republican Police', Irish Defence Microfilm, NLI pos 917, 919.

12. Irish daily papers, 26 November 1919; De Róiste Diaries, op. cit.
13. Collins to Stack, 17–18 May, 20 July 1919, NLI MS 5848.
14. De Róiste Diaries, 26 February, 23 June, 28 October, 21 December 1919, op. cit.; Blythe Papers, op. cit.
15. Mitchell, *Revolutionary Government*, pp. 69, 75.
16. Laffan, *The Resurrection of Ireland*, pp. 304–10.
17. Figgis, Darrell, *Recollections of the Irish War* (London 1977) pp. 219–20, 228–33; Rev. Patrick Gaynor, 'Sinn Féin Days: A Personal Memoir', in private ownership.
18. Blythe Papers, P24/985/9; Gaynor, op. cit.
19. Cope, July 1920, quoted in Kotsonouris, *Retreat from Revolution*, p. 23; *The Nation*, August 1920.
20. For Mountjoy protest see Irish press, 14, 15, 26–9 April 1920. For Wormwood Scrubs protest see Art O'Brien Papers NLI MS 8427.
21. Townshend, Charles, 'The Irish Railway Strike of 1920: Industrial Action and Civil Resistance in the Struggle for Independence', *Irish Historical Studies*, xxi, 1978–9; Cabinet Conference, 26 July 1920, C 41 (20) CAB 23/22.
22. Mitchell, *Revolutionary Government*, pp. 163–5; Fitzpatrick, *Politics and Irish Life*, pp. 143–5.
23. Mitchell, op. cit., pp. 80–98; Blythe Papers, op. cit.; Mitchell, op. cit., pp. 230–2.
24. Mulcahy GHQ Memorandum, P7/A/32; Lynch, undated, ibid. P7/D/70.
25. O'Higgins, *Dáil Debates*, 1 March 1923.
26. Kotsonouris, *Retreat from Revolution*; Mitchell, *Revolutionary Government*, pp. 137–47, 237–9.
27. For local election results see Laffan, *The Resurrection of Ireland*, pp. 323–9. For local government see Mitchell, *Revolutionary Government*, pp. 120–26, 233–66.
28. Sturgis Diaries, 29 September 1920, in Hopkinson, *The Last Days of Dublin Castle: The Diaries of Mark Sturgis* (Dublin 1999), pp. 48–9; Townshend, *British Campaign in Ireland*, pp. 117, 168, 169. For *Freeman's Journal* arrests see Sturgis Diaries 23 December 1920, in Hopkinson, op. cit., pp. 98, 99.
29. Mitchell, *Revolutionary Government*, pp. 99–105, p. 155.
30. Ibid., p. 252.
31. Martin, Hugh, *Ireland in Insurrection* (London 1921).
32. Roger Sweetman's letter in Irish daily press, 30 November 1920; *Dáil Proceedings*, 25 January 1921. On proposal for Collins to go to US see Béaslaí, *Michael Collins*, pp. 141–7; Mulcahy Notes on Discussion with General Costello, 23 May 1963, Mulcahy Papers, P7/D/3; Mulcahy Notes, 22 October 1963, ibid. P7/D/70.
33. Fisher Memorandum, 11 February 1921, Lloyd George Papers, F/17/1/9; *Dáil Proceedings*, 11 March 1921.

Chapter 6 British Security Forces (pages 47–58)

1. Tudor Notes, SIC 4, CAB 27/108; Macpherson Memorandum to Cabinet, CP 827 CAB 24/100.
2. Bonar Law relating what Carson had told him, 30 April 1920, CAB 23A/20 CAB 23/21; Lord Desart, Irish Situation Committee, 3rd Meeting, 15 July 1920, CAB 27/107; Southern Unionist delegation to Bonar Law, 26 April 1920, CP 1795 CAB 24/104.
3. Shaw Memorandum to Cabinet, 25 March 1920, CP 1131 CAB 24/104; Macready Memorandum, 26 July 1920, Anderson Papers, PRO CP 1750; CO 904/188 (1);

Anderson to Greenwood, 20 July 1920, ibid.; Macready note enclosed in letter of Sir Warren Fisher to Prime Minister, 21 July 1920, ibid.

4. *Constabulary Gazette,* volume 41, no. 2, 10 August 1918; volume 36, no. 7, 4 September 1916.
5. French to Lloyd George, 2 July 1919, French Papers, 75/46/11; French memo, 17 December 1919, ibid.; French to Macpherson, 5 January 1920, ibid.
6. Committee of Enquiry into the Detective Organisation of the Irish Police Forces, December 1919–March 1920, CO 904/24/5.
7. Townshend, *British Campaign,* p. 28, and Appendix III, p. 211.
8. RIC Reports from Dripsey Station, 28, 29 September 1919, CO 904/177 (1). For Hunt's shooting see above, p. 117.
9. Duggan (Periscope) 'The Last Days of Dublin Castle'; Coogan, Tim Pat, *Wherever Green is Worn: The Story of the Irish Diaspora* (London 2000) pp. 415–16.
10. Fitzpatrick, David, *The Two Irelands, 1912–1939* (Oxford 1998) p. 90.
11. Wilson Diary for 12 May 1920, quoted in Gilbert, *Winston S. Churchill,* Companion Volume IV, Part II, pp. 1091, 1092; Harvey, A.D., 'Who were the Auxiliaries?' *Historical Journal,* vol. 35, no. 3, September 1992.
12. Hart, Peter, *The IRA and its Enemies,* pp. 27–30.
13. Harvey, op. cit.
14. Crozier, F.P., *Impressions and Recollections* (London 1930); Harvey, op. cit.
15. Bonar Law to French, 30 December 1919, Lloyd George Papers, F/31/1/17 (C); Lloyd George told the Cabinet on 30 April 1920 that they could not declare war on rebels. CAB 23/20.
16. French to Chief Secretary, 16 January 1919, Strathcarron Papers; Shaw Memorandum on the Military Situation, GT 7182 CAB 24/78; Churchill Memorandum, undated, Gilbert, op. cit., pp. 968, 969.
17. Brind, 8 November 1919, Strathcarron Papers; Wilson Diary, 16 April 1920, Imperial War Museum.
18. Loch to French, undated (early 1919), Loch Papers, Imperial War Museum, 71/12/9; Carson at Conference of Ministers with Irish Executive, 30 April 1920, CAB 21, 23A (20).
19. Shaw to Macpherson, 19 September 1919, Strathcarron Papers.
20. *Record of the Rebellion in Ireland,* volume 1; Jeudwine Papers, Imperial War Museum, pp. 11, 12; *The History of the Sixth Division,* Strickland Papers, Imperial War Museum.
21. For Shaw's dismay at being replaced see Shaw to French, 11 July 1920, French Papers 75/46/13; Macready Memorandum, 26 July 1920, CP 1750, Anderson Papers, CO 904/188 (1); Cabinet, 11 May 1920, C 29 (20) Appendix II, CAB 23/21; Anderson to Chief Secretary, 20 July 1920, Bonar Law Papers, 102/5/35.
22. Article on Lucas affair, *Irish Times,* 9 January 1946; *Record of the Rebellion in Ireland,* volume I, p. 15.
23. Tomás Malone, Bureau Statement; Michael Brennan to Florrie O'Donoghue, O'Donoghue Papers, 31423 (3).
24. Sturgis Diaries, 15 August 1920, in Hopkinson (ed.), *The Last Days of Dublin Castle,* pp. 21–2; O'Donoghue, Florence, *No Other Law* (paperback edition, Dublin 1986) pp. 76–86.
25. GOC 5th Division to C-in-C, 23 July 1920, Jeudwine Papers, Imperial War Museum, 72/82/2.

26. Winter Intelligence Report, CO 904/156B.
27. French to Lord Londonderry, 3 January 1920, French Papers, 75/46/12; French, 13 January 1920, ibid.; *The History of the Fifth Division*, pp. 23, 24.
28. *Record of the Rebellion in Ireland*, volume 2, p. 23.
29. For assassinations see below, CO 904/24/5; Report on DMP, op. cit.
30. See material in Anderson Papers, CO 904/188/(1); *Record of the Rebellion*, volume 2, p. 8.
31. O'Halpin, Eunan, 'British Intelligence in Ireland, 1914–1921' in Andrew, Christopher and Dilks, David (eds), *The Missing Dimension: Government and Intelligence Communities in the Twentieth Century* (London 1984) pp. 54–77; Jeffery, Keith, 'British Military Intelligence following World War One' in K. G. Robertson (ed.), *British and American Approaches to Intelligence* (Basingstoke 1987).
32. Putkowski, J.J., 'The Best Secret Service Man We Had: Jack Burns and the IRA', *Lobster* 1994; Collins to Art O'Brien, 28 November, 9 December 1919, Art O'Brien Papers, NLI MS 8429.
33. Collins' Correspondence with O'Brien, 2, 20, 29 January 1920, ibid.; Collins to O'Brien, 2 January 1920, ibid. 8430.
34. Daly, Bureau Statement.
35. Long, quoted in Jones, *Whitehall Diary*, volume III, p. 99, Cabinet Meeting with Irish Executive, 31 May 1920. For Quinlisk see Coogan, *Michael Collins*, pp. 131–2.
36. Anderson to Mark Sturgis, 7 December 1920, Grant–Sturgis Papers.
37. Duggan (Periscope), op. cit.; Sturgis Diaries, 1 September 1920, in Hopkinson, op. cit., p. 32; Jeffery, op. cit.
38. Winter, Brigadier O., *Winter's Tale* (London 1955) pp. 307–8.
39. For raids on Mulcahy Papers on 19 November 1920 and 22 March 1921 see CO 904/168, 1682. For McGrane see Report 31 December 1920, CO 904/44. For raids on Collins's offices see Coogan, *Michael Collins*, p. 168. For raid on Stack's office see Stack to O'Hegarty, 30 May 1921, National Archives, DE 2/51.
40. Winter's Intelligence Report.
41. *Record of the Rebellion in Ireland*, volume II, p. 34.

Chapter 7 British Policy at the Crossroads (pages 59–66)
1. French to Bonar Law, 16 April 1920, French Papers, 75/40/12.
2. Austen Chamberlain to Lloyd George and Bonar Law, 12 May 1920, Lloyd George Papers, F/31/1/32.
3. Fisher Report to Government Ministers, ibid.; Cope and Harwood Report sent to Fisher, 12 May 1920, ibid.; Fisher's Supplementary Report, 15 May 1920, ibid., F/31/1/33.
4. Greenwood to Bonar Law, 8 May 1920, Bonar Law Papers, 103/3/9; Macready to Long, 23 April 1920, ibid., 103/5/3.
5. Anderson Note on Irish Situation, 25 July 1920, Anderson Papers, CO 904/188 (1); Macready to Greenwood, 17 July 1920, ibid.
6. For list of civil servants see Hopkinson, *The Last Days of Dublin Castle*, p. 241.
7. Wheeler-Bennett, Sir J.W., *John Anderson, Viscount Waverley* (London 1962); Wylie Memoir, op. cit.; Duggan (Periscope), op. cit.; Sturgis Diaries, 27 September 1920, in Hopkinson, op. cit., p. 46.
8. Murphy, Brian P., *Patrick Pearse and the Lost Republican Ideal* (Dublin 1991). For Sturgis on Cope, see Sturgis Diaries, 31 August 1920, in Hopkinson, op. cit., p. 31.

9. Hopkinson, op. cit.
10. Wylie Memoir, op. cit.
11. Ibid.; Ó Broin, Leon, *W.E. Wylie and the Irish Revolution, 1916–1921* (Dublin 1989); Wylie to Greenwood, and Wylie Memorandum of September 1920, Wylie Papers, PRO 30/89/3.
12. Cope to Bonar Law, 17 June 1920, Bonar Law Papers, 102/5/27; Duggan (Periscope), op. cit.
13. Duggan (Periscope), op. cit.; Wylie Memoir, op. cit.
14. *Irish Times*, 4 August 1920; *Freeman's Journal*, July 1920.
15. Jones, *Whitehall Diary*, volume III, pp. 16–23.
16. Cabinet Memorandum: 'The Situation in Ireland: Note on a Conference with the Officers of the Irish Government' CP 1693 CAB 24/108; Jones, op. cit., pp. 16–31; Sturgis Diaries, 23 July 1920, in Hopkinson, op. cit., p. 14; Fisher Diary, op. cit.
17. Jones to Prime Minister, 24 July 1920, in Jones, op. cit., pp. 31–2.
18. Campbell, Colm, *Emergency Law in Ireland, 1918–1925* (Oxford 1994) pp. 27–9.
19. *The Times*, 4 August 1920.
20. Sturgis Diaries, 28 February 1921, in Hopkinson, op. cit., p. 134.
21. Fisher Memorandum, 11 February 1921, Lloyd George Papers, F/17/1/9.

Chapter 8 Irish Intelligence System and the Development of Guerrilla Warfare up to the Truce (pages 69–78)

1. Broy in Mulcahy Papers, P7/D/70.
2. Coogan, *Michael Collins*, pp. 64, 76; Neligan, David, *The Spy in the Castle* (London 1968). For Lily Merrin see *Irish Independent*, 13 January 1965. For Nancy O'Brien see Coogan, *Michael Collins*, pp. 81, 82; Frank Thornton, Bureau Statement.
3. For Seán Kavanagh see *An tÓglach*, 1967, winter edition.
4. Mulcahy Notes on proposed book, Mulcahy Papers P7b/134; Thornton, Bureau Statement.
5. Sturgis Diaries, 11 November, 7, 16 December 1920, 1 March 1921, in Hopkinson, op. cit., pp. 69, 87, 93, 151.
6. *Dáil Proceedings*, 12 April 1919; Abbott, Richard, *Police Casualties in Ireland, 1919–1922* (Cork 2000) pp. 298–310.
7. Material on Ashdown ambush in Anderson Papers, CO 904/ 188(1); Note by Macpherson, 20 December 1919, Strathcarron Papers.
8. RIC Reports, August 1919, CO 904/109, for start of process.
9. O'Malley, Ernie, *Raids and Rallies* (Dublin 1982).
10. The GHQ issued *The Irish Republican Army*, Strickland Papers, Imperial War Museum; General IRA Order, 4 October 1920, O'Malley Notebooks, P17b/127.
11. Anderson to Chief Secretary, 17 August 1921, CO 904/232.
12. For discussion of this see: Augusteijn, *From Public Defiance to Guerrilla Warfare*; Hart, *The IRA and its Enemies*; Fitzpatrick, *Politics and Irish Life*, pp. 215–31; Valiulis, Maryann, *Portrait of a Revolutionary: General Richard Mulcahy and the Founding of the Irish Free State* (Dublin 1992) pp. 41–51.
13. 'Memorandum on the Divisional Idea', Mulcahy Papers, P7/A/47; Memoranda on the Second Northern Division, Erris and Connemara, East Clare and South Galway, ibid.; Memorandum on Second Northern Division, ibid. P7/A/16.
14. O'Donoghue, *No Other Law*.

15. *Dáil Proceedings*, 20 August 1919.
16. Collins to O'Brien, undated but probably early May 1921, O'Brien Papers, NLI MS 8430. For Broy's capture see Coogan, *Michael Collins*, pp. 166, 167. For internment figures see Townshend, *British Campaign*, p. 195. Mulcahy's notes on Béaslaí's biography of Collins, Mulcahy Papers, P7b/188.
17. Béaslaí to O'Donoghue, 11 October 1952, and reply, 28 October 1952, NLI MS 31421 (9).
18. O'Donoghue on Italian Arms, O'Donoghue Papers, NLI 31392 O'Malley Notes on interview with Michael Leahy, 29 April 1963, ibid., 31513; Leahy's Statement, ibid.; Art O'Brien to Collins, 1, 14 January, 21 February 1921, O'Brien Papers, NLI MS 8430.
19. Pax Whelan in MacEoin, Uinseann, *Survivors* (Dublin 1980) pp. 139–41.
20. Hart, Peter, 'The Thompson Sub-Machine Gun in Ireland, Revisited', *Irish Sword*, summer 1995; Bell, J. Bowyer, 'The Thompson Sub-Machine Gun in Ireland, 1921', *Irish Sword* 1967.

Chapter 9 The War July–December 1920 (pages 79–91)
1. For Mallow see *Manchester Guardian*, 2 October 1920.
2. Plunkett in *The Times*, 7 September 1920.
3. For Balbriggan see Chief Secretary's Weekly Survey, 2 October 1920, SIC 39 CAB 27/108; Anderson to Sturgis, 2 October 1920, Grant–Sturgis Papers; Sturgis Diaries, 22 September 1920, in Hopkinson, op. cit., p. 43.
4. Fisher to Prime Minister, 16 November 1920, Lloyd George Papers, F/16/7/61.
5. Dwyer, T. Ryle, *Tans, Terror and Troubles*, pp. 230–4.
6. For Smyth see Hopkinson, op. cit., pp. 240, 241; Sturgis Diaries, 10 October 1920, ibid., p. 49.
7. Wilson Diary, 7 July 1920, quoted in Hazelhurst, Cameron, 'Tans Terror' in *Sunday Times*, 7 May 1972; Riddell Diary, British Library; Hankey, quoted in Boyce and Hazelhurst, 'The Unknown Chief Secretary'.
8. Sturgis Diaries, 1, 5 October 1920, in Hopkinson, op. cit., pp. 49, 50, 52. For Macready see ibid., 19 August 1920, p. 25; Macready to CIGS, 27 September 1920, Anderson Papers, CO 904/188 (II).
9. For Greenwood in Commons, 1 November 1920, see *Parliamentary Debates*, 5th Series, volume 134, cols 25–26; Lloyd George to Greenwood, 25 February 1921, Lloyd George Papers, F/19/3/4.
10. Daily press, 13 December 1920; First Meeting Court of Enquiry into Cork Burnings, 16–21 December 1920, WO 35/88/1; D/I Report, 15 December 1920, CO 904/50; GOC Cork to GHQ, 22 December 1920, WO 35/88/1; Sturgis Diaries, 12 December 1920, in Hopkinson, op. cit., p. 89; 'Charlie' to his mother, 16 December 1920, O'Donoghue Papers, NLI MS 31226.
11. Greenwood in Commons, op. cit., volume 136, cols 25–9; Cabinet for 14 February 1921, Jones, *Whitehall Diary*, volume III, p. 50; Sturgis Diaries, 16, 19 December 1920, in Hopkinson, op. cit., pp. 93, 95; 'Charlie', op. cit.
12. Gaynor, 'Sinn Féin Days', *Galway Express*, 24, 31 July 1920.
13. Art O'Brien to D.F., 27 August 1920, O'Brien Papers, NLI MS 8427.
14. Townshend, Charles, 'The Irish Republican Army and the Development of Guerrilla Warfare, 1916–1921', *English Historical Review*, vol. xciv, no. 371, April 1979.

15. Anderson to Chief Secretary, 18 June 1921, CO 904/232.
16. *The Times*, 30 July 1920; Greenwood in Commons, 14 July 1920, *Parliamentary Debates*, 5th Series, volume 131, cols 2386–2391. For Smyth's assassination see O'Donoghue Papers, NLI MS 31312; Seán Culhane, O'Malley Notebooks, P17b/108.
17. Mitchell, *Revolutionary Government*, p. 175.
18. See Costello, Francis J., *Enduring the Most: The Life and Death of Terence MacSwiney* (Dingle 1995). For MacSwiney's arrest see O'Donoghue, *No Other Law*, pp. 87–97; Draft of statement from Anderson, CO 904/168; De Róiste Diary, Cork City Archives, U271/A.
19. Collins in DE 2/4. For Lord Chancellor see Sturgis Diaries, 31 August 1920, in Hopkinson, op. cit., p 32. For debate within Catholic Church see Costello, *Enduring the Most*, pp. 210–16; MacSwiney to Brugha, quoted in Note of 10 February 1929, Mary MacSwiney Papers, UCD Archives, P48c/39. For Griffith's statement see Irish press, 12 November 1920.
20. Blythe Papers, P24/1958–9; Art O'Brien to Collins, 20 October 1920, National Archives, DE 2/4.
21. Lloyd George to Bonar Law, 4 September 1920, Lloyd George Papers F/31/1/44. Sturgis Diaries, 4 September 1920, in Hopkinson, op. cit., p. 36.
22. Ibid., 25 October 1920, pp. 59, 60.
23. See folder on Barry's arrest, CO 904/42.
24. Ibid. French to Chief Secretary, 1 November 1920, French Papers, 75/46/11; O'Donovan, Donal, *Kevin Barry and his Time* (Dublin 1989) pp. 128–9.
25. Sturgis Diaries, 30 October 1920, in Hopkinson, op. cit., p. 62. See Doherty, M.A., 'Kevin Barry and the Anglo-Irish Propaganda War', *Irish Historical Studies*, xxxii, 2000–1.
26. O'Donovan, op. cit., p. 169.
27. For Bloody Sunday see Townshend, Charles, 'Bloody Sunday — Michael Collins Speaks', *European Studies Review*, ix, 1979.
28. Mulcahy on Collins, Mulcahy Papers, P7b/182; Mulcahy comments, 14 April 1959, ibid., P7c/2/(31).
29. Joe O'Connor, O'Malley Notebooks, P17b/64, 105; George White, ibid., P17b/99, 105; MacDonald, ibid., P17b/105; Frank Thornton, Bureau Statement; Larry Nugent, O'Malley Notebooks, P17b/88; Jim Slattery, ibid., P17b/94, 109, 138.
30. Frank Thornton and Vinnie Byrne, Bureau Statements; Andrews, C.S., *Dublin Made Me*, pp. 152, 154. For British casualties see CO 904/168 (3).
31. Pat MacCrea, O'Malley Notebooks, P17b/110. For the convictions see note from AGW, 20 February 1921, CO 904/42; folder on Patrick Moran, CO 904/43; Michael Noyk Statement, NLI MS 18975; folder on Frank Teeling, William Conway, Daniel Healy and Edward Potter, trial for murder of Lieutenant Angliss, CO 904/43. For Teeling escape see Paddy O'Connor, Bureau Statement.
32. Archie Doyle, Liam Kavanagh and Harry Colley, O'Malley Notebooks, P17b/101, 94, 97; report on Croke Park shootings, CO 904/168(3).
33. Charlie Dalton, O'Malley Notebooks, P17b/105; Collins, 15 December 1920, in documents seized at 5 Mespil Road Dublin, CO 904/24/3; Coogan, *Michael Collins*, pp. 160, 162.
34. *Record of the Rebellion*, volume 1, pp. 26, 27; Irish press, 26 November 1920.

35. Fanning, Ronan, 'Michael Collins: An Overview', in Doherty and Keogh (eds), *Michael Collins and the Making of the Irish State*, pp. 204–7; Bowden, Tom, 'Bloody Sunday — A Reappraisal', *European Studies Review*, ii, 1972.

Chapter 10 From the Imposition of Martial Law to the Truce (pages 92–6)

1. See Campbell, *Emergency Law in Ireland*, pp. 30–4. For text of Proclamation see Appendix A. For accompanying proclamations see Campbell, op. cit., pp. 31, 32; CIGS to Acting GOC, 1 December 1920, and reply, 1, 5 December 1920, Jeudwine Papers; Jeudwine to Macready, 7 December 1920, ibid.; Macready letter, 10 December 1920, ibid.; Boyd Memorandum 4 December 1920, ibid.
2. For extension of martial law see Cabinet meeting, 30 December 1920, C81 (20), CAB 23/23; *Record of the Rebellion*, volume I, pp. 28, 29. See Appendix F for Martial Law Proclamation.
3. WO 35/169; Radcliffe to CIGS, 23 September 1920, WO 32/9537, quoted in Townshend; *British Campaign*, p. 119; *The History of the Sixth Division*, Appendix V.
4. Macready to Tudor, 24 February 1921, Anderson Papers, CO 904/188 (II); *The History of the Fifth Division*, pp. 140–2.
5. Macready Memorandum, 18 February 1921, French Papers, 75/46/12. For Castleconnell incident see Townshend, *British Military Campaign*, pp. 166–7.
6. Macready, *Annals of an Active Life*, volume II, p. 517; Macready to Anderson, 7 April 1921, Anderson Papers, CO 904/188/(2); Townshend, Charles, *Making the Peace: Public Order and Public Security in Modern Britain* (Oxford 1993) pp. 76–9.
7. *The History of the Sixth Division*, p. 66; Fisher Memorandum, 11 February 1921, Lloyd George Papers, F/17/1/9.
8. Sturgis Diaries, 6 March 1921, in Hopkinson, op. cit., p. 137.
9. For internment figures see Townshend, *British Campaign*, Appendix XII, p. 223; Sturgis Diaries, 8 June 1921, in Hopkinson, op. cit., p. 186.
10. For armoured cars see WO 35/93 (1)1; Cabinet Paper submitted by Churchill, 27 December 1920, CF 2256, WO 32/9540; *The History of the Fifth Division*, p. 88.
11. Macready Memorandum, 18 February 1921, French Papers, 75/46/12; Fisher Memorandum, 11 February 1921, op. cit.
12. Memo by Colonel Elles of Tank Corps Centre, 24 June 1921, CP 3075 CAB 24/124; Anderson to Chief Secretary, 17 August 1921, CO 904/232. For casualty figures see Townshend, *British Campaign*, Appendix V, p. 214; *The History of the Fifth Division*, p. 141. For British troop numbers see Wilson Papers, 18 May 1921, 2/13/4; Strickland Diary, 11 July 1921, 17 May 1922, Strickland Papers, Imperial War Museum.

Chapter 11 Guerrilla Warfare in Dublin (pages 97–103)

1. Memorandum 'Offensive against Internal Morale of the Enemy', Mulcahy Papers, P7/A/4; Staff Memorandum, 24 March 1921, 'The War as a Whole', ibid., P7/A/17; Ned Broy, O'Malley Notebooks, P17b/128.
2. Mulcahy Memoir, Mulcahy Papers, P7b/200.
3. See Hopkinson (ed.), *Frank Henderson's Easter Rising*; Paddy O'Connor, Bureau Statement; Oscar Traynor Memoir, de Valera Papers, UCD Archives, 1527/2; Henderson, O'Malley Notebooks, P17b/99.
4. Valiulis, *Portrait of a Revolutionary*; Colley, O'Malley Notebooks, P17b/97.

5. Henderson, op. cit.; Henderson, Frank, 'Irish Leaders of our Time, 5: Richard McKee', *An Cosantóir*, v, 1945.

6. Archie Doyle and Brian Holman, O'Malley Notebooks, P17b/95; Paddy Daly, Bureau Statement. For Collinstown raid see Pat MacCrea and Tommy Merrinan, O'Malley Notebooks, P17b/110, 109; Traynor Memoir, op. cit.; *Dublin's Fighting Story, 1916–1921* (Tralee) 1949.

7. McHugh and Lynch, Bureau Statements.

8. Harrington, Niall C., 'The Squad and the Dublin ASU' and Leonard, Joe, 'The Organisation and Activity of Intelligence, ASU and Squad during the Fight for Irish Independence', both in Army Archives; Paddy Daly and Vinnie Byrne, Bureau Statements; Archie Doyle, George White and Jim Slattery, O'Malley Notebooks, P17b/105, 99, 94, 88, 109, 138.

9. Jim Slattery, op. cit.; Archie Doyle, op. cit.; material on shooting of Redmond, CO 904/177 (1).

10. Broy, O'Malley Notebooks, op. cit.

11. Henderson and Andrews, O'Malley Notebooks, op. cit.

12. George White and Tommy Merrinan, O'Malley Notebooks, op. cit.

13. Paddy O'Connor, Bureau Statement and Papers; Leonard, op. cit.; Harrington, op. cit.

14. For detailed record of ASU attacks see Humphreys Papers, UCD Archives; P 106, 1920, 1921, 1922, 1923; Paddy O'Connor, Paddy Daly and Joe McGuinness, Bureau Statements; Madge Clifford, O'Malley Notebooks, P17b/104.

15. Paddy O'Connor, Bureau Statement; Macready to Anderson, 15 February 1921, CO 904/188(1).

16. For attempted MacEoin escape see Paddy Daly, Bureau Statement; Coogan, *Michael Collins*, pp. 180, 181.

17. *Record of the Rebellion*, volume 1, p. 39; Paddy O'Connor, Bureau Statement; Jim Slattery, O'Malley Notebooks, P17b/94, 109, 138; Leonard, op. cit.

18. Memorandum on Baggot Street attack, 26 June 1921, CO 904/168/2; Paddy O'Connor, Bureau Statement and Papers.

19. Traynor, Memoir, op. cit.; Paddy O'Connor, Bureau Statement; Harry Colley, Joe O'Connor and Jim Slattery, O'Malley Notebooks, op. cit.; Mulcahy conversation with Paddy Daly, 28 November 1962, Mulcahy Papers P7b/178; Mulcahy Notes on Béaslaí, *Michael Collins*, volume II, ibid., P7b/188.

20. Paddy O'Connor and Paddy Daly, Bureau Statements; Humphreys Papers, op. cit.

Chapter 12 The War in Cork (pages 104–14)

1. Blythe Memoir, Blythe Papers, P24/1783; Flor Begley, O'Malley Notebooks P17b/111.

2. O'Donoghue, *Tomás MacCurtain*; O'Donoghue, *No Other Law*.

3. O'Donoghue Memoir, O'Donoghue Papers, NLI P31124 (1) (2); Moylan, Bureau Statement; Hart, Peter, *The IRA and its Enemies*, pp. 239–58.

4. O'Donoghue Memoir, op. cit.

5. Moylan, Bureau Statement.

6. Hart, op. cit., pp. 187–225; Deasy, Liam, 'Statement on Ireland's Fight for Independence', Mulcahy Papers, P7/D/45; Deasy, Liam, *Towards Ireland Free* (Cork 1973).

7. Ibid., p. 8.
8. O'Donoghue Memoir, op. cit.
9. O'Donoghue, *No Other Law.*
10. Moylan, Bureau Statement.
11. Barry, *Guerilla Days in Ireland*; Hart, op. cit., pp. 30–2; Butler, Ewan, *Barry's Flying Column* (London 1971).
12. Submission of Siobhán Lankford for a military pension, Lankford Papers, Cork City Archives, U167–169A.
13. O'Donoghue Papers, NLI MS 31124 (3).
14. O'Donoghue, *No Other Law*, pp. 10–19; O'Donoghue Memoir, op. cit.
15. Moylan, Bureau Statement; Babington to O'Donoghue, 2 April 1953, O'Donoghue Papers, NLI MS 31301(1).
16. O'Donoghue, *No Other Law*, pp. 49–59; De Róiste Diary, 15 September 1919, Cork City Archives, U271/A.
17. Talk given by Mulcahy, 31 January 1964, Mulcahy Papers, P7b/142; O'Donoghue, *No Other Law*, p. 56.
18. Inquest on late Alderman Tomás MacCurtain, Lord Mayor of Cork, CO 904/47; Wylie Memoir, PRO 30/89/2; O'Donoghue, *Tomás MacCurtain*, pp. 166–93.
19. For attack on Strickland see *The History of the Sixth Division*, Appendix III; Hart, *The IRA and its Enemies*, pp. 1–18; *Cork Examiner*, 19, 24 November 1920; Stephen Donnelly account, *Western People*, 1 November 1964, with extracts from *Ballina Herald* files.
20. O'Donoghue, *No Other Law*, p. 123.
21. *The History of the Sixth Division*, pp. 63, 64; *Record of the Rebellion*, volume I, p. 27; Hart, op. cit., pp. 21–38. For Barry see Griffith, Kenneth and O'Grady, Timothy, *Curious Journey: An Oral History of Ireland's Unfinished Revolution* (Dublin 1982) pp. 181–2.
22. Hart, op. cit., pp. 27–30; Browne, Charlie, *The Story of the Seventh* (Macroom, undated).
23. Cabinet Conference, 29 December 1920, C 79A (20) CAB 23/23.
24. O'Callaghan, Seán, *Execution* (London 1974); Frank Busteed, O'Malley Notebooks, P17b/12; *The History of the Sixth Division*, pp. 73–5.
25. Records of Meeting in Mallow, 14 January 1951, O'Donoghue Papers; NLI MS 38394; Paddy O'Brien, O'Malley Notebooks, P17b/108, 124; *The History of the Sixth Division*, pp. 80, 83, 84; Lankford Papers, op. cit.; Account of Clonmult, O'Donoghue Papers, NLI MS 31207 (2); Mick Leahy, O'Malley Notebooks, P17b/108; Hart, op. cit., p. 149; File on Siobhán Creedon, CO 904/104.
26. *The History of the Sixth Division*, pp. 92–6; Flor Begley, O'Malley Notebooks, P17b/111; Begley, Diarmuid, *The Road to Crossbarry: The Decisive Battle in the War of Independence* (Cork 1999).
27. Barry, *Guerilla Days*; Moylan, Bureau Statement.
28. *The History of the Sixth Division*, pp. 84–90; Paddy O'Brien and George Power, O'Malley Notebooks, P17b/139, 100; Notes by O'Donoghue, O'Donoghue Papers, NLI MS 31301 (1).
29. Hart, op. cit., p. 256; Tom Kelleher in MacEoin, *Survivors*, pp. 485–91; article in O'Donoghue Papers, NLI MS 31301 (1); *The History of the Sixth Division*, pp. 76–80; article on Upton Station ambush, O'Donoghue Papers, NLI 31301 (1).
30. See O/C Flying Column, O'Donoghue Papers, NLI MS 31205.

31. *The History of the Sixth Division*, p. 125; Paddy O'Brien, O'Malley Notebooks, P17b/139.
32. Moylan Bureau Statement; O'Donoghue Diary, May–June 1921, O'Donoghue Papers, NLI MSS 31176, 31426.
33. Ibid.
34. Ibid.; correspondence with Béaslaí, O'Donoghue Papers, NLI MS 31301 (2).

Chapter 13 The War in Tipperary, Limerick, Waterford, Wexford and Kilkenny (pages 115–24)
1. Breen, Dan, *My Fight for Irish Freedom*; Séamus Robinson, Account of his part in the War of Independence, NLI MS 21265; Ryan, Desmond, *Seán Treacy and the Third Tipperary Brigade* (London 1945); Desmond Ryan Papers, UCD Archives, LA/O/A/30; Mulcahy on IRB and South Tipperary, Mulcahy Papers, P7b/172; Mulcahy discussion on MacEoin Interview, 15 January 1964, ibid., P7/D/3.
2. Breen, *My Fight for Irish Freedom*, p. 30; Andrews, *Dublin Made Me*, p. 115.
3. Ryan, op. cit.; Treacy to Kevin Crowe, 3 May 1918, Desmond Ryan Papers, LA 10/4/33–5; Breen, op. cit.; Brennan, Michael, *The War in Clare, 1911–1921* (Dublin 1980) p. 36; Robinson, op. cit.; Robinson talk on Radio Train, 12 September 1950, NLI MS 21265.
4. Mulcahy Note on the IRB and the South Tipperary Brigade, Mulcahy Papers, P7b/181.
5. Ibid.; Ryan, op. cit., pp. 100–10.
6. Paddy Dwyer, O'Malley Notebooks, P17b/130.
7. For Drumcondra shooting see daily press 13–14 October 1920.
8. O'Dwyer to Editor of *Irish Independent*, 6 November 1920; Robinson Account, op. cit.; Colmcille, Father, 'Tipperary's Fight in 1920', *Capuchin Annual* 1970.
9. Seán Gaynor, Bureau Statement; Mick Kennedy, O'Malley Notebooks, P17b/124.
10. Jim Gibbins and Liam Manahan, O'Malley Notebooks, P17b/129, 106; Tomás Malone, Bureau Statement.
11. Ibid.
12. Malone, Bureau Statement.
13. Gaynor, Bureau Statement; Father Gaynor Memoir, op. cit.; MacEvilly, Michael, *Andy Cooney* (forthcoming); Cooney, O'Malley Notebooks, P17b/107.
14. Father Gaynor Memoir, op. cit.; O'Malley, Ernie, *Raids and Rallies*, pp. 11–26, 41–65.
15. Costello in O'Donoghue Papers, 13 September 1953, NLI MS 31423 (4).
16. Malone, Bureau Statement; Ryan Notes on Treacy, op. cit.; Account of Dromkeen, Anderson Papers, CO 904/188/(2).
17. *The History of the Sixth Division*, p. 104; *Record of Rebellion*, volume I, p. 43; Tomás Malone, Bureau Statement.
18. O'Malley, Ernie, *Raids and Rallies*, pp. 134–55.
19. Seán Fitzpatrick, op. cit.; Augusteijn, op. cit., p. 136; Mossy McGrath, O'Malley Notebooks P17b/123; Material on Tipperary Brigade, NLI MS 17880(1).
20. List of Waterford engagements, O'Donoghue Papers, NLI MS 31150; Divisional Commandant to C/S, 10 June 1921, Mulcahy Papers, P7/A/19. For Tramore ambush see East Waterford Report, May 1921, ibid. For Tramore Enquiry see C/S to O/C First Southern Division, 29 July 1921, ibid., P7/A/22.

21. Divisional Commandant to C/S, 10 June 1921, op. cit. For Waterford in Civil War see Hopkinson, *Green against Green*, pp. 153–5, 168; O'Donoghue Papers, NLI MS 31150.
22. Roche, Richard, 'Events in Wexford 1920', *Capuchin Annual* 1970; GHQ Report, Mulcahy Papers, P7/A/17.
23. Maher, Jim, *The Flying Column — West Kilkenny, 1916–1921*, (Dublin 1988) pp. 14–25, 27–33, 57–61, 67–78, 79–93; O'Malley, *On Another Man's Wound*; C/S to B/C, Kilkenny, 20 April 1921, Mulcahy Papers, P7/A/18p; Edward McPhillips, O'Malley Notebooks, P17b/96, 101, 103, 117, 130.

Chapter 14 The War in Kerry and Clare (pages 125–31)
1. O'Duffy quoted at public meeting in Bandon, 15 October 1933, in Dwyer, *Tans, Terror and Troubles*, p. 7; Augusteijn, *Public Defiance*, p. 19.
2. Tom McEllistrim, O'Malley Notebooks, 17b/102; Abbott, *Police Casualties*, p. 95; Dwyer, op. cit., pp. 228–53.
3. For Greenwood see daily press, 1, 2, 3 November 1920; *Daily News*, 10 November 1920.
4. Dwyer, op. cit., pp. 254–7, 264–5; Johnny Connors, O'Malley Notebooks, P17b/102.
5. Report of 21 March 1921, CO 904/213; Intelligence Summary, H Company, Auxiliary Division RIC 1–15 April 1921; O'Donoghue Papers, NLI MS 31225.
6. Report from R. Ballantyne, 15 April 1921, and Intelligence Summary, 7 April 1921, O'Donoghue Papers, NLI MS 31225.
7. *The History of the Sixth Division*, p. 104; Bertie Scully, O'Malley Notebooks, P17b/102; Dwyer, op. cit., pp. 316–21.
8. Dwyer, op. cit., pp. 43–5.
9. Dinny Daly, O'Malley Notebooks, P17b/102; Liam Deasy, ibid., P17b/85; Con Casey, ibid., P17b/102; Mullins, Billy, *The Memoirs of Billy Mullins: Veteran of the War of Independence* (Tralee 1983); Dwyer, op. cit., pp. 196, 197; Kennedy, O'Malley Notebooks, P17b/102.
10. J.J. Rice, O'Malley Notebooks, P17b/101, 102; Tom O'Connor, ibid.
11. O/C First Southern Division to GHQ, 5 October 1921, Mulcahy Papers, P7/A/28.
12. Cooney, O'Malley Notebooks, P17b/107; MacEvilly, op. cit.
13. C/S to Kerry No. 1 Brigade, Mulcahy Papers, P7/A/29. HQ Inspection Officer, Kerry No. 1 Brigade, 23 June 1921, ibid., P7/A/19.
14. Ibid.; Cooney, op. cit.
15. Fitzpatrick, *Politics and Irish Life*, pp. 198–231.
16. Blythe Papers, op. cit.; Brennan, *The War in Clare*.
17. Ibid.; Fitzpatrick, op. cit., pp. 170, 172, 190, 191; Hopkinson, *Green against Green*, p. 43.
18. Brennan, op. cit.; Fitzpatrick, op. cit., pp. 154–64.
19. Brennan, op. cit.; Fitzpatrick, op. cit., pp. 171–91.
20. Haugh, L., 'The History of the West Clare Brigade', Army Archives, A/0181 Group V; Greenwood Report for week ending 27 September 1920, CO 904/228; Report on Rineen ambush, CO 904/168; Father Gaynor Memoir, op. cit.
21. Ibid.; Haugh, op. cit.; Brennan, op. cit.
22. Haugh, op. cit.; Brennan, op. cit.

234 Notes to pages 131–8

23. Report on Mid-Clare Brigade, Humphreys Papers, UCD Archives, P106/1938(4); Brennan, op. cit.; C/S to B/C Mid-Clare, 23 May 1921, Mulcahy Papers, P7/A/19.
24. D/O to C/S, 6 July 1921, enclosing the Organiser's Report, ibid., P7/A/20.

Chapter 15 The War in the West and North-West Counties (pages 132–40)
1. MacEvilly, Michael, 'The Formation of the West Mayo Brigade', unpublished article.
2. Tommy Heavey in MacEoin, *Survivors*, p. 426; Michael Kilroy, Mark Killilea, Ned Moane, Brodie Malone, Johnny Duffy, P.J. McDonnell and Tommy Heavey, Bureau Statements; Seán Walsh, Bureau Statement.
3. MacEvilly, Michael, 'Séamus MacEvilly', unpublished article; Heavey in MacEoin, *Survivors*, pp. 421–61.
4. Johnny Duffy, O'Malley Notebooks, P17b/109; MacEvilly, Michael, 'Séamus MacEvilly'.
5. Ibid.; Tommy Heavey, Mark Killilea, Paddy Duffy and Jimmy Swift, O'Malley Notebooks, P17b/120, 109, 113, 138, 136; CO 904/102.
6. Malone, Moane, Heavey, op. cit.; Monthly Report from West Mayo, 29 June 1921; Report on Carrowkennedy encounter, Mulcahy Papers, P7/A/19.
7. Tom Maguire in MacEoin, *Survivors*, pp. 283–8; C/S to B/C South Mayo, 25 May 1921, Mulcahy Papers, P7/A/18.
8. Matt Kilcawley and Johnny Grieley, O'Malley Notebooks, P17b/137, 138, 113; C/S to AG, 5 July 1921, Mulcahy Papers, P7/A/20; Report of visit to East Mayo Brigade, 25 August 1921, ibid., P7/A/23.
9. Farry, Michael, *Sligo 1914–1921: A Chronicle of Conflict* (Trim 1992); Farry, Michael, *Aftermath of Revolution: Sligo 1921–1923* (Dublin 2000); Casualty and armament figures, ibid., pp. 8, 9, 15; Augusteijn, *Public Defiance*, p. 19 Table 1.5.
10. Farry, *Sligo 1914–21*, pp. 230, 231; Frank Carty and Tom Scanlon, O'Malley Notebooks, P17b/133, 137; Carty Statement, NLI, Collins Papers, P 914; Linda Kearns Statement, de Valera Papers, UCD Archives, 1406; Jack Brennan, O'Malley Notebooks, P17b/137.
11. Eugene Gilbride, O'Malley Notebooks, P17b/37; Linda Kearns Statement, op. cit.; File on Linda Kearns, CO 904/44; Winter Intelligence Report, CO 904/156B.
12. Farry, *Sligo 1914–21*, pp. 281–4, 308–9; C/S to Sligo O/C, 6 June 1921, Mulcahy Papers, P7/A/19; Sligo O/C to C/S, 22 July 1921, ibid., P7/A/22.
13. Peter Joe McDonnell and John Feehan, Bureau Statements; McDonnell, P.J., 'The Irish in West Connemara, 1921', unpublished.
14. McDonnell, Bureau Statement.
15. Maurteen Brennan and Dr Jack Comer, O'Malley Notebooks P17b/133, 121, 131, 132, 137; McDonnell, Bureau Statement.
16. Ibid.; A/G to C/S, 15 April 1921, Mulcahy Papers, P7/A/19.
17. O/C Tuam Brigade, 28 June 1921, Army Archives; O/C South-East Galway Brigade, Army Archives.
18. 'James Hogan Memoir 1913–37' in Ó Corráin, Donnchadh, *James Hogan: Revolutionary, Historian and Political Scientist* (Dublin 2001) p. 189; O/C East Clare Brigade, 6, 10 November 1921, Mulcahy Papers, P7/A/19, 27; Report on Ballyturin tragedy, CO 904/12 (4).

19. Daily press for 2 November 1920, Ó Laoi, Patrick, 'Father Griffin, 1892–1920' (Galway 1994).
20. D/O to C/S, 26 June 1921, enclosing report from O/C Northern Division, Mulcahy Papers, P7/A/ 22.
21. Joe Sweeney, O'Malley Notebooks, P17b/98; Ó Drisceoil, Donal, *Peadar O'Donnell* (Cork 2001) pp. 17–20; O'Donnell in conversation with Joe Sweeney and Ernie O'Malley, 3 June 1949, O'Malley Notebooks, P17b/98.

Chapter 16 The Irish Midlands, some Surrounding Counties and IRA Activity in Britain (pages 141–9)
1. Mulcahy Notes on Béaslaí, *Michael Collins*, volume II, Mulcahy Papers P7/D/67.
2. RIC Report for Longford, Coleman, 'County Longford 1910–1923'; Longford military service applications, MacEoin Papers; MacEoin Memoir, MacEoin Papers, UCD Archives, 1865; Ernie O'Malley, Draft biography of Collins, O'Malley Notebooks, P17b/152, 153.
3. RIC Report for Longford, CO 904/68; Seán Conway, O'Malley Notebooks, P17b/121; Frank Davis, Bureau Statement.
4. Conway and Davis, Bureau Statements; MacEoin Memoir, MacEoin Papers, 1761.
5. Ibid., 1751, 1753; Davis and Conway, Bureau Statements; Davis, O'Malley Notebooks, P17b/121, 131.
6. *The History of the Fifth Division*, pp. 98, 99; Folder on 'Murder of D.I. McGrath', CO 904/43; Conway, Bureau Statement; MacEoin Memoir, MacEoin Papers, 1752, 1761; Carty, John, 'The Clonfin Ambush', *Journal of Longford Historical Society*, MacEoin Papers, 1739.
7. *The History of the Fifth Division*, pp. 94–97; Conway, Bureau Statement; C/S, 7 June 1921, Mulcahy Papers, P7/A/18.
8. O'Callaghan, Michael, *For Ireland and Freedom: Roscommon's Contribution to the Fight for Independence* (Roscommon 1964); Collins quoted by Mrs Seán McLoughlin (Connolly's sister), O'Malley Notebooks, P17b/131; Davis, O'Malley Notebooks, op. cit.; O'Reilly, O'Malley Notebooks, P17b/121; Bureau Statements; Bureau of Military History Chronology.
9. O'Malley, Draft biography of Collins, op. cit.; Thomas Kelly, Jim Clancy, Matt Kilcawley in O'Malley Notebooks, P17b/91, 96, 100, 101; Connolly to AG, GHQ, 22 June 1920, Army Archives, A/0492 VIII; McCarthy, Veronica, 'The Story of Leitrim 1920', *Capuchin Annual* 1970.
10. *The History of the Fifth Division*, pp. 101, 102; O'Malley, *Raids and Rallies*, pp. 100–115.
11. Coogan, Oliver, *Politics and War in Meath, 1913–23* (Dublin 1983).
12. Ibid., pp. 116, 117, 139, 191–2.
13. C/S to O/C Ist Eastern Division, 27 April 1921, Mulcahy Papers, P7/A/17; McDonnell, Bureau Statement; Kavanagh, Matt, 'Wicklow 1920', *Capuchin Annual* 1970; C/S to B/C Kildare No. 2 Brigade, 22 April 1921, Mulcahy Papers, P7/A/39; Nolan, William, 'Events in Carlow 1920–21', *Capuchin Annual* 1970; Lar Brady, O'Malley Notebooks, P17b/116.
14. C/S to BC, 21 April 1921, referring to report from inspecting officer in Offaly, Mulcahy Papers, P7/A/17; C/S to B/C, 2 April 1921, ibid.; O/C Divisional HQ to C/S, 16 July 1921, ibid., P7/A/20.

15. For Balbriggan see above. C/S to Fingal Brigade, 6 April 1921, Mulcahy Papers, P7/A/17; QMG to C/S, 4 April 1921, ibid.
16. For formation of Fourth Northern Division, C/S to O/C Fourth Northern Division, 26 April 1921, Mulcahy Papers, P7/A/16; Abbott, *Police Casualties*, pp. 113, 257.
17. Ibid., pp. 179, 180; 'Monaghan A', 'Monaghan — 1920', *Capuchin Annual* 1970.
18. Notes from O/C Cavan flying column, 10, 24 May 1921, Mulcahy Papers, P7/A/18; McDermott, Jim, *Northern Divisions: The Old IRA and the Belfast Pogroms, 1920–22* (Belfast 2001) pp. 81–2.
19. Art O'Brien Papers, NLI MS 8921, 8427; Mitchell, *Revolutionary Government in Ireland*, p. 252.
20. Hart, Peter, 'Operations Abroad: The IRA in Britain, 1919–23', *English Historical Review*, vol. cxv, no. 460, February 2000; Paterson, Ian D., 'The Activities of Irish Republican Physical Force Organisations in Scotland', *Scottish Historical Review*, vol. lxxii, no. 193, April 1993. For Collins' arms dealings see Joe Vize to Collins, 26 March, 11 June 1920, Mulcahy Papers, P7/A/1; Tom Craven to Collins, 25 May 1919, ibid.
21. Hart, op. cit. Paddy Daly, O'Malley Notebooks P17b/36, 100; Seán McGrath, ibid., P17b/36; Hugh Early, ibid., P17b/110; Art O'Brien to Collins, 17 December 1920, O'Brien Papers, NLI MS 8460; O'Brien's Memorandum on the organisation in London, ibid., MS 8427.
22. Hart, op. cit.; Billy Aherne and Denis Kelleher, O'Malley Notebooks, P17b/99, 107.
23. Aherne and Early, O'Malley Notebooks, op. cit. For attacks on houses of Black and Tans see *Morning Post*, 7 May 1921. For Brugha's plans see above. Art O'Brien to President, 7 April 1921, O'Brien Papers, NLI MS 8429; O'Brien to GD, 19 May 1921, ibid.

Chapter 17 The North-East and the War of Independence (pages 153–64)
1. PRO, CP103 CAB 27/68, 11 November 1919. For the use of this quotation and an analysis of British attitudes see Fanning, Ronan, 'Anglo-Irish Relations: Partition and the British Dimension in Historical Perspective', *Irish Studies in International Affairs*, vol. 2, no. 1, 1985.
2. Buckland, Patrick, *A History of Northern Ireland* (Dublin 1981); Bowman, John, *De Valera and the Ulster Question, 1917–1973* (Oxford 1982).
3. Walsh in *Dáil Treaty Debate*, 3 January 1922, cols 188–9.
4. Phoenix, Eamon, *Northern Nationalism: Nationalist Politics, Partition and the Catholic Minority in Northern Ireland, 1890–1940* (Belfast 1994).
5. MacDermott, *Northern Divisions*; Townshend, *The British Campaign in Ireland*; Mitchell, *Revolutionary Government.*
6. Kenna, G.B. (Father John Hassan), *Facts and Figures of the Belfast Pogrom, 1920–1922* (Dublin 1922).
7. Séamus Woods Interview with Ernie O'Malley, O'Malley Notebooks, P17b/107; Farrell, Michael, *Northern Ireland: The Orange State* (London 1976) p. 26.
8. Farrell, op. cit., p. 26.
9. Farrell, Michael, *Arming the Protestants* (London 1983) pp. 18–20.
10. See Irish press, 13 July 1920.
11. *Belfast Newsletter*, Letter from 'H.S.' 16 July 1920, and others published on 15, 16 and 17 July.

12. Patterson, Henry, *Class Conflict and Sectarianism* (Belfast 1980); Morgan, Austen, *Labour and Partition* (London 1991).
13. For Smyth's speech see *Parliamentary Debates*, Commons, 14 July 1920, col. 2386. For his death see Seán Culhane interview with Ernie O'Malley, O'Malley Notebooks, P17b/108.
14. Farrell, *The Orange State*, p. 29.
15. Morgan, op. cit., pp. 265–84; Patterson, op. cit., pp. 115–42.
16. Belfast press 23 July–2 August 1920.
17. Hart, *The IRA and its Enemies*, pp. 78–9.
18. Culhane interview with Ernie O'Malley, op. cit.; McDermott, op. cit.
19. Belfast press, 23 August 1920.
20. Report to Ernest Clark by Commandant of Lisburn Special Constables, 24 October 1920, PRONI FIN 18/1/73; McDermott, op. cit.
21. Crawford Notes, PRONI D/640/2/1–2, D/640/8/1–2.
22. Farrell, *Arming the Protestants*, p. 21.
23. PRONI CAB 5/1.
24. Farrell, *Arming the Protestants*, p. 20.
25. Spender to Craig, 29 September 1920, PRONI CAB 5/1.
26. See Crawford Memo, PRONI D/ 640/9/1; 28 June 1921, ibid., D/640/6/18; Spender to Craig, 9 September 1920, PRONI CAB 5/1.
27. Crawford to Craig, 17 May 1920, PRONI D/640/7/7.
28. Spender to C.H. Blackmore (Craig's secretary), 20 October 1920, PRONI CAB 5/1.
29. PRO CP 1693 CAB 24/108; Jones, *Whitehall Diary* III, pp. 25–31.
30. Thomas Jones to Hankey, 2 September 1920, Lloyd George Papers, House of Lords Record Office, F/24/3/8.
31. Bonar Law Papers, House of Lords Record Office, 102/10/3.
32. Farrell, *Arming the Protestants*, pp. 43–8; Clark's reminiscences, PRONI D/1022/7/10. For the establishment of the Northern Irish government and civil service see: McColgan, John, *British Policy and the Irish Administration, 1920–22* (London 1983); Follis, Bryan A., *A State under Siege: The Establishment of Northern Ireland, 1920–1925* (Oxford 1995). Follis worked in the Northern Irish Public Record Office and used material not available to other researchers.
33. Macready Memorandum, September 1920, Bonar Law Papers, 102/10/6.
34. 2 September 1920, ibid., 102/9/1.
35. Undated, PRONI CAB 5/1.
36. For instance, Spender to Craig, 9, 29 September 1920, PRONI CAB 5/1.
37. PRONI FIN 18/1/67; Spender broadcast reminiscences for BBC Northern Ireland, 7 November 1956, Spender Papers, PRONI D 1295/149/4b.
38. McCorley interview with Ernie O'Malley, O'Malley Notebooks, P17b/98.
39. Woods, ibid., P17b/107.
40. Phoenix, *Northern Nationalism*, p. 99.
41. Mitchell, *Revolutionary Government*, p. 168.
42. *Dáil Proceedings*, 6 August 1920.
43. Mitchell, op. cit., p. 171.
44. Collins to Joe McDonagh, National Archives, Dublin, DE/261; Northern Irish Cabinet Meeting, 26 January 1922, PRONI CAB 4/30/1. For the boycott's effects see Johnson, D.J., 'The Belfast Boycott, 1920–22' in Goldstrom, J.M. and

Clarkson, J.A. (eds.), *Irish Population, Economy and Society: Essays in Honour of the late K.H. Connell* (Oxford, 1981).

45. Lindsay to Mrs Childers, 20 January 1922, Childers Papers, TCD MS 7849.
46. Mitchell, op. cit., pp. 291–2.
47. Greenwood to Lloyd George, Lloyd George Papers, F/19/4/5.
48. See Sturgis Diaries, 5 May 1921 in Hopkinson (ed.), *The Last Days of Dublin Castle*, pp. 170–2.
49. See Belfast press in days following meeting.
50. Sturgis Diaries, 6 May 1921, in Hopkinson, op. cit., pp. 172, 173.
51. Ibid., p. 150.
52. Ibid., 2 April, p. 152.
53. Greenwood to Lloyd George, 14 May 1921, Lloyd George Papers, F/19/4/12.
54. Ibid.; Sturgis Diaries, 15 May 1921, in Hopkinson, op. cit., pp. 176, 177.
55. Sturgis Diaries, 27 May 1921, in Hopkinson, op. cit, p. 183.
56. *Belfast Newsletter*, 11 February 1921, quoted in Phoenix, *Northern Nationalism*, p. 397.
57. Buckland, *History of Northern Ireland*, p. 35.
58. Farrell, *The Orange State*, p. 41.
59. See G.W. Tallents' Report after visit to Northern Ireland, July 1922, PRO London, CO 739/16.
60. De Valera to Smuts, 31 July 1921, Lloyd George Papers, F/45/9/51.
61. De Valera to Lloyd George, 10 August 1921, in Jones, *Whitehall Diary*, volume III, pp. 93–4.
62. *Dáil Debates*, 19 September 1922, col. 697.

Chapter 18 The American Dimension (pages 165–76)

1. See Brown, T.N., *Irish-American Nationalism, 1870–1890* (Philadephia 1966); Tansill, C.C., *America and the Fight for Irish Freedom, 1866–1922* (New York 1957); Ward, Alan J., *Ireland and Anglo-American Relations, 1899–1921* (London 1969); Carroll, Francis M., *American Opinion and the Irish Question, 1910–23* (Dublin 1978)
2. Consul Hathaway to State Department, 1 February 1919, National Archives, Washington DC, 841d. 00/22.
3. Ibid., 5 April 1919; *The Gaelic American*, 14 December 1918; *New York World*, 11 December 1918.
4. *Boston Globe*, 23, 24 February 1919; *New York Times*, 24 February 1919; *Philadelphia Public Ledger*, 24 February 1919; William Maloney article, *New York World*, 1 July 1921.
5. Baker's Notebooks for 8 March 1919, Ray Stannard Baker Papers, Library of Congress.
6. Walsh Diary for 17 April 1919, Frank P Walsh Papers, New York Public Library, Box 124.
7. Ibid. for meeting of 17 April. For 11 June meeting see ibid., 11 June 1919, Box 130.
8. For Flood Resolution see Carroll, op. cit., p. 125. For Borah Resolution see Cablegram from Polk, Acting Secretary of State to President Wilson, 6 June 1919, Wilson Papers, Library of Congress, Series 5B, Box 34; *The Times* 9 June 1919; *Boston Globe*, 7 June 1919; *New York Times*, 27 June 1919.

9. Borah to Cohalan, 22 November 1919, Borah Papers, Library of Congress, Box 452; *The Times*, 12 June 1919; Hathaway's Consular Report, 11 July 1919, National Archives, 841d 00/71; *The Times*, 10 June 1919.
10. Report by Sir William Wiseman, *Documents on British Foreign Policy 1919–1935*, First Series, volume 5, pp. 980–83; *The Times*, 23 June, 23 July 1919.
11. *Congressional Record*, volume 59 Part 5, 66th Congress 2nd Session 1920, p. 4457; *New York Times*, 20 March 1920.
12. *The Observer*, 22 June 1919; Maxwell, K.R., 'Irish-Americans and the Fight for Treaty Ratification', *Public Opinion Quarterly*, vol. xxxi, no. 4 winter 1967–8.
13. *The Times* 24 May 1920; *The New York Tribune* quoted in *The Times* 25 May 1920.
14. For a sympathetic account of de Valera's stay in US see McCartney, Donal, 'De Valera's Mission to the United States, 1919–1920' in Cosgrove, Art and McCartney, Donal (eds.), *Studies in Irish History presented to R. Dudley Edwards* (Dublin 1979); *New York Times*, 24 June 1919.
15. McCartan, Patrick, *With de Valera in America* (Dublin 1932) pp. 134, 135; Author's interview with Willard De Lew and Charles T. Rice, October 1967 and February 1968; *New York Times*, 25 June 1919.
16. *Boston Globe*, 30 June 1919; *Irish World*, 19 July 1919; *The Times*, 3 September 1919.
17. Carroll, op. cit., pp. 151–3, 156, 160, 171, 179; Lavelle, Patricia, *James O'Mara: A Staunch Sinn Féiner, 1873–1948*, (Dublin 1961).
18. Frank P. Walsh to James P. Ayward, 5 April 1920, Frank P. Walsh Papers, Box 125; Walsh to Alexander Scott, June 1922, ibid., Box 112. For second drive see *The Washington Post*, 2 January 1925.
19. *Gaelic American*, 16 October 1920; *New York World*, 1 July 1921.
20. *Westminster Gazette* interview, 7 February 1920. See account of John J. Splain, Tansill, op. cit., pp. 366–8; McCartan, op. cit., pp. 166–9; Seán Cronin in *Irish Times*, 17 April 1969.
21. *The Times*, 12 June 1920; *Gaelic American*, 19 June 1920; McCartan, op. cit., p. 193; *Gaelic American*, 26 June 1920.
22. *Gaelic American*, 31 July 1920; *The Times*, 29 June 1920; *New York Times*, 2, 3 July 1920; De Valera quoted in *The Times*, 6 July 1920.
23. *Irish World*, 27 November 1920; Seán Cronin in *Irish Times*, 22 April 1969.
24. *The Times*, 2 December 1920; *Irish World*, 27 November 1920. For de Valera's comment see Béaslaí, *Michael Collins*, volume 2, pp. 18, 19.
25. Longford and O'Neill, *Eamon de Valera*, p. 114; Tansill, op. cit., pp. 395, 396; Frank P. Walsh to Seán T. O'Kelly, 10 May 1921, Frank P. Walsh Papers, Box 110.
26. Cronin in *Irish Times*, op. cit.
27. *The Times*, 2 August 1920. For Mannix' tour see *The Irish World*, 5 June 1920. For Memorial Meeting for Terence MacSwiney see *Irish World*, 6 November 1920.
28. *Report of American Committee for Relief in Ireland* (New York 1922).
29. McCartan, op. cit., p. 210; *The Times*, 22 September 1920.
30. Coyle, Albert (ed.), *Evidence of Conditions in Ireland, comprising the Complete Testimony, Affidavits, and Exhibits placed before the American Commission on Conditions in Ireland* (Washington 1921); Secretary of State Bainbridge Colby to Senator Thomas J. Walsh, 8 February 1921, and reply, 10 February 1921, Thomas J. Walsh Papers, Library of Congress, Box 190.
31. Consul Dumont's Dispatch in J. Howland Shaw of State Department to Secretary of State, 15 April 1921, National Archives, 841d. 00/338; Blanche Seaver to Frank P. Walsh, 10 May 1921, Frank P. Walsh Papers, Box 110.

32. Dumont Dispatch to State Department, 22 March 1921, National Archives, 841d.00/339; *Report of American Committee*, op. cit.; Dumont Dispatch, 28 April 1921, National Archives, 841d.00/353.
33. Clement J. France and James G. Douglas to Morgan J. O'Brien and Judge Campbell, 19 January 1922, McKim–Maloney Papers, New York Public Library, Box 19; Dumont Dispatch, 9 June 1921, National Archives, 841d. 00/381.
34. James O'Mara to Mary MacSwiney, in Lavelle, op. cit., pp. 208, 209.
35. *Irish World*, 7 May 1920; Frank P. Walsh to James O'Mara, 30 April 1921, Frank P. Walsh Papers, Box 128.
36. *Montreal Daily Star*, 6 May 1921; Senator David I. Walsh to William Maloney, 5 July 1921, McKim–Maloney Papers, Box 10.
37. *Irish World*, 16 July 1921.
38. Dispatches from Wright in London Embassy, 29 April, 4 May 1921, National Archives, 841d.00/345, 358; ibid., 31 March 1921, 841d00/332; Dispatch from Ambassador John W. Davis, ibid., 841d.00/299; J.H. Moyle, Assistant Secretary of Treasury, to Secretary of State Hughes, 20 June 1921, ibid., 841d.00/372; Dispatch from London, 12 August 1921, ibid., 841d.00/467.

Chapter 19 The Peace Process (pages 177–91)
1. For the Treaty negotiations see Pakenham, Frank, *Peace by Ordeal* (London 1935); Dwyer, T. Ryle, *Michael Collins and the Treaty: His Differences with de Valera* (Cork 1981). For Treaty, see Appendix I. Fisher to Mark Sturgis, 17 December 1921, Grant–Sturgis Papers.
2. Taylor, A.J.P., *English History, 1914–1945* (Oxford 1965) p. 161; Boyce, D.G., 'How to Settle the Irish Question: Lloyd George and Ireland, 1916–21' in Taylor, A.J.P. (ed.), *Lloyd George: Twelve Essays* (London 1971).
3. Morgan, *Consensus and Disunity*, pp. 42–5; Riddell Diaries, 14 March 1918, *War Diaries*, p. 317.
4. See Sturgis Diaries, 23 February 1921, in Hopkinson, op. cit., p. 131.
5. *Political Diaries of C.P. Scott*, 21 April 1918, p. 342; Bew, Paul, 'Moderate Nationalism and the Irish Revolution, 1916–1923', *Historical Journal*, vol. 42, no. 3, September 1999.
6. Davies to O'Brien, 19 March 1920, Art O'Brien Papers, NLI MS 8427; O'Brien to Collins, 8 July, 19 August 1920, ibid., 8430.
7. James O'Connor to Anderson, 13 June 1920, Anderson Papers, CO 904/188(1); Jones on his meeting with FitzGerald, 10 August 1920, ibid.; B.H. Thomson to Bonar Law, 21 July 1920, Bonar Law Papers, 102/5/36; FitzGerald to Diarmuid O'Hegarty, 29 November 1920, National Archives, DE 234A.
8. Cabinet Meeting, 23 July 1920, in Jones, *Whitehall Diary*, volume III, p. 29. For MacMahon see Sturgis Diaries, 23 October 1920, in Hopkinson, op. cit., p. 59; Cockerill Diary, Cockerill Papers, NLI MS 10606; Cockerill to Prime Minister, 6 October 1920, ibid.; Cockerill to Greenwood, 30 October 1920, Anderson Papers, CO 904/188 (1).
9. Moylett to Mary Bromage, 17 July 1963, de Valera Papers, UCD Archives, 1739; material on Moylett–Steele negotiations, DE 2/251; *Irish Times*, 15 November 1965.
10. *Irish Times*, 15 November 1965; Fisher Diary, 25 October 1920, Fisher Papers, MS 15; Fisher to Prime Minister, 24 December 1920, Lloyd George Papers,

F/16/7/64; quote from Sinn Féin Proposals for Peace, Bonar Law Papers, 102/7/6; Moylett Diary with Chronology of negotiations, Cockerill Papers, NLI MS 10606.

11. C.J. Phillips Note on conversation with Moylett, undated, Lloyd George Papers F/91/7/9; Moylett Diary, 26, 29 November 1920, op. cit.

12. Moylett to Phillip Kerr, 20 December 1920, Lloyd George Papers F/91/7/24, Collins to Art O'Brien, 15 December 1920, DE/251.

13. Macready to Anderson, 2 November 1920, Anderson Papers, CO 904/188(1); Anderson to Sturgis, 2 November 1920, ibid.; Sturgis Diaries, 9 November 1920, in Hopkinson, op. cit., pp. 67–9; Law to Anderson, 9 November 1920, Bonar Law Papers, 102/7/5; Cockerill to Moylett, 10 December 1920, Cockerill Papers, NLI MS 10606.

14. Sturgis Diaries, 26 September 1920, in Hopkinson, op. cit., pp. 45–6; Wylie Memoir, PRO 30/89–1; Murphy, Brian P., *Patrick Pearse and the Lost Republican Ideal*, pp. 114–16; Wheeler-Bennett, *John Anderson*, p. 72.

15. AE to Kerr, 9 December 1920, Lloyd George Papers, F/91/7/5; Collins to Griffith, 2 December 1920, DE234 A; Collins to Joe McDonagh, 2 December 1920, ibid.; *Report of the Labour Commission to Ireland* (London 1921).

16. O'Brien to Griffith, 2 December 1920, DE 234A; Collins to McDonagh, ibid.; Collins to Griffith, 2 December 1920, ibid.

17. Sturgis Diaries, 27 June 1921, in Hopkinson, op. cit., p. 193; Healy to Beaverbrook, 23 December 1920, NLI MS 23628.

18. Bourke, P.A., *The History of the Catholic Church in Western Australia, 1829–1979* (Perth 1979).

19. McMahon, John T., 'The Cream of Their Race' (Clare), undated; Sturgis Diaries, 7 December 1920, in Hopkinson, op. cit., pp. 86–7.

20. McMahon, op. cit.

21. Ibid.; Sturgis Diaries, 7 December 1920, in Hopkinson, op. cit.

22. See Irish daily press, 4–6 December 1920. For Dumont see Mitchell, *Revolutionary Government*, p. 320; Wilson Diary, 8 December 1920, op. cit. For O'Flanagan's admission see Murphy, *Patrick Pearse*, pp. 116–21; Greenwood to Lloyd George, Lloyd George Papers, F/19/2/31.

23. O'Brien Report to Collins, Art O'Brien Papers, NLI MS 8430 and DE 234A; Collins to O'Brien, 15 December 1920, DE 234B; Griffith to Collins, 13 December 1920, DE 234A; Griffith to Collins, 17 December 1920, DE 234B; *Parliamentary Debates, Commons*, 9 December 1920, cols 2601–11; McMahon, op. cit.

24. Griffith to Collins, 13 December 1920, DE 234A; Griffith to Collins, 17 December 1920, DE 234B; O'Brien to Collins, 23 December 1920, ibid.

25. CAB 79A(20) CAB 23/24; Art O'Brien to Collins, 25 December 1920, DE 234B.

26. Cope to Sturgis, Grant–Sturgis Papers; Sturgis Diaries, in Hopkinson, op. cit., p. 129. For Clune's visit to Rome see McMahon, op. cit.; Mrs Gavan Duffy to Art O'Brien, Art O'Brien Papers, NLI MS 8429.

27. Newdegate to Secretary of State for Colonies, 12 January 1921, CO 537/ 1151; Newdegate to Secretary of State for Colonies, Battie Library, Perth AN 395/2; *Western Australian*, 19, 26 February 1921.

28. Sturgis Diaries, 23 March 1921, in Hopkinson, op. cit., p. 146; Collins to Joe McDonagh, 13 December 1920, DE 234A.

29. Sturgis Diaries, 1 January 1921, in Hopkinson, op. cit., p. 103.
30. Ibid.; Lady Greenwood in Sturgis Diaries, 20 January 1920, in Hopkinson, op. cit., pp. 113–14; Collins to Joe McDonagh, 8, 20 January 1921, DE 234B.
31. Sturgis Diaries, 9 January 1921, in Hopkinson, op. cit., pp. 106–8; Lady Greenwood, 11 January, ibid., p. 109; Lloyd George to O'Connor, 12 January 1921, ibid., p. 112; Sturgis to Anderson, 6 January 1921, CO 904/232.
32. Jones Diary, 15 February 1921, in Jones, *Whitehall Diary*, volume III, p. 52; Greenwood to Prime Minister, 26 January 1921, Lloyd George Papers F/19/3/2; Sturgis Diaries, 2 February 1921, in Hopkinson, op. cit., pp. 118–19.
33. Jones Diary, 30 January 1921, in Jones, op. cit., pp. 49–50.
34. Sturgis's Correspondence with Lady Greenwood, Grant–Sturgis Papers; Sturgis Diaries, 16 February 1921, in Hopkinson, op. cit., p. 127.
35. Sturgis Diaries, 20 January 1921, in Hopkinson, op. cit., p. 113; ibid., 23 February 1921, p. 131.
36. Sturgis Diaries, 15, 23, 24, 27 March 1921, ibid., pp. 142, 143, 145, 146. For Sturgis's negotiations with labour leaders see also: Sturgis to Anderson, 23, 29 March, 1 April 1921, CO 904/232; Mitchell, op. cit., p. 293.
37. Sturgis Diaries, 27 March 1921, in Hopkinson, op. cit., p. 148; Sturgis quoted in letter to Anderson, 29 March, op. cit.; Sturgis Diaries, 23 March 1921, in Hopkinson, op. cit., pp. 145–6. For breakdown of talks see Sturgis Diaries, 4 April 1921, ibid., p. 153.
38. See Murray, *Oracles of God*, pp. 6–14; Sturgis Diaries, 6 April 1921, in Hopkinson, op. cit., pp. 154–5.
39. Sturgis Diaries, 12 March 1921, in Hopkinson, op. cit., p. 140–41; *The Times*, 7 March 1921; B. Thomson to Anderson, 14 March 1921, CO 904/232.
40. For Derby visit see Sturgis Diaries, 21, 23, 25, 27 April, in Hopkinson, op. cit., pp. 161–5; Churchill, Randolph S., *Lord Derby, King of Lancashire* (London 1959); Saunderson to Lord Derby, 13 March 1921, ibid., pp. 403–4.
41. Sturgis Diaries, 2 May 1921, in Hopkinson, op. cit., p. 168; *Liverpool Courier*, 30 April 1921; *Daily Express*, 25 April 1921.
42. Churchill, op. cit., pp. 402–24.
43. De Valera to Randolph Churchill, 15 February 1954, ibid., pp. 420–1.

Chapter 20 The Path to the Truce (pages 192–7)
1. For rumours about Greenwood see Sturgis Diaries, 23 April 1921, in Hopkinson, op. cit., p. 163. For Ross see Anderson to Fisher, 22 April 1921, Lloyd George Papers, F/17/1/11.
2. Jones Diary, 8 March 1921, in Jones, *Whitehall Diary*, volume III, pp. 53–5; Anderson to Chief Secretary, 11 May 1921, Lloyd George Papers, F/1914/10.
3. Cabinet discussions, 27 April, 12 May 1921, in Jones, op. cit., pp. 55–70.
4. Irish Situation Committee, 27 May 1921, CP 2983 CAB 24/123; Cabinet Meeting, 2 June 1921, C 47 (21) CAB 23/26. For that meeting see also Jones, op. cit., p. 73.
5. Macready to Miss Stevenson, 20 June 1921, Lloyd George Papers, F/36/2/19; Anderson to Chief Secretary, 18 June 1921, CO 904/232; Irish Situation Committee, 15 June 1921, SIC 9th conclusions, CAB 24/107.
6. Sturgis Diaries, in Hopkinson, op. cit., p. 188; Colonel Maurice Moore to de Valera, August 1929, de Valera Papers, UCD Archives, 1462; Moore to Smuts, 20 August 1921, ibid.

7. Smuts to Prime Minister, 19 June 1921, in Jones, op. cit., pp. 74–5; Jones Diary, 25 June 1921, ibid., pp. 75–6; Daily press, 25 June 1921. For arrest of de Valera see material in CO 904/23/7.

8. Tom Casement Diary, de Valera Papers, UCD Archives, 1321; Seán T. O'Kelly to Art O'Brien, 28 June 1921, Art O'Brien Papers, NLI MS 8421 (35); Art O'Brien to RMG, 5 July 1921, ibid., 8430; Lloyd George to de Valera, 24 June 1921, and reply, 28 June 1921 and de Valera to Unionist representatives, 28 June 1921, both in *Official Correspondence relating to Truce Negotiations, July–September 1921* (Dublin 1921).

9. Casement Diary, op. cit.; Stamfordham to Lord Midleton, 1 July 1921, Midleton Papers, PRO 30/67.45; Midleton's account of his visit to London in 'Memorandum of Meetings between Sinn Féin Leaders and Southern Unionists', 4, 8 July 1921, ibid.; Midleton to Lloyd George, 8, 9 July 1921, ibid.

10. For British version of Truce terms see Cmd 1534 xxix 427; GOC, 9 July 1921, CP 3134 CAB 24/125.

11. Macready to Anderson, 11 June 1921, CO 904/232; Whiskard to Sturgis, 10 July 1921, ibid.; Sturgis Diaries, 10, 11 July 1921, in Hopkinson, op. cit., p. 201.

12. O'Malley, *On Another Man's Wound*, p. 342; Barry, *Guerilla Days in Ireland*, pp. 201–7; Hopkinson, *Green Against Green*, pp. 14–33.

Conclusion (pages 198–203)

1. Andrews, *Dublin Made Me*, pp. 80, 201; O'Faolain, Seán, *Vive Moi! An Autobiography* (London 1965) pp. 150 and 151; O'Connor, Frank, *An Only Child* (London 1958).

2. *Kilkenny People*, 17 June 1922.

3. Ward, *Unmanageable Revolutionaries*, p. 100.

4. Van Voris, Jacqueline, *Constance de Markievicz: In the Cause of Ireland* (Amherst 1967); Clarke, Kathleen, *Revolutionary Woman: Kathleen Clarke, 1878–1972: An Autobiography* (Dublin 1991); Comerford and Humphreys in MacEoin, *Survivors*, pp. 35–55, 331–53; Andrews, *Dublin Made Me*, p. 240.

5. Ward, op. cit.

6. For Kearns and McGrane see above. For prison figures see Ward, op. cit., pp. 145–6.

7. For debate over this see Rumpf, E. and Hepburn A.C., *Nationalism and Socialism in Twentieth-Century Ireland* (Liverpool 1977); Fitzpatrick, David, 'The Geography of Irish Nationalism, 1910–1921', *Past and Present*, February 1978; Hart, Peter, 'The Geography of Revolution in Ireland, 1917–1923', *Past and Present*, May 1997.

8. Hart, *The IRA and its Enemies*; Fitzpatrick, *Politics and Irish Life*; Augusteijn, *From Public Defiance*; Farry, *The Aftermath of Revolution*; Coleman, 'County Longford 1910–1923'; Maguire, Gloria, 'The Political and Military Causes of the Division in the Irish Nationalist Movement, January 1921–August 1922', D.Phil. thesis, University of Oxford, 1985.

9. See Ministry of Defence Archive, A/0396: Microfilm, NLI pos 915; Fitzpatrick, *The Two Irelands, 1912–1939*, p. 85; Jeffery, 'British Security Policy in Ireland, 1919–1921', p. 170.

10. Fitzpatrick, *The Two Irelands*, p. 61. For number of executions see Macready, *Annals of an Active Life*, volume II, p. 518.

11. For a good example see Farrell, J.G., *Troubles* (London 1970); Hopkinson, *Green against Green*.
12. Foster, *Modern Ireland*, p. 506.

BIBLIOGRAPHY

PRIMARY SOURCES

DUBLIN

University College Dublin Archives
Ernest Blythe
Máire Comerford
Eamon de Valera
Desmond FitzGerald
Síghle Humphreys
Seán MacEntee
Seán MacEoin
Mary MacSwiney
Richard Mulcahy
Ernie O'Malley, including Notebooks
Desmond Ryan

National Library of Ireland
F.S. Bourke
G.C. Cockerill
Michael Collins
Michael Collins–Austin Stack Correspondence
John Devoy
Dublin Brigade
Lord French Diary
Frank Gallagher
Michael Hayes
Tim Healy Correspondence with Lord Beaverbrook
Shane Leslie
Diarmuid Lynch
Joe McGarrity
Kathleen McKenna Napoli
Maurice Moore
Michael Noyk
Art O'Brien
J.J. O'Connell

Florence O'Donoghue
Seán T. O'Kelly
Séamus Robinson Statement
Celia Shaw Diary
Dorothy Price

Trinity College Library
Erskine Childers
Frank Gallagher

Irish Military Archives
Michael Collins
Chronology of Bureau of Military History

National Archives
Chief Secretary's Office Registered Files
Dáil Éireann Cabinet Minutes
Proceedings of First and Second Dáil and related documents
Robert Barton
George Gavan Duffy

CORK

Cork Archives Institute
Liam de Róiste
Seán Hegarty
Richard Langford
Siobhán Lankford (Creedon)

BELFAST

Northern Ireland Public Record Office
Cabinet, Prime Minister's Department, Department of Finance
Ernest Clark
Frederick Crawford
Wilfrid Spender

LONDON

Public Record Office
Cabinet
Colonial Office
War Office
Official Publications
Home Office
Midleton
Sturgis Diaries
William Wylie

House of Lords Record Office
Bonar Law
Lloyd George

British Library
Sir Walter Long
Riddell

Imperial War Museum
French
Jeudwine
Loch
Percival
Strickland
Wilson Papers and Diaries

OXFORD

Bodleian Library
Lionel Curtis
H.A.L. Fisher
Strathcarron

TROWBRIDGE

Wiltshire Record Office
Sir Walter Long

BIRMINGHAM

Birmingham University Library
Austen Chamberlain Papers

AUSTRALIA

Perth

Battie Library
Newdegate

Catholic Diocesan Archives
Clune

UNITED STATES OF AMERICA

Washington D.C.

Library of Congress
William E. Borah

Thomas J. Walsh
Woodrow Wilson

National Archives
State Department Files

New York

New York Public Library
McKim–Maloney
Frank P. Walsh

OFFICIAL PUBLICATIONS
Dáil Éireann: Minutes of Proceedings of the First Parliament of the Republic of Ireland, 1919–1921: Official Record (Dublin 1921)
The Authority of Dáil Éireann (Dublin 1919)
Dáil Government Departments, classified under DE in National Archives
Parliamentary Debates, 5th series: *House of Commons*, vols 112–43; *House of Lords*, vols 33–45
1921 Cmd 1220 XV 335. *Report of Mallow Court of Enquiry*
1921 Cmd 1534 XXIX 427. *Arrangements governing the Cessation of Active Operations in Ireland which came into force on 11 July 1921*

PRIVATE SOURCES
Numerous private sources, including Bureau of Military History Statements: see footnotes.

NEWSPAPERS AND PERIODICALS

Belfast Newsletter
Boston Globe
Boston Pilot
Cork Examiner
Clare Champion
Daily News
Daily Mail
Freeman's Journal
Gaelic American
Irish Independent
Irish News
Irish Times
Irish World
Manchester Guardian
Morning Post
Nation
The Nationalist (Clonmel)

New Statesman
New York Times
New York Tribune
Northern Whig
Observer
An tÓglach
Round Table
The Times
Western Australian

SECONDARY SOURCES

Abbott, Richard, *Police Casualties in Ireland, 1919–1922* (Cork 2000)
Andrews, C.S., *Dublin Made Me* (Dublin 1979)
Augusteijn, Joost, *From Public Defiance to Guerrilla Warfare: The Experience of Ordinary Volunteers in the War of Independence, 1916–1921* (Dublin 1996)
—— (ed.), *The Revolution in Ireland* (London 2002)
Barry, Tom, *Guerilla Days in Ireland* (Dublin 1949)
—— 'The Reality of the Anglo-Irish War, 1920–21' in *West Cork: Refutations, Corrections and Comments on Liam Deasy's 'Towards Ireland Free'* (Tralee 1974)
Bartlett, Thomas and Jeffery, Keith, *A Military History of Ireland* (Cambridge 1996)
Béaslaí, Piaras, *Michael Collins and the Making of a New Ireland*, 2 vols, (Dublin 1926)
Begley, Diarmuid, *The Road to Crossbarry: The Decisive Battle in the War of Independence* (Cork 1999)
Bell, J. Bowyer, 'The Thompson Sub-Machine Gun in Ireland, 1921', *Irish Sword* 1967
Bennett, Richard, *The Black and Tans* (London 1959)
Bew, Paul, *Ideology and the Irish Question: Ulster Unionism and Irish Nationalism, 1912–1916* (Oxford 1994)
—— *John Redmond* (Dundalk 1996)
—— 'Moderate Nationalism and the Irish Revolution, 1916–1923', *Historical Journal*, vol. 42, no. 3, September 1999
Bourke, P.A., *The History of the Catholic Church in Western Australia, 1829–1979* (Perth 1979)
Bowden, Tom, *The Breakdown of Public Security: The Case of Ireland, 1919–1921, and Palestine, 1936–1939* (London 1977)
—— 'Bloody Sunday — A Reappraisal', *European Studies Review*, ii, 1972
Bowman, John, *De Valera and the Ulster Question, 1917–1973* (Oxford 1982)
Boyce D.G., *Englishmen and Irish Troubles: British Public Opinion and the Making of Irish Policy 1918–1922* (Cambridge, Mass. 1972)
—— *Nationalism in Ireland* (London 1982)
—— (ed.), *The Revolution in Ireland, 1879–1923* (Dublin 1998)
—— 'How to Settle the Irish Question: Lloyd George and Ireland, 1916–21' in Taylor, A.J.P. (ed.), *Lloyd George: Twelve Essays* (London 1971)
—— and Hazelhurst, Cameron, 'The Unknown Chief Secretary: H.E. Duke and Ireland, 1916–17', *Irish Historical Studies*, xx, 1976–7
—— and O'Day, Alan (eds.),*The Making of Modern Irish History: Revisionism and the Revisionist Controversy* (London 1996)
Bradshaw, Brendan, 'Nationalism and Historical Scholarship in Modern Ireland', *Irish Historical Studies*, xxvi, 1988–9

Brady, Ciaran (ed.), *Interpreting Irish History: The Debate on Historical Revisionism* (Dublin 1994)

Brady, Conor, *Guardians of the Peace* (Dublin 1974)

Breen, Dan, *My Fight for Irish Freedom* (Dublin 1924; Tralee 1964)

Brennan, Michael, *The War in Clare, 1911–1921: Personal Memoirs of the War of Independence* (Dublin 1980)

—— 'James Hogan Memoir, 1913–37' in Ó Corráin, Donnchadh (ed.), *James Hogan: Revolutionary, Historian and Political Scientist* (Dublin 2001)

Brewer, John D., *The Royal Irish Constabulary: An Oral History* (Belfast 1990)

Bric, Deaglan, 'Pierce McCann, MP (1882–1918)' Part II, *Tipperary Historical Journal* 1989

Brown, T.N., *Irish-American Nationalism, 1870–1890* (Philadelphia 1966)

Browne, Charlie, *The Story of the Seventh* (Macroom, undated)

Buckland, Patrick, *Irish Unionism 1: The Anglo-Irish and the New Ireland, 1885–1922* (Dublin 1972)

—— *James Craig* (Dublin 1980)

—— *A History of Northern Ireland* (Dublin 1981)

de Burca, Marcus, *The GAA: A History* (Dublin 1980)

Butler, Ewan, *Barry's Flying Column* (London 1971)

Butler, John (ed.), 'Lord Oranmore's Journal, 1913–27', *Irish Historial Studies*, xxix, 1994–5

Callanan, Frank, *T.M. Healy* (Cork 1996)

Campbell, Colm, *Emergency Law in Ireland, 1918–1925* (Oxford 1994)

Campbell, Fergus, 'Land and Politics in Connacht, 1898–1920', Ph.D. thesis, University of Bristol, 1997.

Carroll, Francis M., *American Opinion and the Irish Question, 1910–1923* (Dublin 1978)

Churchill, Randolph S., *Lord Derby, King of Lancashire* (London 1959)

Clarke, Kathleen, *Revolutionary Woman: Kathleen Clarke, 1878–1972: An Autobiography* (Dublin 1991)

Collins, Michael, *The Path to Irish Freedom* (Dublin 1922)

Coleman, Marie, 'County Longford, 1910–1923: A Regional Study of the Irish Revolution', Ph.D. thesis, University College, Dublin, 1998

Colmcille, Father, 'Tipperary's Fight in 1920', *Capuchin Annual* 1970

Coogan, Oliver, *Politics and War in Meath, 1913–1923* (Dublin 1983)

Coogan, Tim Pat, *Michael Collins: A Biography* (London 1990)

—— *De Valera: Long Fellow, Long Shadow* (London 1993)

—— *The IRA* (London 1970)

—— *Wherever Green is Worn: The Story of the Irish Diaspora* (London 2000)

Cooke, A.B. and Vincent, J., *The Governing Passion: Cabinet Government and Party Politics in Britain, 1885–6* (Brighton 1974)

Costello. Francis J., *Enduring the Most: The Life and Death of Terence MacSwiney* (Dingle 1995)

Cowling, Maurice, *The Impact of Labour, 1920–24* (Cambridge 1971)

Coyle, Albert (ed.), *Evidence of Conditions in Ireland, comprising the Complete Testimony, Affidavits, and Exhibits placed before the American Commission on Conditions in Ireland* (Washington 1921)

Cronin, Seán, *The McGarrity Papers* (Tralee 1972)

Crozier, F.P., *Impressions and Recollections* (London 1930)

Curran, Joseph M., *The Birth of the Irish Free State, 1921–1923* (Alabama 1980)

Dalton, Charles, *With the Dublin Brigade (1917–1921)* (London 1929)

Dangerfield, George, *The Damnable Question: A Study in Anglo-Irish Relations* (London 1977)

Davis, Richard, *Arthur Griffith and Non-Violent Sinn Féin* (Dublin 1974)

Deasy, Liam, *Towards Ireland Free: The West Cork Brigade in the War of Independence, 1917–1921* (Cork 1973)

de Burca, Marcus, *The GAA: A History* (Dublin 1980)

Doherty, Gabriel and Keogh, Dermot (eds), *Michael Collins and the Making of the Irish State* (Cork 1998)

Doherty, M.A., 'Kevin Barry and the Anglo-Irish Propaganda War', *Irish Historical Studies*, xxxii, 2000–1

Dublin's Fighting Story, 1913–1921: told by the men who made it (Tralee 1949)

Duggan, G.C. (Periscope), 'The Last Days of Dublin Castle', *Blackwood's Magazine*, August 1922

Duggan, John P., *A History of the Irish Army* (Dublin 1991)

Dwyer, T. Ryle, *Michael Collins and the Treaty: His Differences with de Valera* (Cork 1981)

—— *Michael Collins: The Man who Won the War* (Cork 1990)

—— *Tans, Terror and Troubles: Kerry's Real Fighting Story, 1913–23* (Cork 2001)

—— *Big Fellow, Long Fellow: A Joint Biography of Collins and de Valera* (Dublin 1999)

Edwards, Owen Dudley, *Eamon de Valera* (Cardiff 1987)

Elliott, Marianne, *The Catholics of Ulster: A History* (London 2000)

English, Richard, *Ernie O'Malley, IRA Intellectual* (Oxford 1998)

—— and Walker, Graham (eds), *Unionism in Modern Ireland* (Dublin 1996)

Fanning, Ronan, *Independent Ireland* (Dublin 1983)

—— 'Michael Collins: An Overview' in Doherty and Keogh (eds), *Michael Collins and the Making of the Irish State*

—— 'Anglo-Irish Relations: Partition and the British Dimension in Historical Perspective', *Irish Studies in International Affairs*, vol. 2, no. 1, 1985

Farrell, Brian, *The Founding of Dáil Eireann: Parliament and Nation-Building* (Dublin 1971)

—— (ed.), *The Creation of the Dáil* (Dublin 1994)

Farrell, J.G., *Troubles* (London 1970)

Farrell, Michael, *Northern Ireland: The Orange State* (London 1975)

—— *Arming the Protestants: The Formation of the Ulster Special Constabulary and the Royal Ulster Constabulary, 1920–27* (London 1983)

Farry, Michael, *Sligo 1914–1921: A Chronicle of Conflict* (Trim 1992)

—— *The Aftermath of Revolution: Sligo 1921–23* (Dublin 2000)

Figgis, Darrell, *Recollections of the Irish War* (London 1927)

Fitzpatrick, David, *Politics and Irish Life, 1913–21: Provincial Experience of War and Revolution* (Dublin 1977)

—— *The Two Irelands, 1912–1939* (Oxford 1998)

—— (ed.), *Revolution? Ireland, 1917–1923* (Dublin 1990)

—— 'The Geography of Irish Nationalism, 1910–1921', *Past and Present*, February 1978

Flanagan, Kieran, 'The Chief Secretary's Office, 1853–1914: A Bureaucratic Enigma', *Irish Historical Studies*, xxiv, 1984–5

Fogarty, L. (ed.), *Collected Writings of James Fintan Lalor* (Dublin 1918)

Follis, Brian, *A State under Siege: The Establishment of Northern Ireland, 1920–1925* (Oxford 1995)

Forester, Margery, *Michael Collins: The Lost Leader* (London 1971; Dublin 1989)

Foster, R.F., *Modern Ireland, 1600–1972* (London 1988)

—— *Paddy and Mr Punch: Connections in Irish and English History* (London 1993)

Gailey, Andrew, *Ireland and the Death of Kindness: The Experience of Constructive Unionism, 1890–1905* (Cork 1987)

Garvin, Tom, *The Evolution of Irish Nationalist Politics* (Dublin 1981)

—— *Nationalist Revolutionaries in Ireland, 1858–1928* (Oxford 1987)

—— *1922: The Birth of Irish Democracy* (Dublin 1996)

Gaughan, J.A., *Austin Stack: Portrait of a Separatist* (Dublin 1977)

Gilbert, Martin, *Winston S. Churchill*, Companion Volume IV: Part 2, *July 1919–March 1921* (London 1977)

Gleeson, J., *Bloody Sunday* (London 1962)

Greaves, C. Desmond, *The Life and Times of James Connolly* (London 1961)

Griffith, Kenneth and O'Grady, Timothy E., *Curious Journey: An Oral History of Ireland's Unfinished Revolution* (Dublin 1982)

Haicéad, Pádraig, *In Bloody Protest: North Tipperary's IRA Roll of Honour, 1916–1926* (Nenagh 1966)

Hammond, J.L., *Gladstone and the Irish Nation* (London 1938)

Hart, Peter, *The IRA and its Enemies: Violence and Community in Cork, 1916–1923* (Oxford 1998)

—— 'The Thompson Sub-Machine Gun in Ireland, Revisited', *Irish Sword*, summer 1995

—— 'Operations Abroad: The IRA in Britain, 1919–23', *English Historical Review*, vol. cxv, no. 460, February 2000

—— 'The Geography of Revolution in Ireland, 1917–1923', *Past and Present*, May 1997

—— 'The Social Structure of the Irish Republican Army, 1916–1923', *Historical Journal*, vol. 42, no. 1, March 1999

Harvey, A.D., 'Who were the Auxiliaries?' *Historical Journal*, vol. 35, no. 3, September 1992

Henderson, Frank, 'Irish Leaders of Our Time, 5: Richard McKee', *An Cosantóir*, v, 1945

Hobson, Bulmer, *Ireland Yesterday and Tomorrow* (Tralee 1968)

—— *Defensive Warfare: A Handbook for Irish Nationalists* (Belfast 1909)

Hogan, David, *The Four Glorious Years* (Dublin 1953)

Holmes, Richard, *The Little Field Marshal: Sir John French* (London 1981)

Holt, Edgar, *Protest in Arms: The Irish Troubles, 1916–1923* (London 1960)

Hopkinson, Michael, *Green against Green: The Irish Civil War* (Dublin 1988)

—— (ed.), *The Last Days of Dublin Castle: The Diaries of Mark Sturgis* (Dublin 1999)

—— (ed.), *Frank Henderson's Easter Rising: Recollections of a Dublin Volunteer* (Cork 1998)

—— 'President Woodrow Wilson and the Irish Question', *Studia Hibernica*, no. 27, 1993

Hoppen, K.T., *Ireland Since 1800: Conflict and Conformity* (London 1989)

Hutchinson, John, *The Dynamics of Cultural Nationalism: The Gaelic Revival and the Creation of the Irish Nation State* (London 1987)

Jackson, Alvin, *Ireland 1798–1998* (Oxford 1999)

—— *Colonel Edward Saunderson: Land and Loyalty in Victorian Ireland* (Oxford 1995)

—— 'What if Irish Home Rule had been enacted in 1912?' in Ferguson, Niall (ed.), *Virtual History: Alternatives and Counterfactuals* (London 1997)

Jalland, Patricia, 'A Liberal Chief Secretary and the Irish question: Augustine Birrell, 1907–14', *Historical Journal*, 19, June 1976

Jeffery, Keith, *Ireland and the Great War* (Cambridge 2000)
—— 'British Security Policy in Ireland, 1919–21' in Collins, Peter (ed.), *Nationalism and Unionism: Conflict in Ireland, 1885–1921* (Belfast 1994)
—— 'British Military Intelligence following World War One' in K.G. Robertson (ed.), *British and American Approaches to Intelligence* (Basingstoke 1987)
Johnson, D.J., 'The Belfast Boycott, 1920–22' in Goldstrom, J.M. and Clarkson, J.A. (eds.), *Irish Population, Economy and Society: Essays in Honour of the late K.H. Connell* (Oxford 1981)
Jones, Thomas (ed. Keith Middlemass), *Whitehall Diary*, volumes I, III (London 1969, 1971)
Kavanagh, Matt, 'Wicklow 1920', *Capuchin Annual* 1970
Kee, Robert, *The Green Flag: A History of Irish Nationalism* (London 1972)
Kendle, John, *Walter Long, Ireland, and the Union, 1905–1920* (Dublin 1992)
Kenna, G.B. (Father John Hassan), *Facts and Figures of the Belfast Pogrom, 1920–1922* (Dublin 1922)
Keogh, Dermot, *Twentieth-Century Ireland: Nation and State* (Dublin 1994)
Kerry's Fighting Story, 1916–21 (Tralee 1949)
Kostick, Conor, *Revolution in Ireland: Popular Militancy, 1917–1923* (London 1996)
Kotsonouris, Mary, *Retreat from Revolution: The Dáil Courts, 1920–24* (Dublin 1994)
Labour Party, *Report of the Labour Commission to Ireland* (London 1920)
Laffan, Michael, *The Partition of Ireland, 1911–1925* (Dublin 1983)
—— *The Resurrection of Ireland: The Sinn Féin Party, 1916–1923* (Cambridge 1999)
Lankford, Siobhán, *The Hope and the Sadness: Personal Recollections of Troubled Times in Ireland* (Cork 1980)
Lavelle, Patricia, *James O'Mara: A Staunch Sinn-Féiner, 1873–1948* (Dublin 1961)
Lawlor, Sheila, *Britain and Ireland, 1914–23* (Dublin 1983)
Lee, J.J., *Ireland 1912–1985: Politics and Society* (Cambridge 1989)
Limerick's Fighting Story, 1916–21: told by the men who made it (Tralee 1948)
Longford, Earl of, and O'Neill T.P., *Eamon de Valera* (London 1970)
Lyons F.S.L., *Ireland since the Famine* (London 1971)
—— *Culture and Anarchy in Ireland, 1890–1939* (Oxford 1979)
Macardle, Dorothy, *The Irish Republic 1911–1925: A Documented Chronicle* (London 1937)
MacBride, Lawrence, *The Greening of Dublin Castle: The Transformation of Bureaucratic and Judicial Personnel in Dublin Castle in Ireland, 1892–1922* (Washington 1991)
McCartan, Patrick, *With de Valera in America* (Dublin 1932)
McCarthy, Veronica, 'The Story of Leitrim, 1920', *Capuchin Annual* 1970
McCartney, Donal, 'De Valera's Mission to the United States, 1919–1920' in Cosgrove, Art and McCartney, Donal (eds), *Studies in Irish History presented to R. Dudley Edwards* (Dublin 1979)
McColgan, John, *British Policy and the Irish Administration, 1920–22* (London 1983)
McDermott, Jim, *Northern Divisions: The Old IRA and the Belfast Pogroms, 1920–22* (Belfast 2001)
McDowell, R.B., *The Irish Administration, 1801–1914* (London 1964)
—— *The Irish Convention, 1917–1918* (London 1970)
MacEoin, Uinseann, *Survivors* (Dublin 1980)
MacEvilly, Michael, *Andy Cooney* (forthcoming)
McMahon, John T., 'The Cream of Their Race' (Clare), undated
Macready, General Sir Nevil, *Annals of an Active Life*, 2 vols (London 1924)

Maguire, Gloria, 'The Political and Military Causes of the Division in the Irish Nationalist Movement, January 1921–August 1922', D.Phil thesis, University of Oxford, 1985

Maher, Jim, *The Flying Column — West Kilkenny, 1916–21* (Dublin 1987)

Mandle W.F., *The Gaelic Athletic Association and Irish Nationalist Politics, 1884–1924* (Dublin 1987)

Mansergh, Nicholas, *The Unresolved Question: The Anglo-Irish Settlement and its Undoing, 1912–72* (New Haven 1991)

Martin, Hugh, *Ireland in Insurrection* (London 1921)

Maume, Patrick, *The Long Gestation: Irish Nationalist Life, 1891–1918* (Dublin 1999)

Maxwell, K.R., 'Irish-Americans and the Fight for Treaty Ratification', *Public Opinion Quarterly*, vol. xxxi, no. 4, winter 1967–8

Maye, Brian, *Arthur Griffith* (Dublin 1997)

Mitchell, Arthur, *Labour in Irish Politics, 1890–1930* (Dublin 1974)

—— *Revolutionary Government in Ireland: Dáil Éireann, 1919–22* (Dublin 1995)

—— and Ó Snodaigh, Padraig, *Irish Political Documents, 1916–1949* (Dublin 1985)

'Monaghan A', 'Monaghan — 1920', *Capuchin Annual* 1970

Morgan, Austen, *Labour and Partition: The Belfast Working Class, 1905–23* (London 1991)

Morgan, K.O., *Consensus and Disunity: The Lloyd George Coalition Government, 1918–1922* (London 1979)

Moynihan, Maurice (ed.), *Speeches and Statements by Eamon de Valera, 1917–1973* (Dublin 1980)

Mullins, Billy, *The Memoirs of Billy Mullins: Veteran of the War of Independence* (Tralee 1983)

Murphy, Brian P., *Patrick Pearse and the Lost Republican Ideal* (Dublin 1991)

Murphy, Cliona, *The Women's Suffrage Movement and Irish Society in the Early Twentieth Century* (Hemel Hempstead 1989)

Murray, Patrick, *Oracles of God: The Roman Catholic Church and Irish Politics, 1922–37* (Dublin 2000)

Neligan, David, *The Spy in the Castle* (London 1968)

Nolan, William, 'Events in Carlow 1920–21', *Capuchin Annual* 1970

O'Brien, Conor Cruise (ed.), *The Shaping of Modern Ireland* (London 1960)

Ó Broin, Leon, *Dublin Castle and the 1916 Rising* (Dublin 1966)

—— *Revolutionary Underground: The Story of the Irish Republican Brotherhood, 1858–1924* (Dublin 1976)

—— *W.E. Wylie and the Irish Revolution, 1916–1921* (Dublin 1989)

O'Callaghan, Michael, *For Ireland and Freedom: Roscommon's Contribution to the Fight for Independence* (Roscommon 1964)

O'Callaghan, Seán, *Execution* (London 1974)

O'Connor, Emmet, *A Labour History of Ireland, 1824–1960* (Dublin 1992)

O'Connor, Frank, *The Big Fellow* (London 1937; Dublin 1965)

—— *An Only Child* (London 1958)

Ó Corráin, Donnchadh (ed.), *James Hogan: Revolutionary, Historian and Political Scientist* (Dublin 2001)

O'Day, Alan, *Irish Home Rule, 1867–1921* (Manchester 1998)

O'Donnell, Peadar, *The Gates Flew Open* (London 1932)

O'Donoghue, Florence, *No Other Law* (Dublin 1954; Dublin 1986)

—— *Tomás MacCurtain: Soldier and Patriot* (Tralee 1971)

O'Donovan, Donal, *Kevin Barry and his Time* (Dublin 1989)

Ó Drisceoil, Donal, *Peadar O'Donnell* (Cork 2001)

O'Faolain, Seán, *Vive Moi! An Autobiography* (London 1965)

O'Farrell, Pádraic, *The Blacksmith of Ballinalee: Seán MacEoin* (Mullingar 1983)

O'Farrell, Patrick, *Ireland's English Question* (London 1971)

O'Halpin, Eunan, *The Decline of the Union: British Government in Ireland, 1892–1920* (Dublin 1987)

—— *Head of the Civil Service: A Study of Sir Warren Fisher* (London 1989)

—— 'Historical Revisions: H.E. Duke and the Irish Administration', *Irish Historical Studies*, xxii, 1980–1

—— 'British Intelligence in Ireland, 1914–1921' in Andrew, Christopher and Dilks, David (eds), *The Missing Dimension: Government and Intelligence Communities in the Twentieth Century* (London 1984)

O'Hegarty, P.S., *The Victory of Sinn Féin* (Dublin 1924)

—— *A History of Ireland Under the Union, 1801–1922* (London 1952)

O'Mahony, Seán, *Frongoch: University of Revolution* (Dublin 1987)

O'Malley, Ernie, *On Another Man's Wound* (London 1936)

—— *Raids and Rallies* (Dublin 1982)

Pakenham, Frank, *Peace by Ordeal* (London 1935)

Paterson, Ian D., 'The Activities of Irish Republican Physical Force Organisations in Scotland', *Scottish Historical Review*, vol. lxxii, no. 193, April 1993

Patterson, Henry, *Class Conflict and Sectarianism: The Protestant Working Class and the Belfast Labour Movement, 1868–1920* (Belfast 1980)

Phillips, W.A., *The Revolution in Ireland, 1906–1923* (London 1923)

Phoenix, Eamon, *Northern Nationalism: Nationalist Politics, Partition and the Catholic Minority in Northern Ireland, 1890–1940* (Belfast 1994)

Putkowski, J.J., 'The Best Secret Service Man We Had: Jack Burns and the IRA', *Lobster* 1994

Regan, John M., *The Irish Counter-Revolution, 1921–1936* (Dublin 1999)

Roche, Richard, 'Events in Wexford, 1920', *Capuchin Annual* 1970

Rumpf, E. and Hepburn, A.C., *Nationalism and Socialism in Twentieth-Century Ireland* (Liverpool 1977)

Ryan, Desmond, *Seán Treacy and the Third Tipperary Brigade* (Tralee 1945)

Stewart, A.T.Q., *The Narrow Ground: Aspects of Ulster, 1609–1969* (London 1977)

Street, C.J.C. (IO), *The Administration of Ireland, 1920* (London 1921)

—— *Ireland in 1921* (London 1922)

Tansill, C.C., *America and the Fight for Irish Freedom, 1866–1922* (New York 1957)

Taylor, A.J.P., *English History, 1914–1945* (Oxford 1965)

—— (ed.), *Lloyd George: Twelve Essays* (London 1971)

Taylor, Rex, *Michael Collins* (London 1958)

Tierney, Michael, *Eoin MacNeill: Scholar and Man of Action, 1867–1945* (Oxford 1980)

Townshend, Charles, *The British Campaign in Ireland, 1919–1921* (Oxford 1975)

—— *Political Violence in Ireland: Government and Resistance since 1848* (Oxford 1983)

—— *Making the Peace: Public Order and Public Security in Modern Britain* (Oxford 1993)

—— 'The Irish Railway Strike of 1920: Industrial Action and Civil Resistance in the Struggle for Independence', *Irish Historical Studies*, xxi, 1978–9

—— 'The Irish Republican Army and the Development of Guerrilla Warfare, 1916–1921', *English Historical Review*, vol. xciv, no. 371, April 1979

—— 'Bloody Sunday — Michael Collins Speaks', *European Studies Review*, ix, 1979

Valiulis, Maryann, *Portrait of a Revolutionary: General Richard Mulcahy and the Founding of the Irish Free State* (Dublin 1992)

Van Voris, Jacqueline, *Constance de Markievicz: In the Cause of Ireland* (Amherst 1967)

Ward, Alan J., *Ireland and Anglo-American Relations, 1899–1921* (London 1969)

—— *The Irish Constitutional Tradition: Responsible Government and Modern Ireland, 1782–1992* (Dublin 1994)

Ward, Margaret, *Unmanageable Revolutionaries: Women and Irish Nationalism* (Dingle 1983)

Wheeler-Bennett, Sir J.W., *John Anderson, Viscount Waverley* (London 1962)

Williams, T.D. (ed.), *The Irish Struggle, 1916–1926* (London 1966)

Wilson, Trevor (ed.), *The Political Diaries of C.P. Scott, 1911–1918* (London 1970)

Winter, Ormonde, *Winter's Tale: An Autobiography* (London 1955)

With the IRA in the Fight for Freedom (Tralee 1955)

INDEX